The Family
Through Literature

The Family Through Literature

Nicholas Tavuchis
Cornell University

William J. Goode
Columbia University

McGraw-Hill Book Company
New York   St. Louis   San Francisco   Düsseldorf   Johannesburg
Kuala Lumpur   London   Mexico   Montreal   New Delhi   Panama   Paris
São Paulo   Singapore   Sydney   Tokyo   Toronto

The Family Through Literature

1234567890MUMU7987654

This book was set in Times Roman by Black Dot, Inc. The editors were
Lyle Linder and Barry Benjamin; the cover was designed by
Jo Jones; the production supervisor was Judi Frey.
The Murray Printing Company was printer and binder.

Library of Congress Cataloging in Publication Data

Tavuchis, Nicholas, date   comp.
   The family through literature.

    1.   Family—Literary collections.   I.   Goode,
William Josiah, joint comp.   II.   Title.
PN6071.F2T3   808.8'0354   74-8935
ISBN 0-07-062919-6

To our beloved children

Contents

Preface

Most literary critics—especially those who profess to abhor sociology even though they are engaged in the amateur practice of it when commenting on modern society—would be astonished to know that a high percentage of excellent sociologists would secretly prefer to be literary artists (but not to be critics). Many sociologists entered the field from the humanities, but few from the sciences. Many indeed have secreted a novel in their files before turning to sociology. Since even good sociology typically attains neither the beauty of fine literature nor the austere elegance of first-rate science, its practitioners do not often report to one another that they really enjoy the work they have done.

Each year, millions of books are bought (and some even read) that utilize or present sociological studies, but surely only a tiny minority of those who read sociology take much pleasure from it. By contrast, although millions of students are forced to read literature, spurred by the edict that only those who complete their B.A. may aspire to a good job, it remains true that most reading of literature (whether high art or popular) is done for fun.

Of course, if high art in literature increasingly follows the path of high art in music, that situation may partly be remedied; sociology will be at least as much fun to read as highbrow fiction. Already, it is safe to say, sociology is more fun to read than modern literary criticism.

Similarly, if sociology becomes more "scientific," so that its practitioners can experience the joys of creation (as does the successful scientist), secure in the knowledge that what they have just discovered was *not* first enunciated by Plato or Aristotle, its practice may become more pleasurable.

In the short run, however, the situation cannot be remedied, and that is good. The two are quite different *métiers,* and we need both. At present, each enriches the other, and could enrich the other still more. The modern novelist can no longer simply *imagine* Johannesburg, or even Houston, just as he or she can no longer simply imagine "the natives" in Assam or Tikopia. The would-be author would do well to consult some good social science data, even if he or she has actually visited those places and people. Almost certainly one's personal experience will not be accurate enough; one needs the help of sober descriptions or data.

Similarly, every sociologist trusts the sober data much more if he or she has actually "been there," has read fiction written by people who have felt life there, has brooded over the meaning of poetry by people whose roots are there, and so on. Even if the sociologist does not fully trust such literary accounts, they may furnish interesting interpretive ideas or hypotheses that deserve testing.

Each, then, needs the other. They have different freedoms and responsibilities. They have before them the whole range of human life, to be ordered and arranged at will—but only if it will make sense. The sociologist is cruelly bound by "the facts," and especially by samples. To locate dramatic stories and to miss the main patterns can be permissible in literature but not in sociology. The artist can be biased in his or her view, distorting reality for artistic reasons; not so the sociologist.

On the other hand, writers are not permitted to be dull; if they are, they lessen their chances of winning success and esteem. If the author wishes to portray dull people (as did Oscar Wilde), his skill must help him avoid writing dully about them. The sociologist bears no such burden. Contrary to the opinions of many critics, the sociologist does not *aim* to be dull or pompous, and the best sociologists do indeed write at least clearly, if not gracefully. And few of them could get away with the turgid analyses of most literary criticism, which has not even the merit of pointing to clearly identifiable relationships.

Since the two activities have different tasks, burdens, and limitations, this book is not designed to confuse them. The best novelist is *not* as good a sociologist as even a good practitioner, and vice versa. The writer does, however, present rich experiences that the sociologist may never get to encounter otherwise and that may challenge his or her sociological imagination. The literary critic or artist, too, might profitably look at the work of his fellows, but now with the questions and tools of the sociologist. Much literary creation is flawed not by a lack of imagination but by a less than adequate sociological eye.

The editors have chosen the selections presented in this book primarily for pleasure—their own and, it is to be hoped, that of their readers. Those who are offended by the idea of literature as sociology can ignore our sociological comments and simply enjoy the excerpts as works of artistic literary creation; those who prefer straight doses of sociology can view the reading as a sober and profitable exercise.

We have been helped by many friends during the years we have been collecting and selecting. We apologize to those whose names, through inadvertence, may have been omitted from this list: Gloria Steinem, Carol Ann Finkelstein, Jonathon Yarowsky, Alice Goode, Cynthia Fuchs Epstein, Allan A. Silver, Ezra Vogel, Walter Goldfrank, Lenore J. Weitzman, Elsie Washington, Robert A. Nisbet, Robert Bierstedt, David Riesman, Marion J. Levy, Wagner P. Thielens, Seymour Spilerman, Norman Birnbaum, and Charles Page. We have benefited greatly from talks with Lewis A. Coser, whose earlier work demonstrated how sociology could illuminate literature and how literature could pose exciting questions for sociology. Finally, our editors have made special efforts to help us with the selection and location of the extracts used here. We are profoundly grateful to everyone concerned.

Nicholas Tavuchis
William J. Goode

Part One

The Genesis of Unions: Constraints and Opportunities

Perhaps only a few people ever succeed in finding happiness within the unions they enter; yet still fewer seek happiness by avoiding any intimate union whatsoever. Almost everyone defines a life alone as intolerable. True, all societies mold and pressure their members to want to be with others—how else could they be controlled?—but the animal needs that are expressed in mating would not be contained by any conceivable social forces. Not all imaginable social structures, not all imaginable marital systems, are really possible.

Two great topics have dominated most of world literature, power seeking (through force and duplicity) and loving, and the second of these has been the more pervasive. Very few societies have encouraged falling in love as the primary basis for a marriage, and in perhaps most major civilizations marriage was considered too weighty a matter to be left to the whim of young people, but literary artists have known just the same that their audiences would feel saddened or triumphant at the fate of people who yearned to be with their beloved.

Perhaps in a deep and even troubling sense one might assert that literature expresses the better qualities of mankind, that it represents an ideal less often attained than praised, the wish to reach out, to open up, to touch, to cherish, to give oneself. Perhaps because that way of life would threaten much of the social structure—property and class systems, monarchies, the authority of elders and kin—it has never been allowed to flourish in any civilization; its proponents in this as in other societies have been scorned when not scourged.

The literary artist is more concerned with yearning balked, rejected, or rewarded than with any abstruse theories about why marriages exist at all, why some kinds of unions are more encouraged than others, or why some kinds of courtship are permitted (and thus occur to him or her as fictional themes) and not others. The sociologist who looks at either life or literature must, however, be concerned with these more prosaic matters, that is, how the social pressures create the scene in which the drama is being played.

Thus, sociology has devoted considerable attention to the problem of why, in almost all societies, people are organized in "families" when even an unfertile imagination could think of many other possible types of unions. We take special note of the term, because "family" is almost a shorthand way of saying that there is a husband and wife (which, in turn, is a shorthand way of referring to nearly universal duties); the two are father and mother, also; incestuous relations are forbidden; they must take physical care of their children and "socialize" them; the family forms an economic unit; and so on. Obviously, one might separate all these activities of the family from one another: social placement, physical care, protection from external threats, socialization, social control—but in fact, except under rare circumstances, they are not separated, not given to other types of "unions." Consequently, the *forms* of family units, of households, even of love relationships (because family structures impinge on all of them), are restricted to a small number out of all possible unions.

The literary artist is little concerned, either, with the curiously intricate, sometimes baffling, interaction between biological forces and the types of marriages or unions that men and women enter. To describe a lover's feelings is enough. But though sociology focuses on cultural and social factors as its domain, it is necessary to understand biological factors at least to this extent: How do biological forces shape the social? and How do social forces transmute the biological? Except for limited areas of life, and even then in only a few societies, men and women have been discouraged from falling in love with or establishing unions with others of the same sex. Obviously, that pressure (1) reduces even the awareness of yearnings for others of the same sex; (2) creates some unhappiness among people who engage in heterosexual unions but whose unconscious or conscious longings are different; (3) maintains the reproductive cycle (we can have children even if our marriage is unsatisfactory); (4) simplifies the organization of kinship and the larger society; and so on. It is likely that the dominant biological forces are heterosexual anyway, but as sociologists we must at least consider the many social forces that support the biological. Similarly, it is easy for the reader to think of dozens of ways in which the social pressures of our society attempt to mold, transmute, or utilize our sexual urges in the service of family unions.

Perhaps the most striking sociological uniformity, one to which writers of all centuries have borne witness, is that (if one may be permitted to personify an abstraction) social structures are not "interested" in the happiness of people in families, are not geared to produce marital contentment—even though social structures do not exist apart from the people who support them. Social structures are far more "interested" in—in other words, their forces are marshaled for—the maintenance of class and property systems; the support of authority and political order; molding children to adjust, not to create; success in war; maximization of goods, not loving; and so on. The reader can doubtless continue the list unaided.

Perhaps this emphasis in human history has been wise. After all, people *could* develop social or family structures that achieved those necessary ends, but no one could have worked out procedures for increasing happiness, either alone or in unions with others. In any event, the poet has more often expressed a very different view: Love, or a loving union, destroyed by a property system, has not been praised as a human triumph but has been lamented as a tragedy. (Of course, the sociologist feels the same way, but nevertheless he gloomily expects class variables to have a pervasive effect on family authority, the dominance of elders in courtship, who has the opportunity to meet whom, who falls in love with whom, who marries whom, etc.).

Sociologists are also likely to believe (along with Bertrand Russell) that unions are more contented where the people entering them have not given much thought to happiness and wild yearnings; where the differences between one person and another are seen as minor; where elders make the major decisions about who marries whom; where people are not required to feel or express emotions (which they cannot control) but to carry out duties (which they *can* do); where other kin press the family members to fulfil their obligations, and indeed the husband-wife relation is made less crucial because of kin interdependence. However, if everyone fitted that pattern, the artist would lack for material in the reality of the society! Again, the sociologist must analyze the background, the framework, the underlying forces, that create the dominant marital or courtship patterns, against which the special, unique dramatic creation is illuminated by the mind of the literary artist.

Where the audience knows all this background in depth, as Homer's did, the poet need not spend much time "explaining" the social structure. By contrast, Jane Austen is constantly "educating" her readers; many would not otherwise be aware of facts essential to their understanding of the narrative (for example, the fact that a middle-class widow could own enough property, independently of any man, to be entitled to make certain decisions by herself). Indeed, we may take some pleasure from being enlightened about such "ethnographic facts," entirely aside from artistic merit. As another example, Hemingway has offered countless readers the shivery excitement (minus the risks) of being inside the bull ring; the opportunity to learn about the social patterns of a safari or to acquire deep-sea lore; in short, social data in their own right, but used in his novels to explain why his characters act as they do.

Of course, life is more complex than either artist or sociologist can comprehend. Both may record the facts that people of similar social backgrounds meet, fall in love, and marry; that young people who defy their elders' wishes will suffer social and economic losses, and most will bend to that will; that the rising talent can sometimes marry the beauty or the heiress; that youth and beauty in a woman is a marketable commodity; that controlling courtship will generally control love and marriage, and so on. But from our own lives we know how subtle and shifting the reality is. Certainly some women have allowed themselves to be "bought" by money, authority, or dazzling talent; but many have also genuinely fallen in love with—what? Surely, some shifting mixture of the man and the magnetism or aura of his other qualities. Although many people have felt constrained in their love and marital lives by class proprieties, most have accepted them as being natural, right, part of the cosmos, so that they rejected others of the "wrong" class not at all because the *class* was wrong, but as simply as one would reject an unattractive smell, taste, or color. Or, class factors subtly shift and blend with taste, guilt, repression, comfort, or physical responses, without the person, the artist, or the sociologist being able to separate them. Unfortunately, only the sociologist is bound by his profession to puzzle over what are "the" facts. The poet can create them. The *person* in real life can reject both puzzle and solution, if he or she wishes.

This large section, on the initiation of various kinds of unions, should offer sufficient richness for anyone who cares to ponder these matters, whether as sociologist or as literary artist.

Chapter 1

The Range of Sex and Love Relations

The higher the animal species, the more complex are its responses to its physical urges. It is for this reason that some have asserted (incorrectly) that man is probably the only animal that laughs and—because of our tragedies—the only one that needs to do so. The events that can occur between the release of sex hormones and a completed sex act range from the ludicrous to the glorious, and human beings never find them boring, not even when the actual final experience is felt as boring.

The sexual impulse is not, as anyone who has felt it can testify, as automatic in its unfolding as is a reflex (e.g., the eye blink) or an instinct (e.g., birds' migration). It is a *drive*, and thus the biological mechanisms do not contain a built-in solution for the hunger that is felt. Our animal nature presents us with a problem; we have to solve it any way we can.

Socialization, mainly within the family, is hardly designed to smooth that way. Contrary to the belief of some essayists, on the other hand, child training is not designed to block that way, either. Rather, all societies harness the sexual drive to their own ends, not those of human beings. More technically, all societies "biologize" or sexualize all sorts of cultural patterns, thus making them more attractive or titillating when intrinsically they are not sexual at all (the little white cottage, the family automobile, perfumes). Reciprocally, all societies transmute and mold the sexual drive *culturally*, so that situations or people that could be sexually attractive are defined as nonsexual, while others are given a seal of approval.

Thus it is not correct to say that the curious sexual and love patterns that vary so much from one society to another are a social or cultural *veneer* on a biological animal, or a constricting armor or shell from which we could escape. There is no such thing as a sexually "natural" human being, and none is possible. We cannot even be human without a complex psychosexual rearing; our deepest impulses are shaped socially.

Especially in the sexual aspects of social life, we are molded greatly by punishment, a technique that all societies use. Punishment teaches swiftly, deeply, constrictedly—and *crudely*. Having been taught (in this culture, a generation ago) to avoid all the dirtiness of the body, many adults approached the sexual experience with a wide array of avoidance feelings. Punishment did not teach them how to enjoy sex even in marriage; it rather implanted in them a vague feeling of ugliness and abhorrence about literally dozens of possible sexual experiences.

We are all socialized, too, so that *whom* we fall in love with is constricted; our culture "tells us" who is attractive. For the most part, that means someone of the opposite sex, near us in age, like us in class, ethnic background, religion, taste in music, etc. Moreover, the continual pressures of neighbors, kin, parents, friends, schools, jobs, and other social regularities maximize the chances that we will mainly meet such people.

Especially in the West, too, we are socialized from the earliest years to fall in love, and to believe that is the appropriate basis for a marriage. Children are asked whom they love, and learn to encourage and invite such feelings in themselves, as well as others. Most societies of the past, by contrast, have played down the importance of love, except as a threat to existing social arrangements, or as a fantasy.

However, precisely because so many events occur between the dim or sharp twitches of affection or love and its consummation, no society succeeds in controlling it fully. Men fall in love with men, and upset dynastic plans. Upper-class women fall in love with lower-class men, creating stubborn problems for many other people. In a perfect world, perhaps not even a cockroach would feel the pangs of unrequited love, but few human beings traverse their life span without such frustrated longings; and some even kill because of them.

In these complexities, liabilities, and even aberrations, no social scientist has charted a clear course for objective analysis, and luckily the literary artist has no such duty. We can point out that no one can control his or her own loving; we can neither force another to love us, nor ourselves to love that other. Yet lovers and would-be lovers feel the "injustice" of unrequited love; while those who are in love continue to believe that their beloved *does* really, underneath it all, requite that love. These stubborn yearnings, demands, hysterical pleas, or vengeful hates, growing from so powerful and so multiplex a set of feelings, can become the source of artistic inspiration even when they are the despair of the sociologist who seeks to make order and regularity out of chaos.

Among the selections that follow we have deliberately included a handful of poems to illustrate this range, and even to remind the reader (if he or she is not in love at the moment) of these emotions that were felt at other times. Both in the prose and the poetry we can note a further psychosocial aspect of sex and love relations—how frequently a need or yearning can seem faintly comic to one observer, a nuisance to another, a catastrophe to another, a quiet joy to yet another. Whoever loves whom, it is likely that all of the people involved are concerned, even fascinated, with the outcome.

Note, too, how the artist can achieve something the sociologist rarely can. In evoking our emotions and recognitions, the writer persuades us that we "understand" why someone behaves as he or she does, that we "know the reasons," but this suggests that the writer has found some order and predictability in the love behavior. Our response suggests that the behavior shows regularities. However, if we try to write down those patterns, chart that order, as a sociologist attempts to do, we shall quickly think of dozens of "exceptions," of qualifications, of still more variables or factors that shape that love or sex behavior. Observe how much information the author feels is necessary to give the reader, in order to make the behavior or emotions "believable."

Advice by a Lover to his Married Mistress

Ovid

Nothing resembling a Kinsey report has survived that would inform us just who, among the Roman upper classes of the first century A.D., engaged in which kinds of sexual relationships. At best, we can infer something from the tone and temper of the frivolous writings of that period, without being able to extract quantitative estimates of the extent of extramarital affairs, premarital sexual intercourse, homosexual relations, and the like.

Whatever the cycles of puritanism or libertinism that have occurred since that time, Ovid's *Art of Love* and *The Loves* continue to delight and instruct generation after generation. Perhaps the philosophical stance that he takes seems very close to what one might call the intellectual cocktail circuit viewpoint. That is, sexual encounters are not seen as simply healthy, animal relationships that call for no excuse or justification. Instead, as in Ovid's accounts, the powers of institutional structures are well recognized: It is imperative that husbands not find out what is going on; flirtation is permitted, but serious involvement deplored; property and class are extremely important in the decisions one makes; and love is a kind of game. He did not assume or even believe that love ought to be a profound or total experience, though he argues that those who wish to win in the game must act as though it is central in importance. Thus, for example, it is all right for the lover to pretend to be pale and wan and to be unable to carry out daily activities because of the great love he or she feels.

In the following brief excerpt, Ovid is telling his married mistress how she should behave at a party. He suggests a form of covert language to his mistress and he tells her how to act in front of others so that they will be deceived (especially her husband). In the final lines, the lover ex-

Ovid, *The Art of Love* and *The Loves*, translated by Rolfe Humphries, University Press, Bloomington, 1957, Bk. 1, Chap. 4, ll. 12-54.

presses the hope that later in the evening they may get some opportunity to be together.

. . . get there before him, and when he reclines, you
      beside him,
Modestly on the couch, give my foot just a touch,
Watch me for every nod, for every facial expression,
Catch my signs and return them, never saying a word.
I can talk with my eyebrows and spell out words with
      my fingers,
I can make you a sign, dipping my finger in wine.
When you think of the tumbles we've had in the hay
      together,
Touch your cheek with your hand; then I will
      understand.
If you're a little bit cross with the way I may be
      behaving,
Let your finger-tip rest light on the lobe of an ear.
If, on the other hand, what I am saying should please
      you,
Darling, keep turning your ring; symbol enough that
      will be.
. . . Let him drink all he wants; keep urging him, only
      don't kiss him.
Keep on filling his glass, secretly, if you can.
Once he passes out cold, perhaps we can figure out
      something—
Time and circumstance maybe will give us a chance.

In Praise of Sex
Ovid

Casanova remarks in his introduction to his memoirs that some men engage in marital exploits so that they can gain glory, others seek money in order to become rich, and still others seek political power so that they can dominate other people. However, he insists that all of them do so simply because they believe that it will make their pursuit of women more effective. Those who succeed in one of the above "games" can trade their winnings for the love of women. Consequently, he argued, he decided early that he would go straight to the goal he wanted, which was of course love relationships.

In this second excerpt, Ovid is extolling the goal of love; he is not talking about a profound lifetime experience with a single woman, but a series of delights and pleasures in successive women. The soldier may seek glory, the trader may seek wealth, and so on, but Ovid himself wishes rather to die in his own bed (but of course, not alone). One should consider, with reference to both of these excerpts from Ovid, the extent to which the dominant cultural patterns of any society urge hard work, dedication to group ends, heroism of various kinds, and a simple life. Simultaneously, however, and not merely in historical succession, other themes are propounded or accepted by some part of the population and continue their life independently of, or in contrast with, the moral exhortations of the classes that rule the social structure. It would be difficult, if not impossible, to find a single period in world history when the dominant classes *officially* expounded such a hedonistic philosophy, but it would be equally difficult to locate a generation in which these themes did not arouse considerable positive response in at least part of the population.

The foregoing helps greatly in understanding how a social structure operates and the extent to which, even after rigorous socialization, every individual remains loyal to his or her own cultural or value orientation, even while obeying

Ibid., Bk. 2, Chap. 10, ll. 26-38.

outwardly the social pressures and influences of others. Even in relatively simple societies, there are dissidents and unbelievers, and many men and women conform outwardly while inwardly feeling very different impulses and even philosophical convictions.

Show me the girl who can say I couldn't answer her
    need.
More than once in the night I have risen to every
    occasion,
Risen, again at dawn, a thoroughly competent man.
Lucky the man who dies in duels with Venus as
    second.
Grant me, gods, such an end, if I must die in my bed.
Let the soldier expose his breast to the darts of the
    foeman,
Let his crimson blood buy him a glorious name,
Let the trader seek wealth, and die in the midst of a
    shipwreck,
Thirsting for more than gain, drinking the salt of the
    sea.
But as for me, let me go in the act of coming to Venus:
In more senses than one, let my last dying be done.
And at my funeral rites, let one of the mourners bear
    witness:
"That was the way, we know, he would have wanted to
    go."

The Symposium

Plato

Plato's symposium is devoted to an analysis of love, in which a succession of speakers express their views of different forms of sexual and love relationships. Sometimes the main protagonist (Socrates) expresses disagreement with one or more of the themes that a given speaker promulgates, but in the long run, as in all of the Platonic dialogues, there is a gradual movement toward some kind ·of agreement.

In Pausanias's speech we encounter a view that is much opposed to the light-hearted and even light-headed view of Ovid. Some part of Pausanias's formulation is in accord with Plato's essential view, but he expresses in part an "exchange relationship" that Plato rejects later on in the dialogue, through the voice of Socrates.

We do, however, encounter one version of what is sometimes called "Platonic love." Here the speaker outlines two kinds of love, one of them basically erotic—the love of a man for a woman. He asserts that the common love is one in which men love women, men, or even boys for their bodies rather than their souls. They enjoy relationships with shallow people, and the relationship itself is not a beautiful one. They may exploit others, and may use any techniques to gain their ends.

Because this is so, the speaker argues, different Greek cities adopt different forms of laws to control these expressions of ordinary or common sexuality. On the other hand, there is a higher form of love, which both Pausanias and Plato believe is to be found only in the relationship of older men with younger boys, preferably those who are coming to an important phase of intellectual growth, which is identified with the beginning of puberty. This form of love is a spiritual one, though the physical aspects are not rejected. The central focus is the beauty and goodness of the mind and soul, and Pausanias would argue that one should love

Plato, *The Symposium*, translated by Suzy Q. Groden, edited by John A. Brentlinger, University of Massachusetts Press, 1970.

such a person, even if that person were not physically beautiful.

In this analysis, as in other analyses that come to us from Plato, we must not assume that homosexuality was rife in Periclean Athens. Without any question, it was viewed as much more tolerable and natural than in our own society. However, contempt was expressed for those who were effeminate, lacked courage or martial spirit, or simply devoted themselves to the love of other men. The ideal homosexual relationship—and again, as with Ovid, we do not know how prevalent such relationships were—was that of an older man with a young boy. The underlying social assumption was that the young boy would himself grow up in time, marry, continue his family line, and engage in normal masculine activities. At some points in his life he might have, in turn, a relationship with a younger man or boy.

It was not, in any event, assumed that the major love relationship in a man's life would be with his wife. Heterosexual domestic relations were accepted as inevitable and a normal part of a man's life cycle. His relationship with boys, or his extramarital relations with hetaerae, who were the educated entertainer-women of Athenian society, were not viewed as basic threats to the marital relationship, which remained a fixed and firm part of the institutional life of Athens.

PAUSANIAS

It seems to me, Phaedrus, that this arrangement won't work out well for us, if we are simply supposed to invent talks in praise of Love. It'd be fine if Love were one thing; but it isn't one. And in view of its not being one it would be better, first, to say which form of Love we're supposed to praise. I'm going to try, then, to set this business straight, beginning with a discussion of the specific Love one ought to praise, and then praising the god appropriately.

We all know that Aphrodite is never without Love. And if she were one there would be a single Love. But since there are actually two Aphrodites, it is necessary to assume two Loves as well. And can anyone challenge the notion of the bifold goddess? On one side we have the ancient one, the motherless daughter of Uranos, whom we even call 'Uranian,' or 'celestial.' Then there is the younger one, the child of Zeus and Dione, whom we address as 'Pandemus'—or 'common.' It is necessary to describe Love, too, as 'common' when he is engaged with the younger Aphrodite and as 'celestial' when with the former. One ought to praise all gods, but I'll try to describe the attributes of each of these two separately.

Every action has this about it: of itself its performance is neither good nor bad. It's this way for our behavior now—if we drink or sing or converse—none of these acts is particularly noble, but rather it's how the deed is done that makes the difference. If it is done in a noble manner and properly it becomes noble, and if improperly, ignoble. Thus I say that even loving and Love are not wholly good, nor worthy of praise, but only that loving which urges us toward noble action.

Now the Love of the common Aphrodite is truly common, and works at random; it is this one your average man loves. First of all, such men love women no less than boys; then, whomever they love, it is their bodies rather than their souls; then, it is the shallowest people they can find, wanting only to have them, without any concern for the beauty of the thing or its lack. These people take it as it happens to come, and go to, good or bad. This is the nature of the god who comes from that younger goddess, whose birth partook of a mixture of female and male.

Then there is the Love of the celestial goddess, who does not partake of the female, only of the male; then, she is older and entirely lacks lust. Men who have been inspired by this Love turn to the male, loving what is most vigorous and more intelligent. And anyone would know, even in this matter of love for young boys, those who are purely involved in this love; they don't desire boys until they are beginning to think, just about the same time that the beard is starting to grow. I believe that people who begin at that point to fall in love, are prepared to share their lives completely, even to live together. They are not deceivers who thoughtlessly will take such a boy, and then laugh and turn away to live with another.

But there must be a law against one's loving young boys, so that a great deal of zeal won't be wasted on an uncertainty. It is uncertain what the boys will grow up to be, what evil or good they will end up having in body and soul. And while good men lay down this law for themselves and hold themselves to it, it is necessary to force the vulgar sort of lovers to adhere to it, just the way we force them, as far as we are able, not to make love to our free women. It is this kind who have introduced the disgrace that makes some men go so far as to say that it is low to gratify lovers—but they say this when they regard the sort I'm describing, observing their importunity and unfairness. If the deed were performed decently and it had a sure legality, they could not justly hold it in reproach.

In other cities the law that deals with love-making is easy to understand, it is simply defined. But the one we have here is complicated. Take Elis, for example, and Boeotia, and places where they are not so articulate. It is set down plainly in the law that to give oneself to lovers is a good thing, nor would anyone, young or old, say it was bad. They wouldn't want, I believe, to have to do the job of convincing the boys of it, and pleading an argument, as they are unskilled in speaking. However, in Ionia, and in many other places it is decreed a bad thing, to the extent that they live under barbarians. Since the barbarians live under tyrants this is made a disgrace, as are philosophy and athletics. It isn't expedient, I imagine, for the rulers, if any deep thoughts develop in their subjects, nor strong friendships and comrade-ships, and actually, all the very things Love delights in engender-ing. The tyrants have learned this fact from the experience here. The love of Aristogeiton and the affection of Harmodius, when it had grown constant, destroyed their power. So, where it has been held an evil to give oneself to lovers, it is because of the evil of those who made the laws. On the one hand it stems from the arrogance of the rulers, and on the other from the emasculated cowardice of the ruled. However, if it has been ruled by law to be entirely good, this is the case because of an intellectual laziness in the lawmakers. Here, the law that deals with these matters is far better, but as I said before, it's not easy to understand.

Consider that it is said to be better to love openly than

secretly, and especially finest to love the highest in mind and the noblest, even when they are uglier than others. Furthermore, one is cheered on marvelously in this love by everybody: one never does anything disgraceful; being won seems a fine thing, and it seems base not to be; and the law grants freedom to a lover who is trying to catch his beloved by doing marvelous deeds to win him praise, while the very same acts, if done by someone pursuing and wanting some other end, would bring the greatest reproach.

If one wanted to get wealth from someone, or to attain an office or some other power, and wanted to use the same methods that lovers use with their youths (making supplications and entreaties in prayers, and swearing oaths and sleeping at their doorsteps, and desiring to perform menial tasks such that no slave would be willing to perform), he would be prevented from acting out this business by his friends and by his enemies alike. The latter would reproach him for his obsequiousness and slavishness, while the former would chastise him and be ashamed over these things. But in a lover who does all these things one sees some grace. He is allowed by law to act without reproach, as if he were performing acts that were thoroughly noble. But what is strangest of all is how the people say that the gods will give pardon to him alone when he swears an oath and then breaks it; for an oath of someone under Aphrodite's rule, they say, doesn't exist—so that both men and gods give complete freedom to the lover, as the law says here.

For this reason a person might well think that it is ruled completely honorable here in this city, both to be a lover, and to be affectionate to lovers. But fathers have appointed tutors for those who are being wooed, so that they won't be allowed to hold intercourse with their lovers, and restrictions are imposed by the tutor to this end, and the boy's comrades and friends reproach him whenever they see this sort of thing taking place, nor do the elders check the reproachers, nor abuse them as speaking out of turn, so that when one has observed such things one would believe rather that this sort of thing is considered execrable here. But I think that this is how it really is: it isn't simple, as I said at the outset, but the granting of one's affection is, of itself, neither a

noble thing, nor deplorable. It is a beautiful act if done beautifully, and if lowly, low. It is done basely when one gives one's
affections to a base person, and does so in a low manner; when
one does so to a good man, and in a noble way, it is done
beautifully. The man who is a lover in the common way is
base—he loves the body rather than the soul. Nor is he constant,
since he loves things which lack constancy. Why, with the flower
of the body fading, his favor, too, *disappearing, is gone*—and his
many speeches and promises are discredited. But the person who
loves the character of a good man endures throughout life,
merging with what is lasting.

Now, our law attempts to prove men in a good and accurate
way, those to whom one should yield, and those one ought to
avoid. By these means it encourages us to pursue some people
and flee from others, acting as referee, and making judgments
about lover and beloved. That's why it's customarily considered
an ignominy to be won quickly. It's so that time might pass, since
time does seem to prove most things well. Then, too, it's held a
lowness to grant favors on account of wealth and political power,
in case one were suffering miserably from fear, lacked endurance,
was unable to scorn the benefits of property or political success,
or else were yielding in the hope of receiving some benefit. These
things seem to lack steadiness and constancy. Besides, genuine
friendship will not arise from this kind of relationship. One path,
then, is left us by our legal institution, if the darling is to gratify
his lover honorably. Just as it is not considered flattery or
anything to be ashamed of when lovers want to serve and act like
slaves for their beloved youths, so in the same way our law allows
one other form of voluntary servility to be kept without shame;
and this is when it is done for the sake of virtue.

To The Virgins, to Make Much of Time
Robert Herrick

Although it is always dangerous to confuse the fantasies of poets with the social realities of their historical era, without question the England of Elizabethan times, as portrayed in literature, seems very alien to, say, the nineteenth-century Victorian England. Perhaps a neat index of the difference is that this is the one period in English history where music-making seems to have been a widespread activity, engaged in by people in barber shops and on the street. There is almost a Latin exuberance about the social life of the era.

Although there is no period since the Elizabethan when one could not encounter here and there a poet who would extol the importance of love, and a dedicated attention to the arts of Venus, it is likely that a higher percentage of the poets of that period expressed such themes. Among the more popular poets whose work has survived to this day is Robert Herrick.

We should also keep in mind, however, while reading Herrick's poetic injunction to enjoy the pleasures of the day, that during this same period among the upper classes marriages were largely arranged by elders; young men and women who fell in love with one another might well be barred from any consummation of that love, both by swords and the threat of disinheritance; that men, especially, were violent in their jealousy and their general protection of their sexual property (whether daughters, sisters, or wives); and that the poet's general suggestion that no serious social consequences were to follow is at variance with much of the reality of the time.

On the other hand, the poet is never writing in a personal vacuum, expressing only his private fantasies. Gallantry between men and women was common, and perhaps more common between married men and women, who had greater freedom than younger unmarried people.

From *The Poems of Robert Herrick*, edited with an introduction by L. E. Martin, Oxford Press, London, 1965, p. 84.

Gather ye rosebuds while ye may,
    Old Time is still a-flying:
And this same flower that smiles today,
    Tomorrow will be dying.

The glorious lamp of heaven, the sun,
    The higher he's a-getting,
The sooner will his race be run,
    And nearer he's to setting.

That age is best which is the first,
    When youth and blood are warmer;
But being spent, the worse, and worst
    Times, still succeed the former.

Then be not coy, but use your time;
    And while ye may, go marry:
For having lost but once your prime,
    You may for ever tarry.

Two Young Men 23 to 24

G. Cavafy

Homosexuality has played a curious role in the history of
marital institutions. On the one hand, every family system
creates a staunch series of barriers against sex relations
between two consenting men or two consenting women.
The reasons are not hard to seek. Each society creates an
elaborate set of socializing and day-to-day pressures that
push men and women into heterosexual relations and
especially into the proper discharge of their marital obligations. Thereby, the birth and socialization of the succeeding
generations is assured. Homosexual relations, if widespread, would weaken the bond between spouses, as well
as the dedication of family heads or wives to the kinship and
marital duties that have been placed on them.

This reading and the one which follows are from *The Complete Poems of Cavafy*,
translated by Rae Dalven, Harcourt, Brace, Jovanovich, New York, 1961.

On the other hand, there is no period when such relationships did not abound. In some historical eras or in particular regions or subsocieties, they are tolerated considerably more; but in others, socialization is so rigorous, and the day-to-day repression so great, that many men and women are "latently homosexual," never discovering the truth about their own emotional responses to others. They enter the phase of courtship and the status of being married, without seriously considering any alternatives. In contemporary literature, we often read accounts of people who have late in life discovered that their deeper sexual love responses are to people of their own sex.

As a consequence of these tensions, poets have sometimes in the past written lyrics in honor of their homosexual loves, without ever identifying the gender of their love object. On the other hand, there have been periods or at least social circles, in which these pretenses were dropped, or in which people could keep their privacy intact, so that the outside world did not punish them for their deviation.

This has been especially so since World War I, and increasingly so for the past fifteen years in the Western world. More recently, of course, there have even been "Gay Liberation Fronts," one of whose aims has been to exhort those who are secretly homosexual to come out into the open.

Relatively few poems or literary accounts in the Western world have freely and frankly treated these love relationships as having the same depth and tenderness that were thought to be ideally characteristic of heterosexual love. Cavafy is one of the few modern poets who have, without explanation or justification, expressed these love feelings with this same seriousness that was typical of poetry about the love between men and women. On the other hand, the reader should not assume that the poet himself, in his day-to-day life, does not suffer difficulties and even social punishment because of his frankly expressed feelings.

He had been in the café since ten-thirty,
expecting to see him come in presently.
Midnight went—and he still waited for him.
Half past one went; the café was

almost entirely empty.
He grew weary of reading newspapers
mechanically. Of his three solitary shillings,
only one was left him: he had waited so long,
he had spent the others on coffees and cognac.
He had smoked all his cigarettes.
Such waiting was exhausting for him. For
as he was also alone for hours
troublesome thoughts took hold of him
of the life that had led him astray.

But when he saw his friend enter—instantly
fatigue, boredom, thoughts vanished.

His friend brought him unexpected news.
He had won sixty pounds at the gambling-house.

Their handsome faces, their marvelous youth,
the sensitive love each felt for the other
were refreshed, reanimated, fortified
by the sixty pounds of the gambling-house.

And full of joy and vigor, feeling, and beauty
they went—not to the homes of their honorable
        families
(where besides, they were no longer wanted):
but to a friend's house, a very particular
house of depravity, and they asked for
a bedroom, and expensive drinks, and again they
        drank.

And when the expensive drinks were finished,
and since it was almost four o'clock in the morning,
they gave themselves happily to love.

The 25th Year of His Life

G. Cavafy

He goes regularly to the tavern
where they had met each other the month before.
He inquired; but they had nothing precise to tell him.
From their words, he understood that his friend had
        made the acquaintance

of some entirely unknown person,
one of the many unknown and suspicious
youthful figures that used to go by there.
But he goes to the tavern regularly, at night,
and he sits and looks toward the entrance;
he looks toward the entrance to the point of weariness.
He may walk in. He may still come tonight.

For almost three weeks he does this.
His mind has grown sick from lust.
The kisses have stayed on his mouth.
All his flesh suffers from the persistent desire.
The touch of that body is over him.
He longs for union with him again.

Naturally he tries not to betray himself.
But sometimes he is almost indifferent.
Besides, he knows to what he is exposing himself,
he has made up his mind. It is not unlikely that this life
of his may bring him to a disastrous scandal.

Gentleman Without Company

Pablo Neruda

The following poem eloquently expresses a particular personal situation, rather than a social status or role, but it is one that many readers will recognize as a period they have experienced themselves at perhaps several times in their lives. The poet is not so much extolling the beauties and wonders of love as expressing his own highly sensitive awareness that he is surrounded by people who are engaging in a wide range of love and sexual relationships—homosexual men, sedately married husbands, masturbating priests, animals and insects, professors and doctors, young cousins in pairs—in short, all about him, in every guise and at every class level, among all the species of life, all are engaging in some form of love, but he himself is alone, "without company."

The poet, Pablo Neruda, is in essence expressing a psychological state that arises in a particular social situation, that is, when he is without attachments but feels within himself a turmoil of desire and awareness. However, it is worth noting that this special state is an outcome of years of socialization, in which we are all sensitized to the stimuli of love and sex, so that we are not only prepared but even eager to enter into relationships when that opportunity is offered. Again, such socializing impulses are built on a biological foundation, but it must be emphasized that the social pressures give us guidance as to what are the appropriate activities in which to engage, and even a measure of the social and personal importance of those activities.

The homosexual young men and the love-mad girls,
and the long widows who suffer from a delirious
    inability to sleep,

From Pablo Neruda, *Twenty Poems*, translated by Robert Bly, Odin House, Madison, Minn., 1967, p. 33.

and the young wives who have been pregnant for thirty
    hours,
and the hoarse cats that cross my garden in the dark,
these, like a necklace of throbbing sexual oysters,
surround my solitary house,
like enemies set up against my soul,
like members of a conspiracy dressed in sleeping
    clothes
who give each other as passwords long and profound
    kisses.

The shining summer leads out the lovers
in low-spirited regiments that are all alike,
made up of fat and thin and cheerful and sullen pairs;
under the elegant coconut palms, near the sea and the
    moon,
there is a steady movement of trousers and petticoats,
and a hum from the stroking of silk stockings,
and women's breasts sparkling like eyes.

The small-time employee, after many things,
after the boredom of the week, and the novels read in
    bed at night,
has once and for all seduced the woman next door
and now he escorts her to the miserable movies,
where the heroes are either colts or passionate princes,
and he strokes her legs sheathed in their sweet down
with his warm and damp hands that smell of cigarettes.

The evenings of the woman-chaser and the nights of
    the husbands
come together like two bed-sheets and bury me,
and the hours after lunch, when the young male
    students
and the young women students, and the priests are
    masturbating,
and the animals are riding each other frankly,
and the bees have an odor of blood, and the flies buzz
    in anger,

and cousins play strange games with their girl-cousins,
and doctors look with rage at the husband of the young
    patient,
and the morning hours, when the professor, as if
    absentminded,
performs his marital duty, and has breakfast,
and still more, the adulterers, who love each other with
    true love
of beds high and huge as ocean liners,
this immense forest, entangled and breathing,
hedges me around firmly on all sides forever
with huge flowers like mouths and rows of teeth
and black roots that look like fingernails and shoes.

Anna Karenina

Leo Tolstoy

The following scene illustrates powerfully the peculiar place of sexual love throughout much of the history of Western society, especially over the past several hundred years. First, in accord with the inner tensions of Christianity, we are led to feel deeply that sexual love is both highly attractive and very dangerous. It is a simultaneous expression of a high spiritual impulse and a base animal deviation. Moreover, because of the social definitions surrounding sexual consummation, once actual sexual intercourse has occurred, the relations between the two parties change radically. If the two are unmarried, they have committed a violation that can be expunged only by marriage; otherwise, some kind of tragedy will result. If married, but not to each other, the marital relationship has been destroyed and the two offending parties must now make a new life together— embark on a road toward either a tragedy or a new fulfill- ment.

From Leo Tolstoy, *Anna Karenina*, translation and foreword by David Magarshack, New American Library, New York, 1961.

Although the husband in nineteenth-century upper-class Russia was powerful, influencing almost all aspects of his wife's decisions, Tolstoy reminds us in *Anna Karenina* that when a married woman became increasingly attached to another man, the husband could not do very much to stop it, if he was not prepared to use force. He could, like Anna's husband, turn away, withdraw into his own thoughts, or simply feel frustrated and hurt by unknown and frightening events that were taking place inside her; but after all no one can control another's love relationships.

Within the literary traditions of his time, Tolstoy was not permitted to describe in great detail the actual sexual encounter. There is, in fact, no description of the purely physical aspects of this consummation, after a long period of increasing emotional involvement between Vronsky and Anna. It can be argued that this was not even necessary, since it plays little part in the unfolding drama itself.

What is central, however, is the awareness on the part of both Anna and Vronsky that they have crossed some great divide and can no longer have the same relations with their kin or social circles that existed before. It is clear, from Anna's expression of "disgust and horror," that the actual physical experience was not itself pleasurable. Again, within the traditions of nineteenth-century European society, the man expresses his sense that this was a great moment of happiness. But though Anna feels a range of upsetting and even degrading emotions, it is clear that she welcomes the new state, having irrevocably moved toward it in the period preceding this scene.

Finally, Tolstoy puts in Anna's mind a fantasy "solution" for her problem, one that doubtless many husbands and wives entertain even today: In her dreams, she now has two husbands, her lover and her real husband, and they both make passionate love to her. In short, she expresses a yearning for an acceptance of both of these relationships, though in her society then, as in most societies now, that would have been impossible.

That which for nearly a whole year had been the sole desire of his life, taking the place of all his former desires; that which for Anna had been an impossible, dreadful, and for that reason all the more fascinating dream of happiness—that desire had been satisfied. Pale, with trembling lower jaw, he stood over her and implored her to be calm, without knowing himself how and why.

"Anna! Anna!" he said in a trembling voice. "Anna, for God's sake!"

But the louder he spoke, the lower she dropped her once proud, gay, but now shameful head, and she bent lower and lower and sank from the sofa on which she was sitting to the floor at his feet; she would have fallen on the carpet if he had not held her.

"Oh God, forgive me!" she said, sobbing and pressing his hand to her bosom.

She felt so culpable and guilty that all that was left to her was to humble herself and beg forgiveness; and since she had no one in the world now but him, she even addressed her prayer of forgiveness to him. Looking at him, she felt her degradation physically and she could not utter another word. He felt what a murderer must feel when he looks at the body he has deprived of life. The body he had deprived of life was their love, the first stage of their love. There was something dreadful and loathsome in the recollection of what had been paid for by this terrible price of shame. Shame at her spiritual nakedness crushed her and communicated itself to him. But in spite of the murderer's great horror before the body of his victim, that body has to be cut up and hidden, for the murderer must enjoy the fruits of his crime.

And the murderer throws himself on the body with a feeling of bitter resentment and as though with passion, and drags it off and cuts it to pieces; so he, too, covered her face and shoulders with kisses. She held his hand and did not stir. Yes, these kisses are what have been bought by that shame. Yes, and this hand, which will always be mine, is the hand of my accomplice. She raised that hand and kissed it. He sank on his knees and tried to see her face; but she hid it and uttered not a word. At last, as though making an effort over herself, she sat up and pushed him away. Her face was still as beautiful as ever, but all the more pitiful for that.

"It's all over," she said. "I've nothing left but you. Remember that."

"How do you expect me not to remember what is life itself to me? For one moment of happiness like this . . ."

"Happiness!" she said with disgust and horror, and her horror involuntarily communicated itself to him. "For God's sake, not a word, not another word!"

She got up quickly and moved away from him.

"Not another word," she repeated, and with a look of cold despair he had never seen on her face before, she left him. She felt that at that moment she could not express in words the feeling of shame, joy, and horror at this entry into a new life, and she did not want to talk about it, to profane this feeling by inexact words. But afterward, too, the next day, and the next, she not only did not find the right words with which she could express the complexity of these feelings, but she could not even find the right thoughts with which she could reflect on all that was in her heart.

She said to herself: "No, I can't think about it now; later, when I am calmer." But that calm for her thoughts never came; every time the thought of what she had done, of what would become of her, and of what she ought to do, occurred to her, she became terrified and she drove these thoughts away.

"Later, later," she kept saying. "When I am calmer."

But when she was asleep and had no control over her thoughts, her situation appeared to her in all its hideous nakedness. She had one and the same dream almost every night. She dreamed that both of them were her husbands and both made passionate love to her. Alexey Karenin wept when kissing her hands and kept saying: "How wonderful it is now!" And Alexey Vronsky was there, too; and he, too, was her husband. And, wondering why this seemed so impossible to her before, she kept explaining to them, laughing, that that was much simpler and that now both of them were happy and contented. But this dream weighed on her like a nightmare, and she woke up in terror.

May We Borrow Your Husband?

Graham Greene

In the following pages from Graham Greene's *May We Borrow Your Husband?*, the writer uses the literary device of an older narrator a biographer, who is thus permitted to express some of his own accumulated wisdom while also being involved in the action of the drama itself. The biographer has become emotionally attached to the young bride and wistfully yearns to have a more open, loving, and sexual relationship with her, but she is simply unaware of his desires; since she is totally absorbed in the failure of her own sexual relationship with her husband.

The core of the young couple's misunderstanding can be found in the sex-role socialization both have experienced up to this point. Both are members of the rural horse-gentry, and neither has had any real sexual experience. The young man has been taught to be masculine and to court in the approved reserved English fashion, and while the young woman has somewhat less reserve, she too has been shielded from any knowledge of the wide range of human sexuality. She is convinced that her husband simply finds her physically unattractive and does not suspect that despite his overt masculinity his basic sexual orientation is toward men.

The reader has already been informed of this situation, however, through a description by the narrator of how a homosexual couple at the same resort hotel is greatly interested in the young husband. They have at once perceived that he is unaware of his own basic sexual interests, but that he will eventually respond to them. Their program for involving the young man in their own lives is sophisticated and sensitive, gradual but persistent.

In the following scene, the young woman inadvertently prevents the older narrator from expressing his own yearnings and from explaining the facts of life to her, both because she would be unable to tolerate them and because

From Graham Greene, *May We Borrow Your Husband? and Other Comedies of the Sexual Life*, The Viking Press, Inc., New York, 1966.

of his own weary acceptance of the inevitability of the outcome. The three men have gone off together for a day's picnic trip, and the narrator is sure that eventually they will engage in a sexual encounter during their absence.

"And you didn't marry again after she left?"

"By that time I was getting too old to marry."

"Picasso does it."

"Oh, I'm not quite as old as Picasso."

The silly conversation went on against a background of fishing-nets draped over a wallpaper with a design of wine bottles—interior-decoration again. Sometimes I longed for a room which had simply grown that way like the lines on a human face. The fish soup steamed away between us, smelling of garlic. We were the only guests there. Perhaps it was the solitude, perhaps it was the directness of her question, perhaps it was only the effect of the *rosé*, but quite suddenly I had the comforting sense that we were intimate friends. "There's always work," I said, "and wine and a good cheese."

"I couldn't be that philosophical if I lost Peter."

"That's not likely to happen, is it?"

"I think I'd die," she said, "like someone in Christina Rossetti."

"I thought nobody of your generation read her."

If I had been twenty years older, perhaps, I could have explained that nothing is quite as bad as that, that at the end of what is called "the sexual life," the only love which has lasted is the love that has accepted everything, every disappointment, every failure and every betrayal, which has accepted even the sad fact that in the end there is no desire so deep as the simple desire for companionship.

She wouldn't have believed me. She said, "I used to weep like anything at that poem about 'Passing Away.' Do you write sad things?"

"The biography I am writing now is sad enough. Two people tied together by love and yet one of them incapable of fidelity. The man dead of old age, burnt-out, at less than forty, and a fashionable preacher lurking by the bedside to snatch his soul. No privacy even for a dying man: the bishop wrote a book about it."

An Englishman who kept a chandler's shop in the old port was talking at the bar, and two old women who were part of the family knitted at the end of the room. A dog trotted in and looked at us and went away again with its tail curled.

"How long ago did all that happen?"

"Nearly three hundred years."

"It sounded quite contemporary. Only now it would be the man from the *Mirror* and not a bishop."

"That's why I wanted to write it. I'm not really interested in the past. I don't like costume pieces."

Winning someone's confidence is rather like the way some men set about seducing a woman; they circle a long way from their true purpose, they try to interest and amuse until finally the moment comes to strike. It came, so I wrongly thought, when I was adding up the bill. She said, "I wonder where Peter is at this moment," and I was quick to reply, "What's going wrong between the two of you?"

She said, "Let's go."

"I've got to wait for my change."

It was always easier to get served at Lou-Lou's than to pay the bill. At that moment everyone always had a habit of disappearing: the old woman (her knitting abandoned on the table), the aunt who helped to serve, Lou-Lou herself, her husband in his blue sweater. If the dog hadn't gone already he would have left at that moment.

I said, "You forget—you told me that he wasn't happy."

"Please, please find someone and let's go."

So I disinterred Lou-Lou's aunt from the kitchen and paid. When we left, everyone seemed to be back again, even the dog.

Outside I asked her whether she wanted to return to the hotel.

"Not just yet—but I'm keeping you from your work."

"I never work after drinking. That's why I like to start early. It brings the first drink nearer."

She said she had seen nothing of Antibes but the ramparts and the beach and the lighthouse, so I walked her around the small narrow back streets where the washing hung out of the

windows as in Naples and there were glimpses of small rooms
overflowing with children and grandchildren; stone scrolls were
carved over the ancient doorways of what had once been
noblemen's houses; the pavements were blocked by barrels of
wine and the streets by children playing at ball. In a low room on
a ground floor a man sat painting the horrible ceramics which
would later go to Vallauris to be sold to tourists in Picasso's old
stamping-ground—spotted pink frogs and mauve fish and pigs
with slits for coins.

She said, "Let's go back to the sea." So we returned to a
patch of hot sun on the bastion, and again I was tempted to tell
her what I feared, but the thought that she might watch me with
the blankness of ignorance deterred me. She sat on the wall and
her long legs in the tight black trousers dangled down like
Christmas stockings. She said, "I'm not sorry that I married
Peter," and I was reminded of a song Edith Piaf sings, "*Je ne
regrette rien.*" It is typical of such a phrase that it is always sung
or spoken with defiance.

I could only say again, "You ought to take him home," but I
wondered what would have happened if I had said, "You are
married to a man who only likes men and he's off now picnicking
with his boy-friends. I'm thirty years older than you, but at least I
have always preferred women and I've fallen in love with you and
we could still have a few good years together before the time
comes when you want to leave me for a younger man." All I said
was, "He probably misses the country—and the riding."

"I wish you were right, but it's really worse than that."

Had she, after all, realized the nature of her problem? I
waited for her to explain her meaning. It was a little like a novel
which hesitates on the verge between comedy and tragedy. If she
recognized the situation it would be a tragedy; if she were
ignorant it was a comedy, even a farce—a situation between an
immature girl too innocent to understand and a man too old to
have the courage to explain. I suppose I have a taste for tragedy. I
hoped for that.

She said, "We didn't really know each other much before we
came here. You know, weekend parties and the odd theatre—and
riding, of course."

I wasn't sure where her remarks tended. I said, "These

occasions are nearly always a strain. You are picked out of ordinary life and dumped together after an elaborate ceremony—almost like two animals shut in a cage who haven't seen each other before."

"And now he sees me he doesn't like me."

"You are exaggerating."

"No." She added with anxiety, "I won't shock you, will I, if I tell you things? There's nobody else I can talk to."

"After fifty years I'm guaranteed shockproof."

"We haven't made love—properly, once, since we came here."

"What do you mean—properly?"

"He starts, but he doesn't finish; nothing happens."

I said uncomfortably, "Rochester wrote about that. A poem called 'The Imperfect Enjoyment.'" I don't know why I gave her this shady piece of literary information; perhaps, like a psychoanalyst, I wanted her not to feel alone with her problem. "It can happen to anybody."

"But it's not his fault," she said. "It's mine. I know it is. He just doesn't like my body."

"Surely it's a bit late to discover that."

"He'd never seen me naked till I came here," she said with the candour of a girl to her doctor—that was all I meant to her, I felt sure.

"There are nearly always first-night nerves. And then if a man worries (you must realize how much it hurts his pride) he can get stuck in the situation for days—weeks even." I began to tell her about a mistress I once had—we stayed together a very long time and yet for two weeks at the beginning I could do nothing at all. "I was too anxious to succeed."

"That's different. You didn't hate the sight of her."

"You are making such a lot of so little."

"That's what he tries to do," she said with sudden school-girl coarseness and giggled miserably.

"We went away for a week and changed the scene, and everything after that was all right. For ten days it had been a flop, and for ten years afterwards we were happy. Very happy. But worry can get established in a room, in the colour of the curtains—it can hang itself up on coat-hangers; you find it smoking away in the ashtray marked Pernod, and when you look at the bed it pokes its head out from underneath like the toes of a pair of shoes." Again I repeated the only charm I could think of. "Take him home."

"It wouldn't make any difference. He's disappointed, that's all it is." She looked down at her long black legs; I followed the course of her eyes because I was finding now that I really wanted her and she said with sincere conviction, "I'm just not pretty enough when I'm undressed."

"You are talking real nonsense. You don't know what nonsense you are talking."

"Oh, no, I'm not. You see—it started all right, but then he touched me"—she put her hands on her breast—"and it all went wrong. I always knew they weren't much good. At school we used to have dormitory inspection—it was awful. Everybody could grow them big except me. I'm no Jayne Mansfield, I can tell you." She gave again that mirthless giggle. "I remember one of the girls told me to sleep with a pillow on top—she said they'd struggle for release and what they needed was exercise. But of course it didn't work. I doubt if the idea was very scientific." She added, "I remember it was awfully hot at night like that."

"Peter doesn't strike me," I said cautiously, "as a man who would want a Jayne Mansfield."

"But you understand, don't you, that, if he finds me ugly, it's all so hopeless."

I wanted to agree with her—perhaps this reason which she had thought up would be less distressing than the truth, and soon enough there would be someone to cure her distrust. I had noticed before that it is often the lovely women who have the least confidence in their looks, but all the same I couldn't pretend to her that I understood it her way. I said, "You must trust me. There's nothing at all wrong with you and that's why I'm talking to you the way I am."

"You are very sweet," she said, and her eyes passed over me rather as the beam from the lighthouse which at night went past the Musée Grimaldi and after a certain time returned and brushed all our windows indifferently on the hotel front. She continued, "He said they'd be back by cocktail time."

"If you want a rest first"—for a little time we had been close, but now again we were getting further and further away. If I pressed her now she might in the end be happy—does conventional morality demand that a girl remain tied as she was tied? They'd been married in church; she was probably a good Christian,—and I know the ecclesiastical rules: at this moment of her life she could be free of him, the marriage could be annulled, but in a day or two it was only too probable that the same rules would say, "He's managed well enough, you are married for life."

And yet I couldn't press her. Wasn't I, after all, assuming far too much? Perhaps it was only a question of first-night nerves; perhaps in a little while the three of them would be back, silent, embarrassed, and Tony in his turn would have a contusion on the cheek. I would have been very glad to see it there; egotism fades a little with the passions which engender it, and I would have been content, I think, just to see her happy.

So we returned to the hotel, not saying much, and she went to her room and I to mine. It was in the end a comedy and not a tragedy, a farce even, which is why I have given this scrap of reminiscence a farcical title.

I was woken from my middle-aged siesta by the telephone. For a moment, surprised by the darkness, I couldn't find the light switch. Scrambling for it, I knocked over my bedside lamp; the telephone went on ringing, and I tried to pick up the holder and knocked over a tooth-glass in which I had given myself a whisky. The little illuminated dial of my watch gleamed up at me, marking eight-thirty. The telephone continued to ring. I got the receiver off, but this time it was the ashtray which fell over. I couldn't get the cord to extend up to my ear, so I shouted in the direction of the telephone, "Hullo!"

A tiny sound came up from the floor which I interpreted as "Is that William?"

I shouted, "Hold on," and now that I was properly awake I realized the light switch was just over my head (in London it was placed over the bedside table). Little petulant noises came up from the floor as I put on the light, like the creaking of crickets.

"Who's that?" I said rather angrily, and then I recognized Tony's voice.

"William whatever's the matter?"

"Nothing's the matter. Where are you?"

"But there was quite an enormous crash. It hurt my eardrum."

"An ashtray," I said.

"Do you usually hurl ashtrays around?"

"I was asleep."

"At eight-thirty? William! William!"

I said, "Where are you?"

"A little bar in what Mrs. Clarenty would call Monty."

"You promised to be back by dinner," I said.

"That's why I'm telephoning you. I'm being *responsible*, William. Do you mind telling Poopy that we'll be a little late? Give her dinner. Talk to her as only you know how. We'll be back by ten."

"Has there been an accident?"

I could hear him chuckling up the phone. "Oh, I wouldn't call it an accident."

"Why doesn't Peter call her himself?"

"He says he's not in the mood."

"But what shall I tell her—" The telephone went dead.

I got out of bed and dressed and then I called her room. She answered very quickly; I think she must have been sitting by the telephone. I relayed the message, asking her to meet me in the bar, and rang off before I had to face answering any questions.

But I found it was not so difficult as I feared to cover up; she was immensely relieved that somebody had telephoned. She had sat there in her room from half past seven onwards thinking of all the dangerous turns and ravines on the Grande Corniche, and when I rang she was half afraid that it might be the police or a hospital. Only after she had drunk two dry martinis and laughed quite a lot at her fears did she say, "I wonder why Tony rang you and not Peter me?"

I said (I had been working the answer out), "I gather he suddenly had an urgent appointment—in the loo."

It was as though I had said something enormously witty.

"Do you think they are a bit tight?" she asked.

"I wouldn't wonder."

"Darling Peter," she said. "He deserved the day off," and I couldn't help wondering in what direction his merit lay.

"Do you want another martini?"

"I'd better not," she said, "You've made me tight too."

Go Tell It on the Mountain

James Baldwin

James Baldwin is one of the few novelists who have been successful in portraying the religious aspects of daily life and the dynamics of the interaction between a preacher and his church or parishioners. In this excerpt from *Go Tell It on the Mountain*, he portrays a familiar scene in Western life (and in Western literature)—the conflict between a vocation or calling and a man's attraction to a woman. In this instance there is a double tension, since the woman is from a lower class, and the preacher perceives her as essentially a loose and sensual woman. He must grant that he himself contributed somewhat to her downfall, but he is able to erase some part of that guilt by the strong condemnation that he feels for her way of life.

He is torn further. Unlike his wife, the "loose and sinful" woman has aroused in him a strong sexual passion, and in addition she is pregnant with his child—while his own wife has been unable to conceive.

However, those subsidiary themes are overshadowed by his realization that if he establishes a liaison with this woman, or even divorces his wife to marry her, he will be giving up the Lord's work. At this level, the conflict is not simply a struggle between sin or salvation, but an awareness that he faces the choice between two very different

James Baldwin, *Go Tell It on the Mountain*, The Dial Press, New York, 1963.

lifestyles, two fundamentally different orientations. Occupationally, his way upward lies in being a success as a preacher. In this theological view, his way upward requires renunciation of his fleshly yearnings.

In the lives of many poets, writers, and even scientists, this conflict has often occurred: whether to espouse a high and ascetic dedication to one's life calling or to accept the pleasures of a simpler existence on a more mundane level.

Baldwin has not, however, made the conflict between the preacher and his woman a simple one, for she is portrayed as a woman of great dignity and strength, if little education, while the preacher is shown to be partly a hypocrite, and not only a noble soul tormented by sexual needs. He wants to get on with his work, and is frightened that he will be exposed and will lose his standing in the community. She would like to have a loving relationship with her man. The scandal means relatively little to her, but she is nevertheless willing to protect him by simply going away.

It should also be noted that even at her lower class level to have a child out of wedlock will bring much social punishment on her head. She recognizes that an illegitimate child will not simply be accepted without question. For her the solution must be to go away, helped by the money that the preacher steals from his wife.

Readers will empathize in varying degrees with a man who wants to abandon a woman in order to devote himself to religion; many would identify with him more easily if he were intending to become a poet or artist. Nevertheless, Baldwin is careful to emphasize that in this man's own eyes, preaching *is* his vocation.

Yet what frightened him, and kept him more than ever on his knees, was the knowledge that, once having fallen, nothing would be easier than to fall again. Having possessed Esther, the carnal man awoke, seeing the possibility of conquest everywhere. He was made to remember that though he was holy he was yet young; the women who had wanted him wanted him still; he had but to stretch out his hand and take what he wanted—even sisters in the church. He struggled to wear out his visions in the marriage bed, he struggled to awaken Deborah, for whom daily his hatred grew.

He and Esther spoke in the yard again as spring was just beginning. The ground was wet still with melting snow and ice; the sun was everywhere; the naked branches of the trees seemed to be lifting themselves upward toward the pale sun, impatient to put forth leaf and flower. He was standing at the well in his shirtsleeves, singing softly to himself—praising God for the dangers he had passed. She came down the porch steps into the yard, and though he heard the soft step, and knew that it was she, it was a moment before he turned around.

He expected her to come up to him and ask for his help in something she was doing in the house. When she did not speak, he turned around. She was wearing a light, cotton dress of light-brown and dark-brown squares, and her hair was braided tightly all around her head. She looked like a little girl, and he almost smiled. Then: "What's the matter?" he asked her; and felt the heart within him sicken.

"Gabriel," she said, "I going to have a baby."

He stared at her; she began to cry. He put the two pails of water carefully on the ground. She put out her hands to reach him, but he moved away.

"Girl, stop that bellering. What are you talking about?"

But, having allowed her tears to begin, she could not stop them at once. She continued to cry, weaving a little where she stood, and with her hands to her face. He looked in panic around the yard and toward the house. "Stop that," he cried again, not daring here and now to touch her, "and tell me what's the matter!"

"I told you," she moaned, "I done told you. I going to have a baby." She looked at him, her face broken up and the hot tears falling. "It's the Lord's truth. I ain't making up no story, it's the Lord's truth."

He could not take his eyes from her, though he hated what he saw. "And when you done find this out?"

"Not so long. I thought maybe I was mistook. But ain't no mistake. Gabriel, what we going to do?"

Then, as she watched his face, her tears began again.

"Hush," he said, with a calm that astonished him, "we *going* to do something, just you be quiet."

"What we going to do, Gabriel? *Tell* me—what you a-fixing in your mind to do?"

"You go on back in the house. Ain't no way for us to talk now."

"Gabriel—"

"Go on in the house, girl. Go *on*!" And when she did not move, but continued to stare at him: "We going to talk about it *tonight*. We going to get to the bottom of *this* thing tonight!"

She turned from him and started up the porch steps. "And dry your *face*," he whispered. She bent over, lifting the front of her dress to dry her eyes, and stood so for a moment on the bottom step while he watched her. Then she straightened and walked into the house, not looking back.

She was going to have his baby—*his* baby? While Deborah, despite their groaning, despite the humility with which she endured his body, yet failed to be quickened by any coming life. It was in the womb of Esther, who was no better than a harlot, that the seed of the prophet would be nourished.

And he moved from the well, picking up, like a man in a trance, the heavy pails of water. He moved toward the house, which now—high, gleaming roof, and spun-gold window— seemed to watch him and to listen; the very sun above his head and the earth beneath his feet had ceased their turning; the water, like a million warning voices, lapped in the buckets he carried on each side; and his mother, beneath the startled earth on which he moved, lifted up, endlessly, her eyes.

They talked in the kitchen as she was cleaning up.

"How come you"—it was his first question—"to be so sure this here's my baby?"

She was not crying now. "Don't you start a-talking that way," she said. "Esther ain't in the habit of lying to *no*body, and I ain't gone with so many men that I'm subject to get my mind confused."

She was very cold and deliberate, and moved about the kitchen with a furious concentration on her tasks, scarcely looking at him.

He did not know what to say, how to reach her.

"You tell your mother yet?" he asked, after a pause. "You been to see a doctor? How come you to be so sure?"

She sighed sharply. "No, I ain't told my mother, I ain't crazy. I ain't told nobody except you."

"How come you to be so sure?" he repeated. "If you ain't seen no doctor?"

"What doctor in this town you want me to go see? I go to see a doctor, I might as well get up and shout it from the housetops. No, I ain't seen no doctor, and I ain't fixing to see one in a hurry. I don't need no doctor to tell me what's happening in my belly."

"And how long you been knowing about this?"

"I been knowing this for maybe a month—maybe six weeks now."

"Six weeks? Why ain't you opened your mouth before?"

"Because I wasn't sure. I thought I'd wait and make sure. I didn't see no need for getting all up in the air before I *knew*. I didn't want to get you all upset and scared and evil, like you is now, if it weren't no need." She paused, watching him. Then: "And you said this morning we was going to do something. What we going to do? That's what we got to figure out now, Gabriel."

"What we going to do?" he repeated at last; and felt that the sustaining life had gone out of him. He sat down at the kitchen table and looked at the whirling pattern on the floor.

But the life had not gone out of her; she came to where he sat, speaking softly, with bitter eyes. "You sound mighty strange to me," she said. "Don't look to me like you thinking of nothing but how you can get shut of this—and me, too—quick as you know how. It wasn't like that always, was it, Reverend? Once upon a time you couldn't think of nothing and nobody *but* me. What you thinking about tonight? I be damned if I think it's *me* you thinking of."

"Girl," he said, wearily, "don't talk like you ain't got good sense. You know I got a wife to think about—" and he wanted to say more, but he could not find the words, and, helplessly, he stopped.

"I know that," she said with less heat, but watching him still with eyes from which the old, impatient mockery was not entirely gone, "but what I mean is, if you was able to forget her once you ought to be able to forget her twice."

He did not understand her at once; but then he sat straight up, his eyes wide and angry. "What you mean, girl? What you trying to say?"

She did not flinch—even in his despair and anger he recognized how far she was from being the frivolous child she had always seemed to him. Or was it that she had been, in so short a space of time, transformed? But he spoke to her at this disadvantage: that whereas he was unprepared for any change in her, she had apparently taken his measure from the first and could be surprised by no change in him.

"You know what I mean," she said. "You ain't never going to have no kind of life with that skinny, black woman—and you ain't never going to be able to make her happy—and she ain't never going to have no children. I be blessed, anyway, if I think you was in your right mind when you married her. And it's *me* that's going to have your baby!"

"You want me," he asked at last, "to leave my wife—and come with you?"

"*I* thought," she answered, "that you had done thought of that yourself, already, many and many a time."

"You know," he said, with a halting anger, "I ain't never said nothing like that. I ain't never told you I wanted to leave my wife."

"I ain't talking," she shouted, at the end of patience, "about nothing you done *said*!"

Immediately, they both looked toward the closed kitchen doors—for they were not alone in the house this time. She sighed, and smoothed her hair with her hand; and he saw then that her hand was trembling and that her calm deliberation was all a frenzied pose.

"Girl," he said, "does you reckon I'm going to run off and lead a life of sin with you somewhere, just because you tell me you got my baby kicking in your belly? How many kinds of a fool you think I am? I got God's work to do—my life don't belong to you. Nor to that baby, neither—if it *is* my baby."

"It's your baby," she said, coldly, "and ain't no way in the world to get around *that*. And it ain't been so very long ago, right here in this very *room*, when looked to me like a life of sin was all you was ready for."

"Yes," he answered, rising, and turning away, "Satan tempted me and I fell. I ain't the first man been made to fall on account of a wicked woman."

"You be careful," said Esther, "how you talk to me. I ain't the first girl's been ruined by a holy man, neither."

"Ruined?" he cried. "You? How you going to be ruined? When you been walking through this town just like a harlot, and a-kicking up your heels all over the pasture? How you going to stand there and tell me you been *ruined*? If it hadn't been me, it sure would have been somebody else."

"But it *was* you," she retorted, "and what I want to know is what we's going to do about it."

He looked at her. Her face was cold and hard—ugly; she had never been so ugly before.

"I don't know," he said, deliberately, "what *we* is going to do. But I tell you what I think *you* better do: you better go along and get one of these boys you been running around with to marry you. Because I can't go off with you nowhere."

She sat down at the table and stared at him with scorn and amazement; sat down heavily, as though she had been struck. He knew that she was gathering her forces; and now she said what he had dreaded to hear:

"And suppose I went through town and told your wife, and the churchfolks, and everybody—supposed I did that, Reverend?"

"And who you think," he asked—he felt himself enveloped by an awful, falling silence—"is going to believe you?"

She laughed. "Enough folks'd believe me to make it mighty hard on you." And she watched him. He walked up and down the kitchen, trying to avoid her eyes. "You just think back," she said, "to that first night, right here on this damn white folks' floor, and you'll see it's too late for you to talk to Esther about how holy you is. I don't care if you want to live a lie, but I don't see no reason for you to make me suffer on account of it."

"You can go around and tell folks if you want to," he said, boldly, "but it ain't going to look so good for you neither."

She laughed again. "But I ain't the holy one. You's a married man, and you's a preacher—and who you think folks is going to blame most?"

He watched her with a hatred that was mixed with his old desire, knowing that once more she had the victory.

"I can't marry you, you know that," he said. "Now, what you want me to do?"

"No," she said, "and I reckon you *wouldn't* marry me even if you *was* free. I reckon you don't want no whore like Esther for your wife. Esther's just for the night, for the dark, where won't nobody see you getting your holy self all dirtied up with Esther. Esther's just good enough to go out and have *your* bastard somewhere in the goddamn woods. Ain't that so, Reverend?"

He did not answer her. He could find no words. There was only silence in him, like the grave.

She rose, and moved to the open kitchen door, where she stood, her back to him, looking out into the yard and on the silent streets where the last, dead rays of the sun still lingered.

"But I reckon," she said slowly, "that I don't want to be with you no more'n you want to be with me. I don't want no man what's ashamed and scared. Can't do me no good, that kind of man." She turned in the door and faced him; this was the last time she really looked at him, and he would carry that look to his grave. "There's just one thing I want you to do," she said. "You do that, and we be all right."

"What you want me to do?" he asked, and felt ashamed.

"I *would* go through this town," she said, "and tell every-body about the Lord's anointed. Only reason I don't is because I don't want my mama and daddy to know what a fool I been. I ain't ashamed of *it*—I'm ashamed of *you*—you done made me feel a shame I ain't never felt before. I shamed before by *God*—to let somebody make me cheap, like you done done."

He said nothing. She turned her back to him again.

"I . . . just want to go somewhere," she said, "*go* some-where, and *have* my baby, and think all this out of my mind. I want to go somewhere and get my mind straight. *That's* what I want you to do—and that's pretty cheap. I guess it takes a holy man to make a girl a real whore."

"Girl," he said, "I ain't got no *money*."

"Well," she said, coldly, "you damn well better find some."

Then she began to cry. He moved toward her, but she moved away.

"If I go out into the field," he said, helplessly, "I ought to be able to make enough money to send you away."

"How long that going to take?"

"A month maybe."

And she shook her head. "I ain't going to stay around here that long."

They stood in silence in the open kitchen door, she struggling against her tears, he struggling against his shame. He could only think: "Jesus Jesus Jesus. Jesus Jesus."

"Ain't you got nothing saved up?" she asked at last. "Look to me like you been married long enough to've saved something!"

Then he remembered that Deborah had been saving money since their wedding day. She kept it in a tin box at the top of the cupboard. He thought of how sin led to sin.

"Yes," he said, "a little. I don't know how much."

"You bring it tomorrow," she told him.

"Yes," he said.

He watched her as she moved from the door and went to the closet for her hat and coat. Then she came back, dressed for the street and, without a word, passed him, walking down the short steps into the yard. She opened the low gate and turned down the long, silent, flaming street. She walked slowly, head bowed, as though she were cold. He stood watching her, thinking of the many times he had watched her before, when her walk had been so different and her laughter had come ringing back to mock him.

He stole the money while Deborah slept. And he gave it to Esther in the morning. She gave notice that same day, and a week later she was gone—to Chicago, said her parents, to find a better job and to have a better life.

Deborah became more silent than ever in the weeks that followed. Sometimes he was certain she had discovered that the money was missing and knew that he had taken it—sometimes he was certain that she knew nothing. Sometimes he was certain that she knew everything: the theft, and the reason for the theft. But she did not speak. In the middle of the spring he went out into the field to preach, and was gone three months. When he came back he brought the money with him and put it in the box again. No money had been added in the meanwhile, so he still could not be certain whether Deborah knew or not.

He decided to let it all be forgotten, and begin his life again.

But the summer brought him a letter, with no return name or address, but postmarked from Chicago. Deborah gave it to him at breakfast, not seeming to have remarked the hand or the postmark, along with the bundle of tracts from a Bible house which they both distributed each week through the town. She had a letter, too, from Florence, and it was perhaps this novelty that distracted her attention.

Esther's letter ended:

What I think is, I made a mistake, that's true, and I'm paying for it now. But don't you think you ain't going to pay for it—I don't know when and I don't know how, but I know you going to be brought low one of these fine days. I ain't holy like you are, but I know right from wrong.

I'm going to have my baby and I'm going to bring him up to be a man. And I ain't going to read to him out of no Bibles and I ain't going to take him to hear no preaching. If he don't drink nothing but moonshine all his natural days he be a better man than his Daddy.

"What Florence got to say?" he asked dully, crumpling this letter in his fist.

Deborah looked up with a faint smile. "Nothing much, honey. But she sound like she going to get married."

Death in Venice

Thomas Mann

The gradual development of psychodynamic thought since World War I has made us increasingly aware that we are all in part bisexual, i.e., there are both masculine and feminine components in our personalities, and we feel attracted to members of our own sex as well as the opposite sex. Most people are still socialized to reject these impulses, or to be ashamed of them, if their existence is recognized. In most social networks throughout Western society, those who act out such tendencies, whether of a bisexual or homosexual character, are ostracized or suffer the contempt of their fellows.

This growing awareness, however, has been accompanied by an increasing permissiveness regarding the behavior that was formerly viewed as deviant. Among the social philosophers of our time are many who urge us to recognize these impulses in ourselves, since doing so will lead to a richer emotional life. In an increasing number of social circles, people no longer have to hide behavior that formerly would have caused them to lose jobs, friends, spouses, and even the ordinary respect of their peers.

Even in this more permissive age, however, for an older man to express his sexual attraction for a young, even a beautiful young, boy, is to confess to a perversion. The most permissive proposals for a new set of laws that would wipe out all legal punishments for sexual intercourse between consenting adults, of any sex and in any number, typically retain this implicit condemnation.

It is in this context that the delicate and sensitive evocation of such feelings by Thomas Mann in *Death in Venice* must be viewed. In this story, he is first of all reminding us of a world long past, the period just before World I, when—if we are to believe the stories told by the upper classes—life for the well-to-do was leisurely, aided by numerous servants, and protected from strife. The writer describes an elderly man who is famous, successful, and alone, when he is suddenly struck by the almost golden appearance of a beautiful boy. He becomes aware of his own feelings, but in the course of the story he makes no attempt to establish a sexual relationship with the boy, nor is that possibility even a remote temptation within his world. He can, however, in his own musings about his feelings and the situation remember the Platonic analyses of love in the *Phaedrus* and *Symposium,* and even enjoy his distant loving of the young boy and a set of feelings that would have horrified his age peers within his class.

As he sat there dreaming thus, deep, deep into the void, suddenly the margin line of the shore was cut by a human form. He gathered up his gaze and withdrew it from the illimitable, and lo, it was the lovely boy who crossed his vision coming from the left along the sand. He was barefoot, ready for wading, the slender legs uncovered above the knee, and moved slowly, yet with such a proud, light tread as to make it seem he had never worn shoes. He looked towards the diagonal row of cabins; and the sight of the Russian family, leading their lives there in joyous simplicity, distorted his features in a spasm of angry disgust. His brow darkened, his lips curled, one corner of the mouth was drawn down in a harsh line that marred the curve of the cheek, his frown was so heavy that the eyes seemed to sink in as they uttered beneath the black and vicious language of hate. He looked down, looked threateningly back once more; then giving it up with a violent and contemptuous shoulder-shrug, he left his enemies in the rear.

A feeling of delicacy, a qualm, almost like a sense of shame, made Aschenbach turn away as though he had not seen; he felt unwilling to take advantage of having been, by chance, privy to this passionate reaction. But he was in truth both moved and exhilarated—that is to say, he was delighted. This childish exhibition of fanaticism, directed against the good-naturedest simplicity in the world—it gave to the godlike and inexpressive the final human touch. The figure of the half-grown lad, a masterpiece from nature's own hand, had been significant enough when it gratified the eye alone; and now it evoked sympathy as well—the little episode had set it off, lent it a dignity in the onlooker's eyes that was beyond its years.

Aschenbach listened with still averted head to the boy's voice announcing his coming to his companions at the sand-heap. The voice was clear, though a little weak, but they answered, shouting his name—or his nickname—again and again. Aschenbach was not without curiosity to learn it, but could make out nothing more exact than two musical syllables, something like Adgio—or, oftener still, Adjiu, with a long-drawn-out *u* at the end. He liked the melodious sound, and found it fitting; said it over to himself a few times and turned back with satisfaction to his papers.

Holding his travelling-pad on his knees, he took his fountain-pen and began to answer various items of his correspondence. But presently he felt it too great a pity to turn his back, and the eyes of his mind, for the sake of mere commonplace correspondence, to this scene which was, after all, the most rewarding one he knew. He put aside his papers and swung round to the sea; in no long time, beguiled by the voices of the children at play, he had turned his head and sat resting it against the chair-back, while he gave himself up to contemplating the activities of the exquisite Adgio.

His eye found him out at once, the red breast-knot was unmistakable. With some nine or ten companions, boys and girls of his own age and younger, he was busy putting in place an old plank to serve as a bridge across the ditches between the sand-piles. He directed the work by shouting and motioning with his head, and they were all chattering in many tongues—French, Polish, and even some of the Balkan languages. But his was the name oftenest on their lips, he was plainly sought after, wooed, admired. One lad in particular, a Pole like himself, with a name that sounded something like Jaschiu, a sturdy lad with brilliantined black hair, in a belted linen suit, was his particular liegeman and friend. Operations at the sand-pile being ended for the time, they two walked away along the beach, with their arms round each other's waists, and once the lad Jaschiu gave Adgio a kiss.

Aschenbach felt like shaking a finger at him. "But you,

Critobulus," he thought with a smile, "you I advise to take a year's leave. That long, at least, you will need for complete recovery." A vendor came by with strawberries, and Aschenbach made his second breakfast of the great luscious, dead-ripe fruit. It had grown very warm, although the sun had not availed to pierce the heavy layer of mist. His mind felt relaxed, his senses revelled in the vast and soothing communion with the silence of the sea. The grave and serious man found sufficient occupation in speculating what name it could be that sounded like Adgio. And with the help of a few Polish memories he at length fixed on Tadzio, a shortened form of Thaddeus, which sounded, when called, like Tadziu or Adziu.

Tadzio was bathing. Aschenbach had lost sight of him for a moment, then descried him far out in the water, which was shallow a very long way—saw his head, and his arm striking out like an oar. But his watchful family were already on the alert; the mother and governess called from the veranda in front of their bathing-cabin, until the lad's name, with its softened consonants and long-drawn *u*-sound, seemed to possess the beach like a rallying-cry; the cadence had something sweet and wild: "Tadziu! Tadziu!" He turned and ran back against the water, churning the waves to a foam, his head flung high. The sight of this living figure, virginally pure and austere, with dripping locks, beautiful as a tender young god, emerging from the depths of sea and sky, outrunning the element—it conjured up mythologies, it was like a primeval legend, handed down from the beginning of time, of the birth of form, of the origin of the gods. With closed lids Aschenbach listened to this poesy hymning itself silently within him, and anon he thought it was good to be here and that he would stop awhile.

Afterwards Tadzio lay on the sand and rested from his bathe, wrapped in his white sheet, which he wore drawn underneath the right shoulder, so that his head was cradled on his bare right arm. And even when Aschenbach read, without looking up, he was conscious that the lad was there; that it would cost him but the slightest turn of the head to have the rewarding vision once more in his purview. Indeed, it was almost as though he sat there to guard the youth's repose; occupied, of course, with his own affairs, yet alive to the presence of that noble human creature close at hand. And his heart was stirred, it felt a father's kindness: such an emotion as the possessor of beauty can inspire in one who has offered himself up in spirit to create beauty.

At midday he left the beach, returned to the hotel, and was carried up in the lift to his room. There he lingered a little time before the glass and looked at his own grey hair, his keen and weary face. And he thought of his fame, and how people gazed respectfully at him in the streets, on account of his unerring gift of words and their power to charm. He called up all the worldly successes his genius had reaped, all he could remember, even his patent of nobility. Then went to luncheon down in the dining-room, sat at his little table and ate. Afterwards he mounted again in the lift, and a group of young folk, Tadzio among them, pressed with him into the little compartment. It was the first time Aschenbach had seen him close at hand, not merely in perspective, and could see and take account of the details of his humanity. Someone spoke to the lad, and he, answering, with indescribably lovely smile, stepped out again, as they had come to the first floor, backwards, with his eyes cast down. "Beauty makes people self-conscious," Aschenbach thought, and considered within himself imperatively why this should be. He had noted, further, that Tadzio's teeth were imperfect, rather jagged and bluish, without a healthy glaze, and of that peculiar brittle transparency which the teeth of chlorotic people often show. "He is delicate, he is sickly," Aschenbach thought. "He will most likely not live to grow old." He did not try to account for the pleasure the idea gave him . . .

. . . Soon the observer knew every line and pose of this form that limned itself so freely against sea and sky; its every loveliness, though conned by heart, yet thrilled him each day afresh; his admiration knew no bounds, the delight of his eye was unending. Once the lad was summoned to speak to a guest who was waiting for his mother at their cabin. He ran up, ran dripping wet out of the sea, tossing his curls, and put out his hand, standing with his weight on one leg, resting the other foot on the toes; as he stood there in a posture of suspense the turn of his body was enchanting, while his features wore a look half shamefaced, half conscious of the duty breeding laid upon him to please. Or he would lie at full length, with his bath-robe around him, one slender young arm resting on the sand, his chin in the hollow of his hand; the lad they called Jaschiu squatting beside him, paying him court. There could be nothing lovelier on earth than the smile and look with which the playmate thus singled out rewarded his humble friend and vassal. Again, he might be at the water's edge, alone, removed from his family, quite close to Aschenbach; standing erect, his hands clasped at the back of his neck, rocking slowly on the balls of his feet, daydreaming away into blue space, while little waves ran up and bathed his toes. The ringlets of honey-coloured hair clung to his temples and neck, the fine down along the upper vertebrae was yellow in the sunlight; the thin envelope of flesh covering the torso betrayed the delicate outlines of the ribs and the symmetry of the breast-structure. His armpits were still as smooth as a statue's, smooth the glistening hollows behind the knees, where the blue network of veins suggested that the body was formed of some stuff more transparent than mere flesh. What discipline, what precision of thought were expressed by the tense youthful perfection of this form! And yet the pure, strong will which had laboured in darkness and succeeded in bringing this godlike work of art to the light of day—was it not known and familiar to him, the artist? Was not the same force at work in himself when he strove in cold fury to liberate from the marble mass of language the slender forms of his art which he saw with the eye of his mind and would body forth to men as the mirror and image of spiritual beauty?

Mirror and image! His eyes took in the proud bearing of that figure there at the blue water's edge; with an outburst of rapture he told himself that what he saw was beauty's very essence; form as divine thought, the single and pure perfection which resides in the mind, of which an image and likeness, rare and holy, was here raised up for adoration. This was very frenzy—and without a scruple, nay, eagerly, the aging artist bade it come. His mind was in travail, his whole mental background in a state of flux. Memory flung up in him the primitive thoughts which are youth's inheritance, but which with him had remained latent, never leaping up into a blaze. Has it not been written that the sun beguiles our attention from things of the intellect to fix it on things of the sense? The sun, they say, dazzles; so bewitching reason and memory that the soul for very pleasure forgets its actual state, to cling with doting on the loveliest of all the objects she shines on. Yes, and then it is only through the medium of some corporeal being that it can raise itself again to contemplation of higher things. Amor, in sooth, is like the mathematician who in order to give children a knowledge of pure form must do so in the language of pictures; so, too, the god, in order to make visible the spirit, avails himself of the forms and colours of human youth, gilding it with all imaginable beauty that it may serve memory as a tool, the very sight of which then sets us afire with pain and longing.

Such were the devotee's thoughts, such the power of his emotions. And the sea, so bright with glancing sunbeams, wove in his mind a spell and summoned up a lovely picture: there was the ancient plane-tree outside the walls of Athens, a hallowed, shady spot, fragrant with willow-blossom and adorned with images and votive offerings in honour of the nymphs and Achelous. Clear ran the smooth-pebbled stream at the foot of the spreading tree. Crickets were fiddling. But on the gentle grassy slope, where one could lie yet hold the head erect, and shelter from the scorching heat, two men reclined, an elder with a younger, ugliness paired with beauty and wisdom with grace. Here Socrates held forth to youthful Phaedrus upon the nature of virtue and desire, wooing him with insinuating wit and charming turns of phrase. He told him of the shuddering and unwonted heat that come upon him whose heart is open, when his eye beholds an image of eternal beauty; spoke of the impious and corrupt, who cannot conceive beauty though they see its image, and are incapable of awe; and of the fear and reverence felt by the noble soul when he beholds a godlike face or a form which is a good image of beauty: how as he gazes he worships the beautiful one and scarcely dares to look upon him, but would offer sacrifice as to an idol or a god, did he not fear to be thought stark mad. "For beauty, my Phaedrus, beauty alone is lovely and visible at once. For, mark you, it is the sole aspect of the spiritual which we can perceive through our senses, or bear so to perceive. Else what should become of us, if the divine, if reason and virtue and truth, were to speak to us through the senses? Should we not perish and be consumed by love, as Semele aforetime was by Zeus? So beauty, then, is the beauty-lover's way to the spirit—but only the way, only the means, my little Phaedrus." . . . And then, sly arch-lover that he was, he said the subtlest thing of all: that the lover was nearer the divine than the beloved; for the god was in the one but not in the other—perhaps the tenderest, most mocking thought that was ever thought, and source of all the guile and secret bliss the lover knows. . . .

Advice to a Young Man on Choosing a Mistress
Benjamin Franklin

Although the popular reputation of Benjamin Franklin remains that of a sober, cautious, moralist devoted to hard work and thrift, "the other Franklin" also continues to live. He was a social success and a gallant with women in the rather tolerant atmosphere of pre-Revolutionary France, where he devoted a quarter of a century to the service of his country. From his eighteenth-century rationalist point of view, sex was a pleasure to be enjoyed, but the promiscuous search after it would only divert one's attention from the important affairs of life. For him, celibacy was not the rational option it appeared to the early Christians. Marriage was a wise arrangement worked out by mankind which promised a secure fountain of contentment if not ecstasy. The present "letter" then is not simply an essay in irony—though many of Franklin's essays are touched with a bit of mockery at human foibles. He makes a genuflection at

From *The Papers of Benjamin Franklin*, edited by Leonard W. Labare and Whitfield J. Bell, Jr., Yale University Press, New Haven, 1961, vol. 3 (January 1, 1745 through June 30, 1750).

eighteenth-century virtue, by beginning and ending his advice with the injunction to marry. Being wise, however, he recognizes that the young man is not yet ready to follow so sensible a course and thus requires additional advice on which *kind* of mistress to choose.

Although Franklin's arguments seem well founded, the reader might consider whether in this age, when sexual liaisons are less attended by scandal and a pressure to marry, an alternative counsel might be wiser, or whether Franklin's notions might be improved by our better knowledge.

June 25, 1745

My dear Friend,

I know of no Medicine fit to diminish the violent natural Inclinations you mention; and if I did, I think I should not communicate it to you. Marriage is the proper Remedy. It is the most natural State of Man, and therefore the State in which you are most likely to find solid Happiness. Your Reasons against entring into it at present, appear to me not well-founded. The circumstantial Advantages you have in View by postponing it, are not only uncertain, but they are small in comparison with that of the Thing itself, the being *married and settled.* It is the Man and Woman united that make the compleat human Being. Separate, she wants his Force of Body and Strength of Reason; he, her Softness, Sensibility and acute Discernment. Together they are more likely to succeed in the World. A single Man has not nearly the Value he would have in that State of Union. He is an incomplete Animal. He resembles the odd Half of a Pair of Scissars. If you get a prudent healthy Wife, your Industry in your Profession, with her good Economy, will be a Fortune sufficient.

But if you will not take this Counsel, and persist in thinking a Commerce with the Sex inevitable, then I repeat my former Advice, that in all your Amours you should *prefer old Women to young ones.* You call this a Paradox, and demand my Reasons. They are these:

1   Because as they have more Knowledge of the World and

their Minds are better stor'd with Observations, their Conversation is more improving and more lastingly agreeable.

2   Because when Women cease to be handsome, they study to be good. To maintain their Influence over Men, they supply the Diminution of Beauty by an Augmentation of Utility. They learn to do a 1000 Services small and great, and are the most tender and useful of all Friends when you are sick. Thus they continue amiable. And hence there is hardly such a thing to be found as an old Woman who is not a good Woman.

3   Because there is no hazard of Children, which irregularly produc'd may be attended with much Inconvenience.

4   Because thro' more Experience, they are more prudent and discreet in conducting an Intrigue to prevent Suspicion. The Commerce with them is therefore safer with regard to your Reputation. And with regard to theirs, if the Affair should happen to be known, considerate People might be rather inclin'd to excuse an old Woman who would kindly take care of a young Man, form his Manners by her good Counsels, and prevent his ruining his Health and Fortune among mercenary Prostitutes.

5   Because in every Animal that walks upright, the Deficiency of the Fluids that fill the Muscles appears first in the highest Part: The Face first grows lank and wrinkled; then the Neck; then the Breast and Arms; the lower Parts continuing to the last as plump as ever: So that covering all above with a Basket, and regarding only what is below the Girdle, it is impossible of two Women to know an old from a young one. And as in the dark all Cats are grey, the Pleasure of corporal Enjoyment with an old Woman is at least equal, and frequently superior, every Knack being by Practice capable of Improvement.

6   Because the Sin is less. The debauching a Virgin may be her Ruin, and make her for Life unhappy.

7   Because the Compunction is less. The having made a young Girl *miserable* may give you frequent bitter Reflections; none of which can attend the making an old Woman *happy.*

8   [thly and Lastly] They are so *grateful!!*

Thus much for my Paradox. But still I advise you to marry directly; being sincerely Your affectionate Friend.

Lament

Dylan Thomas

The following poem needs little comment, celebrating as it does a life devoted to loving and sex. The strong rhythms, almost chanting, deny the title—the old man rejoices in his life and would probably not change any of it, not even the last phase when his children and pious wife surround him with virtue. The poet does not explain the man's extraordinary ability to attract women; instead we see the outrage he created as he swaggered through a field of women. Even "liberated" men can take some delight from this model of indecorum; what changes in our responses to this poem, and to many others that exult in men's sexual pleasures, will the women's liberation movement bring?

When I was a windy boy and a bit
And the black spit of the chapel fold,
(Sighed the old ram rod, dying of women),
I tiptoed shy in the gooseberry wood,   4
The rude owl cried like a telltale tit,
I skipped in a blush as the big girls rolled
Ninepin down on the donkeys' common,
And on seesaw sunday nights I wooed   8
Whoever I would with my wicked eyes,
The whole of the moon I could love and leave
All the green leaved little weddings' wives
In the coal black bush and let them grieve.   12

When I was a gusty man and a half
And the black beast of the beetles' pews,
(Sighed the old ram rod, dying of bitches),
Not a boy and a bit in the wick-   16
Dipping moon and drunk as a new dropped calf,
I whistled all night in the twisted flues,

From *The Collected Poems of Dylan Thomas*, New Directions, New York, 1939.

Midwives grew in the midnight ditches,
And the sizzling beds of the town cried, Quick!—   20
Whenever I drove in a breast high shoal,
Wherever I ramped in the clover quilts,
Whatsoever I did in the coal-
Black night, I left my quivering prints.   24

When I was a man you could call a man
And the black cross of the holy house,
(Sighed the old ram rod, dying of welcome),
Brandy and ripe in my bright, bass prime,   28
No springtailed tom in the red hot town
With every simmering woman his mouse
But a hillocky bull in the swelter
Of summer come in his great good time   32
To the sultry, biding herds, I said,
Oh, time enough when the blood creeps cold,
And I lie down but to sleep in bed,
For my sulking, skulking, coal black soul!   36

When I was half of the man I was
And serve me right as the preachers warn,
(Sighed the old ram rod, dying of downfall),
No flailing calf or cat in a flame   40
Or hickory bull in milky grass
But a black sheep with a crumpled horn,
At last the soul from its foul mousehole
Slung pouting out when the limp time came;   44
And I gave my soul a blind, slashed eye,
Gristle and rind, and a roarers' life,
And I shoved it into the coal black sky
To find a woman's soul for a wife.   48

Now I am a man no more no more
And a black reward for a roaring life,
(Sighed the old ram rod, dying of strangers),
Tidy and cursed in my dove cooed room   52
I lie down thin and hear the good bells jaw—
For, oh, my soul found a sunday wife

In the coal black sky and she bore angels!
Harpies around me out of her womb! 56
Chastity prays for me, piety sings,
Innocence sweetens my last black breath,
Modesty hides my thighs in her wings,
And all the deadly virtues plague my death! 60

Chapter 2

The Nature
of Marriage:
Various Views

Few if any adults have managed to avoid wondering about the
nature of marriage. Doubtless, hunters a thousand centuries ago
sat around campfires at night, complaining about the burdens
their women and children created for them. Every inventor of a
utopia has offered a revised system of marriage for the reader to
ponder. There is not much evidence that all this thinking has
improved marriage by much; but neither can we seriously argue
that so much intellectual work has harmed it either.

It is indeed a peculiar institution in many ways. For example,
it permits very little delegation or transferral of duties. Many
children under parental stress would doubtless be glad to hand
over their responsibilities to another child. Fathers would often
permit another to substitute for them as income-producers. Some
mothering and housekeeping tasks are delegated, but most family
members do not accept alternatives with good grace. The society
still frowns on delegating sexual duties to others.

It is often referred to as a "contract," but it is an unusual one. We are not permitted to negotiate our own personal marriage contracts; if we do, the courts are unlikely to support their provisions. We cannot repudiate the contract, under penalties stipulated in it. In fact, most people never learn what all of its provisions are, and women especially would be reluctant to enter such a contract if they did. Yet almost everyone does in fact enter this relationship. Even in the United States, where the women's liberation movement has made some progress, people remain incurably optimistic, often remarrying soon after a divorce.

Marriage relations remain an inexhaustible well of artistic inspiration because of their complexity and because of a never-ending set of tensions between what the larger society "needs" from families and what individual family members want from one another. These desires overlap, but they also pull and push in very different directions. In sometimes tragic ways, marriage is a last resort: If what we need or want emotionally is not to be found there, the society does not furnish us any other easy source. We are pushed into marriage not because our chances of a high payoff are great, but because other social institutions now in existence offer no such opportunities at all.

That it should have so many paradoxical qualities is not surprising. It is the unique *social* invention designed to handle the problem created by our *biological* heritage: We are not born with instincts, and our offspring cannot care for themselves even after a handful of years' training. Or, reversing that dictum: It is the social invention that has caused human beings to lose gradually any useful instincts they may have had, and that has increased the complexity of the superstructure erected on a biological base. In either case, it is peculiarly an area of interaction between the biological and the social.

The biological qualities of human animals require some kind of "family." The infant does not even become "normal" without human socialization. It cannot survive alone. More important, a *three*-generational link is embodied in this odd social institution: Parents must socialize the child to want to become a parent in turn, to guarantee not so much pregnancy (which would probably happen anyway) but reproduction and care of that *third* generation, and so on *ad infinitum*. As noted before, it is possible to think of other arrangements that would accomplish all the societal ends served by the institution of marriage, but almost always they come all together, as a package. And when "new" societies are created, putting great fervor into creating new family ways, these new patterns soon begin to slip and slide back gradually toward more traditional forms. This need not cause despair, but it does require that we think more seriously about why the system works as it does, if we hope to improve it by much.

The ways of marriage, and the widely divergent views held of it, by philosophers as well as others who suffer through it, guarantee that real marriages are not likely to be works of art; however, they assure the writer an endlessly rich, fascinating flow of dramatic developments from which art can be wrought. Real human beings can take wry satisfaction from undergoing such interesting experiences within this peculiar institution, while the sociologist can view it as an intellectual puzzle that so far cannot be solved.

Marriage

Gregory Corso

In any large-scale urban society the forms of "marriage" in all its possible senses are numerous. Because the kinds of people are many, the range of cultural definitions is wide, and people who are attracted by some uncommon type of union can often locate some social realm or subcircle where they can escape serious censure. Nevertheless, in all societies only a few models of marital unions are widely approved. Everyone is socialized to believe in them, while also being pressed to enter one of them with or without conviction.

In the succeeding poem, Gregory Corso considers whether he should marry, and which kind of marriage he might attempt. In the free marriage market, each person can, at least in fantasy, contract a marriage with others of widely different tastes or social stations, and each person may imagine what life would be like in an urban or a rural setting, in slum or penthouse.

Note, however, that his imagination is limited by his cultural heritage. He does not consider the possibility of joining with several other men to marry one woman, or that of himself marrying several women. He does not entertain the possibility of communal marriage. He does briefly consider and reject a union with another man. Note that he does not even consider, possibly because it would violate the comic note he has chosen, the greater likelihood that his reality will be a marriage to a person who after a while seems banal and ordinary, while he spices this dullness with occasional philanderings.

The increased marital permissiveness over the past decade, which will very likely continue to spread, also increases the likelihood that each of us will in fantasy or reality try out a wider range of marital unions than in the past. Note however that, even now, when most people begin to take seriously the possibility of marriage, the range of

From Gregory Corso, *Selected Poems*, Eyre and Spottiswoode Ltd., London, 1962, pp. 36–40.

alternatives that seem real to them narrows, and indeed the majority gradually or quickly move toward a more traditional union. Here, as with so many other possible utopias, philosophical discourse about them ranges much more widely than the social realities that are put into effect.

Should I get married? Should I be good?
Astound the girl next door
with my velvet suit and faustus hood?
Don't take her to movies but to cemeteries
tell all about werewolf bathtubs and forked clarinets   5
then desire her and kiss her and all the preliminaries
and she going just so far and I understanding why
not getting angry saying You must feel! It's beautiful to
     feel!
Instead take her in my arms
lean against an old crooked tombstone   10
and woo her the entire night the constellations in the
     sky—

When she introduces me to her parents
back straightened, hair finally combed, strangled by a
     tie,
should I sit knees together on their 3rd-degree sofa
and not ask Where's the bathroom?   15
How else to feel other than I am,
a young man who often thinks Flash Gordon soap—
O how terrible it must be for a young man
seated before a family and the family thinking
We never saw him before! He wants our Mary Lou!   20
After tea and homemade cookies they ask What do you
     do?
Should I tell them? Would they like me then?
Say All right get married, we're losing a daughter
but we're gaining a son—
And should I then ask Where's the bathroom?   25

O God, and the wedding! All her family and her friends
and only a handful of mine all scroungy and bearded

just waiting to get at the drinks and food—
And the priest! he looking at me as if I masturbated
asking me Do you take this woman   30
for your lawful wedded wife?
And I, trembling what to say, say Pie Glue!
I kiss the bride all those corny men slapping me on the
     back:
She's all yours, boy! Ha-ha-ha!
And in their eyes you could see   35
some obscene honeymoon going on—
Then all that absurd rice and clanky cans and shoes
Niagara Falls! Hordes of us! Husbands! Wives!
     Flowers!
All streaming into cozy hotels
All going to do the same thing tonight   40
The indifferent clerk he knowing what was going to
     happen
The lobby zombies they knowing what
The whistling elevator man he knowing
The winking bellboy knowing
Everybody knows! I'd be almost inclined not to do
     anything!   45
Stay up all night! Stare that hotel clerk in the eye!
Screaming: I deny honeymoon! I deny honeymoon!
running rampant into those almost climactic suites
yelling Radio belly! Cat shovel!
O I'd live in Niagara forever! in a dark cave beneath
     the Falls   50
I'd sit there the Mad Honeymooner
devising ways to break marriages, a scourge of bigamy
a saint of divorce—

But I should get married I should be good
How nice it'd be to come home to her   55
and sit by the fireplace and she in the kitchen
aproned young and lovely wanting my baby
and so happy about me she burns the roast beef
and comes crying to me and I get up from my big papa
     chair

saying Christmas teeth! Radiant brains! Apple deaf!   60
God what a husband I'd make! Yes, I should get
    married!
So much to do! like sneaking into Mr. Jones' house late
    at night
and cover his golf clubs with 1920 Norwegian books
Like hanging a picture of Rimbaud on the lawnmower
Like pasting Tannu Tuva postage stamps   65
all over the picket fence
Like when Mrs. Kindhead comes to collect
for the Community Chest
grab her and tell her There are unfavorable omens in
    the sky!
And when the mayor comes to get my vote tell him   70
When are you going to stop people killing whales!
And when the milkman comes leave him a note in the
    bottle
Penguin dust, bring me penguin dust, I want penguin
    dust—

Yet if I should get married and it's Connecticut and
    snow
and she gives birth to a child and I am sleepless, worn,   75
up for nights, head bowed against a quiet window,
the past behind me,
finding myself in the most common of situations
a trembling man
knowledged with responsibility not twig-smear   80
nor Roman coin soup—
O what would that be like!
Surely I'd give it for a nipple a rubber Tacitus
For a rattle a bag of broken Bach records
Tack Della Francesca all over its crib   85
Sew the Greek alphabet on its bib
And build for its playpen a roofless Parthenon—

No, I doubt I'd be that kind of father
not rural not snow no quiet window
but hot smelly tight New York City   90

seven flights up, roaches and rats in the walls
a fat Reichian wife screeching over potatoes Get a job!
And five nose-running brats in love with Batman
And the neighbors all toothless and dry haired
like those hag masses of the 18th century   95
all wanting to come in and watch TV
The landlord wants his rent
Grocery store Blue Cross Gas & Electric Knights of
    Columbus
Impossible to lie back and dream Telephone snow,
ghost parking—   100
No! I should not get married I should never get
    married!
But—imagine if I were married to a beautiful
sophisticated woman
tall and pale wearing an elegant black dress
and long black gloves   105
holding a cigarette holder in one hand
and a highball in the other
and we lived high up in a penthouse with a huge
    window
from which we could see all of New York
and even farther on clearer days   110
No, can't imagine myself married to that pleasant
    prison dream—

O but what about love? I forget love
not that I am incapable of love
it's just that I see love as odd as wearing shoes—
I never wanted to marry a girl who was like my mother   115
and Ingrid Bergman was always impossible
And there's maybe a girl now but she's already married
And I don't like men and—
but there's got to be somebody!
Because what if I'm 60 years old and not married,   120
all alone in a furnished room with pee stains on my
    underwear
and everybody else is married! All the universe married
    but me!

Ah, yet well I know that were a woman possible
as I am possible
then marriage would be possible—   125
Like SHE in her lonely alien gaud waiting her Egyptian
    lover
so I wait—bereft of 2,000 years and the bath of life.

The Way of All Flesh
Samuel Butler

When they consider the problem at all, most people who enter a new status position promise to themselves that they will be "the same person" afterwards as before. They assure their friends that if they become boss, their friendship will be unimpaired. If they lose their wealth, they promise that they will not relax their standards for probity, kindness, and attention to others' needs.

So, similarly, friends before marriage promise each other an undying affection. Indeed, the flurry of social activities that precedes marriage would suggest an increased amount of interaction in the future.

However, just as husbands and wives find that they behave very differently toward one another after marriage than before, so do friends. Some two centuries ago, Charles Lamb complained as a bachelor that there was a kind of conspiracy afoot among wives to destroy the friendship between their husbands and their former friends.

Here, the narrator in Samuel Butler's *The Way of All Flesh* confesses self-indulgently that he is like others in this respect: He was annoyed by the protagonists' marriage and they had little to do with one another afterwards; but now that the marriage is foundering, the older man is once more fond of his protégé.

It should be kept in mind, however, that this view of the

Samuel Butler, *The Way of All Flesh*, Hartsdale House, New York, 1935, p. 346.

consequences of marriage is based upon a particular *form* of marriage, one in which husband and wife are supposed to form a unit. On the other hand, it has been fairly common among the working classes in Western nations, and typical among societies where the emphasis is upon the lineage, for the bonds among men to remain fairly strong after marriage. They constitute a social subsystem in which the women have only a peripheral role to play. It may be useful to consider the social conditions that would produce a continuity or constancy of friendship relations (for men or women) that would survive the impact of marriage.

He came to me—not for money, but to tell me his miserable story. I had seen for some time that there was something wrong, and had suspected pretty shrewdly what the matter was, but of course I said nothing. Ernest and I had been growing apart for some time. I was vexed at his having married, and he knew I was vexed, though I did my best to hide it.

A man's friendships are, like his will, invalidated by marriage—but they are also no less invalidated by the marriage of his friends. The rift in friendship which invariably makes its appearance on the marriage of either of the parties to it was fast widening, as it no less invariably does, into the great gulf which is fixed between the married and the unmarried, and I was beginning to leave my *protégé* to a fate with which I had neither right nor power to meddle. In fact I had begun to feel him rather a burden; I did not so much mind this when I could be of use, but I grudged it when I could be of none. He had made his bed and he must lie upon it. Ernest had felt all this and had seldom come near me till now, one evening late in 1860, he called on me, and with a very woe-begone face told me his troubles.

As soon as I found that he no longer liked his wife I forgave him at once, and was as much interested in him as ever. There is nothing an old bachelor likes better than to find a young married man who wishes he had not got married—especially when the case is such an extreme one that he need not pretend to hope that matters will come all right again, or encourage his young friend to make the best of it.

On Marriage

Bertrand Russell

Bertrand Russell belongs to that rare group of first-class minds who have made great contributions to some field of mathematics or science and have in addition made penetrating analyses of social behavior. Though not an especially "moral" man by the standards of his opponents, and often startlingly wrong in some of his assessments, he continually held difficult moral positions that challenged authority, and even some of his wrong judgments made people re-evaluate their easy assumptions.

Both his behavior and his writings relative to marriage scandalized his generation (he came to adulthood at the turn of this century and lived to a great age, shocking to the last). He wrote too well, and too iconoclastically, to be taken seriously as a philosopher, but his analyses could not be ignored.

In this section from his *Marriage and Morals*, Lord Russell suggests what has recently been labeled "open marriage" but would more generally be labeled "promiscuity." His comments are echoed by an acute modern family sociologist, Jessie Bernard, who argues that in the future we can have fidelity or stability in our marriages, but not both. Russell notes that as people have become more differentiated in the modern world, it is more difficult for them to find contentment in marriage; It is no longer true that one man is as good as any other for a husband. But we would be much happier if we gave each other the freedom to seek love and sexual experiences outside the marriage.

These are complex issues, whether viewed esthetically or sociologically. We simply do not know how such marriages would work, that is, whether they would in fact yield more contentment. As we are presently socialized, most of us would not adjust easily to such arrangements. We would be jealous—though perhaps less so if jealousy were not socially approved, and if in fact such extramarital experi-

Bertrand Russell, "Marriage," in *Marriage and Morals,* Liverright, New York, 1929, pp. 135–144.

ences were no threat to our marriages. If both parties to a marriage used their freedom widely, perhaps neither would feel like "returning home," for after all no one would be there to give him or her a welcome.

Russell does not suggest the possibility of communal marriages, or free sexual unions without any commitment at all, although of course the nineteenth century utopias tried those experiments too (and with some success). He envisions civil, kindly people, whose companionship through the years would compensate to some extent for the loss of violent passion, but who would come back from passionate involvements to their life-long companions, perhaps enriched by the experience.

Note, in this connection, how certain kinds of literary conventions have lost their utility in plot construction, because sexual and marital arrangements have become more liberalized: examples are the loss of virginity as a tragedy, or virginity as a supremely great gift; the automatic dismissal of the wife because of her infidelity; the ostracism of the young girl who has stayed out too late at night with her sweetheart; the frustrated longing of the man and woman who want to marry, but divorce is not legal. Consider the problems in novel-writing if the open marriage were to be an accepted part of the family pattern!

When we look round the world at the present day and ask ourselves what conditions seem on the whole to make for happiness in marriage and what for unhappiness, we are driven to a somewhat curious conclusion, that the more civilized people become the less capable they seem of lifelong happiness with one partner. Irish peasants, although until recent times marriages were decided by the parents, were said by those who ought to know them to be on the whole happy and virtuous in their conjugal life. In general, marriage is easiest where people are least differentiated. When a man differs little from other men, and a woman differs little from other women, there is no particular reason to regret not having married someone else. But people with multifarious tastes and pursuits and interests will tend to desire congeniality in their partners, and to feel dissatisfied when they find that they have secured less of it than they might have obtained. The Church, which tends to view marriage solely from the point of view of sex, sees no reason why one partner should not do just as well as another, and can therefore uphold the indissolubility of marriage without realizing the hardship that this often involves.

Another condition which makes for happiness in marriage is paucity of unowned women and the absence of social occasions when husbands meet other women. If there is no possibility of sexual relations with any woman other than one's wife, most men will make the best of the situation and, except in abnormally bad cases, will find it quite tolerable. The same thing applies to wives, especially if they never imagine that marriage should bring much happiness. That is to say, a marriage is likely to be what is called happy if neither party ever expected to get much happiness out of it.

Fixity of social custom, for the same reason, tends to prevent what are called unhappy marriages. If the bonds of marriage are recognized as final and irrevocable, there is no stimulus to the imagination to wander outside and consider that a more ecstatic happiness might have been possible. In order to secure domestic peace where this state of mind exists, it is only necessary that neither the husband nor the wife should fall outrageously below the commonly recognized standard of decent behavior, whatever this may be.

Among civilized people in the modern world, none of these conditions for what is called happiness exist, and accordingly one finds that very few marriages after the first few years are happy. Some of the causes of unhappiness are bound up with civilization, but others would disappear if men and women were more civilized than they are. Let us begin with the latter. Of these the most important is bad sexual education, which is a far commoner thing among the well-to-do than it can ever be among peasants. Peasant children early become accustomed to what are called the facts of life, which they can observe not only among human beings but among animals. They are thus saved from both ignorance and fastidiousness. The carefully educated children of the well-to-do, on the contrary, are shielded from all practical knowledge of sexual matters, and even the most modern parents, who teach children out of books, do not give them that sense of practical familiarity which the peasant child early acquires. The triumph of Christian teaching is when a man and woman marry without either having had previous sexual experience. In nine cases out of ten where this occurs, the results are unfortunate. Sexual behavior among human beings is not instinctive, so that the inexperienced bride and bridegroom, who are probably quite unaware of this fact, find themselves overwhelmed with shame and discomfort. It is little better when the woman alone is innocent but the man has acquired his knowledge from prostitutes. Most men do not realize that a process of wooing is necessary after marriage, and many well-brought-up women do not realize what harm they do to marriage by remaining reserved and physically aloof. All this could be put right by better sexual education, and is in fact very much better with the generation now young than it was with their parents and grandparents. There used to be a widespread belief among women that they were morally superior to men on the ground that they had less pleasure in sex. This attitude made frank companionship between husbands and wives impossible. It was, of course, in itself quite unjustifiable, since failure to enjoy sex, so far from being virtuous, is a mere physiological or psychological deficiency, like a failure to enjoy food, which also a hundred years ago was expected of elegant females.

Other modern causes of unhappiness in marriage are, however, not so easily disposed of. I think that uninhibited civilized people, whether men or women, are generally polygamous in their instincts. They may fall deeply in love and be for some years entirely absorbed in one person, but sooner or later sexual familiarity dulls the edge of passion, and then they begin to look elsewhere for a revival of the old thrill. It is, of course, possible to control this impulse in the interests of morality, but it is very difficult to prevent the impulse from existing. With the growth of women's freedom there has come a much greater opportunity for conjugal infidelity than existed in former times. The opportunity gives rise to the thought, the thought gives rise to the desire, and in the absence of religious scruples the desire gives rise to the act.

Women's emancipation has in various ways made marriage more difficult. In old days the wife had to adapt herself to the husband, but the husband did not have to adapt himself to the wife. Nowadays many wives, on grounds of woman's right to her own individuality and her own career, are unwilling to adapt themselves to their husbands beyond a point, while men who still hanker after the old tradition of masculine domination see no reason why they should do all the adapting. This trouble arises especially in connection with infidelity. In old days the husband was occasionally unfaithful, but as a rule his wife did not know of it. If she did, he confessed that he had sinned and made her believe that he was penitent. She, on the other hand, was usually virtuous. If she was not, and the fact came to her husband's knowledge, the marriage broke up. Where, as happens in many modern marriages, mutual faithfulness is demanded, the instinct of jealousy nevertheless survives, and often proves fatal to the persistence of any deeply rooted intimacy even where no overt quarrels occur.

There is another difficulty in the way of modern marriage, which is felt especially by those who are most conscious of the value of love. Love can flourish only as long as it is free and spontaneous; it tends to be killed by the thought that it is a duty. To say that it is your duty to love so-and-so-is the surest way to cause you to hate him or her. Marriage as a combination of love with legal bonds thus falls between two stools. Shelley says:

I never was attached to that great sect
Whose doctrine is, that each one should select
Out of the crowd a mistress or a friend,
And all the rest, though fair and wise, commend
To cold oblivion, though it is in the code
Of modern morals, and the beaten road
Which those poor slaves with weary footsteps tread,
Who travel to their home among the dead
By the broad highway of the world, and so
With one chained friend, perhaps a jealous foe,
The dreariest and the longest journey go.

There can be no doubt that to close one's mind on marriage against all the approaches of love from elsewhere is to diminish receptivity and sympathy and the opportunities of valuable human contacts. It is to do violence to something which, from the most idealistic standpoint, is in itself desirable. And like every kind of restrictive morality it tends to promote what one may call a policeman's outlook upon the whole of human life—the outlook, that is to say, which is always looking for an opportunity to forbid something.

For all these reasons, many of which are bound up with things undoubtedly good, marriage has become difficult, and if it is not to be a barrier to happiness it must be conceived in a somewhat new way. One solution often suggested, and actually tried on a large scale in America, is easy divorce. I hold, of course, as every humane person must, that divorce should be granted on more grounds than are admitted in the English law, but I do not recognize in easy divorce a solution of the troubles of marriage. Where a marriage is childless, divorce may be often the right solution, even when both parties are doing their best to behave decently; but where there are children the stability of marriage is to my mind a matter of considerable importance. (This is a subject to which I shall return in connection with the family.) I think that where a marriage is fruitful and both parties to it are reasonable and decent, the expectation ought to be that it will be lifelong, but not that it will exclude other sex relations. A marriage which begins with passionate love and leads to children who are desired and loved ought to produce so deep a tie between a man and woman that they will feel something infinitely precious in their companionship, even after sexual passion has decayed, and even if either or both feels sexual passion for someone else. This mellowing of marriage has been prevented by jealousy, but jealousy, though it is an instinctive emotion, is one which can be controlled if it is recognized as bad, and not supposed to be the expression of a just moral indignation. A companionship which has lasted for many years and through many deeply felt events has a richness of content which cannot belong to the first days of love, however delightful these may be. And any person who appreciates what time can do to enhance values will not lightly throw away such companionship for the sake of new love.

It is therefore possible for a civilized man and woman to be happy in marriage, although if this is to be the case a number of conditions must be fulfilled. There must be a feeling of complete equality on both sides; there must be no interference with mutual freedom; there must be the most complete physical and mental intimacy; and there must be a certain similarity in regard to standards of values. (It is fatal, for example, if one values only money while the other values only good work.) Given all these conditions, I believe marriage to be the best and most important relation that can exist between two human beings. If it has not often been realized hitherto, that is chiefly because husband and wife have regarded themselves as each other's policeman. If marriage is to achieve its possibilities, husbands and wives must learn to understand that whatever the law may say, in their private lives they must be free.

Henry Esmond

William Thackeray

William Thackeray is best known now for his *Vanity Fair*, but at the midpoint of the nineteenth century he was hailed for his "masterpiece," *The History of Henry Esmond*. The novel is set amid the turmoil and rivalry of the later seventeenth and early eighteenth centuries, highlighting the question of who was to gain power under Queen Anne. Since his readers could not be expected to know the military events, the political parties, or the social customs of that distant time, Thackeray had to enlighten them accordingly.

The career of Henry Esmond is too complex to summarize in a sentence or two, but what he represents is clear enough. Thackeray lets us see through the flimflam of monarchy and aristocracy and shows us through Esmond's example that aristocrats may be born, but true gentlemen are made—and by their own efforts, their own excellence.

William Thackeray, *The History of Henry Esmond*, Penguin Books, London,1970 (first published 1852).

The novel holds up to scorn the dissoluteness of both the aristocrat and the moneyed title-seeker. The true gentleman can refuse his title, secretly, to avoid hurting the family that once sheltered and cared for him. By ridiculing the sham of titles and court baubles, while extolling natural goodness, Thackeray of course appeals strongly to a middle-class audience.

In the scene that follows, Esmond is still in love with the young lady he has loved throughout the novel (although he will eventually marry her mother when his deeper feelings become clear to him). Like any clever young woman of her day, she is pleased at the courtship, as long as it does not become oppressive to her. After all, Henry Esmond has distinguished himself as an officer, and he is an attractive man. Moreover, a woman in the marriage market *should* have suitors; it informs others how much she is worth. Esmond is not exactly a gay blade, but it is flattering when he pays court to her.

But she is clear-headed about the foolishness of mere love and the lasting value of money. She has beauty and charm as well as the skills that suit her for the aristocratic life. These are doomed to waste away, and she to live in poverty, unless she can find a wealthy buyer. She cannot confer money and a title on a talented, handsome fellow. She wants the best bargain she can get and will not be diverted by any hypocrisy about the virtues of the austere life or the glories of love.

It should be emphasized that her speech is not cold, and the lady herself is not mean or evil. Her society created her, and moreover it generated within her a delight in the very pleasures she *cannot* have, unless she can sell herself at a high price. In our own high-mindedness we may deplore her frivolity, but standards were very different in an age so devoted to hedonism. We may be dismayed at her materialism, her demand for money, but we would be wise to remember that in her world no woman could actually *earn* a living by becoming, say, a physician, professor, or lawyer. She even has spirit enough to assert that she *could* have made a reputation and fortune if she had been a male. Finally, she can even be merry about her plight, and the silliness of her situation, though in fact it required talent and cleverness to surmount it.

This was one view of marriage. In a day when women needed dowries and marriages were arranged, it is likely that many of the gentry would secretly have shared her opinion, whatever cant they may have exchanged among themselves in public.

Doth any young gentleman of my progeny, who may read his old grandfather's papers, chance to be presently suffering under the passion of Love? There is a humiliating cure, but one that is easy and almost specific for the malady—which is, to try an alibi. Esmond went away from his mistress and was cured a half dozen times; he came back to her side, and instantly fell ill again of the fever. He vowed that he could leave her and think no more of her, and so he could pretty well, at least, succeed in quelling that rage and longing he had whenever he was with her; but as soon as he returned he was as bad as ever again. Truly a ludicrous and pitiable object, at least exhausting everybody's pity but his dearest mistress's, Lady Castlewood's, in whose tender breast he reposed all his dreary confessions, and who never tired of hearing him and pleading for him.

Sometimes Esmond would think there was hope. Then again he would be plagued with despair, at some impertinence or coquetry of his mistress. For days they would be like brother and sister, or the dearest friends—she, simple, fond, and charming—he, happy beyond measure at her good behaviour. But this would all vanish on a sudden. Either he would be too pressing, and hint his love, when she would rebuff him instantly, and give his vanity a box on the ear: or he would be jealous, and with perfect good reason, of some new admirer that had sprung up, or some rich young gentleman newly arrived in the town, that this incorrigible flirt would set her nets and baits to draw in. If Esmond remonstrated, the little rebel would say—'Who are you? I shall go my own way, sirrah, and that way is towards a husband, and I don't want *you* on the way. I am for your betters, Colonel, for your betters: do you hear that? You might do if you had an estate and were younger; only eight years older than I, you say! pish, you are a hundred years older. You are an old, old Graveairs, and I should make you miserable, that would be the only comfort I should have in marrying you. But you have not money enough to keep a cat decently after you have paid your man his wages, and your landlady her bill. Do you think I'm going to live in a lodging, and turn the mutton at a string whilst your honour nurses the baby? Fiddlestick, and why did you not get this nonsense knocked out of your head when you were in the wars? You are come back more dismal and dreary than ever. You and mamma are fit for each other. You might be Darby and Joan, and play cribbage to the end of your lives.'

'At least you own to your worldliness, my poor Trix,' says her mother.

'Worldliness—O my pretty lady! Do you think that I am a child in the nursery, and to be frightened by Bogey? Worldliness, to be sure; and pray, madam, where is the harm of wishing to be comfortable? When you are gone, you dearest old woman, or when I am tired of you and have run away from you, where shall I go? Shall I go and be head nurse to my Popish sister-in-law, take the children their physic, and whip 'em, and put 'em to bed when they are naughty? Shall I be Castlewood's upper servant, and perhaps marry Tom Tusher? *Merci*, I have been long enough Frank's humble servant. Why am I not a man? I have ten times his brains, and had I worn the—well, don't let your ladyship be frightened—had I worn a sword and periwig instead of this mantle and commode, to which nature has condemned me— (though 'tis a pretty stuff, too—cousin Esmond! you will go to the Exchange tomorrow, and get the exact counterpart of this riband, sir, do you hear)—I would have made our name talked about. So would Graveairs here have made something out of our name if he had represented it. My Lord Graveairs would have done very well. Yes, you have a very pretty way, and would have made a very decent, grave speaker'; and here she began to imitate Esmond's way of carrying himself, and speaking to his face, and so ludicrously that his mistress burst out a-laughing, and even he himself could see there was some likeness in the fantastical malicious caricature.

'Yes,' says she, 'I solemnly vow, own, and confess, that I want a good husband. Where's the harm of one? My face is my fortune. Who'll come?—buy, buy, buy! I cannot toil, neither can I spin, but I can play twenty-three games on the cards. I can dance the last dance, I can hunt the stag, and I think I could shoot flying. I can talk as wicked as any woman of my years, and know enough stories to amuse a sulky husband for at least one thousand and one nights. I have a pretty taste for dress, diamonds, gambling, and old china. I love sugar plums, Malines lace (that you brought me, cousin, is very pretty), the opera, and everything that is useless and costly. I have got a monkey and a little black boy—Pompey, sir, go and give a dish of chocolate to Colonel Graveairs—and a parrot and a spaniel, and I must have a husband. Cupid, you hear?'

'Iss, Missis,' says Pompey, a little grinning negro Lord Peterborow gave her, with a bird of paradise in his turbant, and a collar with his mistress's name on it.

'Iss, Missis!' says Beatrix, imitating the child. 'And if husband not come, Pompey must go fetch one.'

And Pompey went away grinning with his chocolate tray, as Miss Beatrix ran up to her mother and ended her sally of mischief in her common way, with a kiss—no wonder that upon adying such a penalty her fond judge pardoned her.

Chapter 3

Courtship and Mate Selection

Because young people in a modern industrial society are less dependent for their later success on the goodwill of their parents, they enjoy a greater freedom in personal choice of mate than in most other societies. Nevertheless, in no society are kin and friends unconcerned with who marries whom, or the success of the ensuing marriage. At every point in the life cycle of the individual, from early socialization until death, the individual is pressed toward certain kinds of choices in preference to others. Typically, this means that kin and friends urge the individual to associate most intimately with and to marry others who are of the same class, education, ethnic group, religion, tastes, and so on.

Whether the marriage choice is a "free" market or is determined by elders, it nevertheless occurs in a market. That is, certain types of qualities and performances are valued more than others, and each family or individual seeks as a potential mate someone who has more of these qualities than others, while being restricted in that choice by what the chooser himself or herself can offer. When elders and marriage brokers make these arrangements, they may pay greater attention to money or class than would two young people, but the implicit bargaining is observable even when people do not utilize this rhetoric. That is, even in our own society, where "love" is supposed to be the ideal basis of marital choice, people engaged in courtship do talk freely among one another about which young men will be successful and which will be failures, the amounts of possible inheritance, congeniality of temperament, beauty, indeed all the wide range of traits or performances that are viewed as desirable or undesirable.

Moreover, even when these matters are not articulated, one need only observe actual behavior to see how closely it approximates a bargaining process. A young woman with money somehow seems more "desirable." It is easier to fall in love with a man who seems destined for a great career than one who seems feckless and lazy. Young people in a free marriage market may have friends in all social classes, in different ethnic groups, from different religious backgrounds, and so on, but as they move from casual acquaintance to intimate friendship, through casual dating to steady dating, toward engagement and marriage, it is not merely that the number of "eligibles" decreases. That pool of eligibles becomes more *homogeneous*, and much more like the chooser himself or herself. It is sometimes indeed startling to observe a young person who expresses a general tolerance, a wide tolerance of many kinds of people, even having occasional "crushes" on or brief love relationships with people of whom his or her family would disapprove, but when the final choice is made, it is likely to be almost as traditional as the choice made by someone in his or her social group who had never sought such different experiences.

This is not to urge that the implicit or explicit workings of the market process explain all marriage choices. They rather explain the gradual narrowing of the pool of eligibles. Within that pool, as Robert F. Winch has suggested, we are more likely to choose someone whose personality or psychological needs complement our own. That is, if we are dominant we are more attracted to someone who feeds or supports that dominance, i.e., one who finds submissiveness congenial. If we enjoy nurturing another, we find much more attractive someone who enjoys receiving that nurturance. Up to this point, the foregoing general hypothesis has not been adequately confirmed. However, precisely because of the importance of courtship and mate selection for the happiness of our personal lives (if not for the successful functioning of the society), the problem of just how people choose one another in our kind of society is worth some analytic attention.

Buddenbrooks

Thomas Mann

In all societies, socialization aims at teaching the young to know the difference between good and evil and to *want* to do the things the group values as good. In the phrasing of Christian teaching, people should *love* virtue and *hate* evil. Thereby, in their courtship and marriage behavior, as in all other areas of life, they will autonomously move toward doing the right things, rather than having to consider whether improper actions might simply pay them better.

Socialization also attempts to shape our *view* of what the real alternatives are. We gradually come to reject some alternatives, simply because we can no longer perceive them as "real." Thus, a family like that in Thomas Mann's *Buddenbrooks* develops a rich and strong tradition of what is appropriate to their wealth and social standing, which have risen over many generations in north Germany. Members of this upper-middle-class merchant family are pressed to avoid scandal, to be honorable and upright, and to obey the proprieties and rituals of their privileged class.

They are also taught to obey the *forms* of deference to the status positions in the family, even when the realities are somewhat different. In that nineteenth-century tradition, as in upper-class Europe generally for many generations previously, marriages were "arranged" by elders. However, we should not thereby assume that young men and women were forced brutally into marrying someone they hated, just as we should not assume that in a modern free courtship system people simply choose whomever they fancy. Since in that highly controlled upper-middle-class and upper-class tradition, who associated with whom was also controlled rigorously, young eligibles met only each other, and had few opportunities for even "falling in love" with an inappropriate person. Sometimes young women (but almost never young men) were indeed forced to marry unwillingly,

Thomas Mann, *Buddenbrooks*, translated by H. T. Lowe-Porter, Alfred A. Knopf, Inc., New York, 1959.

but parents who did so were not thought to be wise or loving.

In the letter that follows, we can distinguish several of these underlying strands. Young Thomas Buddenbrooks is now the "head of the family" since he is the lawful heir to the family fortune, and both socially and legally he is in charge of its destiny. On the other hand, he must defer to his mother, and he does so by asking her blessing for his own marriage, though he has contracted it independently of his elders. Nevertheless, he has contracted it *within* a pool of eligibles who, he knows, are appropriate to his station in life.

He is responding, in turn, to her letter in which she asks his permission for his sister to marry. He is head of the family and could reject that marriage, but in fact he knows that he would not have been asked if the elders of his family had not already approved that union. Implicit, too, is the social validation on both sides of the rank of all those who are excluded or included. Thus, Consul Buddenbrooks expresses his approval (and expects hers) of the social standing of all whom he has been seeing during his courtship.

Although the language here seems somewhat stilted to our modern ear, and is a deliberate artistic device that Mann uses to evoke a time past, note to what extent a modern set of communications by telephone and letter would express very similar themes.

Amsterdam, July 30th, 1856
Hotel Het Hassje

My Dear Mother,

I have just received your important letter, and hasten to thank you for the consideration you show me in asking for my consent in the affair under discussion. I send you, of course, not only my hearty agreement, but add my warmest good-wishes, being thoroughly convinced that you and Clara have made a good choice. The fine name Tiburtius is known to me, and I feel sure that Papa had business relations with the father. Clara comes into pleasant connections, in any case, and the position as pastor's wife will be very suited to her temperament.

And Tiburtius has gone back to Riga, and will visit his bride again in August? Well, it will be a gay time then with us in Meng Street—gayer than you realize, for you do not know the reason why I was so joyfully surprised by Mademoiselle Clara's betrothal, nor what a charming company it is likely to be. Yes, my dear good Mother: I am complying with the request to send my solemn consent to Clara's betrothal from the Amstel to the Baltic. But I do so on condition that you send me a similar consent by return of post! I would give three solid gulden to see your face, and even more that of our honest Tony, when you read these lines. But I will come to the point.

My clean little hotel is in the centre of the town with a pretty view of the canal. It is not far from the Bourse; and the business on which I came here—a question of a new and valuable connection, which you know I prefer to look after in person—has gone successfully from the first day. I have still considerable acquaintance here from the days of my apprenticeship; so, although many families are at the shore now, I have been invited out a good deal. I have been at small evening companies at the Van Henkdoms and the Moelens, and on the third day after my arrival I had to put on my dress clothes to go to a dinner at the house of my former chief, van der Kellen, which he had arranged out of season in my honour. Whom did I take in to dinner? Should you like to guess? Fraulein Arnoldsen, Tony's old school-fellow. Her father, the great merchant and almost greater violin artist, and his married daughter and her husband were also of the party.

I well remember that Gerda—if I may call her so—from the beginning, even when she was a young girl at school at Fraulein Weichbrodt's on the Millbrink, made a strong impression on me, never quite obliterated. But now I saw her again, taller, more developed, lovelier, more animated. Please spare me a description, which might so easily sound overdrawn—and you will soon see each other face to face.

You can imagine we had much to talk about at the table, but we had left the old memories behind by the end of the soup, and went on to more serious and fascinating matters. In music I could not hold my own with her, for we poor Buddenbrooks know all too little of that, but in the art of the Netherlands I was more at home, and in literature we were fully agreed.

Truly the time flew. After dinner I had myself presented to old Herr Arnoldsen, who received me with especial cordiality. Later, in the salon, he played several concert pieces, and Gerda also performed. She looked wonderful as she played, and although I have no notion of violin playing, I know that she knew how to sing upon her instrument (a real Stradivarius) so that the tears nearly came into my eyes. Next day I went to call on the Arnoldsens. I was received at first by an elderly companion, with whom I spoke French, but then Gerda came, and we talked as on the day before for perhaps an hour, only that this time we drew nearer together and made still more effort to understand and know each other. The talk was of you Mamma, of Tony, of our good old town, and of my work.

And on that day I had already taken the firm resolve: this one or no one, now or never! I met her again by chance at a garden party at my friend van Svindren's, and I was invited to a musical evening at the Arnoldsens', in the course of which I sounded the young lady by a half-declaration, which was received encouragingly. Five days ago I went to Herr Arnoldsen to ask for permission to win his daughter's hand. He received me in his private office. "My dear Consul," he said, "you are very welcome, hard as it will be for an old widower to part from his daughter. But what does she say? She has already held firmly to her resolve never to marry. Have you a chance?" He was extremely surprised when I told him that Fraulein Gerda had actually given the ground for hope.

He left her some time for reflection, and I imagine that out of pure selfishness he dissuaded her. But it was useless. She had chosen me—since yesterday evening the betrothal is an accomplished fact.

No, my dear Mother, I am not asking a written answer to this letter, for I am leaving to-morrow. But I am bringing with me the Arnoldsens' promise that father, daughter, and married sister will visit us in August, and then you will be obliged to confess that she is the very wife for me. I hope you see no objection in the fact that Gerda is only three years younger than I? I am sure you never thought I would marry a chit out of the Möllendorpf-Langhals, Kistenmaker-Hagenström circle.

And now for the dowry. I am almost frightened to think how Stephan Kistenmaker and Hermann Hagenström and Peter Döhlmann and Uncle Justus and the whole town will blink at me when they hear of the dowry. For my future father-in-law is a millionaire. Heavens, what is there to say? We are such complex, contradictory creatures! I deeply love and respect Gerda Arnoldsen; and I simply will not delve deep down enough in myself to find out how much the thought of the dowry, which was whispered into my ear that first evening, contributed to my feeling. I love her: but it crowns my happiness and pride to think that when she becomes mine, our firm will at the same time gain a very considerable increase of capital.

I must close this letter, dear Mother; considering that in a few days, we shall be talking over my good fortune together, it is already too long. I wish you a pleasant and beneficial stay at the baths, and beg you to greet all the family most heartily for me. Your loving and obedient son,

T.

You Were Perfectly Fine

Dorothy Parker

If the 1920's were "gay" or "mad," this was so only for a tiny segment of the United States population. The writers who sketched that period focused on young people who were rebelling against the stiffness of the period prior to World War I, while nevertheless seeking no fundamental alteration

Dorothy Parker, "You Were Perfectly Fine," in Philip Van Doren (ed.), *The Pocket Book of Modern American Short Stories*, Copyright 1939 by Dorothy Parker; by permission of the Viking Press, New York.

in the economic or power structure of their generation. The public read about them with some disapproval and more envy, for they seemed to be having a delightful time while suffering none of the perils or catastrophes to which ordinary people were subjected. It was a time when prohibition had, in a burst of national puritanism, been imposed upon the country along with political persecution of radicals. Carefree young people were expected to be rich enough to obtain bootleg liquor, and as a rebellious act to drink heavily.

Dorothy Parker depicts in this little story some of these contrasting themes. On the one hand, drunkenness and its aftermath were viewed as a subject of amusement rather than an indicator of alcoholism. Friends meet the following day, as they do now in some circles, to exclaim over how wild and daring they were under the influence of liquor (or drugs). At the same time, friends assure the most drunken or stoned person (here the young man) that he or she did not engage in any really destructive or hurtful behavior. With each reluctant disclosure by the young woman of her companion's obnoxious performance the previous evening, he is more contrite and upset, while she remains—note the womanly stereotype—reassuring: "You were perfectly fine."

Note also, however, that in the social customs of that time, and in spite of the publicly proclaimed sexual permissiveness, to ask for a young woman's hand in marriage was a serious matter. The rebellion, as already noted, was on the surface, not fundamental. Consequently the most upsetting element in the disclosure is that while intoxicated he has "confessed" to her and wants to marry her, while she has accepted him. She is also wise enough (again, note the stereotypical womanly behavior) to avoid asking him whether he "really meant it." Instead she dwells upon how happy they will be when they are married. She gives him no escape from his commitment.

Although Parker consciously creates the farcical pattern this conflict takes in the succeeding exchange, the reader will recognize how difficult it is, even today—when engagement is not so irrevocable as in the past—for a young man to retract his marriage proposal the following day, even if it was given under the temporary impulse of a bright moon and romantic music, the courage and ardor of alcohol, or the disorientation from a psychotropic drug.

The pale young man eased himself carefully into the low chair, and rolled his head to the side, so that the cool chintz comforted his cheek and temple.

"Oh, dear," he said. "Oh, dear, oh, dear, oh, dear. Oh."

The clear-eyed girl, sitting light and erect on the couch, smiled brightly at him.

"Not feeling so well today?" she said.

"Oh, I'm great," he said. "Corking, I am. Know what time I got up? Four o'clock this afternoon, sharp. I kept trying to make it, and every time I took my head off the pillow, it would roll under the bed. This isn't my head I've got on now. I think this is something that used to belong to Walt Whitman. Oh, dear, oh, dear, oh, dear."

"Do you think maybe a drink would make you feel better?" she said.

"The hair of the mastiff that bit me?" he said. "Oh, no, thank you. Please never speak of anything like that again. I'm through. I'm all, all through. Look at that hand; steady as a humming-bird. Tell me, was I very terrible last night?"

"Oh, goodness," she said, "everybody was feeling pretty high. You were all right."

"Yeah," he said. "I must have been dandy. Is everybody sore at me?"

"Good heavens, no," she said. "Everyone thought you were terribly funny. Of course, Jim Pierson was a little stuffy, there for a minute at dinner. But people sort of held him back in his chair, and got him calmed down. I don't think anybody at the other tables noticed it at all. Hardly anybody."

"He was going to sock me?" he said. "Oh, Lord. What did I do to him?"

"Why, you didn't do a thing," she said. "You were perfectly fine. But you know how silly Jim gets, when he thinks anybody is making too much fuss over Elinor."

"Was I making a pass at Elinor?" he said. "Did I do that?"

"Of course you didn't," she said. "You were only fooling, that's all. She thought you were awfully amusing. She was having a marvelous time. She only got a little tiny bit annoyed just once, when you poured the clam-juice down her back."

"My God," he said. "Clam-juice down that back. And every vertebra a little Cabot. Dear God. What'll I ever do?"

"Oh, she'll be all right," she said. "Just send her some flowers, or something. Don't worry about it. It isn't anything."

"No, I won't worry," he said. "I haven't got a care in the world. I'm sitting pretty. Oh, dear, oh, dear. Did I do any other fascinating tricks at dinner?"

"You were fine," she said. "Don't be so foolish about it. Everybody was crazy about you. The maître d'hôtel was a little worried because you wouldn't stop singing, but he really didn't mind. All he said was, he was afraid they'd close the place again, if there was so much noise. But he didn't care a bit, himself. I think he loved seeing you have such a good time. Oh, you were just singing away, there, for about an hour. It wasn't so terribly loud, at all."

"So I sang," he said. "That must have been a treat. I sang."

"Don't you remember?" she said. "You just sang one song after another. Everybody in the place was listening. They loved it. Only you kept insisting that you wanted to sing some song about some kind of fusiliers or other, and everybody kept shushing you, and you'd keep trying to start it again. You were wonderful. We were all trying to make you stop singing for a minute, and eat something, but you wouldn't hear of it. My, you were funny."

"Didn't I eat any dinner?" he said.

"Oh, not a thing," she said. "Every time the waiter would offer you something, you'd give it right back to him, because you said that he was your long-lost brother, changed in the cradle by a gypsy band, and that anything you had was his. You had him simply roaring at you."

"I bet I did," he said. "I bet I was comical. Society's Pet, I must have been. And what happened then, after my overwhelming success with the waiter?"

"Why, nothing much," she said. "You took a sort of dislike to some old man with white hair, sitting across the room, because you didn't like his necktie and you wanted to tell him about it. But we got you out, before he got really mad."

"Oh, we got out," he said. "Did I walk?"

"Walk! Of course you did," she said. "You were absolutely all right. There was that nasty stretch of ice on the sidewalk, and you did sit down awfully hard, you poor dear. But good heavens, that might have happened to anybody."

"Oh, sure," he said. "Louisa Alcott or anybody. So I fell down on the sidewalk. That would explain what's the matter with my— Yes. I see. And then what, if you don't mind?"

"Ah, now, Peter!" she said. "You can't sit there and say you don't remember what happened after that! I did think that maybe you were just a little tight at dinner—oh, you were perfectly all right, and all that, but I did know you were feeling pretty gay. But you were so serious, from the time you fell down—I never knew you to be that way. Don't you know, how you told me I had never seen your real self before? Oh, Peter, I just couldn't bear it, if you didn't remember that lovely long ride we took together in the taxi! Please, you do remember that, don't you? I think it would simply kill me, if you didn't."

"Oh, yes," he said. "Riding in the taxi. Oh, yes, sure. Pretty long ride, hmm?"

"Round and round and round the park," she said. "Oh, and the trees were shining so in the moonlight. And you said you never knew before that you really had a soul."

"Yes," he said. "I said that. That was me."

"You said such lovely, lovely things," she said. "And I'd never known, all this time, how you had been feeling about me, and I'd never dared to let you see how I felt about you. And then last night—oh, Peter dear, I think that taxi ride was the most important thing that ever happened to us in our lives."

"Yes," he said. "I guess it must have been."

"And we're going to be so happy," she said. "Oh, I just want to tell everybody! But I don't know—I think maybe it would be sweeter to keep it all to ourselves."

"I think it would be," he said.

"Isn't it lovely?" she said.

"Yes," he said. "Great."

"Lovely!" she said.

"Look here," he said, "do you mind if I have a drink? I mean, just medicinally, you know. I'm off the stuff for life, so help me. But I think I feel a collapse coming on."

"Oh, I think it would do you good," she said. "You poor boy, it's a shame you feel so awful. I'll go make you a whisky and soda."

"Honestly," he said, "I don't see how you could ever want to speak to me again, after I made such a fool of myself, last night. I think I'd better go join a monastery in Tibet."

"You crazy idiot!" she said. "As if I could ever let you go away now! Stop talking like that. You were perfectly fine."

She jumped up from the couch, kissed him quickly on the forehead, and ran out of the room.

The pale young man looked after her and shook his head long and slowly, then dropped it in his damp and trembling hands.

"Oh, dear," he said. "Oh, dear, oh, dear, oh, dear."

The Importance of Being Earnest

Oscar Wilde

Farce makes us laugh by so exaggerating the ordinary that we perceive how ridiculous it is. It requires our awareness and even acceptance of the ordinary as proper behavior, so that we hold in tension, simultaneoulsy, the absurdity in commonplace reality and the truth in the exaggeration. In sociology, the result is sometimes called an "ideal type."

The great conversationalist, poet, and speed reader Oscar Wilde lampooned the customs of the odd upper-class English natives whom he studied as a participant observer so assiduously until public scandal drove him from the

Oscar Wilde, *The Importance of Being Earnest*, Avon Books, Inc., New York, 1965.

country. Although all his plays are "dated," since they focus on the specifically time-bound behavior of the upper class at the turn of the century, the recurring success of revivals decade after decade attests to the fact that we are amused by his wit because we can still see around us much of the behavior that he found so hilarious.

As we know, even in Wilde's time a pretty, brainless, sheltered upper-class English girl was not often hustled into a marriage she hated; nor were dominant mothers all like Lady Bracknell, though such caricatures were common enough in all generations and numerous even in those circum-Mediterranean societies where fathers are reputed to be so powerful and typically able to insist that girls should have nothing to do with the decision to marry. On the other hand, however subtly or indirectly it may be done, young men in our generation, as in Oscar Wilde's, are in fact interrogated by prospective mothers-in-law about their present family position and possible financial and social future.

Moreover, although we may chuckle at Lady Bracknell's apparently silly statements in *The Importance of Being Earnest*, we would not find them amusing if they did not cut a bit close to the bone: for some upper-class men, smoking could indeed be described as a major occupation in social life; education does not alter their understanding, and, if it did, it might threaten the upper classes; some upper-class mothers do have a "list of eligible young men," written or not; in some circles to have lost both parents may not necessarily arouse compassion, but a bit of suspicion; and more than one prospective bride or groom has been forced to "produce" some relatives, however spurious, for the engagement and marriage. The reader will doubtless perceive still other correct social descriptions disguised in Wilde's jocularities.

Lady Bracknell: Mr Worthing! Rise, sir, from this semirecumbent posture. It is most indecorous.

Gwendolen: Mamma! (*He tries to rise; she restrains him.*) I must beg you to retire. This is no place for you. Besides, Mr. Worthing has not quite finished yet.

Lady Bracknell: Finished what, may I ask?

Gwendolen: I am engaged to Mr Worthing, mamma. (*They rise together.*)

Lady Bracknell: Pardon me, you are not engaged to any one. When you do become engaged to some one, I, or your father, should his health permit him, will inform you of the fact. An engagement should come on a young girl as a surprise, pleasant or unpleasant, as the case my be. It is hardly a matter that she could be allowed to arrange for herself. . . . And now I have a few questions to put to you, Mr Worthing. While I am making these inquiries, you, Gwendolen, will wait for me below in the carriage.

Gwendolen (*Reproachfully*): Mamma!

Lady Bracknell: In the carriage, Gwendolen! (GWENDOLEN *goes to the door. She and* JACK *blow kisses to each other behind* LADY BRACKNELL*'s back.* LADY BRACKNELL *looks vaguely about as if she could not understand what the noise was. Finally turns round.*) Gwendolen, the carriage!

Gwendolen: Yes, mamma. (*Goes out, looking back at* JACK.)

Lady Bracknell (*Sitting down*): You can take a seat, Mr Worthing. (*Looks in her pocket for note-book and pencil.*)

Jack: Thank you, Lady Bracknell, I prefer standing.

Lady Bracknell (*Pencil and note-book in hand*): I feel bound to tell you that you are not down on my list of eligible young men, although I have the same list as the dear Duchess of Bolton has. We work together, in fact. However, I am quite ready to enter your name, should your answers be what a really affectionate mother requires. Do you smoke?

Jack: Well, yes, I must admit I smoke.

Lady Bracknell: I am glad to hear it. A man should always have an occupation of some kind. There are far too many idle men in London as it is. How old are you?

Jack: Twenty-nine.

Lady Bracknell: A very good age to be married at. I have always been of opinion that a man who desires to get married should know either everything or nothing. Which do you know?

Jack (*After some hesitation*): I know nothing, Lady Bracknell.

Lady Bracknell: I am pleased to hear it. I do not approve of anything that tampers with natural ignorance. Ignorance is like a delicate exotic fruit; touch it and the bloom is gone. The whole theory of modern education is radically unsound. Fortunately in England, at any rate, education produces no effect whatsoever. If it did, it would prove a serious danger to the upper classes, and probably lead to acts of violence in Grosvenor Square. What is your income?

Jack: Between seven and eight thousand a year.

Lady Bracknell (*Makes a note in her book*): In land, or in investments?

Jack: In investments, chiefly.

Lady Bracknell: That is satisfactory. What between the duties expected of one during one's lifetime, and the duties exacted from one after one's death, land has ceased to be either a profit or a pleasure. It gives one position, and prevents one from keeping it up. That's all that can be said about land.

Jack: I have a country house with some land, of course, attached to it, about fifteen hundred acres, I believe; but I don't depend on that for my real income. In fact, as far as I can make out, the poachers are the only people who make anything out of it.

Lady Bracknell: A country house! How many bedrooms? Well, that point can be cleared up afterwards. You have a town house, I hope? A girl with a simple, unspoiled nature, like Gwendolen, could hardly be expected to reside in the country.

Jack: Well, I own a house in Belgrave Square, but it is let by the year to Lady Bloxham. Of course, I can get it back whenever I like, at six months' notice.

Lady Bracknell: Lady Bloxham? I don't know her.

Jack: Oh, she goes about very little. She is a lady considerably advanced in years.

Lady Bracknell: Ah, nowadays that is no guarantee of respectability of character. What number in Belgrave Square?

Jack: 149.

Lady Bracknell (*Shaking her head*): The unfashionable side. I thought there was something. However, that could easily be altered.

Jack: Do you mean the fashion, or the side?

Lady Bracknell (*Sternly*): Both, if necessary, I presume. What are your politics?

Jack: Well, I am afraid I really have none. I am a Liberal Unionist.

Lady Bracknell: Oh, they count as Tories. They dine with us. Or come in the evening, at any rate. Now to minor matters. Are your parents living?

Jack: I have lost both my parents.

Lady Bracknell: To lose one parent, Mr Worthing, may be regarded as a misfortune; to lose both looks like carelessness. Who was your father? He was evidently a man of some wealth. Was he born in what the Radical papers call the purple of commerce, or did he rise from the ranks of the aristocracy?

Jack: I am afraid I really don't know. The fact is, Lady Bracknell, I said I had lost my parents. It would be nearer the truth to say that my parents seem to have lost me. . . . I don't actually know who I am by birth. I was . . . well, I was found.

Lady Bracknell: Found!

Jack: The late Mr Thomas Cardew, an old gentleman of a very charitable and kindly disposition, found me, and gave me the name of Worthing, because he happened to have a first-class ticket for Worthing in his pocket at the time. Worthing is a place in Sussex. It is a seaside resort.

Lady Bracknell: Where did the charitable gentleman who had a first-class ticket for this seaside resort find you?

Jack (*Gravely*): In a hand-bag.

Lady Bracknell: A hand-bag?

Jack (*Very seriously*): Yes, Lady Bracknell. I was in a hand-bag—a somewhat large, black leather hand-bag, with handles to it—an ordinary hand-bag in fact.

Lady Bracknell: In what locality did this Mr James, or Thomas, Cardew come across this ordinary hand-bag?

Jack: In the cloak-room at Victoria Station. It was given to him in mistake for his own.

Lady Bracknell: The cloak-room at Victoria Station?

Jack: Yes. The Brighton line.

Lady Bracknell: The line is immaterial. Mr Worthing, I confess I feel somewhat bewildered by what you have just told me. To be born, or at any rate bred, in a hand-bag, whether it had handles or not, seems to me to display a contempt for the ordinary decencies of family life that reminds one of the worst excesses of the French Revolution. And I presume you know what that unfortunate movement led to? As for the particular locality in which the hand-bag was found, a cloak-room at a railway station might serve to conceal a social indiscretion—has probably, indeed, been used for that purpose before now—but it could hardly be regarded as an assured basis for a recognized position in good society.

Jack: May I ask you then what you would advise me to do? I need hardly say I would do anything in the world to ensure Gwendolen's happiness.

Lady Bracknell: I would strongly advise you, Mr Worthing, to try and acquire some relations as soon as possible, and to make a definite effort to produce at any rate one parent, of either sex, before the season is quite over.

Jack: Well, I don't see how I could possibly manage to do that. I can produce the hand-bag at any moment. It is in my dressing-room at home. I really think that should satisfy you, Lady Bracknell.

Lady Bracknell: Me, sir! What has it to do with me? You can hardly imagine that I and Lord Bracknell would dream of allowing our only daughter—a girl brought up with the utmost care—to marry into a cloak-room, and form an alliance with a parcel. Good morning, Mr Worthing!

The Family Carnovsky

I. J. Singer

The meaning of "class" in real life is never exhausted, as it is in most of sociology, by the variables of wealth, education, and occupation. Nor are the additional variables to be called "intangible" or "subjective." They include such matters as style of life, the achievements of *past* generations,

I. J. Singer, *The Family Carnovsky*, The Vanguard Press, New York, 1969.

the *kinds* of achievements the family can boast of (e.g., learning as contrasted with business), the moral rectitude of its members, and even the prospective future of its younger members. At the upper reaches of the class system, such traits loom as crucial in deciding against a family alliance, though in view from the bottom everyone "up there" appears to be enviable.

In Singer's *The Family Carnovsky*, we see a confrontation of two classes and two styles of life, both represented by emigrants from Russia to Germany. The Carnovskys are a great family, rich in honor; the Buraks are rich in money, but uncultured. True, the daughter is, in herself, beautiful, cultured, and well-educated, but both by class within the ethnic group and by the tastes that express his assimilationist philosophy, young Georg Carnovsky is actually repelled by Ruth's "Jewish Mother"-liness.

At this place and time, not long before Hitler's accession to power, it is a cultural assumption that marriages can be arranged (or manipulated if not arranged,) but that only rarely will the young man be pressed into a marriage with a woman he detests. However, the elder Carnovsky would oppose such an alliance in any case, for with a generation of scholars behind him he views the Buraks as hopelessly boorish, and their attractive daughter as a surprising exception rather than a desirable match. By contrast, his own wife, who was herself elevated by marrying him, sees no objection to the union, because she does not share the high and austere tastes of the Carnovskys.

We also note a characteristic pattern of behavior in familistic groups, that is, the extent to which each individual not only identifies with other members of the family but feels free to intervene, to protest, and even to intrigue with outsiders, secretly trying to make arrangements they view as desirable for the family or for one individual whom they love. Solomon Burak has for years suffered because of the pride of the Carnovskys, and he knows in his heart that not only is he in many ways "as good as" many of the Carnovskys, but his daughter Ruth is equal to anyone. Because he loves her, he is willing to humiliate himself (and, as it turns out, her) in order to get her what she most wants, a marriage with Georg Carnovsky. Note, too, the artist's achievement in depicting these subtle interrelations among class, philosophical, and personality variables, for we are moved to identify with Ruth's tragedy—perhaps because we have all felt the pangs of unrequited love; yet the modern sophisticate also cherishes values by which Ruth would be measured and found wanting.

In Solomon Burak's usually cheerful apartment, the phonograph no longer played gay Yiddish theater tunes as it once did.

This was not because Solomon Burak's business was going badly. On the contrary, he had recently enlarged not only his store but also the sign bearing his name, to the distress of his German-Jewish neighbors. It was said on Dragonerstrasse that Solomon Burak himself did not know how much he was worth. Still, neither he nor his wife Yetta was content.

What good was their money to them when their daughter Ruth was pining away from love for Georg Carnovsky, who did not even know she existed?

She had loved him since their first meeting. She took every opportunity to accompany her mother to the Carnovskys, allegedly to see Georg's sister, Rebecca, of whom she was so fond. But Leah knew that the girl was infatuated with her son. She saw it in Ruth's eyes, and in the love she lavished upon the child whom she fondled by the hour, transferring to the little girl the passion she felt for her brother. Yetta Burak did not try to hide her feelings. Each time she saw the two young people together she said: "What a handsome couple."

Leah could not understand why her son avoided Ruth. "Why are you so rude to her?" she asked. "Such a fine, pretty, educated girl. What do you have against her?"

Georg was puzzled himself. Ruth was everything his mother said. Her eyes were velvety black, soft and full of love, especially for him. She was cultured, played the piano, and knew all the operas. But she did not excite him as other girls did. The billowy softness of her ripe curves was more maternal than virginal. She was a mother through and through, from her stolidity to her excessive love of children. Her bosom was also too large and puffy, making her look even shorter and fatter than she was. Although he was normally attracted to voluptuous women, Ruth's rounded bosom left him as cold as would the breast of a mother nursing her baby. He could not work up a passion for the plump and placid girl whose piteous eyes begged him to love her, to marry her, and to beget her with a flock of children. Her softness, sweetness, and goodness reminded him of the strudel his mother baked for the Sabbath. Although her obvious devotion boosted his ego, it also smothered all desire for her. He had even concocted a secret nickname for her—Madame Rebbetzin.

Ruth did everything she could to make Georg want her. She read the latest books in case he should decide to discuss literature; she came to his house often on the pretext of giving Rebecca piano lessons. She put all her emotion into the mournful chords that she directed toward Georg's room, and through Chopin's Nocturne bared her deep longing for him. Leah Carnovsky wiped away a tear at the girl's anguish crying out from the ivory keys. It reminded her of her own youth and of the years forever gone.

She kissed Ruth's soft hair and the girl hungrily snuggled up to Leah's bosom. Even David Carnovsky, deep in some ponderous volume in his study, heard the haunting chords and wondered how two boors like the Buraks could have produced such a talented daughter. The only one unaffected was Georg himself. The moment he found out that Ruth Burak was visiting, he ran from the house.

"Where are you off to?" his mother said. "Don't you see we have a guest?"

"Yes, yes," Georg said innocently. "But I haven't a moment to spare. I'm sure Fräulein Ruth will excuse me. Won't you, Fräulein?"

And he smiled ingratiatingly to persuade Fräulein Ruth to excuse him, which naturally she did, the tears welling up in her eyes.

Feeling a complete fool for coming, humiliated by Georg's indifference and embarrassed by Leah's pity, she hurried to leave before her tears began to fall in earnest.

"Good-by," she blurted out and ran downstairs, vowing never to return. She even determined to stay away from the street where he lived. But in a few days she felt herself drawn to the apartment again, to every room, to every piece of furniture. She envied Georg's neighbors who lived in the same house and could see him every day. Berating herself for her weakness, disgusted with her lack of pride and filled with shame, she crawled back to Oranienburger Strasse for another glimpse of her beloved. Even if he avoided her and offered transparent excuses to run away, she treasured the short moments she could be near him, hear his voice, see the smile on his swarthy face and the sparkle of his eyes.

For hours before the visit she primped and fussed in front of a full-length mirror, wondering what kept him from wanting her. Sometimes she thought she was ugly, awkward, and frumpish and she didn't blame Georg for his indifference. But soon she began a more detailed examination, feature by feature. She compared herself quite objectively to other girls, to her friends, and she decided that she was much more alluring and desirable. She fell in love with her own image. She stroked her hair, admired her soft downy arms, grew ecstatic over her legs, and even fondled her full, milk-white breasts. Filled with self-admiration and tingling with a warm, moist rapture, she could not understand how any man could resist her. She was convinced that if only he would take the time to look at her closely and see her full-blooming, ripening beauty, he would fall to his knees before her and cover her with kisses. But the fact remained that he did not bother to look at her and ignored her shamelessly. Even on those rare moments when she did manage to spend some time with him, she grew so distraught from her deep feelings for him that she behaved like a tongue-tied ninny.

Before she left her house she rehearsed what she would say and how she would say it. But when they came together she forgot all her plans and gaped at him like a lovesick schoolgirl. Georg enjoyed her discomfort and assumed an infuriatingly patronizing manner. Ruth felt a contempt for herself that flustered her even further, and to conceal her confusion she launched into an involved discussion about music, a subject in which she felt superior. But Georg refused to be serious and maintained his mocking tone.

Lying in bed, Ruth berated herself over her gaucheness. She recalled every word that was said—each of his mocking questions, each of her halting replies. Now she thought of clever retorts but the damage was already done. She had exhausted every means of attracting him. She read up on the psychology of sex, wore the most enticing clothes she dared, used the recommended perfumes, and dieted to lose weight, especially from her bosom. She paid particular attention to her grooming and wore her hair differently each time. She also begged God to grant her the beauty and wisdom that she needed to win the one she loved. She spent restless nights tortured by an emotion with which her innocent mind was not equipped to cope.

"Tell me what to do, God!" she cried.

Her parents shared her anguish. "I don't have a word of advice to give the girl," Yetta sighed, lying next to her husband. "She's wasting away before my eyes. . . ."

"And for whom? A nothing, a lout," he muttered.

He was even more indignant than his daughter that anyone would have the audacity to reject her. Such fine, decent, good-looking, and intelligent children as his could not be found anywhere—not even in a royal household. And she, Ruth, was the best of the lot!

When Yetta had first told him about his daughter's infatuation, Solomon Burak felt both hurt and exalted. On the one hand, it disturbed him that his daughter had chosen, of all people, the son of the haughty and insolent David Carnovsky. On the other, he felt a certain thrill because his life would again be linked with that self-appointed aristocrat. Like any successful businessman who believes in the power of money, Solomon Burak was certain that he could overcome any of young Carnovsky's objections with a large enough dowry, whether the boy's father approved of the match or not. He was prepared to turn over to the young man a huge sum of money, more than he could afford; to heap presents on the couple, and to furnish a house for them as only Solomon Burak could. Convinced that he would win out, he relished the prospect of forcing David Carnovsky to become his in-law. To bring things to a head, Solomon Burak arranged a great party to celebrate Ruth's graduation from the Academy, to which he invited all the merchants with whom he did business as well as all of Ruth's friends. He engaged a cook from the finest Jewish restaurant and hired an army of waiters and servants. The apartment was filled with flowers. Ruth's piano teacher, a dignified gentleman with an artistic beard and a great shock of hair, was present to add a cultural note to the festivities. The new grand piano that was Ruth's graduation present gleamed with an ebony glow in the brightly lit parlor. Among those invited first had been Leah and young Georg Carnovsky. Solomon Burak planned that while Ruth and her teacher performed on the piano he would tactfully take Georg aside for a man-to-man talk.

"A ducat more, a ducat less," he would say, "as long as you two will be happy and have a good life together."

But Georg never showed up. Everyone was there, even Leah Carnovsky, but the one for whom the whole thing had been intended merely sent a long, congratulatory telegram. After the guests had gone, Ruth began to cry.

"May he be buried a hundred feet deep!" Solomon Burak swore, trying to console his daughter. "Just you wait, I'll find you a bridegroom a thousand times nicer and better-looking. Just leave it to me!"

To spite the Carnovskys, he was prepared to sacrifice all he had to find the most eligible husband in all Berlin for his daughter. If she wanted a businessman, he would get her the biggest. If she wanted an educated man—a lawyer, a doctor, even a professor—he would arrange it.

"Don't cry, silly girl," he soothed her. "No daughter of Solomon Burak need ever cry. . . ."

But Ruth wanted to cry. She did not want a big dowry or expensive gifts or even a professor—she wanted Georg. "What can I do if he doesn't love me?" she wailed to her mother.

To this, Yetta had no answer.

Solomon Burak tried letting the matter run its course. He was sure that time, the best cure for all ills, would take care of this problem too. To get his daughter's mind off her troubles, he threw a series of large parties to which he invited the gayest and most attractive young men in Berlin's Jewish community.

Dancing with his wife, he would say, "Well, Yetta, what's happening? Anything yet?"

"No, Shlomele," Yetta would say anxiously, keeping in step with him, "nothing at all. . . ."

When Ruth began to lose her appetite and the will to go out, her father decided to do something that went against his grain and did not befit a man in his position. Without a word to Ruth or his wife, he decided to face David Carnovsky and to talk things out with him frankly. Finding it inconceivable that a young man could reject a girl with Ruth's attributes, Solomon laid all the blame on Georg's father, that arrogant, stiff-necked snob. It was he, the self-inflated ass, who prevented the match because the Buraks didn't measure up to his standards. Like any experienced merchant, Solomon knew that the best way to triumph over an enemy was to buy his friendship. Without telling anyone, he put on his most conservative dark suit and black shoes and, feeling very solid and respectable, went to David Carnovsky's house on Oranienburger Strasse.

Shaky and worried, unlike his usual self, Solomon Burak walked up the painted stairs to David Carnovsky's apartment. He even lingered for a few moments before the door, like a poor relative coming for a handout. Finally he rang the doorbell. He was ready for any humiliation for the sake of his daughter. Waiting in Carnovsky's study, he lit a cigarette, took a few puffs, ground it out, and lit another. From all sides books faced him, books and more books. He didn't believe that in a lifetime anybody could read a tenth of the books collected here, and he was convinced that Carnovsky bought them not to study but out of false pride and the need to show off. Still, they filled him with a kind of awe and a feeling of inadequacy.

When David Carnovsky came in with his brisk stride, his neatly trimmed beard, and spotless frock coat, Solomon bowed too deeply, realized his *faux pas* and, from confusion, bowed once more. Carnovsky was polite but reserved. The tilt of his sharp nose displayed the contempt he felt toward one beneath him. Although he knew Solomon Burak's name, he pretended to have forgotten it. "I . . . believe we've met. What is the name again?"

"Solomon Burak, originally Shlomo," Solomon blurted out "A townsman of yours . . . that is, of your wife's, Leah's. . . ."

"Of course, of course, Herr Burak," Carnovsky acknowledged. "How can I be of service to you? Do sit down."

"I'd rather stand, Herr Carnovsky, if you don't mind. As we say among us merchants: 'Better to stand on one's own two feet than to sit badly' " . . . and he laughed nervously.

Not even a hint of a smile crossed Carnovsky's icy features. Stroking his abbreviated beard, he waited for the visitor to come to the point. Solomon was crushed. He always found it easier to express himself with a joke.

He cleared his throat several times, swallowed, and began to speak.

Rambling, adding irrelevant details, repeating himself often, quoting what he had said to his wife and what she had said to him, becoming more and more entangled and often straying from the subject, he finally managed to communicate to David Carnovsky the reason for his visit.

During the whole time Solomon Burak was speaking and despite a strong temptation to shout: "Get on with it!" David Carnovsky did not utter a single word. Although the frequent "So I said to my wife and she said to me" tried his patience, he remained silent because he subscribed to the theory that a Talmudic scholar must listen and not interrupt.

Only after Solomon Burak had finished describing his daughter's qualities and had clapped his hands boldly, as if having succeeded in emerging from a deep morass, did David Carnovsky begin to stroke his beard and to examine his visitor from head to foot, as if seeing him for the first time. He had ascertained what Burak wanted from his first few sentences.

"What is it you actually want, Herr Burak?" he asked in a cool voice.

"I want you not to stand in the way of my daughter's happiness, Herr Carnovsky," Solomon Burak said. "A ducat more, a ducat less, it can't be a matter of money, since I'm ready to go all the way for the sake of my child."

For a moment David Carnovsky said nothing. His custom was to consider every matter with deliberation, although what Solomon Burak now proposed was simply out of the question. To link his family with an ignorant boor from Melnitz, and a former peddler at that, was preposterous, and David pondered the best means of letting Burak know that such a match was impossible. For a moment he thought to say that a Berlin university student was not a Yeshiva boy from Melnitz and that here a father had no say in such matters. The best lie is often the truth, it occurred to him. But soon he decided that it would not be wise to reveal to Solomon Burak that he had no control over his own son. "No, Herr Burak," he said firmly, "what you propose cannot be."

"Why not, Herr Carnovsky?" Solomon Burak asked too quickly. "Why not?"

"First of all, my son is still in school. Secondly, a man must be established financially before thinking about marriage. That's the way things are done in this part of the world."

Solomon Burak waved his hand impatiently. "Don't let that part of it disturb you for a second, Herr Carnovsky. I'm prepared to pay for your son's tuition and board and everything else besides."

"Thank you, I am quite capable of supporting my own son," David Carnovsky said frostily.

Solomon Burak felt that he had committed another *faux pas* and he tried to correct it. "Herr Carnovsky, I didn't mean to imply that you needed anyone's help. But in my house your child would be like one of my own. . . ."

"Thirdly," Carnovsky continued, ignoring the other, "my son is still young and has plenty of time to think about marriage. At his age a boy must study, only study, and not fill his head with other things."

Ever the businessman, Solomon Burak brought the matter around to the subject of money. "Herr Carnovsky, I'll make your son a very rich man. . . ."

"No," Carnovsky replied.

"He'll be a big man in Berlin. I've got thousands of friends in the city. I'll get him the best job available. Leave it to me. When Solomon Burak wants something, nothing can stop him."

"No," Carnovsky said again.

Solomon Burak hooked his thumbs in his vest pockets. "I'm not good enough for you, is that it?" he asked with a crooked smile.

"What are you trying to force me to say, Herr Burak?" Carnovsky asked.

Solomon Burak took several puffs on the cigarette and threw it into the ashtray. He came up so close to Carnovsky that he almost stepped on his feet and said thickly: "Listen, if it was up to me only, I would never come here. I'm a proud man too. I made my fortune with these two hands and I don't have to back away from anybody. But since it concerns my daughter's happiness, my self-respect doesn't mean a thing, not a thing."

"I don't understand what you are trying to say," Carnovsky mumbled.

"I'm an ignorant man, a common man, and I don't try to hide it. But my daughter is educated. She is bright, refined, and decent. You can be ashamed of me all you like, but never of her. For her I'd do anything in the world, even crawl before you, Herr Carnovsky, even beg. Because she is my baby. She is unhappy. She cries!"

Carnovsky remained polite but unmoved. "I am sorry for your daughter, Herr Burak, but it isn't my fault. Everyone must stick to his principles."

Solomon Burak left Carnovsky's study without even saying good-by. As he was leaving, Leah invited him into the dining room. Although she hadn't heard anything the men had said, she guessed the reason for Solomon Burak's visit and she was deeply ashamed. She herself had no objection to her son marrying Ruth Burak. On the contrary, she pitied the girl. Nor did she consider the Buraks in any way inferior. Her own father had been neither a great scholar nor an aristocrat.

"Shlomele, at least have a glass of tea before you go," she urged him, embarrassed beyond words.

Solomon Burak could not wait to leave the apartment. "I might contaminate one of Carnovsky's glasses," he said. "Please let me go."

When Ruth found out what her father had done she got into

bed, buried her face in a pillow, and refused to get up. Her father caressed her and pleaded with her at least to look at him. "I did it for you, child. Please forgive me!" he cried.

"Leave me alone, don't even look at me!" she cried, sobbing into the pillow. "I don't want to see anyone! Not anyone!"

She was so filled with shame and humiliation, she wanted to die.

The Bride Comes to Yellow Sky
Stephen Crane

Historians have waged continuous battles about the issue of the frontier ever since Frederick Jackson Turner pro- pounded his famous thesis at the time of the closing of the frontier, namely, that it had played a crucial role in American development. Even in recent years, historians have argued that its importance has been given too much weight. How- ever, whatever the scholarly verdict, for about a century thousands of readers have been addicted to stories set on the Western frontier.

Contrasting with the encroachments of bureaucracy, the myth of the West suggests a personal freedom from rules; far from the dullness of the city, these stories evoke imminent danger of death; instead of the domesticity of family life, this literature recalls the fraternal bond among men who avoid the burdens of wife and children. The reader is persuaded to move back into a history that is older than its dates. There was no place on the frontier for the baggage of customs and even technology that were taken for granted in the settled urban communities of the East. Here in Stephen Crane's "The Bride Comes to Yellow Sky," we witness the inner turmoil of the traditionally brave town marshal who vaguely feels he has violated a "community custom": he has not informed the town of his sudden

Stephen Crane, *Twenty Stories*, introduction by Carl van Doren, Alfred A. Knopf, Inc., New York, 1940.

marriage. A simple, taciturn man, he cannot easily articulate the community "rules," but recognizes that a mature man should give his friends time to absorb such an event; that a person as important as he is in the town should allow its members to be part of the wedding; and that he should be welcomed at the train station by the band on his return from the metropolis (San Antonio). Unable to muster the urbane glibness that would ease his reentrance into the community, he merely hopes to sneak into his own house before anyone is aware of his new status.

As a way of generating our belief in this confrontation between the town marshal and the gun fighter, Crane introduces several bits of cultural description: the talkative salesman, so unlike the Texans; the implicit community rule that Mexican sheep-herders did not have the privilege of talking in the bar at all, being there only on sufferance; the seriousness (but not fear) with which the men view Scratchy Wilson's homicidal intent.

However, our deeper insight into the social patterns of the community comes from the final confrontation. It would be difficult to formulate the *general* customs which Scratchy's decision represents, but Crane's prior evocation of the West convinces us at once that that *is* a rule: You may kill a man afterwards in fair fight or in ambush but you may not require him to duel with you when he has just come home, unarmed, with his new bride.

To the left, miles down a long purple slope, was a little ribbon of mist where moved the keening Rio Grande. The train was approaching it at an angle, and the apex was Yellow Sky. Presently it was apparent that, as the distance from Yellow Sky grew shorter, the husband became commensurately restless. His brick-red hands were more insistent in their prominence. Occasionally he was even rather absent-minded and far-away when the bride leaned forward and addressed him.

As a matter of truth, Jack Potter was beginning to find the shadow of a deed weighing upon him like a leaden slab. He, the town marshal of Yellow Sky, a man known, liked, and feared in his corner, a prominent person, had gone to San Antonio to meet a girl he believed he loved, and there, after the usual prayers, had actually induced her to marry him, without consulting Yellow Sky for any part of the transaction. He was now bringing his bride before an innocent and unsuspecting community.

Of course people in Yellow Sky married as it pleased them, in accordance with a general custom; but such was Potter's thought of his duty to his friends, or of their idea of his duty, or of an unspoken form which does not control men in these matters, that he felt he was heinous. He had committed an extraordinary crime. Face to face with this girl in San Antonio, and spurred by his sharp impulse, he had gone headlong over all the social hedges. At San Antonio he was like a man hidden in the dark. A knife to sever any friendly duty, any form, was easy to his hand in that remote city. But the hour of Yellow Sky—the hour of daylight—was approaching.

He knew full well that his marriage was an important thing to his town. It could only be exceeded by the burning of the new hotel. His friends could not forgive him. Frequently he had reflected on the advisability of telling them by telegraph, but a new cowardice had been upon him. He feared to do it. And now the train was hurrying him toward a scene of amazement, glee, and reproach. He glanced out of the window at the line of haze swinging slowly in toward the train.

Yellow Sky had a kind of brass band, which played painfully, to the delight of the populace. He laughed without heart as he thought of it. If the citizens could dream of his prospective arrival with his bride, they would parade the band at the station and escort them, amid cheers and laughing congratulations, to his adobe home.

He resolved that he would use all the devices of speed and plains-craft in making the journey from the station to his house. Once within that safe citadel, he could issue some sort of vocal bulletin, and then not go among the citizens until they had time to wear off a little of their enthusiasm.

The bride looked anxiously at him. "What's worrying you, Jack?"

He laughed again. "I'm not worrying, girl; I'm only thinking of Yellow Sky."

She flushed in comprehension.

A sense of mutual guilt invaded their minds and developed a

finer tenderness. They looked at each other with eyes softly aglow. But Potter often laughed the same nervous laugh; the flush upon the bride's face seemed quite permanent.

The traitor to the feelings of Yellow Sky narrowly watched the speeding landscape. "We're nearly there," he said.

Presently the porter came and announced the proximity of Potter's home. He held a brush in his hand, and, with all his airy superiority gone, he brushed Potter's new clothes as the latter slowly turned this way and that way. Potter fumbled out a coin and gave it to the porter, as he had seen others do. It was a heavy and muscle-bound business, as that of a man shoeing his first horse.

The porter took their bag, and as the train began to slow they moved forward to the hooded platform of the car. Presently the two engines and their long string of coaches rushed into the station of Yellow Sky.

"They have to take water here," said Potter, from a constricted throat and in mournful cadence, as one announcing death. Before the train stopped his eye had swept the length of the platform, and he was glad and astonished to see there was none upon it but the station-agent, who, with a slightly hurried and anxious air, was walking toward the water-tanks. When the train had halted, the porter alighted first, and placed in position a little temporary step.

"Come on, girl," said Potter, hoarsely. As he helped her down they each laughed on a false note. He took the bag from the Negro, and bade his wife cling to his arm. As they slunk rapidly away, his hang-dog glance perceived that they were unloading the two trunks, and also that the station-agent, far ahead near the baggage-car, had turned and was running toward him, making gestures. He laughed, and groaned as he laughed, when he noted the first effect of his marital bliss upon Yellow Sky. He gripped his wife's arm firmly to his side, and they fled. Behind them the porter stood, chuckling fatuously.

II

The California express on the Southern Railway was due at Yellow Sky in twenty-one minutes. There were six men at the bar of the Weary Gentleman saloon. One was a drummer who talked a great deal and rapidly; three were Texans who did not care to talk at that time; and two were Mexican sheep-herders, who did not talk as a general practice in the Weary Gentleman saloon. The barkeeper's dog lay on the board-walk that crossed in front of the door. His head was on his paws, and he glanced drowsily here and there with the constant vigilance of a dog that is kicked on occasion. Across the sandy street were some vivid green grass-plots, so wonderful in appearance, amid the sands that burned near them in a blazing sun, that they caused a doubt in the mind. They exactly resembled the grass mats used to represent lawns on the stage. At the cooler end of the railway station, a man without a coat sat in a tilted chair and smoked his pipe. The fresh-cut bank of the Rio Grande circled near the town, and there could be seen beyond it a plum-colored plain of mesquit.

Save for the busy drummer and his companions in the saloon, Yellow Sky was dozing. The new-comer leaned gracefully upon the bar, and recited many tales with the confidence of a bard who has come upon a new field.

"—and at the moment that the old man fell downstairs with the bureau in his arms, the old woman was coming up with two scuttles of coal, and of course—"

The drummer's tale was interrupted by a young man who suddenly appeared in the open door. He cried: "Scratchy Wilson's drunk, and has turned loose with both hands." The two Mexicans at once set down their glasses and faded out of the rear entrance of the saloon.

The drummer, innocent and jocular, answered: "All right, old man. S'pose he has? Come in and have a drink, anyhow."

But the information had made such an obvious cleft in every skull in the room that the drummer was obliged to see its importance. All had become instantly solemn. "Say," said he, mystified, "what is this?" His three companions made the introductory gesture of eloquent speech; but the young man at the door forestalled them.

"It means, my friend," he answered, as he came into the saloon, "that for the next two hours this town won't be a health resort."

The barkeeper went to the door, and locked and barred it;

reaching out of the window, he pulled in heavy wooden shutters, and barred them. Immediately a solemn, chapel-like gloom was upon the place. The drummer was looking from one to another.

"But say," he cried, "what is this, anyhow? You don't mean there is going to be a gun-fight?"

"Don't know whether there'll be a fight or not," answered one man, grimly; "but there'll be some shootin'—some good shootin'."

The young man who had warned them waved his hand, "Oh, there'll be a fight fast enough, if any one wants it. Anybody can get a fight out there in the street. There's a fight just waiting."

The drummer seemed to be swayed between the interest of a foreigner and a perception of personal danger.

"What did you say his name was?" he asked.

"Scratchy Wilson," they answered in chorus.

"And will he kill anybody? What are you going to do? Does this happen often? Does he rampage around like this once a week or so? Can he break in that door?"

"No; he can't break down that door," replied the barkeeper. "He's tried it three times. But when he comes you'd better lay down on the floor, stranger. He's dead sure to shoot at it, and the bullet may come through."

Thereafter the drummer kept a strict eye upon the door. The time had not yet been called for him to hug the floor, but, as a minor precaution, he sidled near to the wall. "Will he kill anybody?" he said again.

The men laughed low and scornfully at the question.

"He's out to shoot, and he's out for trouble. Don't see any good in experimentin' with him."

"But what do you do in a case like this? What do you do?"

A man responded: "Why, he and Jack Potter—"

"But," in chorus the other men interrupted, "Jack Potter's in San Anton'."

"Well, who is he? What's he got to do with it?"

"Oh, he's the town marshal. He goes out and fights Scratchy when he gets on one of these tears."

"Wow!" said the drummer, mopping his brow. "Nice job he's got."

The voices had toned away to mere whisperings. The drummer wished to ask further questions, which were born of an increasing anxiety and bewilderment; but when he attempted them, the men merely looked at him in irritation and motioned him to remain silent. A tense waiting hush was upon them. In the deep shadows of the room their eyes shone as they listened for sounds from the street. One man made three gestures at the barkeeper; and the latter, moving like a ghost, handed him a glass and a bottle. The man poured a full glass of whisky, and set down the bottle noiselessly. He gulped the whisky in a swallow, and turned again toward the door in immovable silence. The drummer saw that the barkeeper, without a sound, had taken a Winchester from beneath the bar. Later he saw this individual beckoning to him, so he tiptoed across the room.

"You better come with me back of the bar."

"No, thanks," said the drummer, perspiring; "I'd rather be where I can make a break for the back door."

Whereupon the man of bottles made a kindly but peremptory gesture. The drummer obeyed it, and, finding himself seated on a box with his head below the level of the bar, balm was laid upon his soul at sight of various zinc and copper fittings that bore a resemblance to armor-plate. The barkeeper took a seat comfortably upon an adjacent box.

"You see," he whispered, "this here Scratchy Wilson is a wonder with a gun—a perfect wonder; and when he goes on the war-trail, we hunt our holes—naturally. He's about the last one of the old gang that used to hang out along the river here. He's a terror when he's drunk. When he's sober he's all right—kind of simple—wouldn't hurt a fly—nicest fellow in town. But when he's drunk—whoo!"

There were periods of stillness. "I wish Jack Potter was back from San Anton'," said the barkeeper. "He shot Wilson up once—in the leg—and he would sail in and pull out the kinks in this thing."

Presently they heard from a distance the sound of a shot, followed by three wild yowls. It instantly removed a bond from the men in the darkened saloon. There was a shuffling of feet. They looked at each other. "Here he comes," they said.

III

A man in a maroon-colored flannel shirt, which had been pur-
chased for purposes of decoration, and made principally by some
Jewish women on the East Side of New York, rounded a corner
and walked into the middle of the main street of Yellow Sky. In
either hand the man held a long, heavy, blue-black revolver.
Often he yelled, and these cries rang through a semblance of a
deserted village, shrilly flying over the roofs in a volume that
seemed to have no relation to the ordinary vocal strength of a
man. It was as if the surrounding stillness formed the arch of a
tomb over him. These cries of ferocious challenge rang against
walls of silence. And his boots had red tops with gilded imprints,
of the kind beloved in winter by little sledding boys on the
hillsides of New England.

The man's face flamed in a rage begot of whisky. His eyes,
rolling, and yet keen for ambush, hunted the still doorways and
windows. He walked with the creeping movement of the midnight
cat. As it occurred to him, he roared menacing information. The
long revolvers in his hands were as easy as straws; they were
moved with an electric swiftness. The little fingers of each hand
played sometimes in a musician's way. Plain from the low collar
of the shirt, the cords of his neck straightened and sank,
straightened and sank, as passion moved him. The only sounds
were his terrible invitations. The calm adobes preserved their
demeanor at the passing of this small thing in the middle of the
street.

There was no offer of fight—no offer of fight. The man called
to the sky. There were no attractions. He bellowed and fumed
and swayed his revolvers here and everywhere.

The dog of the barkeeper of the Weary Gentleman saloon
had not appreciated the advance of events. He yet lay dozing in
front of his master's door. At sight of the dog, the man paused
and raised his revolver humorously. At sight of the man, the dog
sprang up and walked diagonally away, with a sullen head, and
growling. The man yelled, and the dog broke into a gallop. As it
was about to enter an alley, there was a loud noise, a whistling,
and something spat the ground directly before it. The dog

screamed, and, wheeling in terror, galloped headlong in a new direction. Again there was a noise, a whistling, and sand was kicked viciously before it. Fear-stricken, the dog turned and flurried like an animal in a pen. The man stood laughing, his weapons at his hips.

Ultimately the man was attracted by the closed door of the Weary Gentleman saloon. He went to it and, hammering with a revolver, demanded drink.

The door remaining imperturbable, he picked a bit of paper from the walk, and nailed it to the framework with a knife. He then turned his back contemptuously upon this popular resort and, walking to the opposite side of the street and spinning there on his heel quickly and lithely, fired at the bit of paper. He missed it by half-inch. He swore at himself, and went away. Later he comfortably fusilladed the windows of his most intimate friend. The man was playing with this town; it was a toy for him.

But still there was no offer of fight. The name of Jack Potter, his ancient antagonist, entered his mind, and he concluded that it would be a glad thing if he should go to Potter's house, and by bombardment induce him to come out and fight. He moved in the direction of his desire, chanting Apache scalp-music.

When he arrived at it, Potter's house presented the same still front as had the other adobes. Taking up a strategic position, the man howled a challenge. But this house regarded him as might a great stone god. It gave no sign. After a decent wait, the man howled further challenges, mingling with them wonderful epithets.

Presently there came the spectacle of a man churning himself into deepest rage over the immobility of a house. He fumed at it as the winter wind attacks a prairie cabin in the North. To the distance there should have gone the sound of a tumult like the fighting of two hundred Mexicans. As necessity bade him, he paused for breath or to reload his revolvers.

IV

Potter and his bride walked sheepishly and with speed. Sometimes they laughed together shamefacedly and low.

"Next corner, dear," he said finally.

They put forth the efforts of a pair walking bowed against a strong wind. Potter was about to raise a finger to point the first appearance of the new home when, as they circled the corner, they came face to face with a man in a maroon-colored shirt, who was feverishly pushing cartridges into a large revolver. Upon the instant the man dropped his revolver to the ground and, like lightning, whipped another from its holster. The second weapon was aimed at the bridegroom's chest.

There was a silence. Potter's mouth seemed to be merely a grave for his tongue. He exhibited an instinct to at once loosen his arm from the woman's grip, and he dropped the bag to the sand. As for the bride, her face had gone as yellow as old cloth. She was a slave to hideous rites, gazing at the apparitional snake.

The two men faced each other at a distance of three paces. He of the revolver smiled with a new and quiet ferocity.

"Tried to sneak up on me," he said. "Tried to sneak up on me!" His eyes grew more baleful. As Potter made a slight movement, the man thrust his revolver venomously forward. "No; don't you do it, Jack Potter. Don't you move a finger toward a gun just yet. Don't you move an eyelash. The time has come for me to settle with you, and I'm goin' to do it my own way, and loaf along with no interferin'. So if you don't want a gun bent on you, just mind what I tell you."

Potter looked at his enemy. "I ain't got a gun on me, Scratchy," he said. "Honest, I ain't." He was stiffening and steadying, but yet somewhere at the back of his mind a vision of the Pullman floated: the sea-green figured velvet, the shining brass, silver, and glass, the wood that gleamed as darkly brilliant as the surface of a pool of oil—all the glory of the marriage, the environment of the new estate. "You know I fight when it comes to fighting, Scratchy Wilson; but I ain't got a gun on me. You'll have to do all the shootin' yourself."

His enemy's face went livid. He stepped forward, and lashed his weapon to and fro before Potter's chest. "Don't you tell me you ain't got no gun on you, you whelp. Don't tell me no lie like that. There ain't a man in Texas ever seen you without no gun. Don't take me for no kid." His eyes blazed with light, and his throat worked like a pump.

"I ain't takin' you for no kid," answered Potter. His heels

had not moved an inch backward. "I'm takin' you for a damn fool. I tell you I ain't got a gun, and I ain't. If you're goin' to shoot me up, you better begin now; you'll never get a chance like this again."

So much enforced reasoning had told on Wilson's rage; he was calmer. "If you ain't got a gun, why ain't you got a gun?" he sneered. "Been to Sunday-school?"

"I ain't got a gun because I've just come from San Anton' with my wife. I'm married," said Potter. "And if I'd thought there was going to be any galoots like you prowling around when I brought my wife home, I'd had a gun, and don't you forget it."

"Married!" said Scratchy, not at all comprehending.

"Yes, married. I'm married," said Potter, distinctly.

"Married?" said Scratchy. Seemingly for the first time, he saw the drooping, drowning woman at the other man's side. "No!" he said. He was like a creature allowed a glimpse of another world. He moved a pace backward, and his arm, with the revolver, dropped to his side. "Is this the lady?" he asked.

"Yes; this is the lady," answered Potter.

There was another period of silence.

"Well," said Wilson at last, slowly, "I s'pose it's all off now."

"It's all off if you say so, Scratchy. You know I didn't make the trouble." Potter lifted his valise.

"Well, I 'low it's off, Jack," said Wilson. He was looking at the ground. "Married!" He was not a student of chivalry; it was merely that in the presence of this foreign condition he was a simple child of the earlier plains. He picked up his starboard revolver, and, placing both weapons in their holsters, he went away. His feet made funnel-shaped tracks in the heavy sand.

The Magic Barrel
Bernard Malamud

Although educated people in industrial societies are likely to view the marriage broker as a hopelessly outdated and even laughable social institution, yet the activity itself will not die as long as anyone, whether prospective spouse or family elder, believes that somewhere there is a better choice to be made. We should therefore look on the marriage broker not as a quaint custom of some ethnic groups, but as a social role that appears under many guises. For example, we go to some stores rather than others because we have learned that they have already done much of the choosing for us. They have sifted, from the myriad kinds of articles of commerce the market affords, a limited range that better fits our needs.

Even in modern Japan, the marriage broker has not disappeared. In one of the intellectually most sophisticated literary reviews, personal advertisements appear as a way of reaching out among the anonymous multitude to find that ideal partner whom the seekers might otherwise never encounter in their own social circles. Those who feel unloved, rootless, and alone, who think they are in the wrong social network, who are resentfully emphatic about their own worth but receive few affirmations of it from the people about them, hope that somehow the "right person" will be found, through an intermediary, a friend or relative, a social director at a singles resort, or even a marriage broker.

Thus, in *The Magic Barrel*, Bernard Malamud is not simply painting a portrait of a time past, or describing a peculiar ethnic custom when he describes the conflict that arises when the Yeshivah student Leo finally seeks a marriage broker in order to obtain a wife. Each introduction to a prospective bride that Salzman produces shows, in Leo's opinion, a complete misunderstanding of what he wants. Each encounter is abrasive and humiliating, but Salzman

Reprinted by permission from Bernard Malamud, *The Magic Barrel,* Farrar, Straus & Giroux, Inc., New York, 1954.

persists, for, the writer is telling us, the broker in his wisdom sees more deeply into Leo's heart than Leo himself.

Anyone who has been alone in a great city will recognize the common experience that Leo undergoes. At one point, we may wish to work out a rational plan for locating candidates—whether for a dating relationship, a deeply emotional love affair, or marriage. At other times we may view this as abjectly humiliating, proposing instead to devote ourselves to work and career, or to allow the chance happenings of our normal daily life to produce someone with whom we can create a life together. It should not seem strange in our society (where arranged marriages are not common, and young people meet one another freely) for elders to seek out appropriate marriage partners through intermediaries. Wherever the importance of the relationship between two loving human beings is viewed as crucial to happiness, few men or women can be sure that they should be content with what is displayed during their casual strolls through the social marketplace.

Finally, although some readers may object to the romantic response of Leo to the *face* in a picture, it is a common enough phenomenon, and one for which the sociologist has no ready explanation. Because of many complex elements in our social and psychological backgrounds, we do respond to faces differently, attribute various qualities to the person who owns the face, impute to him or her many characteristics that may or may not correspond with reality. Whatever that correspondence, however, the reality of the reaction itself cannot be denied. For many people, their faces are part of their destinies, part of the social burdens they have to carry, or unearned advantages that smooth their pathways.

Not long ago there lived in uptown New York, in a small, almost meager room, though crowded with books, Leo Finkle, a rabbinical student in the Yeshivah University. Finkle, after six years of study, was to be ordained in June and had been advised by an acquaintance that he might find it easier to win himself a congregation if he were married. Since he had no present prospects of marriage, after two tormented days of turning it over in his mind, he called in Pinye Salzman, a marriage broker whose two-line advertisement he had read in the *Forward.*

The matchmaker appeared one night out of the dark fourth-floor hallway of the graystone rooming house where Finkle lived, grasping a black, strapped portfolio that had been worn thin with use. Salzman, who had been long in the business, was of slight but dignified build, wearing an old hat, and an overcoat too short and tight for him. He smelled frankly of fish, which he loved to eat, and although he was missing a few teeth, his presence was not displeasing, because of an amiable manner curiously contrasted with mourning eyes. His voice, his lips, his wisp of beard, his bony fingers were animated, but give him a moment of repose and his mild blue eyes revealed a depth of sadness, a characteristic that put Leo a little at ease although the situation, for him, was inherently tense.

He at once informed Salzman why he had asked him to come, explaining that his home was in Cleveland, and that but for his parents, who had married comparatively late in life, he was alone in the world. He had for six years devoted himself almost entirely to his studies, as a result of which, understandably, he had found himself without time for a social life and the company of young women. Therefore he thought it the better part of trial and error—of embarrassing fumbling—to call in an experienced person to advise him on these matters. He remarked in passing that the function of the marriage broker was ancient and honorable, highly approved in the Jewish community, because it made practical the necessary without hindering joy. Moreover, his own parents had been brought together by a matchmaker. They had made, if not a financially profitable marriage—since neither had possessed any worldly goods to speak of—at least a successful one in the sense of their everlasting devotion to each other. Salzman listened in embarrassed surprise, sensing a sort of apology. Later, however, he experienced a glow of pride in his work, an emotion that had left him years ago, and he heartily approved of Finkle.

The two went to their business. Leo had led Salzman to the only clear place in the room, a table near a window that overlooked the lamp-lit city. He seated himself at the matchmaker's side but facing him, attempting by an act of will to suppress the unpleasant tickle in his throat. Salzman eagerly unstrapped his portfolio and removed a loose rubber band from a thin packet of much-handled cards. As he flipped through them, a gesture and sound that physically hurt Leo, the student pretended not to see and gazed steadfastly out the window. Although it was still February, winter was on its last legs, signs of which he had for the first time in years begun to notice. He now observed the round white moon, moving high in the sky through a cloud menagerie, and watched with half-open mouth as it penetrated a huge hen, and dropped out of her like an egg laying itself. Salzman, though pretending through eyeglasses he had just slipped on, to be engaged in scanning the writing on the cards, stole occasional glances at the young man's distinguished face, noting with pleasure the long, severe scholar's nose, brown eyes heavy with learning, sensitive yet ascetic lips, and a certain, almost hollow quality of the dark cheeks. He gazed around at shelves upon shelves of books and let out a soft, contented sigh.

When Leo's eyes fell upon the cards, he counted six spread out in Salzman's hand.

"So few?" he asked in disappointment.

"You wouldn't believe me how much cards I got in my office," Salzman replied. "The drawers are already filled to the top, so I keep them now in a barrel, but is every girl good for a new rabbi?"

Leo blushed at this, regretting all he had revealed of himself in a curriculum vitae he had sent to Salzman. He had thought it best to acquaint him with his strict standards and specifications, but in having done so, felt he had told the marriage broker more than was absolutely necessary.

He hesitantly inquired, "Do you keep photographs of your clients on file?"

"First comes family, amount of dowry, also what kind promises," Salzman replied, unbuttoning his tight coat and settling himself in the chair. "After comes pictures, rabbi."

"Call me Mr. Finkle. I'm not yet a rabbi."

Salzman said he would, but instead called him doctor, which he changed to rabbi when Leo was not listening too attentively.

Salzman adjusted his horn-rimmed spectacles, gently cleared his throat and read in an eager voice the contents of the top card:

"Sophie P. Twenty four year. Widow one year. No children. Educated high school and two years college. Father promises eight thousand dollars. Has wonderful wholesale business. Also real estate. On the mother's side comes teachers, also one actor. Well known on Second Avenue."

Leo gazed up in surprise. "Did you say a widow?"

"A widow don't mean spoiled, rabbi. She lived with her husband maybe four months. He was a sick boy she made a mistake to marry him."

"Marrying a widow has never entered my mind."

"This is because you have no experience. A widow, especially if she is young and healthy like this girl, is a wonderful person to marry. She will be thankful to you the rest of her life. Believe me, if I was looking now for a bride, I would marry a widow."

Leo reflected, then shook his head.

Salzman hunched his shoulders in an almost imperceptible gesture of disappointment. He placed the card down on the wooden table and began to read another:

"Lily H. High school teacher. Regular. Not a substitute. Has savings and new Dodge car. Lived in Paris one year. Father is successful dentist thirty-five years. Interested in professional man. Well Americanized family. Wonderful opportunity."

"I knew her personally," said Salzman. "I wish you could see this girl. She is a doll. Also very intelligent. All day you could talk to her about books and theyater and what not. She also knows current events."

"I don't believe you mentioned her age?"

"Her age?" Salzman said, raising his brows. "Her age is thirty-two years."

Leo said after a while, "I'm afraid that seems a little too old."

Salzman let out a laugh. "So how old are you, rabbi?"

"Twenty-seven."

"So what is the difference, tell me, between twenty-seven and thirty-two? My own wife is seven years older than me. So what did I suffer?—Nothing. If Rothschild's a daughter wants to marry you, would you say on account her age, no?"

"Yes," Leo said dryly.

Salzman shook off the no in the yes. "Five years don't mean a thing. I give you my word that when you will live with her for one week you will forget her age. What does it mean five years—that she lived more and knows more than somebody who is younger? On this girl, God bless her, years are not wasted. Each one that it comes makes better the bargain."

"What subject does she teach in high school?"

"Languages. If you heard the way she speaks French, you will think it is music. I am in the business twenty-five years, and I recommend her with my whole heart. Believe me, I know what I'm talking, rabbi."

"What's on the next card?" Leo said abruptly.

Salzman reluctantly turned up the third card:

"Ruth K. Nineteen years. Honor student. Father offers thirteen thousand cash to the right bridegroom. He is a medical doctor. Stomach specialist with marvelous practice. Brother in law owns own garment business. Particular people."

Salzman looked as if he had read his trump card.

"Did you say nineteen?" Leo asked with interest.

"On the dot."

"Is she attractive?" He blushed. "Pretty?"

Salzman kissed his finger tips. "A little doll. On this I give you my word. Let me call the father tonight and you will see what means pretty."

But Leo was troubled. "You're sure she's that young?"

"This I am positive. The father will show you the birth certificate."

"Are you positive there isn't something wrong with her?" Leo insisted.

"Who says there is wrong?"

"I don't understand why an American girl her age should go to a marriage broker."

A smile spread over Salzman's face.

"So for the same reason you went, she comes."

Leo flushed. "I am pressed for time."

Salzman, realizing he had been tactless, quickly explained. "The father came, not her. He wants she should have the best, so he looks around himself. When we will locate the right boy he will introduce him and encourage. This makes a better marriage than if a young girl without experience takes for herself. I don't have to tell you this."

"But don't you think this young girl believes in love?" Leo spoke uneasily.

Salzman was about to guffaw but caught himself and said soberly, "Love comes with the right person, not before."

Leo parted dry lips but did not speak. Noticing that Salzman had snatched a glance at the next card, he cleverly asked, "How is her health?"

"Perfect," Salzman said, breathing with difficulty. "Of course, she is a little lame on her right foot from an auto accident that it happened to her when she was twelve years, but nobody notices on account she is so brilliant and also beautiful."

Leo got up heavily and went to the window. He felt curiously bitter and upbraided himself for having called in the marriage broker. Finally, he shook his head.

"Why not?" Salzman persisted, the pitch of his voice rising.

"Because I detest stomach specialists."

"So what do you care what is his business? After you marry her do you need him? Who says he must come every Friday night in your house?"

Ashamed of the way the talk was going, Leo dismissed Salzman, who went home with heavy, melancholy eyes.

Though he had felt only relief at the marriage broker's departure, Leo was in low spirits the next day. He explained it as arising from Salzman's failure to produce a suitable bride for him. He did not care for his type of clientele. But when Leo found himself hesitating whether to seek out another matchmaker, one more polished than Pinye, he wondered if it could be—his protestations to the contrary, and although he honored his father and mother— that he did not, in essence, care for the matchmaking institution? This thought he quickly put out of mind yet found himself still upset. All day he ran around in the woods—missed an important appointment, forgot to give out his laundry, walked out of a Broadway cafeteria without paying and had to run back with the ticket in his hand; had even not recognized his landlady in the street when she passed with a friend and courteously called out, "A good evening to you, Doctor Finkle." By nightfall, however, he had regained sufficient calm to sink his nose into a book and there found peace from his thoughts.

Almost at once there came a knock on the door. Before Leo could say enter, Salzman, commercial cupid, was standing in the room. His face was gray and meager, his expression hungry, and he looked as if he would expire on his feet. Yet the marriage broker managed, by some trick of the muscles, to display a broad smile.

"So good evening. I am invited?"

Leo nodded, disturbed to see him again, yet unwilling to ask the man to leave.

Beaming still, Salzman laid his portfolio on the table. "Rabbi, I got for you tonight good news."

"I've asked you not to call me rabbi. I'm still a student."

"Your worries are finished. I have for you a first-class bride."

"Leave me in peace concerning this subject." Leo pretended lack of interest.

"The world will dance at your wedding."

"Please, Mr. Salzman, no more."

"But first must come back my strength," Salzman said weakly. He fumbled with the portfolio straps and took out of the leather case an oily paper bag, from which he extracted a hard, seeded roll and a small, smoked white fish. With a quick motion of his hand he stripped the fish out of its skin and began ravenously to chew. "All day in a rush," he muttered.

Leo watched him eat.

"A sliced tomato you have maybe?" Salzman hesitantly inquired.

"No."

The marriage broker shut his eyes and ate. When he had finished he carefully cleaned up the crumbs and rolled up the remains of the fish, in the paper bag. His spectacled eyes roamed the room until he discovered, amid some piles of books, a one-burner gas stove. Lifting his hat he humbly asked, "A glass tea you got, rabbi?"

Conscience-stricken, Leo rose and brewed the tea. He served it with a chunk of lemon and two cubes of lump sugar, delighting Salzman.

After he had drunk his tea, Salzman's strength and good spirits were restored.

"So tell me, rabbi," he said amiably, "you considered some more the three clients I mentioned yesterday?"

"There was no need to consider."

"Why not?"

"None of them suits me."

"What then suits you?"

Leo let it pass because he could give only a confused answer.

Without waiting for a reply, Salzman asked, "You remember this girl I talked to you—the high school teacher?"

"Age thirty-two?"

But, surprisingly, Salzman's face lit in a smile. "Age twenty-nine."

Leo shot him a look. "Reduced from thirty-two?"

"A mistake," Salzman avowed. "I talked today with the dentist. He took me to his safety deposit box and showed me the birth certificate. She was twenty-nine years last August. They made her a party in the mountains where she went for her vacation. When her father spoke to me the first time I forgot to write the age and I told you thirty-two, but now I remember this was a different client, a widow."

"The same one you told me about? I thought she was twenty-four?"

"A different. Am I responsible that the world is filled with widows?"

"No, but I'm not interested in them, nor for that matter, in school teachers."

Salzman pulled his clasped hands to his breast. Looking at the ceiling he devoutly exclaimed, "Yiddishe kinder, what can I say to somebody that he is not interested in high school teachers? So what then you are interested?"

Leo flushed but controlled himself.

"In what else will you be interested," Salzman went on, "if you not interested in this fine girl that she speaks four languages and has personally in the bank ten thousand dollars? Also her father guarantees further twelve thousand. Also she has a new car, wonderful clothes, talks on all subjects, and she will give you a first-class home and children. How near do we come in our life to paradise?"

"If she's so wonderful, why wasn't she married ten years ago?"

"Why?" said Salzman with a heavy laugh. "—Why? Because she is *partikiler.* This is why. She wants the *best.*"

Leo was silent, amused at how he had entangled himself. But Salzman had aroused his interest in Lily H., and he began seriously to consider calling on her. When the marriage broker observed how intently Leo's mind was at work on the facts he had supplied, he felt certain they would soon come to an agreement.

Late Saturday afternoon, conscious of Salzman, Leo Finkle walked with Lily Hirschorn along Riverside Drive. He walked briskly and erectly, wearing with distinction the black fedora he had that morning taken with trepidation out of the dusty hat box on his closet shelf, and the heavy black Saturday coat he had thoroughly whisked clean. Leo also owned a walking stick, a present from a distant relative, but quickly put temptation aside and did not use it. Lily, petite and not unpretty, had on something signifying the approach of spring. She was au courant, animatedly, with all sorts of subjects, and he weighed her words and found her surprisingly sound—score another for Salzman, whom he uneasily sensed to be somewhere around, hiding perhaps high in a tree along the street, flashing the lady signals with a pocket mirror; or perhaps a cloven-hoofed Pan, piping nuptial ditties as he danced his invisible way before them, strewing wild buds on the walk and purple grapes in their path, symbolizing fruit of a union, though there was of course still none.

Lily startled Leo by remarking, "I was thinking of Mr. Salzman, a curious figure, wouldn't you say?"

Not certain what to answer, he nodded.

She bravely went on, blushing, "I for one am grateful for his introducing us. Aren't you?"

He courteously replied, "I am."

"I mean," she said with a little laugh—and it was all in good taste, or at least gave the effect of being not in bad—"do you mind that we came together so?"

He was not displeased with her honesty, recognizing that she meant to set the relationship aright, and understanding that it took a certain amount of experience in life, and courage, to want to do it quite that way. One had to have some sort of past to make that kind of beginning.

He said that he did not mind. Salzman's function was traditional and honorable—valuable for what it might achieve, which, he pointed out, was frequently nothing.

Lily agreed with a sigh. They walked on for a while and she said after a long silence, again with a nervous laugh, "Would you mind if I asked you something a little bit personal? Frankly, I find the subject fascinating." Although Leo shrugged, she went on half embarrassedly, "How was it that you came to your calling? I mean was it a sudden passionate inspiration?"

Leo, after a time, slowly replied, "I was always interested in the Law."

"You saw revealed in it the presence of the Highest?"

He nodded and changed the subject. "I understand that you spent a little time in Paris, Miss Hirschorn?"

"Oh, did Mr. Salzman tell you, Rabbi Finkle?" Leo winced but she went on, "It was ages ago and almost forgotten. I remember I had to return for my sister's wedding."

And Lily would not be put off. "When," she asked in a trembly voice, "did you become enamored of God?"

He stared at her. Then it came to him that she was talking not about Leo Finkle, but of a total stranger, some mystical figure, perhaps even passionate prophet that Salzman had dreamed up for her—no relation to the living or dead. Leo trembled with rage and weakness. The trickster had obviously sold her a bill of goods, just as he had him, who'd expected to become acquainted with a young lady of twenty-nine, only to behold, the moment he laid eyes upon her strained and anxious face, a woman past thirty-five and aging rapidly. Only his self control had kept him this long in her presence.

"I am not," he said gravely, "a talented religious person," and in seeking words to go on, found himself possessed by shame and fear. "I think," he said in a strained manner, "that I came to God not because I loved Him, but because I did not."

This confession he spoke harshly because its unexpectedness shook him.

Lily wilted. Leo saw a profusion of loaves of bread go flying like ducks high over his head, not unlike the winged loaves by which he had counted himself to sleep last night. Mercifully, then, it snowed, which he would not put past Salzman's machinations.

He was infuriated with the marriage broker and swore he would throw him out of the room the minute he reappeared. But Salzman did not come that night, and when Leo's anger had subsided, an unaccountable despair grew in its place. At first he thought this was caused by his disappointment in Lily, but before long it became evident that he had involved himself with Salzman without a true knowledge of his own intent. He gradually realized—with an emptiness that seized him with six hands—that he had called in the broker to find him a bride because he was incapable of doing it himself. This terrifying insight he had derived as a result of his meeting and conversation with Lily Hirschorn. Her probing questions had somehow irritated him into revealing—to himself more than her—the true nature of his relationship to God, and from that it had come upon him, with shocking force, that apart from his parents, he had never loved anyone. Or perhaps it went the other way, that he did not love God so well as he might, because he had not loved man. It seemed to Leo that his whole life stood starkly revealed and he saw himself for the first time as he truly was—unloved and loveless. This bitter but somehow not fully unexpected revelation brought him to a point of panic, controlled only by extraordinary effort. He covered his face with his hands and cried.

The week that followed was the worst of his life. He did not eat and lost weight. His beard darkened and grew ragged. He stopped attending seminars and almost never opened a book. He seriously considered leaving the Yeshivah, although he was deeply troubled at the thought of the loss of all his years of study—saw them like pages torn from a book, strewn over the city—and at the devastating effect of this decision upon his parents. But he had lived without knowledge of himself, and never in the Five Books and all the Commentaries—mea culpa—had the truth been revealed to him. He did not know where to turn, and in all this desolating loneliness there was no *to whom*, although he often thought of Lily but not once could bring himself to go downstairs and make the call. He became touchy and irritable, especially with his landlady, who asked him all manner of personal questions; on the other hand, sensing his own disagreeableness, he waylaid her on the stairs and apologized abjectly, until mortified, she ran from him. Out of this, however, he drew the consolation that he was a Jew and that a Jew suffered. But gradually, as the long and terrible week drew to a close, he regained his composure and some idea of purpose in life: to go on as planned. Although he was imperfect, the idea was not. As for his quest of a bride, the thought of continuing afflicted him with anxiety and heartburn, yet perhaps with this new knowledge of himself he would be more successful than in the past. Perhaps love would now come to him and a bride to that love. And for this sanctified seeking who needed a Salzman?

The marriage broker, a skeleton with haunted eyes, returned that very night. He looked, withal, the picture of frustrated expectancy—as if he had steadfastly waited the week at Miss Lily Hirschorn's side for a telephone call that never came.

Casually coughing, Salzman came immediately to the point: "So how did you like her?"

Leo's anger rose and he could not refrain from chiding the matchmaker: "Why did you lie to me, Salzman?"

Salzman's pale face went dead white, the world had snowed on him.

"Did you not state that she was twenty-nine?" Leo insisted.

"I give you my word—"

"She was thirty-five, if a day. *At least* thirty-five."

"Of this don't be too sure. Her father told me—"

"Never mind. The worst of it was that you lied to her."

"How did I lie to her, tell me?"

"You told her things about me that weren't true. You made me out to be more, consequently less than I am. She had in mind a totally different person, a sort of semi-mystical Wonder Rabbi."

"All I said, you was a religious man."

"I can imagine."

Salzman sighed. "This is my weakness that I have," he confessed. "My wife says to me I shouldn't be a salesman, but when I have two fine people that they would be wonderful to be married, I am so happy that I talk too much." He smiled wanly. "This is why Salzman is a poor man."

Leo's anger left him. "Well, Salzman, I'm afraid that's all."

The marriage broker fastened hungry eyes on him.

"You don't want any more a bride?"

"I do," said Leo, "but I have decided to seek her in a different way. I am no longer interested in an arranged marriage. To be frank, I now admit the necessity of premarital love. That is, I want to be in love with the one I marry."

"Love?" said Salzman, astounded. After a moment he remarked "For us, our love is our life, not for the ladies. In the ghetto they—"

"I know, I know," said Leo. "I've thought of it often. Love, I have said to myself, should be a by-product of living and worship rather than its own end. Yet for myself I find it necessary to establish the level of my need and fulfill it."

Salzman shrugged but answered, "Listen, rabbi, if you want love, this I can find for you also. I have such beautiful clients that you will love them the minute your eyes will see them."

Leo smiled unhappily. "I'm afraid you don't understand."

But Salzman hastily unstrapped his portfolio and withdrew a manila packet from it.

"Pictures," he said, quickly laying the envelope on the table.

Leo called after him to take the pictures away, but as if on the wings of the wind, Salzman had disappeared.

March came. Leo had returned to his regular routine. Although he felt not quite himself yet—lacked energy—he was making plans for a more active social life. Of course it would cost something, but he was an expert in cutting corners; and when there were no corners left he would make circles rounder. All the while Salzman's pictures had lain on the table, gathering dust. Occasionally as Leo sat studying, or enjoying a cup of tea, his eyes fell on the manila envelope. but he never opened it.

The days went by and no social life to speak of developed with a member of the opposite sex—it was difficult, given the circumstances of his situation. One morning Leo toiled up the stairs to his room and stared out the window at the city. Although the day was bright his view of it was dark. For some time he watched the people in the street below hurrying along and then turned with a heavy heart to his little room. On the table was the packet. With a sudden relentless gesture he tore it open. For a half-hour he stood by the table in a state of excitement, examining the photographs of the ladies Salzman had included. Finally, with a deep sigh he put them down. There were six, of varying degrees of attractiveness, but look at them long enough and they all became Lily Hirschorn: all past their prime, all starved behind bright smiles, not a true personality in the lot. Life, despite their frantic yoohooings, had passed them by; they were pictures in a brief case that stank of fish. After a while, however, as Leo attempted to return the photographs into the envelope, he found in it another, a snapshot of the type taken by a machine for a quarter. He gazed at it a moment and let out a cry.

Her face deeply moved him. Why, he could at first not say. It gave him the impression of youth—spring flowers, yet age—a sense of having been used to the bone, wasted; this came from the eyes, which were hauntingly familiar, yet absolutely strange. He had a vivid impression that he had met her before, but try as he might he could not place her although he could almost recall her name, as if he had read it in her own handwriting. No, this couldn't be; he would have remembered her. It was not, he affirmed, that she had an extraordinary beauty—no, though her face was attractive enough; it was that *something* about her moved him. Feature for feature, even some of the ladies of the photographs could do better; but she leaped forth to his heart—and *lived*, or wanted to—more than just wanted, perhaps regretted how she had lived—had somehow deeply suffered; it could be seen in the depths of those reluctant eyes, from the way the light enclosed and shone from her, and within her, opening realms of possibility: this was her own. Her he desired. His head ached and eyes narrowed with the intensity of his gazing, then as if an obscure fog had blown up in the mind, he experienced fear of her and was aware that he had received an impression, somehow, of evil. He shuddered, saying softly, it is thus with us all. Leo brewed some tea in a small pot and sat sipping it without sugar, to calm himself. But before he had finished drinking, again with excitement he examined the face and found it good: good for Leo Finkle. Only such a one could understand him and help him seek whatever he was seeking. She might, perhaps, love him. How she had happened to be among the discards in Salzman's barrel he could never guess, but he knew he must urgently go find her.

Leo rushed downstairs, grabbed up the Bronx telephone book, and searched for Salzman's home address. He was not listed, nor was his office. Neither was he in the Manhattan book. But Leo remembered having written down the address on a slip of paper after he had read Salzman's advertisement in the "personals" column of the *Forward.* He ran up to his room and tore through his papers, without luck. It was exasperating. Just when he needed the matchmaker he was nowhere to be found. Fortunately Leo remembered to look in his wallet. There on a card he found his name written and a Bronx address. No phone number was listed, the reason—Leo now recalled—he had originally communicated with Salzman by letter. He got on his coat, put a hat on over his skull cap and hurried to the subway station. All the way to the far end of the Bronx he sat on the edge of his seat. He was more than once tempted to take out the picture and see if the girl's face was as he remembered it, but he refrained, allowing the snapshot to remain in his inside coat pocket, content to have her so close. When the train pulled into the station he was waiting at the door and bolted out. He quickly located the street Salzman had advertised.

The building he sought was less than a block from the subway, but it was not an office building, nor even a loft, nor a store in which one could rent office space. It was a very old tenement house. Leo found Salzman's name in pencil on a soiled tag under the bell and climbed three dark flights to his apartment. When he knocked, the door was opened by a thin, asthmatic, gray-haired woman, in felt slippers.

"Yes?" she said, expecting nothing. She listened without listening. He could have sworn he had seen her, too, before but knew it was an illusion.

"Salzman—does he live here? Pinye Salzman," he said, "the matchmaker?"

She stared at him a long minute. "Of course."

He felt embarrassed. "Is he in?"

"No." Her mouth, though left open, offered nothing more.

"The matter is urgent. Can you tell me where his office is?"

"In the air." She pointed upward.

"You mean he has no office?" Leo asked.

"In his socks."

He peered into the apartment. It was sunless and dingy, one large room divided by a half-open curtain, beyond which he could see a sagging metal bed. The near side of the room was crowded with rickety chairs, old bureaus, a three-legged table, racks of cooking utensils, and all the apparatus of a kitchen. But there was no sign of Salzman or his magic barrel, probably also a figment of the imagination. An odor of frying fish made Leo weak to the knees.

"Where is he?" he insisted. "I've got to see your husband."

At length she answered, "So who knows where he is? Every time he thinks a new thought he runs to a different place. Go home, he will find you."

"Tell him Leo Finkle."

She gave no sign she had heard.

He walked downstairs, depressed.

But Salzman, breathless, stood waiting at his door.

Leo was astounded and overjoyed. "How did you get here before me?"

"I rushed."

"Come inside."

They entered. Leo fixed tea, and a sardine sandwich for Salzman. As they were drinking he reached behind him for the packet of pictures and handed them to the marriage broker.

Salzman put down his glass and said expectantly, "You found somebody you like?"

"Not among these."

The marriage broker turned away.

"Here is the one I want." Leo held forth the snapshot.

Salzman slipped on his glasses and took the picture into his trembling hand. He turned ghastly and let out a groan.

"What's the matter?" cried Leo.

"Excuse me. Was an accident this picture. She isn't for you." Salzman frantically shoved the manila packet into his portfolio. He thrust the snapshot into his pocket and fled down the stairs.

Leo, after momentary paralysis, gave chase and cornered the marriage broker in the vestibule. The landlady made hysterical outcries but neither of them listened.

"Give me back the picture, Salzman."

"No." The pain in his eyes was terrible.

"Tell me who she is then."

"This I can't tell you. Excuse me."

He made to depart, but Leo, forgetting himself, seized the matchmaker by his tight coat and shook him frenziedly.

"Please," sighed Salzman, "*Please.*"

Leo ashamedly let him go. "Tell me who she is," he begged. "It's very important for me to know."

"She is not for you. She is a wild one—wild, without shame. This is not a bride for a rabbi."

"What do you mean wild?"

"Like an animal. Like a dog. For her to be poor was a sin. This is why to me she is dead now."

"In God's name, what do you mean?"

"Her I can't introduce to you," Salzman cried.

"Why are you so excited?"

"Why, he asks," Salzman said, bursting into tears. "This is my baby, my Stella, she should burn in hell."

Leo hurried up to bed and hid under the covers. Under the covers he thought his life through. Although he soon fell asleep he could not sleep her out of his mind. He woke, beating his breast. Though he prayed to be rid of her, his prayers went unanswered. Through days of torment he endlessly struggled not to love her; fearing success, he escaped it. He then concluded to convert her to goodness, himself to God. The idea alternately nauseated and exalted him.

He perhaps did not know that he had come to a final decision until he encounted Salzman in a Broadway cafeteria. He was sitting alone at a rear table, sucking the bony remains of a fish. The marriage broker appeared haggard, and transparent to the point of vanishing.

Salzman looked up at first without recognizing him. Leo had grown a pointed beard and his eyes were weighted with wisdom.

"Salzman," he said, "love has at last come to my heart."

"Who can love from a picture?" mocked the marriage broker.

"It is not impossible."

"If you can love her, then you can love anybody. Let me show you some new clients that they just sent me their photographs. One is a little doll."

"Just her I want," Leo murmured.

"Don't be a fool, doctor. Don't bother with her."

"Put me in touch with her, Salzman," Leo said humbly. "Perhaps I can be of service."

Salzmán had stopped eating and Leo understood with emotion that it was now arranged.

Leaving the cafeteria, he was, however, afflicted by a tormenting suspicion that Salzman had planned it all to happen this way.

Leo was informed by letter that she would meet him on a certain corner, and she was there one spring night, waiting under a street lamp. He appeared, carrying a small bouquet of violets and rosebuds. Stella stood by the lamp post, smoking. She wore white with red shoes, which fitted his expectations, although in a troubled moment he had imagined the dress red, and only the shoes white. She waited uneasily and shyly. From afar he saw that her eyes—clearly her father's—were filled with desperate innocence. He pictured, in her, his own redemption. Violins and lit candles revolved in the sky. Leo ran forward with flowers outthrust.

Around the corner, Salzman, leaning against a wall, chanted prayers for the dead.

Part Two

The Conjugal Family: Its Phases and Forms

We no longer subscribe to the myth that a few generations ago almost everyone lived in large, multi-generational households, presided over by the eldest couple and ruled by a strong but just patriarch. Whenever we obtain quantitative data from the past, from this or any other major country, we find that most households were relatively small, and that a conjugal family was the main unit within it.

We should not, however, swallow the reverse myth, so common in popular essays, that in modern industrial systems the conjugal family has "lost all its functions"—that it has been reduced to the isolated nuclear family, devoid of important links with other extended kin. In fact, no family system as a whole has ever been made up of such isolated units, and there are good sociological reasons why this should be so. Whenever we obtain good data, whether in England, Holland, France, or the United States, we learn that conjugal families typically interact with a large number of kin.

In some complex kinship systems, the conjugal family unit of parents and children may be less important than in a modern urban society, but almost everywhere it is within that unit that most people have their deepest familial experiences. The graying man in his fifties will still flush with childish shame and anger when called to account by his retired parents—who continue to scold their "children" for their failures of decades ago. Polygyny does not wipe out all jealousy among spouses. Wives and husbands may stray, but remain central in each other's emotional lives.

Within that unit a division of labor is observed which often appears as a source of tension in fiction because of the authority that is based on it. In all societies, until recently at any rate, there were some tasks that were defined as strictly male, such as sea mammal hunting or stone quarrying. Others were defined as mostly female, such as nursing infants or cooking. Others were and are divided differently in different societies, but divided between the sexes just the same. In general, men get the jobs that require much strength or speed, but women do much hard work in all societies. However divided, one large generalization remains: *honorific* jobs have typically belonged to men. Jobs that are exciting or fun, yield honor or authority, or give freedom, are still mainly defined as tasks that only men *can* do. Moreover, custom enforces that opinion, since it has generally been thought to be a violation if women try their hand at such tasks.

But though men do stack the cards in their own favor, by rearing sons to develop a personality that seeks mastery, initiative, aggressiveness, and competence in the outside world, while persuading their daughters to become nurturants, supportive, self-effacing, and devoted to the needs of husband and children, literary artists have always known that the facts about real life in the family are very different.

Of course, if all boys were thoroughly male by psychophysical heritage, and all girls entirely "female," all that energy devoted to shaping them for their conjugal roles as husbands and wives would not be necessary. Whatever the efforts of parents to mold their children into appropriately conforming males and females, it is clear that many men feel most comfortable as nurturant, self-effacing people, and that many women would feel more comfortable as heads of corporations. Few parents have ever really believed that their own children are plastic beings, malleable according to whatever role behaviors society wants from those children.

Of course, if husbands or wives, parents or children, brothers and sisters, *were* easily molded according to doctrine, then literary creation would be severely limited. It is precisely the tensions between those aims and the reality, between the wish to fulfil one's duties as brother, mother, sister, or father and the temptations of real life, or between and among all those conflicting demands of other family members, that generate so infinite a range of behavior, and so powerful an array of emotions.

Needless to say, it was not the modern world that invented the dominant woman. In both Greek and Roman plays we can observe men complaining about "modern" women. Some can rule because they can best their husbands in a fair battle of tongues. Others are, in Willard Waller's phrase, better fighting machines. Many are aware that men possess the legal authority, but they challenge it just the same.

Indeed, if we review the great women in the literature of the past, few of them fit the ideal that was held up as a model in their time. Whether evil or noble, the most successful evocations of womanhood in literature are persons in their own right. By contrast, the fictional characters who do fit the feminine ideal are dull. Even worse (from the viewpoint of artistic creation), the roles they are given to play are not important.

Relations within the conjugal family have been significant in much of the world's literature. However, we can discern a major change that has occurred within the modern period—perhaps as late as the eighteenth century. In the modern era, much of the drama (whether tragedy, comedy, or bittersweet irony) occurs *within* the family or the group of people who are caught up in it. In the past, by contrast, when literature focused far more on glory, conquest, Grail-seeking, war, and rulership—in short, the world of noble men—the great events occurred *outside* the conjugal family. What happened within it often had crucial, even fatefully tragic consequences for those outside events (for example, the entire Oedipus cycle), but the emotions of the audience hung on the outcome of those grander events. That difference doubtless reflects both a changed literary stance and the altered place of the conjugal family within the larger social structure of kith and kin.

But though the literary artist has rescued reality from the kinship stereotypes and myths sometimes perpetrated by the social scientist, literature has, until very recently, remained as silent as the sociologist about the conjugal family of the lower classes. It was primarily men who created works of literature, and they saw with men's eyes; thus we cannot be surprised that fiction is so replete with men's attitudes—about men, women, and children. However, because they *were* artists, and above all aimed at making their characters full-bodied and alive, their women often do speak from their own inner worlds. By contrast, literature has mostly been aristocratic, and only rarely do we hear members of the lower classes tell their own story.

In the selections that follow, people of different centuries and cultures appear. They are complex and highly individual, different from all others. Yet it is startling how quickly, thanks to the writer's skill, we perceive an underlying similarity with the emotions and experiences we have within our own conjugal families.

Chapter 4

Marital Interaction

In fairy tales, as indeed in much of Western literature, the narrative ends with marriage. In the classical story, the plot describes how, in spite of various difficulties (class differences, evil machinations, misunderstandings), the boy and girl finally marry: "Boy meets girl. Boy loses girl. Boy gets girl." A common variant, especially frequent in Japanese and Chinese literature where the class barriers may have been stronger, is tragic: love ends in death.

All such stories express our hopeful fantasies ("they lived happily ever after," love is all-important) and give us advice (courtship must end at marriage, for it is final; loving the wrong person may be tragic; true worth will be rewarded by love, etc.).

However, their reticence about life within marriage suggests several dour speculations. The first is that in many literatures it is the love encounter, usually before marriage, that is dramatic and fascinating, while marital interaction is seen to be banal if not boring. Second, the drama of courtship is about the unformed young, who still have a promising future before them, while marital interaction occurs between people socially defined as mature (however young in years), whose duty it is to live out their lives peacefully.

Third, the conflict in courtship stories is artistically organized so as to *end*, whether with marriage or tragedy, while folk wisdom perceives that conflict in marriage will continue for decades ending only with death, not tragedy.

This focus on love and courtship also suggests that among all the family variables it is only passionate love that is perceived to be powerful enough to threaten the really fundamental social factors, such as wealth and inheritance, kingdoms and military might, etc.

But perhaps deeper than these possible causes for literature's reticence in portraying marital interaction is a further, cognitive problem, namely, that folk wisdom can embody in stories only what it can grasp and understand, while the rich, subtle life of people in marriage resists our efforts to describe it in formulas or neat rules for behavior. Beyond such advice as "follow the traditional sex role definition" (e.g., women should bow to their husbands' will) and "a good spouse is a rare jewel to be cherished," common sense does almost as little to instruct us as family sociology.

The sociologist of the family can, of course, apply a range of analytic frameworks to marital interaction, because it is after all a form of social behavior, and almost any sociological tool can be used to some extent. For example, considerable work has been done in sociology on decision making, and that approach can therefore be applied equally well to the decisions of husbands and wives. The family is a social microunit, and some part of the interaction within it can be analyzed by asking the questions of ethnomethodology, or those so brilliantly posed by Erving Goffman—about the presentation of self, deception, civility, body language, and so on. Although economists have typically viewed the family as a consuming unit, we can nevertheless view it as a microworld in which exchanges take place.

All these approaches contribute something to our understanding of marital interaction, but no overarching framework has been created that would encompass and exploit all these narrower views, so as to state a satisfactory set of analytical propositions of any substantial penetration or generality.

Family sociology has been, up to now, far less successful in ordering this body of observations, so central to the life of the family as a whole, than any other aspect of this great social institution. Consequently it has lost some of the rich concreteness of the individual case, which remains the domain of the literary artist, without moving far in its quest for scientific generalizations.

Thus, in reading the following selections we feel closer to the reality of marital interaction (in spite of their particularity, because lives are created before our eyes), than in reading sociological accounts of the same types of marital processes.

This contrast between the few (but clearly delineated) lives portrayed by the literary artist and the range of marriages the sociologist tries to encompass can be carried a step further. A major additional difference lies in their access to information.

The writer can know all that he or she needs to know, because the writer creates the story. Even the writer who reports that once the character has been created he need only observe that person in action remains nevertheless the only source of information. The sociologist, by contrast, knows only what the interviewees want to report.

Moreover, the sociological information has been obtained, typically, at one point in time. The effort to grasp the marital process over a longer period of time—the most penetrating data—is hampered when the questioner must reconstruct the past from one or two interviews.

Then again, most information comes from women. This bias arises from two main sources: (a) the fact that more women than men are at home to be interviewed; and (b) a conviction that women know more about marital life because that is their primary concern. Both of these assumptions are less valid now than in the past, but both have barred us from a deeper understanding of marital life. If almost half the labor force is made up of women, the difference in accessibility is not large enough to justify omitting the men if *their* experiences would enlighten us.

When sociologists have compared the experiences of both the man and the woman, they have reported important differences in opinions: namely, views about the success of the marriage, areas of good or poor adjustment, authority, and so on. This is not surprising; after all, they occupy different positions from which to observe their own married life. When sociologists have looked at the marital concerns of men, they have reported a wider range of family behavior, a greater emotional commitment, a higher percentage of time devoted to family than had been assumed. Thus their experiences should also be analyzed. At least, we should ascertain how each sex divides or invests its time and emotion among the different areas of marital interaction.

At present, then, the biases and gaps in our knowledge and sympathetic understanding of marital life are to be encountered in both the creations of the literary artist and the analyses of the sociologist. What one is missing, the other may not fully supply. The contrasts between the two forms of discovery, as well as our need for deeper wisdom about marital life, remain a continuing challenge to all of us.

The White Stocking
D. H. Lawrence

In all societies of which we have sure knowledge, the men
rule, enjoy the most challenging and exciting occupations,
hold the important political posts, and make the larger
decisions within the family itself. However, it cannot escape
anyone's observation that whatever the definition of sex
roles, or the weight of resources in the hands of males,
some wives rule just the same. Sometimes, as remarked
earlier, it is because the woman is simply a "better fighting
machine" than her husband. Sometimes he perceives that
she is more often right in her judgment than he is. She may
also come from a higher social class, and may be supported
by her family in her battle of wills with her husband. In
societies that have permitted her to own wealth independently, she may control the family finances and thus
be able to impose her decisions.

There are many structural reasons why husbands are
less likely to be dominated by love than are their wives, but
that happens too, as illustrated by D. H. Lawrence's story,
"The White Stocking." In both familistic and industrial
societies, the adult male is pressed by others, as by the
values he has absorbed over his lifetime, to invest more of
his attention, energy, and emotion in activities outside the
conjugal unit. If he fails there, he cannot recoup by being an
affectionate or dutiful husband. By contrast, women are
pressed centripetally. Even today the woman who fails as a
wife but succeeds in the outside world will be criticized far
more than a man would be. Her contentment depends more
on his caring for her than his does upon her caring.

This relationship can be summed up in Waller's *Principle of Lesser Interest*, i.e., the person who cares less is
better able to dominate the other. However, that person is
sometimes the wife, not the husband, as in this story. The
young wife loved Whiston passionately, and has not ceased

From *The Complete Short Stories of D. H. Lawrence*, 1961, vol. I, (Compass
Edition), by permission of the Viking Press, Inc., Lawrence Pollinger Ltd., and estate of
late Frieda Lawrence.

to love him, but her dedication to him is not as complete as before. She does not reject him. Instead, he is the air she breathes, the house she inhabits. She has experienced an emotional change that was perhaps more common when divorce was an unthinkable solution to marital conflict: a young girl before her marriage had to watch her every act, lest she destroy her chances of a good marriage, bring shame on her family, or suffer punishment from her elders. After marriage, in spite of her husband's control, she could feel more free, being endowed with a new set of rights as an adult and feeling secure about the continuity of her marriage—but note the contrast with our modern era.

Whiston cannot control her flirtation with Adams, except for some parts of her external behavior. He can threaten or beat her physically, take away the jewels Adams gave her, but he cannot force her to give her heart to him unreservedly. No one can, after all, control another's loving, or even his or her own loving. On the other hand, that is central to Whiston's needs. He feels his "love-property" is being threatened, that the purity of their marital relationship is being polluted by her coquettishness with Adams. He feels humiliated by this encroachment and betrayed by her frivolity, but all the social and cultural definitions he can muster, all the weight of resources cannot achieve the goal that is central to his husbandly needs.

She refused to go to her work at Adams's any more. Her father had to submit and she sent in her notice—she was not well. Sam Adams was ironical. But he had a curious patience. He did not fight.

In a few weeks, she and Whiston were married. She loved him with passion and worship, a fierce little abandon of love that moved him to the depths of his being, and gave him a permanent surety and sense of realness in himself. He did not trouble about himself any more: he felt he was fulfilled and now he had only the many things in the world to busy himself about. Whatever troubled him, at the bottom was surety. He had found himself in this love.

They spoke once or twice of the white stocking.

"Ah!" Whiston exclaimed. "What does it matter?"

He was impatient and angry, and could not bear to consider the matter. So it was left unresolved.

She was quite happy at first, carried away by her adoration of her husband. Then gradually she got used to him. He always was the ground of her happiness, but she got used to him, as to the air she breathed. He never got used to her in the same way.

Inside of marriage she found her liberty. She was rid of the responsibility of herself. Her husband must look after that. She was free to get what she could out of her time.

So that, when, after some months, she met Sam Adams, she was not quite as unkind to him as she might have been. With a young wife's new and exciting knowledge of men, she perceived he was in love with her, she knew he had always kept an unsatisfied desire for her. And, sportive, she could not help playing a little with this, though she cared not one jot for the man himself.

When Valentine's day came, which was near the first anniversary of her wedding day, there arrived a white stocking with a little amethyst brooch. Luckily Whiston did not see it, so she said nothing of it to him. She had not the faintest intention of having anything to do with Sam Adams, but once a little brooch was in her possession, it was hers, and she did not trouble her head for a moment how she had come by it. She kept it.

Now she had the pearl ear-rings. They were a more valuable and a more conspicuous present. She would have to ask her mother to give them to her, to explain their presence. She made a little plan in her head. And she was extraordinarily pleased. As for Sam Adams, even if he saw her wearing them, he would not give her away. What fun, if he saw her wearing his ear-rings! She would pretend she had inherited them from her grandmother, her mother's mother. She laughed to herself as she went down-town in the afternoon, the pretty drops dangling in front of her curls. But she saw no one of importance.

Whiston came home tired and depressed. All day the male in him had been uneasy, and this had fatigued him. She was curiously against him, inclined, as she sometimes was nowadays, to make mock of him and jeer at him and cut him off. He did not understand this, and it angered him deeply. She was uneasy before him.

She knew he was in a state of suppressed irritation. The veins stood out on the backs of his hands, his brow was drawn stiffly. Yet she could not help goading him.

"What did you do wi' that white stocking?" he asked, out of a gloomy silence, his voice strong and brutal.

"I put it in a drawer—why?" she replied flippantly.

"Why didn't you put it on the fire-back?" he said harshly. "What are you hoarding it up for?"

"I'm not hoarding it up," she said. "I've got a pair."

He relapsed into gloomy silence. She, unable to move him, ran away upstairs, leaving him smoking by the fire. Again she tried on the ear-rings. Then another little inspiration came to her. She drew on the white stockings, both of them.

Presently she came down in them. Her husband still sat immovable and glowering by the fire.

"Look!" she said. "They'll do beautifully."

And she picked up her skirts to her knees, and twisted round, looking at her pretty legs in the neat stockings.

He filled with unreasonable rage, and took the pipe from his mouth.

"Don't they look nice?" she said. "One from last year and one from this, they just do. Save you buying a pair."

And she looked over her shoulders at her pretty calves, and at the dangling frills of her knickers.

"Put your skirts down and don't make a fool of yourself," he said.

"Why a fool of myself?" she asked.

And she began to dance slowly round the room, kicking up her feet half reckless, half jeering, in ballet-dancer's fashion. Almost fearful, yet in defiance, she kicked up her legs at him, singing as she did so. She resented him.

"You little fool, ha' done with it," he said. "And you'll backfire them stockings, I'm telling you." He was angry. His face flushed dark, he kept his head bent. She ceased to dance.

"I shan't," she said. "They'll come in very useful."

He lifted his head and watched her, with lighted, dangerous eyes.

"You'll put 'em on the fire-back, I tell you," he said.

It was a war now. She bent forward, in a ballet-dancer's fashion, and put her tongue between her teeth.

"I shan't back-fire them stockings," she sang, repeating his words, "I shan't, I shan't, I shan't."

And she danced round the room doing a high kick to the tune of her words. There was a real biting indifference in her behaviour.

"We'll see whether you will or not," he said, "trollops! You'd like Sam Adams to know you was wearing 'em, wouldn't you? That's what would please you."

"Yes, I'd like him to see how nicely they fit me, he might give me some more then."

And she looked down at her pretty legs.

He knew somehow that she *would* like Sam Adams to see how pretty her legs looked in the white stockings. It made his anger go deep, almost to hatred.

"Yer nasty trolley," he cried. "Put yer petticoats down, and stop being so foul-minded."

"I'm not foul-minded," she said. "My legs are my own. And why shouldn't Sam Adams think they're nice?"

There was a pause. He watched her with eyes glittering to a point.

"Have you been havin' owt to do with him?" he asked?

"I've just spoken to him when I've seen him," she said. "He's not as bad as you would make out."

"Isn't he?" he cried, a certain wakefulness in his voice. "Them who has anything to do wi' him is too bad for me, I tell you."

"Why, what are you frightened of him for?" she mocked.

She was rousing all his uncontrollable anger. He sat glowering. Every one of her sentences stirred him up like a red-hot iron. Soon it would be too much. And she was afraid herself; but she was neither conquered nor convinced.

A curious little grin of hate came on his face. He had a long score against her.

"What am I frightened of him for?" he repeated automatically. "What am I frightened of him for? Why, for you, you stray-running little bitch."

She flushed. The insult went deep into her, right home.

"Well, if you're so dull—" she said, lowering her eyelids, and speaking coldly, haughtily.

"If I'm so dull I'll break your neck the first word you speak to him," he said, tense.

"Pf!" she sneered. "Do you think I'm frightened of you?" She spoke coldly, detached.

She was frightened, for all that, white round the mouth.

His heart was getting hotter.

"You *will* be frightened of me, the next time you have anything to do with him," he said.

"Do you think *you'd* ever be told—ha!"

Her jeering scorn made him go white-hot, molten. He knew he was incoherent, scarcely responsible for what he might do. Slowly, unseeing, he rose and went out of doors, stifled, moved to kill her.

He stood leaning against the garden fence, unable either to see or hear. Below him, far off, fumed the lights of the town. He stood still, unconscious with a black storm of rage, his face lifted to the night.

Presently, still unconscious of what he was doing, he went indoors again. She stood, a small, stubborn figure with tight-pressed lips and big, sullen, childish eyes, watching him, white with fear. He went heavily across the floor and dropped into his chair.

There was a silence.

"*You're* not going to tell me everything I shall do, and everything I shan't," she broke out at last.

He lifted his head.

"I tell you *this*," he said, low and intense. "Have anything to do with Sam Adams, and I'll break your neck."

She laughed, shrill and false.

"How I hate your word 'break your neck'," she said, with a grimace of the mouth. "It sounds so common and beastly. Can't you say something else—"

There was a dead silence.

"And besides," she said, with a queer chirrup of mocking laughter, "what do you know about anything? He sent me an amethyst brooch and a pair of pear ear-rings."

"He what?" said Whiston, in a suddenly normal voice. His eyes were fixed on her.

"Sent me a pair of pearl ear-rings, and an amethyst brooch," she repeated, mechanically, pale to the lips.

And her big, black, childish eyes watched him, fascinated, held in her spell.

He seemed to thrust his face and his eyes forward at her, as he rose slowly and came to her. She watched transfixed in terror. Her throat made a small sound, as she tried to scream.

Then, quick as lightning, the back of his hand struck her with a crash across the mouth, and she was flung back blinded against the wall. The shock shook a queer sound out of her. And then she saw him still coming on, his eyes holding her, his fist drawn back, advancing slowly. At any instant the blow might crash into her.

Mad with terror, she raised her hands with a queer clawing movement to cover her eyes and her temples, opening her mouth in a dumb shriek. There was no sound. But the sight of her slowly arrested him. He hung before her, looking at her fixedly, as she stood crouched against the wall with open, bleeding mouth, and wide-staring eyes, and two hands clawing over temples. And his lust to see her bleed, to break her and destroy her, rose from an old source against her. It carried him. He wanted satisfaction.

But he had seen her standing there, a piteous, horrified thing, and he turned his face aside in shame and nausea. He went and sat heavily in his chair, and a curious ease, almost like sleep, came over his brain.

She walked away from the wall towards the fire, dizzy, white to the lips, mechanically wiping her small, bleeding mouth. He sat motionless. Then, gradually, her breath began to hiss, she shook, and was sobbing silently, in grief for herself. Without looking, he saw. It made his mad desire to destroy her come back.

At length he lifted his head. His eyes were glowing again, fixed on her.

"And what did he give them you for?" he asked, in a steady, unyielding voice.

Her crying dried up in a second. She also was tense.

"They came as valentines," she replied, still not subjugated, even if beaten.

"When, to-day?"

"The pearl ear-rings to-day—the amethyst brooch last year."

"You've had it a year?"

"Yes."

She felt that now nothing would prevent him if he rose to kill her. She could not prevent him any more. She was yielded up to him. They both trembled in the balance, unconscious.

"What have you had to do with him?" he asked, in a barren voice.

"I've not had anything to do with him," she quavered.

"You just kept 'em because they were jewellery?" he said.

A weariness came over him. What was the worth of speaking any more of it? He did not care any more. He was dreary and sick.

She began to cry again, but he took no notice. She kept wiping her mouth on her handkerchief. He could see it, the blood-mark. It made him only more sick and tired of the responsibility of it, the violence, the shame.

When she began to move about again, he raised his head once more from his dead, motionless position.

"Where are the things?" he said.

"They are upstairs," she quavered. She knew the passion had gone down in him.

"Bring them down," he said.

"I won't," she wept, with rage. "You're not going to bully me and hit me like that on the mouth."

And she sobbed again. He looked at her in contempt and compassion and in rising anger.

"Where are they?" he said.

"They're in the little drawer under the looking-glass," she sobbed.

He went slowly upstairs, struck a match, and found the trinkets. He brought them downstairs in his hand.

"These?" he said, looking at them as they lay in his palm.

She looked at them without answering. She was not interested in them any more.

He looked at the little jewels. They were pretty.

"It's none of their fault," he said to himself.

And he searched round slowly, persistently, for a box. He

tied the things up and addressed them to Sam Adams. Then he
went out in his slippers to post the little package.

When he came back she was still sitting crying.

"You'd better go to bed," he said.

She paid no attention. He sat by the fire. She still cried.

"I'm sleeping down here," he said. "Go to bed."

In a few moments she lifted her tear-stained, swollen face
and looked at him with eyes all forlorn and pathetic. A great flash
of anguish went over his body. He went over, slowly, and very
gently took her in his hands. She let herself be taken. Then as she
lay against his shoulder, she sobbed aloud:

"I never meant—"

"My love—my little love—" her cried, in anguish of spirit,
holding her in his arms.

The Adventurous History of Hsi Men and His Six Wives

Chin P'ing Mei

We must shift both our literary and our sociological per-
spectives in order to comprehend marital interaction in
polygyny. The literary conventions or devices are different,
because such stories are laid in non-Western countries. We
must be quick to note, as we need not in our reading of
Western literature, the varied cultural assumptions that the
artist does not discuss, for to him they are part of the
background, not to be questioned or explained. In spite of
the differences in marital structure, however—in this instance the husband has a great household of five wives
(another has died) so that it forms in effect a community—
we note the operation of a set of social relations that after all
are not so alien to our own. Let us consider several of the
cultural patterns that are woven into the narrative before us.

From Chin P'ing Mei, *The Adventurous History of Hsi Men and His Six Wives*,
Capricorn Books, New York, 1960.

Whether or not true polygyny was practiced during the past several Chinese dynasties is open to argument. By a very rigorous definition, perhaps it was not. Note that in anger Moon Lady asserts that *she* was lawfully married (unlike Gold Lotus). But in marriage forms, as in most other social patterns we must think of *degrees* rather than sharp divisions. However, concubinage was common among the upper classes (it is obvious that only under very special and temporary conditions can the average man enjoy the delights, if any, of multiple union); and some concubines did enjoy specific rights as "wives," in harmony with the differing forms and ceremonials that preceded the union. In any event the author did not consider or question these subtle points: to him these women *are* wives, and perhaps they were.

Next, in a polygynous system one of the devices or levers by which a woman may come to play a more influential role in her relations with her husband is to produce children, especially *sons*. Consequently, Gold Lotus is resentful because she wants very much to become pregnant and has been taking a magic potion, but she was not allowed to entice Hsi Men to her couch that night.

Further, Moon Lady is the Number One wife. In all polygynous systems, but especially in the Chinese system, the first wife enjoyed a much higher social rank and influence. She was older than other wives (since new wives were likely to be very young) and more accustomed to running the entire household. The senior marriage was usually an alliance with another great family, while later alliances might well have as their motive the acquisition of a beautiful young woman to entertain the older man. In a household headed by an ideal Number One wife, it was wise policy to welcome new wives, since the ultimate authority was in the hands of the husband, and a clever wife thus pleased him. At the same time, she was the guardian of the proprieties, which always included a respect for the feelings of other wives. Even an enticing and clever young woman could not be permitted for long to make the husband her adoring slave. Moreover, in a showdown, both the members of the household and the husband himself would defer to the senior wife, because her broader resources of rank and the influence of her family weighed heavily in these matters; the Chinese great family ideally always respected the traditional rights and obligations of each rank in a hierarchy.

At the time of the present scene from Chin P'ing Mei's story about Hsi Men and his six wives, Moon Lady is pregnant with her husband's child; Gold Lotus is still an exciting but barren plaything. The scene also illustrates a point that is too often forgotten in our imaginings about a polygynous household: even though these women (in contrast to their American counterparts who became polygynists in Mormon society) were socialized from birth to accept polygyny as normal, and were trained to be appropriately subordinate and to accept their fellow wives, in fact—precisely because their contentment with their day-to-day existence depended so completely on the master's goodwill—they were likely to be highly sensitive to the least threat to their positions, to each failure in equality or justice, or to any neglect. Polygyny does not, in short, eradicate jealousy, simply because a mere ideology of nonjealousy was imposed by men from the top, and in any event real stakes were at issue. A secondary wife was, in fact, threatened if another wife came to dominate the attention of the one husband.

He had been nestling closer and closer, and now he had found his way.

"I did beg you not to bother me with your nonsense!" she said, still feigning to resist him. But very soon her mouth was making those quivering, snapping motions which one may observe in a dog that is snapping at flies, and her lips without ceasing, uttered their tender cry of "*Ta ta.*" With redoubled efforts Hsi Men endeavored that night to atone for the injustice with which he had treated his Third. But Gold Lotus sought her lonely couch with a heart full of bitter resentment. She had been shamefully cheated of her hope of testing the nun's magic potion on this seven-times-seventh day of the sixty-day cycle.

Next morning, at the family breakfast table, Moon Lady, turning to Jade Fountain, asked whether the wax pills had benefited her.

"I was sick twice more early this morning, but now I feel quite well again."

Gold Lotus did not appear at breakfast. Moon Lady wanted to send Little Jewel for her.

"Little Jewel is in the kitchen, baking the cakes; I'll go instead," said Jade Flute; and off she went.

"I must tell you what happened last night," she said to Gold Lotus. "When you had gone my mistress said just what she thought about you. She said you were shameless, that you ruined the peace of the household, and that you and Master Hsi Men ate out of one platter. You had completely monopolized him; you ordered him about as if he had been your wife, and never let him show himself in the women's apartments. And then she sent him to the Third. He spent the night with her. What's more, she told her sister-in-law and the two nuns that you had ruined Spring Plum, and it was your fault that she had no manners. Master Hsi Men wanted to send Spring Plum to the blind singer; she was to apologize to her and take her an ounce of silver as compensation."

Gold Lotus made no reply, but what she had heard she stored up in her heart.

"Where is the Fifth?" asked Moon Lady, as Jade Flute returned.

"The Fifth mistress will be here directly."

"You see," said Moon Lady, turning to Sister-in-law Wu, "one said barely two words to her yesterday, and she's behaving as though she had been insulted. I expect there'll be another scene today."

"Who dares to say that I've monopolized him?" suddenly cried Gold Lotus's voice, from behind the curtain of the veranda door. She had crept up to the door unnoticed.

"Do you wish to deny it?" cried Moon Lady, angrily. "Day after day, since his return, you have seized upon him and kept him for yourself. The rest of us barely see the edge of his shadow. You behave as though you were his only wife, as though the rest of us didn't exist. Yes, that was exactly what I said."

"And it's a pack of lies! He wasn't with me yesterday, nor the day before."

"*You* are lying! Hadn't you the insolence to come in here last night, when he was quietly sitting with me, and order him to come to you, as though it were a matter of course that he would do so? He is man enough to know what he ought to do and leave undone. How do you contrive to fetter him with cords of pig's hair and rob him of his freedom of movement? You are always running after him and trying to catch him for yourself. Is that seemly? Is it the reserve that one expects of a decent woman? Moreover, you appropriated the sable cloak of the Sixth behind my back. Couldn't you have spoken to me about it first? And what of the unmannerly way in which your maid behaved to the singing-girl, who was my guest, who frequents a hundred houses, and will of course gossip about us and bring us into disrepute? Can't you teach her better manners?"

"Well, chastise her yourself! She's as much your maid as mine. I've nothing to say to that. As for the fur, I didn't appropriate it; it was given to me. As far as that goes, on the same occasion he presented somebody else with various articles from the Sixth wife's wardrobe. Why do you blame only me for unseemly conduct?"

Moon Lady mistakenly believed that this last remark was aimed at her, though it actually referred to the nurse Ju I and her secret relations with her master. Angered beyond all control, her cheeks crimson with fury, she burst into voluble speech: "I suppose that means that I myself am guilty of unseemly behavior? No, I at all events know what is right and proper. I was decently brought up in an honorable family, and I was lawfully married to him; I am an honest and respectable wife, not a shameless harlot like yourself, who runs after every man she sees!"

"Big Sister, don't be so angry!" said Jade Fountain, seeking to appease her. "In your excitement you quite overlook the fact that you are hitting us with the same club!" And turning to Gold Lotus: "Sister Five," she said, "do let there be an end of all this controversy! Must you always have the last word?"

"This dispute is not exactly pleasant for your guests," added Sister-in-law Wu. "If it continues perhaps one had better get into one's palanquin and leave the house."

Gold Lotus, who was beside herself with rage at these rebukes, threw herself down at full length. Her hair became unfastened, tears of rage flooded her cheeks, and like a madwoman she struck herself and beat her head upon the floor.

"I will endure this aimless life no longer! I would rather die!" she cried in despair. "I am supposed to have run after him when he took me into his household! Very well, as soon as he comes home I shall ask him for a letter of divorce, and go. Then no one can ever say again that I ran after him."

Jade Fountain could endure this squabbling no longer. She took Gold Lotus by the hand and tried to lead her away to her own pavilion.

"You really ought to control yourself better! We are making ourselves a laughing stock to our guests! Come! Stand up!" And with the help of Jade Flute she pulled the resisting woman to her feet and escorted her to her pavilion.

"One always enjoys one's visits to you when everyone is cheerful and contented," said Sister-in-law Wu, when Gold Lotus had gone. "But under these circumstances one loses all desire to remain any longer."

The two nuns had already made their preparations for departure, and now came to make their farewells, carrying food boxes in their hands.

"This has been very painful," said Moon Lady, in an apologetic tone. "I do hope you won't think us too ridiculous."

"My dear Bodhisattva, you needn't apologize!" replied Sister Pi. "In every household it sometimes happens that the chimney smokes. But the dusting of a soul tablet is a work pleasing to the gods. You should just try to be a little more indulgent to each other. One must contrive to master whatever monkey feelings and horse thoughts one may harbor. And now, dear Bodhisattva, many thanks for all your kindness! The simple nun takes her leave of you."

Moon Lady responded with a double *Wan fu*, sending Hsi Men's daughter and Sunflower to see her to the gate, so that she would not be molested by the watchdog.

"See how my shoulders are twitching with excitement, and my hands are icy cold," said Moon Lady to her Sister-in-law Wu.

"The cup of tea which I drank before this unpleasantness is splashing about inside me undigested."

"I have always warned you against excitement, but you wouldn't obey me. You ought to have more consideration for your state of advanced pregnancy."

"Sister-in-law, you have been visiting this house for years. Have you ever seen me quarrel with her before? But this time I was in the right, and she behaved like a nocturnal brawler who storms at the night watchman when the latter bids him be quiet. I am certainly a tolerant person, but she is really intolerable. We are five women to one man, but she wants him for herself alone. Instead of taking the lamp and turning it upon herself she dares to accuse other people of invented improprieties. When the Sixth was alive she made things difficult for her, and did everything possible to humiliate her. Now I shall have to wash my eyes and take care that she does not bring me to the grave. She has the face of a human being, but the heart of a beast. Everything about her is false. She herself doesn't believe in her declamations and her oaths; she is only trying to impress people. With the best of intentions I invited her to breakfast this morning with her mother. Who could have guessed that she had already sent her mother home? She had made up her mind beforehand to have a quarrel with me. And think how she suddenly came creeping in, after listening outside on the veranda! She's really becoming quite gruesome! I am only concerned with what she may tell him when he comes home. Probably it will come to this, that he will give the letter of divorce not to her, but to me!"

"Jade Flute and I were in the room, attending to the stove, when the Fifth mistress suddenly came in," Little Jewel interposed. "Neither of us saw her or heard her outside on the veranda."

"She creeps about as silently as a ghost," said Snowblossom. "No wonder; she has felt soles to her slippers. She once forced such a quarrel on me, and abused me so to the master that he struck me."

"Truly," agreed Moon Lady, "none of us is safe from her attacks. Who knows what I have to expect? Did you see how she beat her head upon the floor? Of course she's reckoning that when he sees her bruises he'll pity her and be furious with me."

"But that would be turning the world upside down!" cried Snowblossom.

"You don't know her. She's a nine-tailed vixen. She's capable of any sort of witchcraft. Think of her insolence last night, when she came into my room and called out to him that she couldn't wait any longer for him, and was going on ahead! As though he were her sole possession! Not for a single night does she allow us to have him; she has no respect even for a birthday! Surely as a child she must have put all ten fingers in her mouth in her gluttony!"

"My dear, you shouldn't take the matter to heart so; you must put it out of your mind, or you'll be quite ill!" said Sister-in-law Wu. "What good will it do you to quarrel with her? Show more pride, and ignore her!"

Moon Lady, complaining of pain in her head and her body, retired to her bedroom, in order to lie down for a brief rest. Hsi Men was not a little surprised to find her lying tired and languid on the kang when he returned from the yamen at noon. When he asked her what had happened she did not reply; nor were her maids more communicative. His surprise increased when he found Gold Lotus lying on her bed. She seemed to be quite distracted; she had a headache, her eyes were red with weeping, and she too was dumb when he questioned her.

It was from Jade Fountain that he at last learned what had been happening. In consternation he hurried back to Moon Lady.

"You must have regard for your condition," he said, gently raising her. "How could you allow yourself to be involved in a quarrel with that silly woman?"

"It was not my fault; it was she who forced the quarrel on me. Ask the others if I am not speaking the truth. I am terribly anxious about the little one I am carrying under my heart. For there is a commotion in my body as though a great toad were kicking and struggling there. My head pains me and my shoulders are quite limp and lifeless, and I cannot digest my food. What I should like to do more than anything else today is to take a cord and hang myself."

Shocked by her words, Hsi Men pressed her to his breast.

"Dear big sister, don't take the thing to heart so! You mustn't pay any serious attention to the irresponsible chatter of this uncultivated person, who can't tell high from low, or stench from perfume. I'll go straight to her now and call her to account."

"It's no use doing that. She'll simply entangle you in a hog's-hair string of lies until you don't know which way to turn."

"She had better not anger me, or I'll give her such a kicking. . . . Do you feel a little better now?"

"I don't know. Although I've had only a cup of tea today, there's such a commotion in my body, the pain in my head hasn't stopped, and my limbs are numb and heavy. If you don't believe me, feel my cold, trembling hands and see for yourself. . . . I haven't been able to take hold of anything since."

"Then I'll send for Doctor Yen at once."

"He can't help me. If it comes to that, it simply depends on fate whether one lives or dies. And why so much fuss about me? A humble grave by the city wall; I don't ask for more."

"But my love, what a way to talk! Don't worry about the mud that miserable woman throws at you! The doctor must certainly come. I want to know whether the fruit of your body is unharmed."

"Then let old Liu come. A few of her drops and two pricks of her cauterizing needle in my head; that's all I need."

"Nonsense! What does that old quack know of diagnosis and midwifery? You must have the doctor."

And he then and there bade his groom Kiu Tung saddle a horse and ride off to fetch Doctor Yen. But he came back without the doctor, who was that day the guest of the prefect. However, his wife would send him early in the morning. At first Hsi Men absolutely refused to leave his first wife's side, although Neighbor Kiao had repeatedly sent for him; for Kiao had invited him to his house that afternoon. Moon Lady persuaded him that he ought not to ignore this invitation.

At last he gave way to her, and left the house. Early that evening he was back again. The first thing he did was to visit Moon Lady. She had already left her bed. Sister-in-law Wu, Sunflower, and Jade Fountain were keeping her company.

"Well, are you better?" he asked sympathetically.

"Thanks, I have managed to take a little rice soup. My body has quieted down pretty well, only I still have rather a headache."

"And tomorrow you will be quite well again, when the doctor has given you something."

"Please don't have him! I feel so awkward in his presence. I won't in any circumstances show myself to a strange man."

But the next morning, when Doctor Yen came, she did, after persistent refusal, show herself to him, to please her husband. With her hair carefully arranged, and fully dressed, she agreed to a short, ceremonious interview in the veranda room. He could not, of course, enter her bedroom; her strict views on such matters as good form and decency made this impossible. Sitting stiffly and demurely in her chair, she laid her right hand, which was hidden in the wide sleeve, on the damask cloth of the table which divided her from the doctor, and timidly allowed her delicate bamboo-shoot fingertips and her jade knuckles to peep forth beyond the hem of her sleeve. After Doctor Yen had felt her pulse for some time he thanked her with a bow, whereupon she rose, breathed a second *Wan fu*, and withdrew with measured step to her bedchamber.

While the doctor was refreshing himself with a cup of tea, the lad Kiu Tung appeared, having been sent by Moon Lady to facilitate his diagnosis by explaining in detail just how his mistress was feeling, and the nature of her various troubles.

"All that I knew beforehand," said the doctor pompously.

"My great and honorable First is pregnant and near delivery," Hsi Men added by way of further explanation. "Her troubles are due to the annoyance and excitement which she suffered yesterday. I have confidence in your supramundane power of intellect; you will surely take measures for her quick recovery. You may count on a generous reward."

"This tyro," said the physician, "gives ear to your instructions and will not fail to do the utmost that is in his power to restore to her womb the necessary peace and to her breath the accustomed harmony."

He thereupon launched into a learned and long-winded description of the case, in which he spoke of "too little blood," "too much air," "fire in the liver," and "impeded flow in the veins." He then wrote his prescription, and he had also to prescribe a remedy for the Third wife's stomach trouble. This done, he pocketed his fee and took his leave.

In the meantime Jade Fountain had paid a visit to Gold Lotus, when she tried to bring about a reconciliation between the Fifth and Moon Lady. She found Gold Lotus undressed and unkempt, sitting on the edge of her bed. She was pale, and looked as though she had had a sleepless night.

"Why, Sister Five, not dressed yet?" she began. "Today is Moon Lady's birthday; you surely won't be missing from the table! Do at least bury your resentment and wear a cheerful face again! She is quite ready to make it up. Just go to her room, make a kowtow of apology, and add a few friendly words. Then the whole thing will be dead and buried. A kind word in winter makes us forget the cold, an angry word makes us shiver on a midsummer day. So the proverb tells us. You have both spoken your minds; now you must make it up again. Otherwise you will let yourself in for further trouble, if Hsi Men comes to see you and wants to discuss the affair."

"How can I ever show myself to her again?" Gold Lotus objected. "After she has said that she is a respectable and lawfully married wife, not such a creature as you or I, who had to run after our husband, and who before that used to sleep in the grass and the dew. . . . No, after such words as those, women like you and me can't venture within reach of her highly respectable toes!"

"I know, I know. But I've already answered that on behalf of the rest of us: don't you remember? I told her that she was beating us all with the same stick, for we were all of us married later than Moon Lady. But after all, our entry into this household was made in a perfectly respectable fashion. Weren't the matchmakers employed, weren't witnesses summoned, in the proper manner? No, there can be no question of our having run after anybody. There she is quite in the wrong, and she really sees it herself. It only needs a little tolerance on either side, and all will be forgotten. What will our guests and acquaintances be thinking if they find such discord prevailing in the household? So dress yourself quickly and come with me."

Gold Lotus pondered awhile; then she made up her mind. She would control herself, and swallow the words that were on her tongue. So she sat down to the mirror and put up her hair and dressed herself. Jade Foùntain took her by the hand and led her to Moon Lady's apartments.

"I have brought her!" she cried, raising the curtain and triumphantly dragging her hesitating captive into the room. Gold Lotus went humbly up to Moon Lady, raised her eyes from the ground, and said in a low voice: "Cousin, I have come to apologize. In my youthful lack of thought I have annoyed you. I beg that you will this time overlook it. If I am ever so ill-mannered again your hand may chastise me as it will; I shall not move."

She knelt and performed four kowtows before Moon Lady. No sooner had she risen to her feet than she nimbly sprang at Jade Fountain and gave her a gentle slap, crying, in a jesting tone: "Wicked woman, through your fault yet another 'New One' has entered the household!"

At this all the wives, including the dignified Moon Lady, burst out laughing. With two words Gold Lotus had contrived to change the painful solemnity of the moment into merriment.

"When you are all so happy and cheerful it is pleasant to be with you," said Sister-in-law Wu, in a gratified tone. "If you would always be so friendly and peaceable! A peony blossom is a very lovely thing, but it is seen at its best only in the green wreath of its foliage."

"One must admit that there is no one like our Fifth for speaking the right word at the right time," added Moon Lady, with a smile.

And so peace was restored in the women's apartments.

The Portrait of a Lady

Henry James

The great psychologist William James considered the work
of his brother Henry to be bloodless, indeed lifeless, and
there are few details in Henry James's writings about sexual
behavior, war, violence, and physical bravery, dramatic
incidents on the frontier, or generally the world of men.
Even when he was the most important writer in this country,
he was not popular. Nevertheless, his work has continued to
be read, while the work of far more popular writers has
disappeared, partly because we have ourselves become
subtler and more sophisticated in our understanding of
people's inner emotions, the realm in which he excelled.
Perhaps also we have gradually acquired at least some
rudiments of understanding about the feelings and
thoughts of women, who in his time were usually presented
as vapid, hyperromantic idealizations.

In addition, the much-touted virtues of the simple life,
usually rural or lower-class life, became predominant as
themes in much English and American literature after World
War I, with the result that Henry James's work seemed less
appealing. Now, however, we understand better that James
was not so much extolling the virtues of the upper class as
he was dissecting them with the calm deliberation of a
first-rate surgeon.

In the following section from *The Portrait of a Lady*, we
see with what subtlety a literary artist can present the
deepest conflict, without exaggerated or violent language.
An upper-class couple has come to a parting of the ways.
(That they live in separate rooms is not an index of their
coolness but of their class position.) The husband is cold
and self-righteous, but that is his personality rather than his
class. He is aware of his legal and social power as a
husband, but instead wishes to have his way simply because
inwardly he feels morally justified.

Once again, even when the wife is at a great dis-

From Henry James, *The Portrait of a Lady*, Modern Library, Inc., New York, pp.
352–358.

advantage in her conflict with her husband, he can control only a part of the behavior that he wishes to elicit from her. He is jealous of her cousin, and as an act of what he considers compassion has tolerated the cousin's presence in their social circle; but he had hoped that *in exchange* she would not continue to visit him. Now the cousin is dying, and she wishes to see him. But at this point the husband cannot feel triumph at the death; he only feels moral indignation that the relationship was not completely ended already.

In his view of the marital relationship, she has no choice. The marriage cannot continue if she intends to thwart his will. He cannot imagine a union in which she will have freedom independently of his wishes, especially to see another man (even if that man is dying). If she insists, she will—in the phrasing of a much earlier generation—be no longer under his protection.

The husband feels that both should be bound by tradition, even though (since the story takes place in the latter part of the nineteenth century in the United States) that social tradition was in fact of very short duration. He is content with an "empty-shell marriage" if the form of that shell is adequately maintained by proper public behavior. By contrast, she is pained by the shallowness of their union, the lack of real emotion between them. Thus, though the language is less violent and dramatic than it would be now, even in the same social class, the aims and philosophies being expressed could easily be observed today.

Isabel stood a moment looking at the latter missive; then, thrusting it into her pocket, she went straight to the door of her husband's study. Here she again paused an instant, after which she opened the door and went in. Osmond was seated at the table near the window with a folio volume before him, propped against a pile of books. This volume was open at a page of small coloured plates, and Isabel presently saw that he had been copying from it the drawing of an antique coin. A box of water-colours and fine brushes lay before him, and he had already transferred to a sheet of immaculate paper the delicate, finely-tinted disk. His back was turned toward the door, but he recognised his wife without looking round.

"Excuse me for disturbing you," she said.

"When I come to your room I always knock," he answered, going on with his work.

"I forgot; I had something else to think of. My cousin's dying."

"Ah, I don't believe that," said Osmond, looking at his drawing through a magnifying glass. "He was dying when we married; he'll outlive us all."

Isabel gave herself no time, no thought, to appreciate the careful cynicism of this declaration; she simply went on quickly, full of her own intention: "My aunt has telegraphed for me; I must go to Gardencourt."

"Why must you go to Gardencourt?" Osmond asked in the tone of impartial curiosity.

"To see Ralph before he dies."

To this, for some time, he made no rejoinder; he continued to give his chief attention to his work, which was a sort that would brook no negligence. "I don't see the need of it," he said at last. "He came to see you here. I didn't like that; I thought his being in Rome a great mistake. But I tolerated it because it was to be the last time you should see him. Now you tell me it's not to have been the last. Ah, you're not grateful!"

"What am I to be grateful for?"

Gilbert Osmond laid down his little implements, blew a speck of dust from his drawing, slowly got up, and for the first time looked at his wife. "For my not having interfered while he was here."

"Oh yes, I am. I remember perfectly how distinctly you let me know you didn't like it. I was very glad when he went away."

"Leave him alone then. Don't run after him."

Isabel turned her eyes away from him; they rested upon his little drawing. "I must go to England," she said, with a full consciousness that her tone might strike an irritable man of taste as stupidly obstinate.

"I shall not like it if you do," Osmond remarked.

"Why should I mind that? You won't like it if I don't. You like nothing I do or don't do. You pretend to think I lie."

Osmond turned slightly pale; he gave a cold smile. "That's why you must go then? Not to see your cousin, but to take a revenge on me."

"I know nothing about revenge."

"I do," said Osmond. "Don't give me an occasion."

"You're only too eager to take one. You wish immensely that I would commit some folly."

"I should be gratified in that case if you disobeyed me."

"If I disobeyed you?" said Isabel in a low tone which had the effect of mildness.

"Let it be clear. If you leave Rome to-day it will be a piece of the most deliberate, the most calculated, opposition."

"How can you call it calculated? I received my aunt's telegram but three minutes ago."

"You calculate rapidly; it's a great accomplishment. I don't see why we should prolong our discussion; you know my wish." And he stood there as if he expected to see her withdraw.

But she never moved; she couldn't move, strange as it may seem; she still wished to justify herself; he had the power, in an extraordinary degree, of making her feel this need. There was something in her imagination he could always appeal to against her judgment. "You've no reason for such a wish," said Isabel, "and I've every reason for going. I can't tell you how unjust you seem to me. But I think you know. It's your own opposition that's calculated. It's malignant."

She had never uttered her worst thought to her husband before, and the sensation of hearing it was evidently new to Osmond. But he showed no surprise, and his coolness was apparently a proof that he had believed his wife would in fact be unable to resist forever his ingenious endeavour to draw her out. "It's all the more intense then," he answered. And he added almost as if he were giving her a friendly counsel: "This is a very important matter." She recognised that; she was fully conscious of the weight of the occasion; she knew that between them they had arrived at a crisis. Its gravity made her careful; she said nothing, and he went on. "You say I've no reason? I have the

very best. I dislike, from the bottom of my soul, what you intend
to do. It's dishonourable; it's indelicate; it's indecent. Your
cousin is nothing whatever to me, and I'm under no obligation to
make concessions to him. I've already made the very hand-
somest. Your relations with him, while he was here, kept me on
pins and needles; but I let that pass, because from week to week I
expected him to go. I've never liked him and he has never liked
me. That's why you like him—because he hates me," said
Osmond with a quick, barely audible tremor in his voice. "I've an
ideal of what my wife should do and should not do. She should
not travel across Europe alone, in defiance of my deepest desire,
to sit at the bedside of other men. Your cousin's nothing to you;
he's nothing to us. You smile most expressively when I talk about
us, but I assure you that *we*, *we*, Mrs. Osmond, is all I know. I take
our marriage seriously; you appear to have found a way of not
doing so. I'm not aware that we're divorced or separated; for me
we're indissolubly united. You are nearer to me than any human
creature, and I'm nearer to you. It may be a disagreeable
proximity; it's one, at any rate, of our deliberate making. You
don't like to be reminded of that, I know; but I'm perfectly
willing, because—because—" And he paused a moment, looking
as if he had something to say which would be very much to the
point. "Because I think we should accept the consequences of
our actions, and what I value most in life is the honour of a
thing!"

He spoke gravely and almost gently; the accent of sarcasm
had dropped out of his tone. It had a gravity which checked his
wife's quick emotion; the resolution with which she had entered
the room found itself caught in a mesh of fine threads. His last
words were not a command, they constituted a kind of appeal;
and, though she felt that any expression of respect on his part
could only be a refinement of egotism, they represented something transcendent and absolute, like the sign of the cross or the
flag of one's country. He spoke in the name of something sacred
and precious—the observance of a magnificent form. They were
as perfectly apart in feeling as two disillusioned lovers had ever
been; but they had never yet separated in act. Isabel had not
changed; her old passion for justice still abode within her; and

now, in the very thick of her sense of her husband's blasphemous sophistry, it began to throb to a tune which for a moment promised him the victory. It came over her that in his wish to preserve appearances he was after all sincere, and that this, as far as it went, was a merit. Ten minutes before she had felt all the joy of irreflective action—a joy to which she had so long been a stranger; but action had been suddenly changed to slow renunciation, transformed by the blight of Osmond's touch. If she must renounce, however, she would let him know she was a victim rather than a dupe. "I know you're a master of the art of mockery," she said. "How can you speak of an indissoluble union—how can you speak of your being contented? Where's our union when you accuse me of falsity? Where's your contentment when you have nothing but hideous suspicion in your heart?"

"It is in our living decently together, in spite of such drawbacks."

"We don't live decently together!" cried Isabel.

"Indeed we don't if you go to England."

"That's very little; that's nothing. I might do much more."

He raised his eyebrows and even his shoulders a little: he had lived long enough in Italy to catch this trick. "Ah, if you've come to threaten me I prefer my drawing." And he walked back to his table where he took up the sheet of paper on which he had been working and stood studying it.

"I suppose that if I go you'll not expect me to come back," said Isabel.

He turned quickly round, and she could see this movement at least was not designed. He looked at her a little, and then, "Are you out of your mind?" he enquired.

"How can it be anything but a rupture?" she went on; "especially if all you say is true?" She was unable to see how it could be anything but a rupture; she sincerely wished to know what else it might be.

He sat down before his table. "I really can't argue with you on the hypothesis of your defying me," he said. And he took up one of his little brushes again.

After the Party

John Updike

The modern conjugal union tries to carry, as many analysts have noted, too great a weight, and consequently the chances of its foundering are high. Its burden is least in a society where a monolithic cultural tradition offers few alternatives for behavior and no alternative spouses; where kin have an active stake in the continuity of the family; where the emotional investment of people is less in the husband-wife relationship and more in other kin relations or friendships; where role definitions require specific kinds of *acts* from its members (bringing hot tea to one's mother-in-law in the morning, walking behind the husband, chopping firewood, etc.) rather than deep, positive, emotional responses; and where there is a profound conviction that once one has married, there is no second chance: one must adjust.

In all these ways, the modern marriage is different from those of the past, and the secular trend in that direction continues.

In the novel *Couples,* John Updike has sharply drawn an extreme subsegment of our society. A husband and wife have settled in a well-to-do village in Cape Cod whose inhabitants maximize the importance of the family and are ostensibly focused on children, but where as a consequence the least failure in understanding, sympathy, loving and giving, and even sex is likely to hurt the other spouse.

They are all linked in a social network, watching and gossiping about each other constantly—as do all intimate groups. They try to make sure their children "have all the advantages" of their economic success, but in fact they are much more concerned with each other as couples.

Married, they are constantly engaged in flirtation, sexual liaisons, and love affairs, an implicit set of goals that is disguised by their social definition of frequent parties as simply an expression of unity and friendship. The writer depicts their outwardly placid, warm relationships as shallow, competitive, and anxiety-laden.

This contrast is paralleled in the intimate relations between husband and wife, and thereby Updike implicitly argues that he is describing modern society generally, though without any suggestions for replacing it with a better one. Piet and Angela are "a loving couple" to outsiders, but Angela is repelled by his physical impulses—"bully," she calls him. He is successful in his seduction of other women, but not in that of his own wife, who asserts her individuality and strength by refusing sex to him. Attracted by her, he resents her moral superiority and moral instruction. Their lives are so closely shared that every error in communication, every disagreement, and every thwarted wish taints all the good things they have in common. Note, too, the peculiar tensions in sexual interaction that are socially imposed by our contemporary definition of freedom and love: Angela might (in a different cultural system) engage in sexual intercourse with her husband as a *duty*; and in many societies of the past he could insist upon his marital rights even by force. However, it is precisely a culturally imposed need that he feels, that she must *want* to make love with him, not simply enact the appropriate sexual behavior.

Now, thinking of this house from whose purchase he had escaped and from whose sale he had realized a partner's share of profit, Piet conservatively rejoiced in the house he had held. He felt its lightly supporting symmetry all around him. He pictured his two round-faced daughters asleep in its shelter. He gloated upon the sight of his wife's body, her fine ripeness.

Having unclasped her party pearls, Angela pulled her dress, the black décolleté knit, over her head. Its soft wool caught in her hairpins. As she struggled, lamplight struck zigzag fire from her slip and static electricity made its nylon adhere to her flank. The slip lifted, exposing stocking-tops and garters. Without her head she was all full form, sweet, solid.

Pricked by love, he accused her: "You're not happy with me."

She disentangled the bunched cloth and obliquely faced him.

The lamplight, from a bureau lamp with a pleated linen shade, cut shadows into the line of her jaw. She was aging. A year ago, she would have denied the accusation. "How can I be," she asked, "when you flirt with every woman in sight?"

"In sight? Do I?"

"Of course you do. You know you do. Big or little, old or young, you eat them up. Even the yellow ones, Bernadette Ong. Even poor little soused Bea Guerin, who has enough troubles."

"You seemed happy enough, conferring all night with Freddy Thorne."

"Piet, we can't keep going to parties back to back. I come home feeling dirty. I hate it, this way we live."

"You'd rather we went belly to belly? Tell me"—he had stripped to his waist, and she shied from that shieldlike breadth of taut bare skin with its cruciform blazon of amber hair—"what do you and Freddy find to talk about for hours on end? You huddle in the corner like children playing jacks." He took a step forward, his eyes narrowed and pink, party-chafed. She resisted the urge to step backwards, knowing that this threatening mood of his was supposed to end in sex, was a plea.

Instead she reached under her slip to unfasten her garters. The gesture, so vulnerable, disarmed him; Piet halted before the fireplace, his bare feet chilled by the hearth's smooth bricks.

"He's a jerk," she said carelessly, of Freddy Thorne. Her voice was lowered by the pressure of her chin against her chest; the downward reaching of her arms gathered her breasts to a dark crease. "But he talks about things that interest women. Food. Psychology. Children's teeth."

"What does he say psychological?"

"He was talking tonight about what we all see in each other."

"Who?"

"You know. Us. The couples."

"What Freddy Thorne sees in me is a free drink. What he sees in you is a gorgeous fat ass."

She deflected the compliment. "He thinks we're a circle. A magic circle of heads to keep the night out. He told me he gets frightened if he doesn't see us over a weekend. He thinks we've made a church of each other."

"That's because he doesn't go to a real church."

"Well Piet, you're the only one who does. Not counting the Catholics." The Catholics they knew socially were the Gallaghers and Bernadette Ong. The Constantines had lapsed.

"It's the source," Piet said, "of my amazing virility. A stiffening sense of sin." And in his chalkstripe suit pants he abruptly dove forward, planted his weight on his splayed raw-knuckled hands, and stood upside down. His tensed toes reached for the tip of his conical shadow on the ceiling; the veins in his throat and forearms bulged. Angela looked away. She had seen this too often before. He neatly flipped back to his feet; his wife's silence embarrassed him. "Christ be praised," he said, and clapped, applauding himself.

"Shh. You'll wake the children."

"Why the hell shouldn't I, they're always waking me, the little blood-suckers." He went down on his knees and toddled to the edge of the bed. "Dadda, dadda, wake up-up, Dadda. The Sunday paper's here, guess what? Jackie Kennedy's having a *ba*by!"

"You're so cruel," Angela said, continuing her careful undressing, parting vague obstacles with her hands. She opened her closet door so that from her husband's angle her body was hidden. Her voice floated free. "Another thing Freddy thinks, he thinks the children are suffering because of it."

"Because of what?"

"Our social life."

"Well I have to have a social life if you won't give me a sex life."

"If you think *that* approach is the way to a lady's heart, you have a lot to learn." He hated her tone; it reminded him of the years before him, when she had instructed children.

He asked her, "Why shouldn't children suffer? They're supposed to suffer. How else can they learn to be good?" For he felt that if only in the matter of suffering he knew more than she, and that without him she would raise their daughters as she had been raised, to live in a world that didn't exist.

She was determined to answer him seriously, until her patience dulled his pricking mood. "That's positive suffering," she said. "What we give them is neglect so subtle they don't even notice it. We aren't abusive, we're just evasive. For instance, Frankie Appleby is a bright child, but he's just going to waste, he's just Jonathan Little-Smith's punching bag because their parents are always together.

"Hell. Half the reason we all live in this silly hick town is for the sake of the children."

"But we're the ones who have the fun. The children just get yanked along. They didn't enjoy all those skiing trips last winter, standing in the T-bar line shivering and miserable. The girls wanted all winter to go some Sunday to a museum, a nice warm museum with stuffed birds in it, but we wouldn't take them because we would have had to go as a family and our friends might do something exciting or ghastly without us. Irene Saltz finally took them, bless her, or they'd never have gone. I like Irene; she's the only one of us who has somehow kept her freedom. Her freedom from crap."

"How much did you drink tonight?"

"It's just that Freddy didn't let me talk enough."

"He's a jerk," Piet said and, suffocated by an obscure sense of exclusion, seeking to obtain at least the negotiable asset of a firm rejection, he hopped across the hearth-bricks worn like a passageway in Delft and sharply kicked shut Angela's closet door, nearly striking her. She was naked.

He too was naked. Piet's hands, feet, head, and genitals were those of a larger man, as if his maker, seeing that the cooling body had been left too small, had injected a final surge of plasma which at these extremities had ponderously clotted. Physically he held himself, his tool-toughened palms curved and his acrobat's back a bit bent, as if conscious of a potent burden.

Angela had flinched and now froze, one arm protecting her breasts. A luminous polleny pallor, the shadow of last summer's bathing suit, set off her surprisingly luxuriant pudenda. The slack forward cant of her belly remembered her pregnancies. Her thick-thighed legs were varicose. But her tipped arms seemed, simple and symmetrical, a maiden's; her white feet were high-arched and neither little toe touched the floor. Her throat, wrists and triangular bush appeared the pivots from some undeniable effort of flight, but like Eve on a portal she crouched in shame, stone. She held rigid. Her blue irises cupped light catlike, shallowly. Her skin breathed hate. He did not dare touch her, though her fairness gathered so close dried his tongue. Their bodies hung upon them as clothes too gaudy. Piet felt the fireplace draft on his ankles and became sensitive to the night beyond her hunched shoulders, an extensiveness pressed tight against the bubbled old panes and the frail mullions, a blackness charged with the ache of first growth and the suspended skeletons of Virgo and Leo and Gemini.

She said, "Bully."

He said, "You're lovely."

"That's too bad. I'm going to put on my nightie."

Sighing, immersed in a clamor of light and paint, the Hanemas dressed and crept to bed, exhausted.

Poems

e. e. cummings

Cummings denied the rules of English syntax and wildly created his own. Readers who cannot free themselves from the rules in their heads will be offended and will claim that they cannot understand what he is saying. However, his message is a clear and moving one. It is especially clear when we begin to feel the rhythms and the pauses he has inserted in and between lines. It is moving even when we do not completely succeed in grasping his new grammatical rules.

Here he is honoring the joy of small people in their deeply loving marriage, their warm and gay companionship through life. That other people did not take notice of them while living, or pay great tribute when they died, is of no consequence. The poet does not tell us how to achieve so

From e. e. cummings, *Poems 1923–1954*, Harcourt, Brace, and World, New York, 1954.

glowing an inner pleasure, but we rejoice with them for having had it.

anyone lived in a pretty how town
(with up so floating many bells down)
spring summer autumn winter
he sang his didn't he danced his did.   4

Women and men(both little and small)
cared for anyone not at all
they sowed their isn't they reaped their same
sun moon stars rain   8

children guessed(but only a few
and down they forgot as up they grew
autumn winter spring summer)
that noone loved him more by more   12

when by now and tree by leaf
she laughed his joy she cried his grief
bird by snow and stir by still
anyone's any was all to her   16

someones married their everyones
laughed their cryings and did their dance
(sleep wake hope and then)they
said their nevers they slept their dream   20

stars rain sun moon
(and only the snow can begin to explain
how children are apt to forget to remember
with up so floating many bells down)   24

one day anyone died i guess
(and noone stooped to kiss his face)
busy folk buried them side by side
little by little and was by was   28

all by all and deep by deep
and more by more they dream their sleep

noone and anyone earth by april
wish by spirit and if by yes.   32

Women and men(both dong and ding)
summer autumn winter spring
reaped their sowing and went their came
sun moon stars rain   36

Chapter 5

Parenting: Pleasures, Perils, and Prisms

It is especially in the area of relations between parents and children that the task of the sociologist appears to be more difficult than that of the writer-artist. The sociologist, hampered to begin with by his or her disciplinary exclusion from psychological tools, transforms the problem into "socialization," i.e., the ways in which various forms of child rearing succeed or fail in shaping the emotions, values, attitudes, or role definitions of the next generation. The rearing of children is a prime role obligation of parents (and other kin) in all societies; the continuity of the society requires that children be socialized to want to become parents much like *their* parents. And the stratification system (how wealth, political influence, and prestige are allocated among the classes) depends on the effectiveness of parents in their interaction with children.

However, these interactions are so complex and are so much the outcome of a rich interplay among biological, maturational, psychological, and sociological factors, that few sociological generalizations of great power have been confirmed by the thousands of researches done over the past two generations. Perhaps we can outline some child rearing patterns that can harm children greatly, but it is much less clear what the optimal socialization patterns are.

By contrast the author need not shoulder such a burden. Hundreds of autobiographical novels of the past half century have told the story of the young man who gradually perceives he is creative (the protagonist is almost never a woman), but he need not explain why creative people are more likely to come from one rather than another type of child-parent relationship. Indeed most novelists do not give much credit to their parents for their own achievements.

The author need not bother about the fact that most children do not rebel very much against their parents: *he* did, and so did the other artists he knows. He need not try to explain how our type of industrial society probably generates more parent-youth conflict than most others of the past, because he focuses only on *his* particular conflict. Most parent-child conflict is not between bourgeois parents and a bohemian, artistic son or daughter, but a high percentage of novels focus on that theme.

Authors are much more likely than their readers to believe in rebellion, conflict against parents, abandonment and rejection of their parents, leaving the neighborhood or home town, early sexual freedom, and for that matter a generally uncommitted attitude toward all traditional family institutions. It would be fair to say that over the past century they were prophets rather than true chroniclers: Succeeding generations have gradually moved toward the opinions they expressed. In a way, they have often been successful propagandists for the future with regard to parent-child relations.

Note that just as the sociologist of the family has usually failed to obtain the views of children, so does literature typically omit the experiences and reports of the parents of the writer, who are not often given much opportunity to justify their behavior. This is a bias of information, of framework, and of generations: Each sees the same "reality" but through a different prism. Here again literature and sociology can be a "corrective" to one another.

Family sociology has obtained much of its information from women, thus filling part of the gap left by writers, who mostly describe men. However, both have neglected the serious concern with the stakes, interests, goals, and needs of women and mothers. They have not looked through womanly prisms in order to treat the world of women and mothers in their own right. That chapter, in literature as in sociology, has not as yet been written.

King Lear

William Shakespeare

For over three centuries the role of King Lear has remained a colossal challenge to the actor's art, far beyond the difficulty of Hamlet, for few have been able to transcend the ranting and bombast that can too easily dominate the portrayal. At first glance, it is surprising that Lear moves us so much, for certainly most of us would not wish to identify with him as a person: he is self-centered, arrogant, blind to the emotions of those about him, and foolish in his judgments.

On the other hand, the very exaggerations in the plot and characterization touch upon themes and experiences that are socially universal. For though we are not Cordelia, most of us have had the experience of being pushed into proclaiming our love when we did love but felt it was false to make a formal statement about it. Those who have been parents have been hurt by feeling that one or another child did not love in return, or gave only a dutiful conformity without deep affection. Those who have grown up with brothers and sisters have sometimes learned, or believed, that their siblings plotted against them or sought to profit from them. Children who love their parents have felt betrayed or attacked by them. Thus, though we are fascinated and horrified when Shakespeare places us in this mad world, we soon come to recognize familiar landscapes and emotional crises.

Note, to begin with, the outrageous proposition of exchange that Lear states at the beginning of this scene, that the daughter who loves him most shall have the largest part of his kingdom. We at once object to it, on many grounds, not the least of which is our understanding that love cannot be compelled. On the other hand, we should recognize that at a deeper level we all do accept this proposition to some extent: we are likely to be partial to the child who expresses his or her love the most, just as the child in turn is likely to favor most the parent who expresses the most love for him or her.

From *Shakespeare: The Complete Works*, edited by G. B. Harrison, Harcourt, Brace & World, Inc., New York, 1968, p. 1141, lines 49–122.

We are repelled by the speeches of Goneril and Regan, for we at once recognize their falsity. On the other hand, we have doubtless all experienced some situations in which a clever manipulator is able to get his or her way by expressing a love that was not truly felt. Moreover, if we coolly examine our own behavior, we might well have to confess that we may have, to achieve some goal in a family situation, refrained from expressing our anger or hostility, or positively expressed a warmth or conciliatory attitude that was false. Cordelia's true love and honesty by contrast move us to admiration, but if we put ourselves in the position of parent, we would have to recognize that so flat and cool an expression of affection would hurt us deeply. We do not want only duty, but an expression of deep affection. And though we recognize the correctness of Cordelia's assertion that if her sisters loved their father as fully as they claimed, they would not have married, yet that statement would only hurt us the more.

As sociologists, we know of course that such a division by a great king would be statistically most unlikely, and in any event the chances are high that there would be traditional rules for any division of a king's inheritance. Surely, too, a single, unmarried daughter would not be permitted to rule over a third of the kingdom or more. Finally, it would be equally unlikely that a father would rely on one single statement on such a formal occasion for his ultimate decision about dividing the kingdom, for he would already have had many years of knowledge about the affection of his daughters.

These particularities do not, however, undermine the accuracy of Shakespeare's plot development, once we have accepted them as real, just as in any literary creation a master writer can compel us to accept the conditions, contingencies, and cultural definitions that he or she has created for the purposes of enlightening our understanding about family relations.

From Act I, Scene I. King Lear
Lear: . . . Tell me, my daughters,
    Since now we will divest us both of rule,   50
    Interest of territory, cares of state,
    Which of you shall we say doth love us most? That we our

largest bounty may extend
Where nature doth with merit challenge.
 Goneril,   55
Our eldest-born, speak first.

Goneril: Sir, I love you more than words can wield the matter,
 Dearer than eye-sight, space and liberty,
 Beyond what can be valued, rich or rare,
 No less than life, with grace, health, beauty, honor, 60
 As much as child e'er loved or father found;
 A love that makes breath poor and speech unable;
 Beyond all manner of so much I love you.

Cordelia: (*Aside*) What shall Cordelia do? Love, and be silent.

Lear: Of all these bounds, even from this line to this, 65
 With shadowy forests and with champains rich'd,
 With plenteous rivers and wide-skirted meads,
 We make thee lady. To thine and Albany's issue
 Be this perpetual. What says our second daughter,
 Our dearest Regan, wife to Cornwall? Speak. 70

Regan: I am made of that self metal as my sister,
 And prize me at her worth. In my true heart
 I find she names my very deed of love;
 Only she comes too short; that I profess
 Myself an enemy to all other joys 75
 Which the most precious square of sense possesses,
 And find I am alone felicitate
 In your dear highness' love.

Cordelia: (*Aside*) Then poor Cordelia!
 And yet not so, since I am sure my love's
 More ponderous than my tongue. 80

Lear: To thee and thine hereditary ever
 Remain this ample third of our fair kingdom,
 No less in space, validity and pleasure,
 Than that conferr'd on Goneril. Now, our joy,
 Although the last, not least, to whose young love 85
 The vines of France and milk of Burgundy
 Strive to be interess'd, what can you say to draw
 A third more opulent than your sisters? Speak.

Cordelia: Nothing, my lord.

Lear: Nothing!   90
Cordelia: Nothing.
Lear: Nothing will come of nothing; speak again.
Cordelia: Unhappy that I am, I cannot heave
　My heart into my mouth: I love your majesty
　According to my bond; nor more nor less.   95
Lear: How, how, Cordelia! mend your speech a little,
　Lest it may mar your fortunes.
Cordelia: Good my lord,
　You have begot me, bred me, loved me: I
　Return those duties back as are right fit,
　Obey you, love you, and most honour you.   100
　Why have my sisters husbands, if they say
　They love you all? Haply, when I shall wed,
　That lord whose hand must take my plight shall carry
　Half my love with him, half my care and duty:
　Sure, I shall never marry like my sisters,   105
　To love my father all.
Lear: But goes thy heart with this?
Cordelia: Aye, good my lord.
Lear: So young, and so untender?
Cordelia: So young, my lord, and true.
Lear: Let it be so; thy truth, then, be thy dower: 110
　For, by the sacred radiance of the sun,
　The mysteries of Hecate, and the night;
　By all the operation of the orbs
　From whom we do exist, and cease to be;
　Here I disclaim all my paternal care,   115
　Propinquity and property of blood,
　And as a stranger to my heart and me
　Hold thee, from this, for ever. The barbarous Scythian,
　Or he that makes his generation messes
　To gorge his appetite, shall to my bosom   120
　Be as well neighbour'd, pitied, and relieved,
　As thou my sometime daughter.

Gulliver's Travels

Jonathan Swift

Most young Americans eventually read the part of *Gulliver's Travels* that takes place in Lilliput, where Gulliver is a giant among tiny people. Only a few have followed Gulliver through the rest of his travels, where Swift pokes fun at intellectuals, makes his hero himself a tiny man among giants, or has him encounter the Houyhnhnms. Jonathan Swift's indignation at the imbecility, cruelty, and repellent physical qualities of human beings was vast, and thus it was fitting that he should (through the attitudes of Gulliver) view a race of horses—the most physical of our domestic animals —as the wisest, gentlest, and most kindly of beings he has known. Perhaps modern literary tastes would prefer the creation of a race of beings whose impulses would be natural but passionate, impulsive but attuned to the cosmos, serene in the acceptance of their own dirt and smells, and completely without hostility. As a man of the eighteenth century, Swift rather admired rationalism, moderation, factual proofs, and an avoidance of overwhelming passion. Thus, his horse-humans have no conception of lying, do not cunningly seek their own interest, and find it difficult to understand how anyone can "argue" about matters on which facts are unobtainable.

Consequently, in their socialization of their own children, they strive to educate them slowly by the dictates of reason. Parents do not stay with their children, thus avoiding an attachment that might prevent the young from offering benevolence and friendship to strangers as well as acquaintances. Everyone's allegiance is to everyone else, not to his or her own kin. Even in their mating practices, it is the group (parents and friends) that determines who marries whom, since they do not lay any stress on the particularistic or exclusive relations that are ruled by jealous passion.

From Jonathan Swift, *Gulliver's Travels*, Dodd, Mead and Company, Inc., New York, 1950.

Swift constantly shows us how degraded and inferior are the Yahoos, who are most like human beings (Gulliver is finally exiled from the land of the Houyhnhnms, because they believe that though he is an especially superior Yahoo, he might in time become dangerous as a leader of these brutish creatures). They grow up like beasts, while the Houyhnhnms train their offspring to follow the Platonic ideals of temperance, industry, exercise, and cleanliness.

Swift's suggestions for socialization do not now seem effective to us, but Swift did not fully accept the widespread hypothesis of his time that a rational child rearing would be sufficient; obviously, he also believes that if we give an excellent education to a pig, the result is an educated pig, but a pig nonetheless. He does not see any evidence, and the Houyhnhnms deny the notion completely, that a Yahoo could ever be trained to become as thoughtful, kindly, or virtuous as a Houyhnhnm.

Having lived three years in this country, the reader I suppose will expect that I should, like other travelers, give him some account of the manners and customs of its inhabitants, which it was indeed my principal study to learn.

As these noble Houyhnhnms are endowed by nature with a general disposition to all virtues, and have no conceptions or ideas of what is evil in a rational creature, so their grand maxim is to cultivate reason, and to be wholly governed by it. Neither is reason among them a point problematical as with us, where men can argue with plausibility on both sides of the question; but strikes you with immediate conviction; as it must needs do where it is not mingled, obscured, or discolored by passion and interest. I remember it was with extreme difficulty that I could bring my master to understand the meaning of the word *opinion*, or how a point could be disputable; because reason taught us to affirm or deny only where we are certain, and beyond our knowledge we cannot do either. So that controversies, wranglings, disputes, and positiveness in false or dubious propositions, are evils unknown among the Houyhnhnms. In the like manner when I used to explain to him our several systems of natural philosophy, he would laugh that a creature pretending to reason should value itself upon the knowledge of other people's conjectures, and in things where that knowledge, if it were certain, could be of no use. Wherein he agreed entirely with the sentiments of Socrates, as Plato delivers them; which I mention as the highest honor I can do that prince of philosophers. I have often since reflected what destruction such a doctrine would make in the libraries of Europe, and how many paths to fame would be then shut up in the learned world.

Friendship and benevolence are the two principal virtues among the Houyhnhnms, and these not confined to particular objects, but universal to the whole race. For a stranger from the remotest part is equally treated with the nearest neighbor, and wherever he goes looks upon himself as at home. They preserve decency and civility in the highest degrees, but are altogether ignorant of ceremony. They have no fondness for their colts or foals, but the care they take in educating them proceeds entirely from the dictates of reason. And I observed my master to show the same affection to his neighbor's issue that he had for his own. They will have it that nature teaches them to love the whole species, and it is reason only that makes a distinction of persons, where there is a superior degree of virtue.

When the matron Houyhnhnms have produced one of each sex, they no longer accompany with their consorts, except they lose one of their issue by some casualty, which very seldom happens; but in such a case they meet again; or when the like accident befalls a person whose wife is past bearing, some other couple bestow on him one of their own colts, and then go together again till the mother is pregnant. This caution is necessary to prevent the country from being overburdened with numbers. But the race of inferior Houyhnhnms bred up to be servants is not so strictly limited upon this article; these are allowed to produce three of each sex, to be domestics in the noble families.

In their marriages they are exactly careful to choose such colors as will not make any disagreeable mixture in the breed. Strength is chiefly valued in the male, and comeliness in the female; not upon the account of love, but to preserve the race from degenerating; for where a female happens to excel in strength, a consort is chosen with regard to comeliness. Court-ship, love, presents, jointures, settlements, have no place in their thoughts, or terms whereby to express them in their language. The young couple meet and are joined, merely because it is the determination of their parents and friends: it is what they see done every day, and they look upon it as one of the necessary actions of a rational being. But the violation of marriage, or any other unchastity, was never heard of; and the married pair pass their lives with the same friendship and mutual benevolence that they bear to all others of the same species who come in their way; without jealousy, fondness, quarrelling, or discontent.

In educating the youth of both sexes, their method is admirable, and highly deserves our imitation. These are not suffered to taste a grain of oats, except upon certain days, till eighteen years old; nor milk, but very rarely; and in summer they graze two hours in the morning, and as long in the evening, which their parents likewise observe; but the servants are not allowed above half that time, and a great part of their grass is brought home, which they eat at the most convenient hours, when they can be best spared from work.

Temperance, industry, exercise and cleanliness, are the lessons equally enjoined to the young ones of both sexes; and my master thought it monstrous in us to give the females a different kind of education from the males, except in some articles of domestic management; whereby, as he truly observed, one half of our natives were good for nothing but bringing children into the world; and to trust the care of our children to such useless animals, he said, was yet a greater instance of brutality.

But the Houyhnhnms train up their youth to strength, speed, and hardiness, by exercising them in running races up and down steep hills, and over hard stony grounds; and when they are all in a sweat, they are ordered to leap over head and ears into a pond or river. Four times a year the youth of a certain district meet to show their proficiency in running and leaping, and other feats of strength and agility; where the victor is rewarded with a song made in his or her praise. On this festival the servants drive a herd of Yahoos into the field, laden with hay and oats and milk, for a repast to the Houyhnhnms; after which these brutes are immediately driven back again, for fear of being noisome to the assembly.

Every fourth year, at the vernal equinox, there is a representative council of the whole nation, which meets in a plain about twenty miles from our house, and continues about five or six days. Here they inquire into the state and condition of the several districts; whether they abound or be deficient in hay or oats, or cows or Yahoos. And wherever there is any want (which is seldom) it is immediately supplied by unanimous consent and contribution. Here likewise the regulation of children is settled: as for instance, if a Houyhnhnm has two males, he changes one of them with another that has two females; and when a child has been lost by any casualty, where the mother is past breeding, it is determined what family in the district shall breed another to supply the loss.

Memoirs of a Dutiful Daughter
Simone de Beauvoir

Although the writings by Simone de Beauvoir about women and about her own life have elicited worldwide acclaim, far more than any of her other literary works, their position in French literature is more singular than the Anglo-Saxon reader is likely to sense. In England by the beginning of the nineteenth century, and in the United States by the 1840s, a growing stream of rebellious writings by women appeared, but this movement was slight in France. True enough, there were women writers in France, but in the early part of the nineteenth century they were almost always upper-class women who primarily wrote about court events or composed romances (George Sand was, of course, a prominent exception). It is fair to say that no French writer of the first

Simone de Beauvoir, *Memoirs of a Dutiful Daughter*, translated by James Kirkup, The World Publishing Company, Cleveland–New York, 1959, pp. 111–115. Reprinted by permission of The World Publishing Company, André Deutsch Limited, Publishers, and Weidenfeld and Nicholson. Copyright © 1959 by the World Publishing Company.

rank was a woman, but English literature produced at least two, George Eliot and Jane Austen. It is only very recently that family laws in France have given women the rights that have been theirs in England and the United States for over fifty years. Except for the very brief flurry of egalitarianism during the French Revolution, French law as well as its literature have remained relatively impervious to any challenge directed at man's dominion over women.

De Beauvoir's refusal to accept the rigid sexual definitions imposed upon her by her society is the more striking when we understand her personal background. She had little to gain and much to lose by rebelling. Her family had a high social standing, adequate wealth, and she herself was given both respect and affection. Her talents in school were encouraged, as appropriate ornaments to herself and to her family. And indeed, in her earliest childhood years, she was "a dutiful daughter." Thus, she titles her book *Memoirs of a Dutiful Daughter*. Even when she begins to rebel inwardly, she continues to see the necessity of conforming outwardly to her parents' domination.

Several elements in this account should be noted here. One is that her rebellion is not at this early stage a political one, centering on a view of how the society should be organized. Her objections are on an *ethical* level and are also focused on the appropriate role for women to play. She is greatly concerned with a problem that the parent sees through an entirely different prism: the conflict and contradiction among different precepts. On the one hand, the child is told to tell the truth, but one should not contradict one's parents even if they are wrong, and a child should not tell his mother that she is an idiot even if she is. The child's money is her own, but she has no right (if her parents object) to spend it as she wishes.

Another point to be noted, though it is one that we know as an immediate experience rather than as an ideal, is the extent to which communication between parent and child is often impaired or nonexistent. Her parents simply do not know the extent of her rebellion. They recognize her anger, but do not understand (for she takes pains not to tell them) that she is gradually evolving a philosophical position that runs counter to their definitions and beliefs. They will not indeed find that out until much later in her life. Needless to say, this is often true of communication among all members of the family, and at times only the most acute perception can bridge the barrier.

Finally we come to a problem that often prevents the sociologist from reducing to regularity and order some of the observations that he can make as an individual: in one sense the events described here are very ordinary, if not banal. Nothing very dramatic occurs, and certainly nothing that seems great enough to cause the profound alterations that occur in the child's perceptions and attitudes. These are the result of perhaps hundreds of such small incidents that gradually press or move the child to become a very different person. They are, however, so complex and interwoven that the sociologist cannot describe them easily as a set of generalizations.

A DUTIFUL DAUGHTER REBELS

I had lost the sense of security childhood gives, and nothing had come to take its place. My parents' authority remained inflexible, but as my critical sense developed I began to rebel against it more and more. I couldn't see the point of visits, family dinners, and all those tiresome social duties which my parents considered obligatory. Their replies, "It's your duty" or "That just isn't done," didn't satisfy me at all. My mother's eternal solicitude began to weigh me down. She had her own "ideas" which she did not attempt to justify, and her decisions often seemed to me quite arbitrary. We had a violent argument over a missal which I wanted to give my sister for her First Communion; I wanted to choose one bound in pale fawn leather, like those which the majority of my schoolmates had; Mama thought that one with a blue cloth cover would do just as well; I protested that the money in my money box was for me to do what I liked with; she replied that one should not pay out twenty francs for a thing that could be bought for fourteen. While we were buying bread at the baker's and all the way up the stairs and in the house itself I held my own against her. But in the end I had to give in, with rage in my heart, vowing never to forgive her for what I considered to be an abuse of her power over me. If she had often stood in my way, I think she would have provoked me to open rebellion. But in the really important things—my studies and the choice of my friends—she very rarely meddled; she respected my work and my leisure too, only asking me to do little odd jobs for her like grinding the coffee or carrying the trash downstairs. I had the habit of obedience, and I believed that, on the whole, God expected me to be dutiful: the conflict that threatened to set me against my mother did not break out; but I was uneasily aware of its underlying presence. My mother's whole education and upbringing had convinced her that for a woman the greatest thing was to become the mother of a family; she couldn't play this part unless I played the dutiful daughter, but I refused to take part in grown-up pretense just as much as I did when I was five years old. At the Cours Désir, on the eve of our First Communion, we were exhorted to go and cast ourselves down at our mothers' feet and ask them to forgive our faults; not only had I not done this, but when my sister's turn came, I persuaded her not to do so either. My mother was vexed about it. She was aware of a certain reticence in me which made her bad-tempered, and she often rebuked me. I held it against her for keeping me so dependent upon her and continuing to impose her will upon me. In addition, I was jealous of the place she held in my father's affections because my own passion for him had continued to grow.

The more difficult life became for him, the more I was dazzled by my father's superior character; it did not depend on money or success, and so I used to tell myself that he had deliberately ignored these; that did not prevent me from being sorry for him: I thought he was not appreciated for his true value, that he was misunderstood and the victim of obscure cataclysms. . . .

As long as he approved of me, I could be sure of myself. For years he had done nothing but heap praises on my head. But when I reached the awkward age, he was disappointed in me: he appreciated elegance and beauty in women. Not only did he fail to conceal his disillusionment from me, but he began to show more interest than before in my sister, who was still a pretty girl.

He glowed with pride when she paraded up and down dressed as "The Queen of the Night." He sometimes took part in productions which his friend Monsieur Jeannot—a great advocate of religious drama—organized in the local church clubs; Poupette often played with him. Her face framed in her long fair hair, she played the part of the little girl in Max Maury's *Le Pharmacien*. He taught her to recite fables, putting in gestures and expressions. Though I would not admit it to myself, I was hurt by the understanding between them, and felt a vague resentment against my sister.

But my real rival was my mother. I dreamed of having a more intimate relationship with my father; but even on the rare occasions when we found ourselves alone together we talked as if she were there with us. When there was an argument, if I appealed to my father, he would have said: "Do what your mother tells you!" I only once tried to get him on my side. He had taken us to the races at Auteuil; the course was black with people, it was hot, there was nothing happening, and I was bored; finally the horses were off: the people rushed toward the barriers, and their backs hid the track from my view. My father had hired folding chairs for us and I wanted to stand on mine to get a better view. "No!" said my mother, who detested crowds and had been irritated by all the pushing and shoving. I insisted that I should be allowed to stand on my folding chair. "When I say no, I *mean* no!" my mother declared. As she was looking after my sister, I turned to my father and cried furiously: "Mama is being ridiculous! Why can't I stand on my folding chair?" He simply lifted his shoulder in an embarrassed silence, and refused to take part in the argument.

At least this ambiguous gesture allowed me to assume that as far as he was concerned my father sometimes found my mother too domineering; I persuaded myself that there was a silent conspiracy between us. But I soon lost this illusion. One lunchtime there was talk of a wild-living cousin who considered his mother to be an idiot: on my father's own admission she actually was one. Yet he declared vehemently: "A child who sets himself up as a judge of his mother is an imbecile." I went scarlet and left the table, pretending I was feeling sick. I was judging my mother, and my father had struck a double blow at me by affirming their solidarity and by referring to me indirectly as an imbecile. What upset me even more was that I couldn't help passing judgment on the very sentence my father had just uttered: since my aunt's stupidity was plain to everyone, why shouldn't her son acknowledge it? It is no sin to tell oneself the truth, and besides, quite often one tells oneself the truth unintentionally; at that very moment, for example, I couldn't help thinking what I thought: was that wrong of me? In one sense it was not, and yet my father's words made such a deep impression on me that I felt at once irreproachable and a monster of imbecility. After that, and perhaps partly because of that incident, I no longer believed in my father's absolute infallibility. Yet my parents still had the power to make me feel guilty; I accepted their verdicts while at the same time I looked upon myself with different eyes than theirs. My essential self still belonged to them as much as to me: but paradoxically the self they knew could only be a decoy now; it could be false. There was only one way of preventing this strange confusion: I would have to cover up superficial appearances, which were deceptive. I was used to guarding my tongue; I redoubled my vigilance. I took a further step. As I was not now admitting everything I thought, why not venture unmentionable acts?[1] I was learning how to be secretive.

[1]These "unmentionable acts" consisted of reading forbidden books.

The Way of All Flesh
Samuel Butler

We are likely to feel less tolerance for the Victorian parent's harshness to children than for that of our Puritan forefathers, because we sense that Puritan parents were harsh toward themselves as well. Victorian parents seem far more self-indulgent, hypocritical, and self-righteous. Children

From Samuel Butler, *The Way of All Flesh*, Hartsdale House, New York, 1935, pp. 96–99.

were expected to meet the needs of parents rather than to conform to moral rules that applied to everyone, regardless of age.

Whether parents were in fact more hypocritical (i.e., there was a greater discrepancy between their moral presentation of self and the reality) we may be unable to test, for historical questions of that kind require detailed intimate "inside" data captured from the participants. The reliable information which we *do* have is mainly statistical and demographic, with details of large and small political actions, for example; there are also moral exhortations (in letters or sermons) and even diaries meant to be seen later. But those on whom the moral burden fell left few data: what children felt, knew, or experienced is mostly lost to us.

It is for this reason that we need the accounts of novelists, for though they transform their private experiences into an artistic account (and thus intentionally distort) they also convince us they were *there*. This scene from Samuel Butler's *The Way of All Flesh* depicts the moral trickery and self-pleasing domination of parents who would have been incredulous had they been charged with cruelty to children. Consider, however, parallel instances in the lives of modern children.

I was there on a Sunday, and observed the rigor with which the young people were taught to observe the Sabbath; they might not cut out things, nor use their paint box on a Sunday, and this they thought rather hard, because their cousins the John Pontifexes might do these things. Their cousins might play with their toy train on Sunday, but though they had promised that they would run none but Sunday trains, all traffic had been prohibited. One treat only was allowed them—on Sunday evenings they might choose their own hymns.

In the course of the evening they came into the drawing-room, and, as an especial treat, were to sing some of their hymns to me, instead of saying them, so that I might hear how nicely they sang. Ernest was to choose the first hymn, and he chose one about some people who were to come to the sunset tree. I am no botanist, and do not know what kind of tree a sunset tree is, but the words began, "Come, come, come; come to the sunset tree, for the day is past and gone." The tune was rather pretty and had taken Ernest's fancy, for he was unusually fond of music and had a sweet little child's voice which he liked using.

He was, however, very late in being able to sound a hard "c" or "k," and, instead of saying "Come," he said "Tum, tum, tum."

"Ernest," said Theobald, from the armchair in front of the fire, where he was sitting with his hands folded before him, "don't you think it would be very nice if you were to say 'come' like other people, instead of 'tum'?"

"I do say tum," replied Ernest, meaning that he had said "come."

Theobald was always in a bad temper on Sunday evening. Whether it is that they are as much bored with the day as their neighbors, or whether they are tired, or whatever the cause may be, clergymen are seldom at their best on Sunday evening; I had already seen signs that evening that my host was cross, and was a little nervous at hearing Ernest say so promptly, "I do say tum," when his papa had said he did not say it as he should.

Theobald noticed the fact that he was being contradicted in a moment. He got up from his armchair and went to the piano.

"No, Ernest, you don't," he said, "you say nothing of the kind, you say 'tum,' not 'come.' Now say 'come' after me, as I do."

"Tum," said Ernest, at once; "is that better?" I have no doubt he thought it was, but it was not.

"Now, Ernest, you are not taking pains: you are not trying as you ought to do. It is high time you learned to say 'come'; why, Joey can say 'come,' can't you, Joey?"

"Yeth, I can," replied Joey, and he said something which was not far off "come."

"There, Ernest, do you hear that? There's no difficulty about it, nor shadow of difficulty. Now, take your own time, think about it, and say 'come' after me."

The boy remained silent a few seconds and then said "tum" again.

I laughed, but Theobald turned to me impatiently and said, "Please do not laugh, Overton; it will make the boy think it does not matter, and it matters a great deal;" then turning to Ernest he said, "Now, Ernest, I will give you one more chance, and if you don't say 'come,' I shall know that you are self-willed and naughty."

He looked very angry, and a shade came over Ernest's face, like that which comes upon the face of a puppy when it is being scolded without understanding why. The child saw well what was coming now, was frightened, and, of course, said "tum" once more.

"Very well, Ernest," said his father, catching him angrily by the shoulder. "I have done my best to save you, but if you will have it so, you will," and he lugged the little wretch, crying by anticipation, out of the room. A few minutes more and we could hear screams coming from the dining room, across the hall which separated the drawing-room from the dining room, and knew that poor Ernest was being beaten.

"I have sent him up to bed," said Theobald, as he returned to the drawing-room, "and now, Christina, I think we will have the servants in to prayers," and he rang the bell for them, red-handed as he was.

Report to Greco

Nikos Kazantzakis

When, through the prism of our modern thinking about sex roles and how they are shaped by parent-child relations, we examine either contemporary or historical defenses of men's privileges, they seem factually wrong, ethically unjust, and hollow in their pretensions. We now smile patronizingly at the bravado and braggadocio of a Hemingway, a Lawrence, or a Mailer. They seem as anachronistic and vapid as sentimental popular novels of not so long ago, like *Elsie Dinsmore* or *Girl of the Limberlost*.

From Nikos Kazantzakis, *Report to Greco*, Simon & Schuster, Inc., New York, 1965.

Modern essayists or sociologists have not come forward to explain men in any adequate fashion, perhaps because it is an unaccustomed task; after all, it has always been the unspoken assumption of this and all other great cultures that *women* were the puzzle.

To do so requires that we drop the easy intellectual assumption that the prime goal of men was the domination and exploitation of women. Rather, as Kazantzakis suggests implicitly in *Report to Greco,* some part of their domination grew from caring much less about women than women cared about them. Men's attention was focused on other things, such as glory, revenge, political freedom and revolution (here, the fight of the Greeks against the Turks), land and wealth. In addition, as one could not infer from most modern writers, and however uneasy we may feel about the idea, Kazantzakis reminds us that some types of cultures do produce men who are brave, willing to risk everything for a principle or a cause, joyful in violence. As a child, the male role models he is led to emulate are a succession of patriarchs who *merit* his admiration and press him to be heroic in turn. Consider, then, the social conditions that might be created in our time to furnish adequate heroic role models for young men and women—models which did not focus on masculine issues of the past but on a set of ideals closer to the real problems of the present and the future.

My father spoke only rarely, never laughed, never engaged in brawls. He simply grated his teeth or clenched his fist at certain times, and if he happened to be holding a hard-shelled almond, rubbed it between his fingers and reduced it to dust. Once when he saw an aga place a packsaddle on a Christian and load him down like a donkey, so completely did his anger overcome him that he charged toward the Turk. He wanted to hurl an insult at him, but his lips had become contorted. Unable to utter a human word, he began to whinny like a horse. I was still a child. I stood there and watched, trembling with fright. And one midday as he was passing through a narrow lane on his way home for dinner, he heard women shrieking and doors being slammed. A huge drunken Turk with drawn yataghan was pursuing Christians. He rushed upon my father the moment he saw him. The heat was torrid, and my father, tired from work, felt in no mood for a brawl. It occurred to him momentarily to turn into another lane and flee—no one was looking. But this would have been shameful. Untying the apron he had on, he wrapped it around his fist, and just as the colossal Turk began to raise the yataghan above his head, he gave him a punch in the belly and sprawled him out on the ground. Stooping, he wrenched the yataghan out of the other's grip and strode homeward. My mother brought him a clean shirt to put on—he was drenched in sweat—and I (I must have been about three years old) sat on the couch and gazed at him. His chest was covered with hair and steaming. As soon as he had changed and cooled off, he threw the yataghan down on the couch next to me. Then he turned to his wife.

"When your son grows up and goes to school," he said, "give him this as a pencil sharpener."

I cannot recall ever hearing a tender word from him—except once when we were on Naxos during the revolution. I was attending the French school run by Catholic priests and had won a good many examination prizes—large books with gilded bindings. Since I could not lift them all by myself, my father took half. He did not speak the entire way home; he was trying to conceal the pleasure he felt at not being humiliated by his son. Only after we entered the house did he open his mouth.

"You did not disgrace Crete," he said with something like tenderness, not looking at me.

But he felt angry with himself immediately; this display of emotion was a self-betrayal. He remained sullen for the rest of the evening and avoided my eyes.

He was forbidding and insufferable. When relatives or neighbors who happened to be visiting the house began to laugh and exchange small talk, if the door suddenly opened and he came in, the conversation and laughter always ceased and a heavy shadow overwhelmed the room. He would say hello halfheartedly, seat himself in his customary place in the corner of the sofa next to the courtyard window, lower his eyes, open his tobacco pouch, and roll a cigarette, without saying a word. The guests would clear their throats dryly, cast secret, uneasy glances at one another, and after a discreet interval, rise and proceed on tiptoe to the door.

He hated priests. Whenever he met one on the street, he crossed himself to exorcise the unfortunate encounter, and if the frightened priest greeted him with a "Good day, Captain Michael," he replied, "Give me your curse!" He never attended Divine Liturgy—to avoid seeing priests. But every Sunday when the service was over and everyone had left, he entered the church and lighted a candle before the wonder-working icon of Saint Minas. He worshiped Saint Minas above all Christs and Virgin Marys, because Saint Minas was the captain of Megalo Kastro.

His heart was heavy, unliftable. Why? He was healthy, his affairs were going well, he had no complaints regarding either his wife or children. People respected him. Some, the most inferior, rose and bowed when he passed, placed their palms over their breasts, and addressed him as Captain Michael. On Easter Day the Metropolitan invited him to the episcopal palace after the Resurrection, along with the city's notables, and offered him coffee and a paschal cake with a red egg. On Saint Minas's day, the eleventh of November, he stood in front of his house and said a prayer when the procession passed.

But his heart never lightened. One day Captain Elias from Messará dared to ask him, "Why is there never a laugh on your lips, Captain Michael?" "Why is the crow black, Captain Elias?" my father replied, spitting out the cigarette butt he was chewing. Another day I heard him say to the verger of Saint Minas's, "You should look at my father, not at me, at my father. He was a real ogre. What am I next to him? A jellyfish!" Though extremely old and nearly blind, my grandfather had taken up arms again in the Revolution of 1878. He went to the mountains to fight, but the Turks surrounded him, caught him by throwing lassos, and slaughtered him outside the Monastery of Savathianá. The monks kept his skull in the sanctuary. One day I looked through the tiny window and saw it—polished, anointed with sanctified oil from the watch lamp, deeply incised by sword blows.

"What was my grandfather like?" I asked my mother.

"Like your father. Darker."

"What was his job?"

"Fighting."

"And what did he do in peacetime?"

"He smoked a long chibouk and gazed at the mountains."

Being pious when I was young, I asked still another question: "Did he go to church?"

"No. But on the first of every month he brought a priest home with him and had him pray that Crete would take up arms again. Your grandfather fretted, naturally, when he had nothing to do. Once when he was arming himself again I asked him, 'Aren't you afraid to die, Father?' But he neither answered nor even turned to look at me."

When I grew older, I wanted to ask my mother: Did he ever love a woman? I was ashamed to, however, and never found out. But he surely must have loved many women, because when he was killed and the family opened his coffer, a cushion was found there, stuffed with black and brown tresses.

The Father

Björnstjerne Björnson

Kingsley Davis has pointed out that much of the energy devoted to child rearing must be aimed at persuading young people that it is desirable to become adequate parents when they grow up, while very little attention need be paid to persuading people to adopt effective medical or health techniques. This is because the advantages of being a parent are not obvious, while the worth of saving one's own life *is* obvious. Many analyses have probed the reasons why parents have children; one powerful motive is somewhat difficult for modern people to confess, a wish for a kind of immortality, a way of continuing to live through successive generations.

In the following story, Björnstjerne Björnson's is "The

From Björnstjerne Björnson *The Bridal March, and Other Stories*, translated by Rasmus Anderson, Books For Libraries Press, Freeport, New York, 1969, pp. 148–153.

Father," the author has attempted a difficult literary technique which perhaps fails more often than it succeeds. His tone is flat and unemotional, and it imitates the style of a saga or a traditional folk story. It does not dwell on inner motivations, and nothing is described in dramatic language. There is only a simple succession of events.

It is a moving story. Although it has no specific place or time, we recognize at least the possibility of ourselves being part of it, primarily as the father but also perhaps as the son. We perceive the farmer's pride in his own wealth and influence. We also sense the farmer's real love for his son, although the word would not have easily fallen from his tongue. Surely most of us would also like to have so excellent a son, to carry on our name, to keep us in his memory.

And, because all of us have experienced total frustration at times, we feel great sympathy with the father, though in his style and philosophy he is alien to the modern temperament: he is reserved, cold, oriented toward his wealth and family line, obviously self-centered.

The world that Björnson describes here has mostly gone, and industrial contemporary life does not encourage such dynastic dreams. Nevertheless, it seems likely that as long as parents have children, and live through them, some part of these actions and emotions will remain an experience that we will understand, even if we do not try to imitate it.

The man whose story is here to be told was the wealthiest and most influential person in his parish; his name was Thord Overaas. He appeared in the priest's study one day, tall and earnest.

"I have got a son," said he, "and I wish to present him for baptism."

"What shall his name be?"

"Finn—after my father."

"And the sponsors?"

They were mentioned, and proved to be the best men and women of Thord's relations in the parish.

"Is there anything else?" inquired the priest, and looked up. The peasant hesitated a little.

"I should like very much to have him baptized by himself," said he, finally.

"That is to say on a weekday?"

"Next Saturday, at twelve o'clock noon."

"Is there anything else?" inquired the priest.

"There is nothing else"; and the peasant twirled his cap, as though he were about to go.

Then the priest rose. "There is yet this, however," said he, and walking toward Thord, he took him by the hand and looked gravely into his eyes: "God grant that the child may become a blessing to you!"

One day sixteen years later, Thord stood once more in the priest's study.

"Really, you carry your age astonishingly well, Thord," said the priest; for he saw no change whatever in the man.

"That is because I have no troubles," replied Thord.

To this the priest said nothing, but after a while he asked: "What is your pleasure this evening?"

"I have come this evening about that son of mine who is to be confirmed tomorrow."

"He is a bright boy."

"I did not wish to pay the priest until I heard what number the boy would have when he takes his place in church tomorrow."

"He will stand number one."

"So I have heard; and here are ten dollars for the priest."

"Is there anything else I can do for you?" inquired the priest, fixing his eyes on Thord.

"There is nothing else."

Thord went out.

Eight years more rolled by, and then one day a noise was heard outside of the priest's study, for many men were approaching, and at their head was Thord, who entered first.

The priest looked up and recognized him.

"You come well attended this evening, Thord," said he.

"I am here to request that the banns may be published for my son; he is about to marry Karen Storliden, daughter of Gudmund, who stands here beside me."

"Why, that is the richest girl in the parish."

"So they say," replied the peasant, stroking back his hair with one hand.

The priest sat a while as if in deep thought, then entered the names in his book, without making any comments, and the men wrote their signatures underneath. Thord laid three dollars on the table.

"One is all I am to have," said the priest.

"I know that very well; but he is my only child. I want to do it handsomely."

The priest took the money.

"This is now the third time, Thord, that you have come here on your son's account."

But now I am through with him," said Thord, and folding up his pocketbook he said farewell and walked away.

The men slowly followed him.

A fortnight later, the father and son were rowing across the lake, one calm, still day, to Storliden to make arrangements for the wedding.

"This thwart is not secure," said the son, and stood up to straighten the seat on which he was sitting.

At the same moment the board he was standing on slipped from under him; he threw out his arms, uttered a shriek, and fell overboard.

"Take hold of the oar!" shouted the father, springing to his feet and holding out the oar.

But when the son had made a couple of efforts he grew stiff.

"Wait a moment!" cried the father, and began to row toward his son.

Then the son rolled over on his back, gave his father one long look, and sank.

Thord could scarcely believe it; he held the boat still, and stared at the spot where his son had gone down, as though he must surely come to the surface again. There rose some bubbles, then some more, and finally one large one that burst; and the lake lay there as smooth and bright as a mirror again.

For three days and three nights people saw the father rowing round and round the spot, without taking either food or sleep; he was dragging the lake for the body of his son. And toward morning of the third day he found it, and carried it in his arms up over the hills to his gard.

It might have been about a year from that day, when the priest, late one autumn evening, heard someone in the passage outside of the door, carefully trying to find the latch. The priest opened the door, and in walked a tall, thin man, with bowed form and white hair. The priest looked long at him before he recognized him. It was Thord.

"Are you out walking so late?" said the priest, and stood still in front of him.

"Ah, yes! it is late," said Thord, and took a seat.

The priest sat down also, as though waiting. A long, long silence followed. At last Thord said:

"I have something with me that I should like to give to the poor; I want it to be invested as a legacy in my son's name."

He rose, laid some money on the table, and sat down again. The priest counted it.

"It is a great deal of money," said he.

"It is half the price of my gard. I sold it today."

The priest sat long in silence. At last he asked, but gently:

"What do you propose to do now, Thord?"

"Something better."

They sat there for a while, Thord with downcast eyes, the priest with his eyes fixed on Thord. Presently the priest said, slowly and softly:

"I think your son has at last brought you a true blessing."

"Yes, I think so myself," said Thord, looking up, while two big tears coursed slowly down his cheeks.

My Oedipus Complex
Frank O'Connor

Whether or not the so-called Oedipus complex is a universal human phenomenon remains almost as little tested now as it was fifty years ago. However, children do (male and female) experience most of their first pleasurable human contacts through their mothers; most mothers continue to give their children much love and attention, and most children are jealous of the love that spouses give to one another.

Freud once spoke of the special grace a young boy receives if he is the favorite child of his mother. In the following scene from Frank O'Connor's "My Oedipus Complex," the author reports through the eyes of the young child he was at the end of World War I, when he had enjoyed a long monopoly of the affections of his mother during his soldier-father's absence. As he comments, he had prayed that his father would live through the war, but now that the family is reunited he has grave doubts about the wisdom of those prayers.

To him, as perhaps to many children, the relation between his mother and father seems a bit mysterious, and he cannot understand why it should conflict with what he views as his absolute moral right to primacy in her affections and concern.

In this scene, we trace the altered relationships among the members of the family; first, the child's rage at being displaced by his father—an indignation which he has not yet been taught to hide. Second, although he had believed that the advent of a brother would improve matters, it soon becomes apparent that in fact he *and* his father have now been removed from the center of the mother's attention. Finally, he himself makes overtures to his father—who is admittedly "bony, but better than nothing."

At a deeper level, we can see one of the patterns by which male role identification may be shaped. Two males

From Frank O'Connor, *Stories*, Alfred A. Knopf and Random House, Inc., New York, 1956, pp. 256–262.

feel some sharing of destiny, in this instance because they are forced to be together if they are to get any love at all. The outside society will, in addition, identify them both as having a common fate. And, to the mother, "the men" represent a set of duties that she owes to the males, who will of course eventually be pushed out still further, for their lives are to be lived primarily outside the home. Although the events and the child's view of things are comic, the laughter we feel is simply an index of the extent to which we recognize in this fierce battle for possession an experience that we may well have had ourselves.

"Mummy," I said with equal firmness, "I think it would be healthier for Daddy to sleep in his own bed."

That seemed to stagger her, because she said nothing for a while.

"Now, once for all," she went on, "you're to be perfectly quiet or go back to your own bed. Which is it to be?"

The injustice of it got me down. I had convicted her out of her own mouth of inconsistency and unreasonableness, and she hadn't even attempted to reply. Full of spite, I gave Father a kick, which she didn't notice but which made him grunt and open his eyes in alarm.

"What time is it?" he asked in a panic-stricken voice, not looking at Mother but at the door, as if he saw someone there.

"It's early yet," she replied soothingly. "It's only the child. Go to sleep again. . . . Now, Larry," she added, getting out of bed, "you've wakened Daddy and you must go back."

This time, for all her quiet air, I knew she meant it, and knew that my principal rights and privileges were as good as lost unless I asserted them at once. As she lifted me, I gave a screech, enough to wake the dead, not to mind Father. He groaned.

"That damn child! Doesn't he ever sleep?"

"It's only a habit, dear," she said quietly, though I could see she was vexed.

"Well, it's time he got out of it," shouted Father, beginning to heave in the bed. He suddenly gathered all the bedclothes about him, turned to the wall, and then looked back over his shoulder with nothing showing only two small, spiteful, dark eyes. The man looked very wicked.

To open the bedroom door, Mother had to let me down, and I broke free and dashed for the farthest corner, screeching. Father sat bolt upright in bed.

"Shut up, you little puppy!" he said in a choking voice.

I was so astonished that I stopped screeching. Never, never had anyone spoken to me in that tone before. I looked at him incredulously and saw his face convulsed with rage. It was only then that I fully realized how God had coddled me, listening to my prayers for the safe return of this monster.

"Shut up, you!" I bawled, beside myself.

"What's that you said?" shouted Father, making a wild leap out of the bed.

"Mick, Mick!" cried Mother. "Don't you see the child isn't used to you?"

"I see he's better fed than taught," snarled Father, waving his arms wildly. "He wants his bottom smacked."

All his previous shouting was as nothing to these obscene words referring to my person. They really made my blood boil.

"Smack your own!" I screamed hysterically. "Smack your own! Shut up! Shut up!"

At this he lost his patience and let fly at me. He did it with the lack of conviction you'd expect of a man under Mother's horrified eyes, and it ended up as a mere tap, but the sheer indignity of being struck at all by a stranger, a total stranger who had cajoled his way back from the war into our big bed as a result of my innocent intercession, made me completely dotty. I shrieked and shrieked, and danced in my bare feet, and Father, looking awkward and hairy in nothing but a short grey army shirt, glanced down at me like a mountain out for murder. I think it must have been then that I realized he was jealous too. And there stood Mother in her nightdress, looking as if her heart was broken between us. I hoped she felt as she looked. It seemed to me that she deserved it all.

From that morning out my life was a hell. Father and I were enemies, open and avowed. We conducted a series of skirmishes against one another, he trying to steal my time with Mother and I his. When she was sitting on my bed, telling me a story, he took to looking for some pair of old boots which he alleged he had left behind him at the beginning of the war. While he talked to Mother I played loudly with my toys to show my total lack of concern. He created a terrible scene one evening when he came in from work and found me at his box, playing with his regimental badges, Gurkha knives and buttonsticks. Mother got up and took the box from me.

"You mustn't play with Daddy's toys unless he lets you, Larry," she said severely. "Daddy doesn't play with yours."

For some reason Father looked at her as if she had struck him and then turned away with a scowl.

"Those are not toys," he growled, taking down the box again to see had I lifted anything. "Some of those curios are very rare and valuable."

But as time went on I saw more and more how he managed to alienate Mother and me. What made it worse was that I couldn't grasp his method or see what attraction he had for Mother. In every possible way he was less winning than I. He had a common accent and made noises at his tea. I thought for a while that it might be the newspapers she was interested in, so I made up bits of news of my own to read to her. Then I thought it might be the smoking, which I personally thought attractive, and took his pipes and went round the house dribbling into them till he caught me. I even made noises at my tea, but Mother only told me I was disgusting. It all seemed to hinge round that unhealthy habit of sleeping together, so I made a point of dropping into their bedroom and nosing round, talking to myself, so that they wouldn't know I was watching them, but they were never up to anything that I could see. In the end it beat me. It seemed to depend on being grown-up and giving people rings, and I realized I'd have to wait.

But at the same time I wanted him to see that I was only waiting, not giving up the fight. One evening when he was being particularly obnoxious, chattering away well above my head, I let him have it.

"Mummy," I said, "do you know what I'm going to do when I grow up?"

"No, dear," she replied. "What?"

"I'm going to marry you," I said quietly.

Father gave a great guffaw out of him, but he didn't take me in. I knew it must only be pretence. And Mother, in spite of everything, was pleased. I felt she was probably relieved to know that one day Father's hold on her would be broken.

"Won't that be nice?" she said with a smile.

"It'll be very nice," I said confidently. "Because we're going to have lots and lots of babies."

"That's right, dear," she said placidly. "I think we'll have one soon, and then you'll have plenty of company."

I was no end pleased about that because it showed that in spite of the way she gave in to Father she still considered my wishes. Besides, it would put the Geneys in their place.

It didn't turn out like that, though. To begin with, she was very preoccupied—I supposed about where she would get the seventeen and six—and though Father took to staying out late in the evenings it did me no particular good. She stopped taking me for walks, became as touchy as blazes, and smacked me for nothing at all. Sometimes I wished I'd never mentioned the confounded baby—I seemed to have a genius for bringing calamity on myself.

And calamity it was! Sonny arrived in the most appalling hullabaloo—even that much he couldn't do without a fuss—and from the first moment I disliked him. He was a difficult child—so far as I was concerned he was always difficult—and demanded far too much attention. Mother was simply silly about him, and couldn't see when he was only showing off. As company he was worse than useless. He slept all day, and I had to go round the house on tiptoe to avoid waking him. It wasn't any longer a question of not waking Father. The slogan now was "Don't-wake-Sonny!" I couldn't understand why the child wouldn't sleep at the proper time, so whenever Mother's back was turned I woke him. Sometimes to keep him awake I pinched him as well. Mother caught me at it one day and gave me a most unmerciful flaking.

One evening, when Father was coming in from work, I was playing trains in the front garden. I let on not to notice him; instead, I pretended to be talking to myself, and said in a loud voice: "If another bloody baby comes into this house, I'm going out."

Father stopped dead and looked at me over his shoulder.

"What's that you said?" he asked sternly.

"I was only talking to myself," I replied, trying to conceal my panic. "It's private."

He turned and went in without a word. Mind you, I intended it as a solemn warning, but its effect was quite different. Father started being quite nice to me. I could understand that, of course. Mother was quite sickening about Sonny. Even at mealtimes she'd get up and gawk at him in the cradle with an idiotic smile, and tell Father to do the same. He was always polite about it, but he looked so puzzled you could see he didn't know what she was talking about. He complained of the way Sonny cried at night, but she only got cross and said that Sonny never cried except when there was something up with him—which was a flaming lie, because Sonny never had anything up with him, and only cried for attention. It was really painful to see how simple-minded she was. Father wasn't attractive, but he had a fine intelligence. He saw through Sonny, and now he knew that I saw through him as well.

One night I woke with a start. There was someone beside me in the bed. For one wild moment I felt sure it must be Mother, having come to her senses and left Father for good, but then I heard Sonny in convulsions in the next room, and Mother saying: "There! There! There!" and I knew it wasn't she. It was Father. He was lying beside me, wide awake, breathing hard and apparently as mad as hell.

After a while it came to me what he was mad about. It was his turn now. After turning me out of the big bed, he had been turned out himself. Mother had no consideration now for anyone but that poisonous pup, Sonny. I couldn't help feeling sorry for Father. I had been through it all myself, and even at that age I was magnanimous. I began to stroke him down and say: "There! There!" He wasn't exactly responsive.

"Aren't you asleep either?" he snarled.

"Ah, come on and put your arm around us, can't you?" I

said, and he did, in a sort of way. Gingerly, I suppose, is how you'd describe it. He was very bony but better than nothing.

At Christmas he went out of his way to buy me a really nice model railway.

The Rainbow

D. H. Lawrence

The fairy tales and myths of most cultures contain many accounts of the cruel fate of stepchildren. Examined somewhat more closely, they almost always focus on the cruelty of step*mothers*. As sociologists, we can recognize that it is in fact the stepmother who would bear most of the burden represented by a stepchild. In most cases, the father would not be at home during the day and thus in a position to protect his offspring. We also recognize that the stepmother might well have some bases for resenting the stepchild, for the latter might represent some threat to her relationship with the husband.

Here we observe the slow, sensitive, development of warmth between a stepfather and a stepdaughter. Note that this relationship is facilitated by the fact that the child is very young and has no alternative. Her mother loves Tom, and she makes it clear that the situation is irrevocable. The child needs love, and her farmer stepfather is willing to give it—as long as he himself is given his full respect. The farm setting permits a range of possible relationships between stepfather and stepdaughter, so that they are not always required to be intimate: the child can play at a distance, go off on errands, and explore, but then also return to intimate touches and caresses.

There are deeper elements within the larger chronicle, that cannot be included here. *The Rainbow* is an account

From D. H. Lawrence, *The Rainbow*, The Viking Press Inc., New York, 1945 (1961).

spanning three generations. The wife comes from a higher class than does the farmer, and she is moreover a "foreigner." The farmer recognizes that both wife and daughter are of a finer mold than he, but by and large he does not resent this. He rather rejoices in it. Thus, he does not treat the stepdaughter roughly, for she is delicate. He wants her love, for he wants to make a genuine family unit. In the relations between stepdaughter and stepfather, there are no references to the wife's prior marriage.

Finally, note how fully the wife and husband accept the finality of the union, Tom's absolute headship of the family, the fact that it is *his* house and farm they have entered, and the conviction that it is the child who must adjust, whether slowly or quickly. Consider in this connection the extent to which the modern stepchild might have somewhat different experiences, especially because of the widespread belief that the child's interests should come first.

The first morning after his marriage he had discovered it would not be so easy with the child. At the break of dawn he had started awake hearing a small voice outside the door saying plaintively:

"Mother!"

He rose and opened the door. She stood on the threshold in her night-dress, as she had climbed out of bed, black eyes staring round and hostile, her fair hair sticking out in a wild fleece. The man and child confronted each other.

"I want my mother," she said, jealously accenting the "my."

"Come on then," he said gently.

"Where's my mother?"

"She's here—come on."

The child's eyes, staring at the man with ruffled hair and beard, did not change. The mother's voice called softly. The little bare feet entered the room with trepidation.

"Mother!"

"Come, my dear."

The small bare feet approached swiftly.

"I wondered where you were," came the plaintive voice. The mother stretched out her arms. The child stood beside the high

bed. Brangwen lightly lifted the tiny girl, with an "up-a-daisy",
then took his own place in the bed again.

"Mother!" cried the child, as in anguish.

"What, my pet?"

Anna wriggled close into her mother's arms, clinging tight,
hiding from the fact of the man. Brangwen lay still, and waited.
There was a long silence.

Then suddenly, Anna looked round, as if she thought he
would be gone. She saw the face of the man lying upturned to the
ceiling. Her black eyes stared antagonistic from her exquisite
face, her arms clung tightly to her mother, afraid. He did not
move for some time, not knowing what to say. His face was
smooth and soft-skinned with love, his eyes full of soft light. He
looked at her, scarcely moving his head, his eyes smiling.

"Have you just wakened up?" he said.

"Go away," she retorted, with a little darting forward of the
head, something like a viper.

"Nay," he answered, "*I'm* not going. You can go."

"Go away," came the sharp little command.

"There's room for you," he said.

"You can't send your father from his own bed, my little
bird," said her mother, pleasantly.

The child glowered at him, miserable in her impotence.

"There's room for you as well," he said. "It's a big bed
enough."

She glowered without answering, then turned and clung to
her mother. She would not allow it.

During the day she asked her mother several times:

"When are we going home, mother?"

"We are at home, darling, we live here now. This is our
house, we live here with your father."

The child was forced to accept it. But she remained against
the man. As night came on, she asked:

"Where are you going to sleep, mother?"

"I sleep with the father now."

And when Brangwen came in, the child asked fiercely:

"*Why* do you sleep with *my* mother? My mother sleeps with
me," her voice quivering.

"You come as well, an' sleep with both of us," he coaxed.

"Mother!" she cried, turning, appealing against him.

"But I must have a husband, darling. All women must have a husband."

"And you like to have a father with your mother, don't you?" said Brangwen.

Anna glowered at him. She seemed to cogitate.

"No," she cried fiercely at length, "no, I don't *want*." And slowly her face puckered, she sobbed bitterly. He stood and watched her, sorry. But there could be no altering it.

Which, when she knew, she became quiet. He was easy with her, talking to her, taking her to see the live creatures, bringing her the first chickens in his cap, taking her to gather the eggs, letting her throw crusts to the horse. She would easily accompany him, and take all he had to give, but she remained neutral still.

She was curiously, incomprehensibly jealous of her mother, always anxiously concerned about her. If Brangwen drove with his wife to Nottingham, Anna ran about happily enough, or unconcerned, for a long time. Then, as afternoon came on, there was only one cry—"I want my mother, I want my mother—" and a bitter, pathetic sobbing that soon had the soft-hearted Tilly sobbing too. The child's anguish was that her mother was gone, gone.

Yet as a rule, Anna seemed cold, resenting her mother, critical of her. It was:

"I don't like you to do that, mother," or "I don't like you to say that." She was a sore problem to Brangwen and to all the people at the Marsh. As a rule, however, she was active, lightly flitting about the farmyard, only appearing now and again to assure herself of her mother. Happy she never seemed, but quick, sharp, absorbed, full of imagination and changeability. Tilly said she was bewitched. But it did not matter so long as she did not cry. There was something heart-rending about Anna's crying, her childish anguish seemed so utter and so timeless, as if it were a thing of all the ages.

She made playmates of the creatures of the farmyard, talking to them, telling them the stories she had from her mother, counselling them and correcting them. Brangwen found her at the gate leading to the paddock and to the duckpond. She was peering through the bars and shouting to the stately white geese, that stood in a curving line:

"You're not to call at people when they want to come. You must not do it."

The heavy, balanced birds looked at the fierce little face and the fleece of keen hair thrust between the bars, and they raised their heads and swayed off, producing the long, can-canking, protesting noise of geese, rocking their ship-like, beautiful white bodies in a line beyond the gate.

"You're naughty, you're naughty," cried Anna, tears of dismay and vexation in her eyes. And she stamped her slipper.

"Why, what are they doing?" said Brangwen.

"They won't let me come in," she said, turning her flushed little face to him.

"Yi, they will. You can go in if you want to," and he pushed open the gate for her.

She stood irresolute, looking at the group of bluey-white geese standing monumental under the grey, cold day.

"Go on," he said.

She marched valiantly a few steps in. Her little body started convulsively at the sudden, derisive can-cank-ank of the geese. A blankness spread over her. The geese trailed away with uplifted heads under the low grey sky.

"They don't know you," said Brangwen. "You should tell 'em what your name is."

"They're *naughty* to shout at me," she flashed.

"They think you don't live here," he said.

Later he found her at the gate calling shrilly and imperiously:

"My name is Anna, Anna Lensky, and I live here, because Mr. Brangwen's my father now. He *is*, yes he *is*. And I live here."

This pleased Brangwen very much. And gradually, without knowing it herself, she clung to him, in her lost, childish, desolate moments, when it was good to creep up to something big and warm, and bury her little self in his big, unlimited being. Instinctively he was careful of her, careful to recognize her and to give himself to her disposal.

She was difficult of her affections. For Tilly, she had a

childish, essential contempt, almost dislike, because the poor woman was such a servant. The child would not let the serving-woman attend to her, do intimate things for her, not for a long time. She treated her as one of an inferior race. Brangwen did not like it.

"Why aren't you fond of Tilly?" he asked.

"Because—because—because she looks at me with her eyes bent."

Then gradually she accepted Tilly as belonging to the household, never as a person.

For the first weeks, the black eyes of the child were forever on the watch. Brangwen, good humored but impatient, spoiled by Tilly, was an easy blusterer. If for a few minutes he upset the household with his noisy impatience, he found at the end the child glowering at him with intense black eyes, and she was sure to dart forward her little head, like a serpent, with her biting:

"Go away."

"I'm *not* going away," he shouted, irritated at last. "Go yourself—hustle—stir thysen—hop." And he pointed to the door. The child backed away from him, pale with fear. Then she gathered up courage, seeing him become patient.

"We don't live with *you*," she said, thrusting forward her little head at him. "You—you're—you're a bomakle."

"A what?" he shouted.

Her voice wavered—but it came.

"A bomakle."

"Ay, an' you're a comakle."

She meditated. Then she hissed forwards her head.

"I'm not."

"Not what?"

"A comakle."

"No more am I a bomakle."

He was really cross.

Other times she would say:

"My mother *doesn't* live here."

"Oh, ay?"

"I want her to go away."

"Then want's your portion," he replied laconically.

So they drew nearer together. He would take her with him when he went out in the trap. The horse ready at the gate, he came noisily into the house, which seemed quiet and peaceful till he appeared to set everything awake.

"Now then, Topsy, pop into thy bonnet."

The child drew herself up, resenting the indignity of the address.

"I can't fasten my bonnet myself," she said haughtily.

"Not man enough yet," he said, tying the ribbons under her chin with clumsy fingers.

She held up her face to him. Her little bright-red lips moved as he fumbled under her chin.

"You talk—nonsents," she said, re-echoing one of his phrases.

"*That* face shouts for th' pump," he said, and taking out a big red handkerchief, that smelled of strong tobacco, began wiping round her mouth.

"Is Kitty waiting for me?" she asked.

"Ay," he said. "Let's finish wiping your face—it'll pass wi' a cat-lick."

She submitted prettily. Then, when he let her go, she began to skip, with a curious flicking up of one leg behind her.

"Now my young buck-rabbit," he said. "Slippy!"

She came and was shaken into her coat, and the two set off. She sat very close beside him in the gig, tucked tightly, feeling his big body sway, against her, very splendid. She loved the rocking of the gig, when his big, live body swayed upon her, against her. She laughed, a poignant little shrill laugh, and her black eyes glowed.

Portnoy's Complaint
Philip Roth

In some societies, parents respect a postpartum taboo, i.e., they refrain from sexual relations for a long time after the birth of a child. Breast feeding is continued for a year or more, and the child sleeps with the mother. Because the relation between son and mother becomes very strong, many such societies practice harsh adolescent initiation ceremonies designed to break the mother-son link and to integrate boys more closely with the male adult group. We can see that sending children away to boarding schools might weaken a very intense tie between mother and child. What, however, happens in a society where mothers are in fact encouraged to continue an intense emotional relationship with their children?

When *Portnoy's Complaint* was a runaway best seller, some critics expressed surprise at its popularity, for it seemed so narrowly focused on a small segment of American life that few people knew well, i.e., middle class Jewish family life. In turn, many Jews expressed annoyance, for they felt that Roth's exaggerated description of his own private experiences might be taken as an ethnic stereotype.

The average reader enjoyed the book, however— perceiving in Roth's apparent exaggerations many of his or her own past experiences. That is, Roth managed to evoke a wide range of emotions and events that many recognized at once to be general in our society, and perhaps in other societies as well. Let us take note of a few of these.

One, of course, is that a severe repression of sexuality within the family may lead to impotence with "nice girls" or sometimes even with one's own wife, while one is sexually potent with outsiders, "loose girls," or those one does not take very seriously as potential mates.

For more than half a century there has been a decline in the formality between parents and children, permitting much more expression of emotion, especially by the

From Philip Roth, *Portnoy's Complaint*, Random House, New York, 1967.

mother. Indeed, she may be encouraged to lavish special affection on her son. This is the other side of the oedipal tie, somewhat neglected by Freud: the strong attachment of the mother to the son, and her insistence on intruding herself even into his love life. Parents often consider even an adult to be their child still, and the adult in turn may respond emotionally just as he or she did as a child. Especially in a society where parents do not arrange marriages, parents continue to demand that their child marry, "settle down," produce a family for *their* needs, not the needs of the child.

Finally, we should consider the hypothesis that a society which attempts to repress free sexuality but titillates us constantly with sexual stimuli may rear adults who are afraid of their sexual impulses, yet at the same time think about sex obsessively.

The reader may wish to consider further themes or elements in *Portnoy's Complaint* that are pervasive throughout much of Western society and not merely confined to one ethnic group within it.

I am reminded at this joyous little juncture of when we lived in Jersey City, back when I was still very much my mother's papoose, still very much a sniffer of her body perfumes and a total slave to her *kugel* and *grieben* and *ruggelech*—there was a suicide in our building. A fifteen-year-old boy named Ronald Nimkin, who had been crowned by the women in the building "José Iturbi the Second," hanged himself from the shower head in his bathroom. "With those golden hands!" the women wailed, referring of course to his piano playing—"With that talent!" Followed by, "You couldn't look for a boy more in love with his mother than Ronald!"

I swear to you, this is not bullshit or a screen memory, these are the very words these women use. The great dark operatic themes of human suffering and passion come rolling out of those mouths like the prices of Oxydol and Del Monte canned corn! My own mother, let me remind you, when I returned this past summer from my adventure in Europe, greets me over the phone with the following salutation: "Well, how's my lover?" Her *lover* she calls me, while her husband is listening on the other extension! And it never occurs to her, if I'm her lover, who is he, the *schmegeggy* she lives with? No, you don't have to go digging where these people are concerned—they wear the old unconscious on their *sleeves!*

Mrs. Nimkin, weeping in our kitchen: "Why? Why? Why did he do this to us?" Hear? Not what might *we* have done to *him*, oh no, never that—why did he do this *to us*? To us! Who would have given our arms and legs to make him happy and a famous concert pianist into the bargain! Really, can they be this blind? Can people be so abysmally stupid and live? Do you *believe* it? Can they actually be equipped with all the machinery, a brain, a spinal cord, and the four apertures for the ears and eyes—equipment, Mrs. Nimkin, nearly as impressive as color TV—and still go through life without a single clue about the feelings and yearnings of anyone other than themselves? Mrs. Nimkin, you shit, I remember you, I was only six, but I remember you, and what killed your Ronald, the concert-pianist-to-be is obvious: YOUR FUCKING SELFISHNESS AND STUPIDITY! "All the lessons we gave him," weeps Mrs. Nimkin . . . Oh look, look, why do I carry on like this? Maybe she means well, surely she must—at a time of grief, what can I expect of these simple people? It's only because in her misery she doesn't know what else to say that she says that God-awful thing about all the lessons they gave to somebody who is now a corpse. What are they, after all, these Jewish women who raised us up as children? In Calabria you see their suffering counterparts sitting like stones in the churches, swallowing all that hideous Catholic bullshit; in Calcutta they beg in the streets, or if they are lucky, are off somewhere in a dusty field hitched up to a plow . . . Only in America, Rabbi Golden, do these peasants, our mothers, get their hair dyed platinum at the age of sixty, and walk up and down Collins Avenue in Florida in pedalpushers and mink stoles—and with opinions on every subject under the sun. It isn't their fault they were given a gift like speech—look, if cows could talk, they would say things just as idiotic. Yes, yes, maybe that's the solution then: think of them as cows, who have been given the twin miracles of speech and mahjohgg. Why not be charitable in one's thinking, right, Doctor?

My favorite detail from the Ronald Nimkin suicide: even as

he is swinging from the shower head, there is a note pinned to the dead young pianist's short-sleeved shirt—which is what I remember most about Ronald: this tall emaciated teen-age catatonic, swimming around all by himself in those oversized short-sleeved sport shirts, and with their lapels starched and ironed back so fiercely they looked to have been bulletproofed . . . And Ronald himself, every limb strung so tight to his backbone that if you touched him, he would probably have begun to hum . . . and the fingers, of course, those long white grotesqueries, seven knuckles at least before you got down to the nicely gnawed nail, those Bela Lugosi hands that my mother would tell me—and tell me—*and tell me*—because nothing is ever said once—nothing!—were "the hands of a born pianist."

Pianist! Oh, that's one of the words they just love, almost as much as *doctor*, Doctor. And *residency*. And best of all, *his own office. He opened his own office in Livingston.* "Do you remember Seymour Schmuck, Alex?" she asks me, or Aaron Putz or Howard Shlong, or some yo-yo I am supposed to have known in grade school twenty-five years ago, and of whom I have no recollection whatsoever. "Well, I met his mother on the street today, and she told me that Seymour is now the biggest brain surgeon in the entire Western Hemisphere. He owns six different split-level ranch-type houses made all of fieldstone in Livingston, and belongs to the boards of eleven synagogues, all brand-new and designed by Marc Kugel, and last year with his wife and his two little daughters, who are so beautiful that they are already under contract to Metro, and so brilliant that they should be in college—he took them all to Europe for an eighty-million dollar tour of seven thousand countries, some of them you never even heard of, that they made them just to honor Seymour, and on top of that, he's so important, Seymour, that in every single city in Europe that they visited he was asked by the mayor himself to stop and do an impossible operation on a brain in hospitals that they also built for him right on the spot, and—listen to this—where they pumped into the operating room during the operation the theme song from *Exodus* so everybody would know what religion he is—and that's how big your friend Seymour is today! *And how happy he makes his parents!*"

And you, the implication is, when are *you* going to get married already? In Newark and the surrounding suburbs this apparently is the question on everybody's lips: WHEN IS ALEXANDER PORTNOY GOING TO STOP BEING SELFISH AND GIVE HIS PARENTS, WHO ARE SUCH WONDERFUL PEOPLE, GRANDCHILDREN? "Well," says my father, the tears brimming up in his eyes, "well," he asks, *every single time I see him*, "is there a serious girl in the picture? Big shot? Excuse me for asking, I'm only your father, but since I'm not going to be alive forever, and you in case you forgot carry the family name, I wonder if maybe you could let me in on the secret."

Yes, shame, shame, on Alex P., the only member of his graduating class who hasn't made grandparents of his Mommy and Daddy.

Honeymoon, Bittermoon

Ramón Pérez de Ayala

Any revolutionary program faces the problem of developing a new generation that will not be contaminated by the attitudes, values, and social relations of the old. In Pérez de Ayala's fantasy, *Honeymoon, Bittermoon*, half farce and half tragedy, two sets of parents, both fiercely puritanical in sexual matters, strive to rear their children in complete innocence about sex or about any of life's uglier aspects. Their aim is not a revolutionary program for the whole society, but for their own children; still, the consequences the author describes might well apply to such programs as well. A similar situation is where an author creates a set of circumstances in which a child is reared on a desert island or in a jungle forest, isolated from other adults who would contaminate him or her.

The writer of a farce requires that we accept his initial

From Ramón Pérez de Ayala, *Honeymoon, Bittermoon*, University of California Press, Berkeley, Los Angeles, London, 1972.

conditions or premises, in this case that the parents actually succeed in insulating their children to this extent. The books they read, the people they see, are all screened, so that when the two young people encounter one another, they are nearly adult but are completely unaware of the impulses of their own bodies or emotions. The author is mocking the harsh asceticism of Spanish Catholicism, but we come to believe in the reality of his characters and are willing to tolerate for a while our disbelief in the effectiveness of that socialization.

To such innocents, all sorts of common occurrences are surprises: the sexual or love activities between adults, the appearance of babies, the mating of animals. They do know even how to label their own feelings when these feelings seem to overpower them. Communication with others is difficult, because many things which seem mysterious to these two young people are taken for granted by others. Note that both the questioning and the observation process are hampered, crippled, or distorted when we do not know the context or framework within which things appear before our eyes or into which the answers must be fitted. It is as though we were asking directions in an isolated rural region and cannot comprehend the answers because the native assumes knowledge of a local map that is completely foreign to us. Pérez de Ayala is heaping scorn on this particular attempt at socialization, but the problem of socializing a "new generation" is a significant one both scientifically and pragmatically.

Leoncio, now a partner in The Nineteenth Century and orphaned, married Micaela. The couple settled down in a middle class neighborhood. Her ascetic type of religiosity, frigid puritanical fervor, infused Micaela with fortitude to undergo the conjugal initiations without repulsion, with resigned passivity.

Urbano was born, and after a while the second of the fundamental ideas in Doña Micaela's mind took shape. At times she had been overwhelmed by a longing: "Why can't I be a man?"

Now a mother, one day while holding in her hands the little creature—soft, pliable, and unaware, like clay that awaits the shape the potter may wish to give it—she thought, "Now I am a man; my son is I myself; I will make of him whatever I like. Here I have life, blind life, which can be evil and sorrow or goodness and happiness, subject to my decision." She suddenly glimpsed twenty years' future compressed into the present moment. Her skin grew cold, and she nearly fainted. She would make of her son the exact opposite of what she had been. She knew everything repugnant in life at the age of eight. Her son would come to marriage without having suspected let alone known anything. He would be the first example of a perfect man. Like an apprehension or a buzzing, she thought she heard inside her head: "What a foolish dream!" Rigid, Micaela replied aloud, "It will be! It will be! It will be, just as I make it!" with such desperate energy that she drove her fingers into the baby's flesh and made him cry.

For four years she kept the child close to her breast without anyone else's touching him. This was the time when she brought him as companion and tutor Don Cástulo.

Don Cástulo was so addlepated that he had failed in everything. He had tried for several professorships, but on taking the orals he panicked and was overcome by dizziness. He was living then as a private tutor with a meager income.

Doña Micaela placed complete confidence in Don Cástulo's honesty and learning. He was the mentor destined by the Almighty for Urbano.

"Listen to me carefully," Doña Micaela told him. "My son will be a man and he must get married pure as the snow."

Then she gave him precise orders and outlined for him the blueprint of the future, with the aplomb of an architect who has checked all the calculations and tolerances. Her severe face was not set vaingloriously, but with firmness and confidence.

Don Cástulo exclaimed, "I always proclaimed you an extraordinary woman. That plan, without your knowing it, had already occurred to none less than Plato and to Calderón de la Barca."

"Who are those gentlemen? People of old lineages?"

"Very old indeed; the one goes back more than two centuries and the other more than twenty-four. So then. And not only to those two gentlemen did your plan occur, but also to a king. May I read you a short paragraph from one of my books?"

Don Cástulo returned with a slender volume.

"This book is called *Novellino*; it's in Italian and was written in the fourteenth century." He searched for the passage and read: "*Of how a king brought up a son of his in a cave, and afterward, showing him all things, what pleased him most were women.* To a king was born a son. The wise astrologers forewarned that he must remain twenty years without seeing the light of day. Then they kept watch over him and kept him in a dark cave. After the stated time they took him out and set before him many precious things and beautiful maidens, calling each thing by its name, and of the maidens they told him they were demons. They asked him then what was the thing that he liked most. He replied, 'the demons.' Then the king marveled exceedingly, exclaiming: 'How much tyranny and beauty there is in woman!'"

"It's not that my son," replied Doña Micaela, "must not see women. For now he won't be leaving my side. Neither will it be possible to avoid his seeing women in the street or in church. The point is that my son not see the woman in women. I've already told you; Urbano must arrive at marriage pure as the snow, with his mind as clean and unsullied as a newborn babe's."

"But, carried to that extreme, won't that be impossible?"

"I only condemn as impossible what should not be, even though it be and right before the eyes. If tomorrow you were to relate to me something obscene my son had done, I would reply to you: impossible. And I will not mean that it might not be true, but that it cannot continue being true. But everything, all that should be, can be and must be; it's a question of deciding it. Are you in doubt? Remember, I'm the woman who has seen the inferno."

"You're an extraordinary woman. Whatever you want, you'll achieve."

And with what assiduity and sharpsightedness did Doña Micaela, assisted by Don Cástulo, go about imposing arbitrary form on the helpless clay of Urbano! Over the course of many years, Don Cástulo characterized Urbano's education as a sublime work of energy, ingenuity, and art. Don Cástulo was proud of his collaboration as a journeyman; the master artist was Doña Micaela.

Doña Micaela expurgated the books her son studied, beginning with the Catechism, in which she found coarse and overly explicit references. She likewise censored in the Devotionary certain expressions about divine love conceived in terms of erotic love. She instructed Urbano's confessor so that he might not ask him indiscreet questions, which most of the time, instead of serving as relief and outlet for troubled consciences, are disquieting and suggestive of sin for virginal consciences.

In the household there was no other woman servant than the cook, a recluse who stuck close by her stove. Doña Micaela cleaned the house and a young peasant boy, changed periodically, waited on the table with white cotton gloves.

Don Cástulo did not part from Urbano's side. They slept in the same bedroom. The child did not leave the house, except for mass very early on Sundays with his mother and for a walk to the village, on occasional afternoons, with Don Cástulo. On the country walks Don Cástulo sometimes used to tell Urbano fairy tales and stories of enchantments, those most infantile ones which were approved by Doña Micaela, for example, "Open Sesame"; but most of the time they enjoyed themselves in puerile games, for the tutor was as ingenuous as the pupil.

Don Cástulo was, yes, superlatively ingenuous in his heart and conduct; not so in his imagination. Don Cástulo lived two parallel lives, autonomous and without mutual contact; a real life and a fantasy life. His spare and leisure time was spent in reading erotic authors, Greek and Latin. His imagination was crammed full of literary and vaporous eroticism, which was never inserted in real life, for want of empirical data and experiential points of reference. In his head, he was always going about lamenting, with epigrammatic atticism, the indifference of some Ionic, Corinthian, or perhaps Boetian courtesan: Erisila, Prodicea, Melissa, Heliodora, Berenice. Some nights, Urbano in bed, Don Cástulo said that he was going out for a breath of air. It was the conjuncture at which his imaginary ramblings assumed form and action. He lost himself in the back alleys, and sitting down on the threshold of some unknown mansion, supposed residence of the disdainful courtesan of the moment, would sigh, with the words of Callimachus, "Sleep without care, while I am lain on your porch, beneath the frost. May you some day come to find yourself in a bed like this in which you leave, cruel one! your lover. And you are merciless. The neighbors pity me; but you, not even in dreams. Soon enough white hairs will remind you of these wintry rigors and will avenge me." Afterward he returned home, quite refreshed. These erotic escapades belonged only to his fantasy life, and they were like an esoteric exercise that Don Cástulo permitted himself. He would rather have bitten off his own tongue than mention love in Urbano's presence: *maxima debetur pueris reverentia.*

On Urbano's reaching the age of eight, they enrolled him as a nonresident in the institute. Doña Micaela reviewed the text-books beforehand and tore out the pages she considered suggestive or dangerous. In the history books she blotted out any reference to bastards, court favorites, and the tribute of the hundred maidens. On discovering in the physiology and organography text a chapter with plates on sex and its functions, Doña Micaela went white with rage.

"This," she declared, "is a plot of Jews and Freemasons to pervert Spanish youth."

Don Cástulo accompanied Urbano even to the point of going into the room where they gave him his final examination and waited for him to leave, so that he might not speak with and be contaminated by any other student. Thus he concluded his secondary education.

For the law course, Don Cástulo abridged the lessons of each subject into respective synopses, which then, after being well scrutinized by Doña Micaela, were given to Urbano to study, until he repeated them by heart, without giving them nor seeking in them the least meaning. Moreover, Doña Micaela snipped out chapters and even entire sections from the texts, without fear of penalty in the examination, since shortly before the end of the course Don Leoncio, on his wife's orders, bribed the professors by sending them objects from the store as gifts—plaster of paris figurines, lamps, and razor cases.

Don Leoncio disapproved of Micaela's system of education; but, stymied by his wife's despotism, he did not dare to grumble. On one occasion, he asked Don Cástulo secretly, "Don't you think that the education being given to Urbano is absurd?"

"Psss. In this manner royal princes are educated."

Nevertheless, as the years went by, Don Cástulo was assailed by serious doubts whether Micaela would not be making—with unheard of thoroughness and talent, true enough, and even as it were with genius—an enormous and horrible mistake, because the fact is that Micaela achieved the full measure of her idea. At the age of twenty, in love and set to marry, Urbano was as innocent of the mysteries of physical love as at the moment of coming into the world. Or, in the words of Don Cástulo, "*Tanquam tabula rasa*, strange as it might seem."

Polonius's Advice to Laertes
William Shakespeare

Shakespeare doubtless intended his audiences to perceive Polonius as a great bore. By contrast, the latter sees himself as weighty with wisdom and good sense, and he cannot imagine that others do not wish to listen to it.

What he says seems to us a set of clichés, but this is not only because so many of Shakespeare's phrases have become part of our heritage; it is rather that they represent the distillation of cautious, unimaginative conformity with the world. Polonius is less penetrating or witty than Lord Chesterfield in his advice to his son, though both represent the same type of "wisdom." Our modern temperament, with its Dionysiac or romantic thrust, asks us to dare all, to risk greatly, to violate common sense for some greater achievement. As a consequence, Polonius's advice comes all too

From *Shakespeare: The Complete Works*, edited by G. B. Harrison, Harcourt Brace Jovanovich, New York, 1968, pp. 891–892. This excerpt is from Act I, Scene 3, ll. 55–81.

close to the kind of parental counsel that young people with imagination have always wanted to escape.

On the other hand, while rejecting philosophically what Polonius says, we ought also to consider the extent to which these clichés do in fact promise a higher chance of worldly success than the precepts we ourselves would wish to follow: be warm to others, but not vulgar; try to keep one's good friends; avoid quarrels, but make one's true enemy fearful; dress so that others are aware of one's worth; and so on. Moreover, though modern parents are not likely to express their thought with such grace as Shakespeare possessed, they do continue–even in the face of this generation's great emphasis on rebellion and individuality—to offer such advice to their children from the earliest phases of childhood onward.

In analyzing this speech from *Hamlet*, the reader might consider the question of why parents continue to do this, even though they are aware that it irritates their children, and even though they rarely observe any great changes in their children's behavior as a result.

Polonius: Yet here, Laertes? Aboard, aboard, for shame!
  The wind sits in the shoulder of your sail,
  And you are stay'd for. There; my blessing with you!
  And these few precepts in thy memory
  See thou character. Give thy thoughts no tongue,
  Nor any unproportion'd thought his act.
  Be thou familiar, but by no means vulgar.
  The friends thou hast, and their adoption tried,
  Grapple them to thy soul with hoops of steel;
  But do not dull thy palm with entertainment
  Of each [new]-hatch'd, unfledg'd comrade. Beware
  Of entrance to a quarrel; but being in,
  Bear't that the opposed may beware of thee.
  Give every man thine ear, but few thy voice;
  Take each man's censure, but reserve thy judgement.
  Costly thy habit as thy purse can buy,
  But not express'd in fancy; rich, not gaudy;
  For the apparel oft proclaims the man,

And they in France of the best rank and station
Are most select and generous in that.
Neither a borrower nor a lender be;
For loan oft loses both itself and friend,
And borrowing dulls the edge of husbandry.
This above all: to thine own self be true,
And it must follow, as the night the day,
Thou canst not then be false to any man
Farewell; my blessing season this in thee!

The Man Who Loved Children

Christina Stead

The Man Who Loved Children belongs to that small class of
novels which are greeted with some critical acclaim by a
small discerning public, then fall into comparative oblivion,
while enjoying an "underground" reputation among a small
group who pride themselves on not confusing popularity
with quality. Such novels are likely to be "rediscovered" from
time to time, as Christina Stead's was a few years ago.

Unfortunately for the popularity of the book, it is difficult for us to locate major characters in it with whom we
can identify. It is easy to identify with a great hero and heroine, and even with a bold, bad scoundrel. In this work, however, it is hard to empathize with either the husband or his
wife, although we feel compassion for the latter.

The title of Stead's novel is partly ironic, for we eventually realize that the husband has been able to impose on
others his self-perception as someone who rejoices in
children. "Everyone knows" that he is a man who loves
children. Indeed, he does in a very particular sense, and
here we must look about us for examples among our

Christina Stead, *The Man Who Loved Children*, Holt, Rinehart and Winston, New
York, 1940.

acquaintances; for he maintains his own childlike ways, his own refusal to accept anything as reality except his own fantasies.

Moreover (and here the irony cuts more deeply still: he loves children because he loves himself), he insists that he be given priority as the prime child among all the children in his family. He is the eldest child and the favorite child. Again, note that we do not wish to identify ourselves with such a character, though of course we may be able to recognize these traits in others.

With such a set of attitudes, and with social reinforcement from his own children's acceptance of his role, he can remain serene and cheerful (and be praised for being cheerful) in the midst of catastrophes. After all, those catastrophes must be truly faced and solved by other people. Consequently, he also manages to avoid perceiving the great burdens his wife must assume in bearing and rearing all these children—a theme that is well expressed in the succeeding scene.

Sanguine and sun-haired Sam Pollit, waiting for the birth of his seventh child, had not slept all night. Louie, after some attendance at the door of the birth room, had slept well, downstairs, in Henny's big bed, with Evie. Kind Bonnie had stayed all night. The four boys, used to wind cries and human cries, had slept very well on mattresses on the floor in the sunroom, exactly as they had on the day of the great gale in 1933 when Sam feared the chimney pots would blow down. One or two of them woke once or twice and, hearing their mother cry out, saw nothing in it at all but an ordinary connubial quarrel between her and Sam, and turned and slept again. There were torments in the Himalayas, windspouts in the Grand Canyon, and Judges of the Supreme Court got into sacred rages. What could little boys do, too, about differences between their hearthstones, Mother and Father? They listened for a while, turned, and slept again.

At four o'clock the sky grew lighter and, one by one, the birds began to creak, some like rusty winches, some like door hinges, and some like fishing lines unreeled at a great rate. There was one that sang joyously like the water burbling down a choked drain. At any rate, to Sam's ear, all of these were singing hymns of praise to the rising dawn, and congratulating themselves on their broods and him on his new child. "All Nature is awake," thought Sam, prowling amongst the chance-sown seedlings of pine at the bottom of the orchard, "and my latest young one, in a new suit of flesh, is trying to greet the dawn, too." At five-thirty the flame-red sun, so heralded, was kicked out of the horizon's waist and visibly jerked upwards. Not even a breeze stirred the hundred-year-old elms on the south-facing bluff of Tohoga Place. Overhead stretched an immense, tender spring sky. The budding trees, already root-hid in weeds, ran up the hill on all sides. The surrounding streets, their hollows, the lesser heights, and dome bubbles of reeking Washington were visible; the world was a milky cameo at sunup. The neglected garden thronged upwards with all its plants into the new sun, with its guava trees, peach trees, magnolia trees, apple trees, seedling pines and forsythia, and the wild double narcissus that grew so rank and green on the possums' graves.

From the girls' bedroom that looked due south into Virginia, carried on the sloping airs to Sam, his wife's screams began coming louder and closer together. No doubt their neighbors with the small, pinched brick faces, feverishly avoiding the sunspots on their spoiled sheets in bedrooms on Reservoir Street, and the encroachers on old Tohoga House Estate, slums of Thirty-fifth Street, back-bedroom dwellers, who rested their hot eyes on green Tohoga's wilderness, if they were awake, heard the sound too. The air was still and lazy. Sam plied fast his long legs and reached the house in a minute.

"It's the end," said Sam. Both leaves of the tall south door stood open letting in the moist air, and he raced from the porch through them and along the hall to Henny's bedroom where the two girls were fast asleep. Brick-colored light fell through the shutters of the French windows on to the ceiling, and moved quickly in bars farther and farther into the room. The air breathed heat and nightlong sweat mixed with the dewy morning coming through the shutter slits. The windows were open. Louie's long

hair was spread out in a fan on the pillow, and the rumpled sheet
was kicked to the bottom of the bed on her side, though it still half
embraced Evie. Sam, standing at the foot of the bed, whistled
Louie's whistle. When she opened her eyes, he said quickly, "Get
the kids up and dressed, Looloo: I want 'em to hear the new baby
come."

"Is it here?" asked the girl, half awake. He pointed in the
direction of the noises, "Coming, coming; hurry. That means the
end. I'll get the boys."

His daughter jumped out of bed, after shaking Evie.

"Little-Womey, hurry, hurry," said Sam, stooping to the
level of her vague, surprised eyes, on the bed. "New bimbo, new
bambino!"

Evie sat up suddenly, her face pulled into a grotesque and
comical grin, "Have we got a new bimbo?"

"Not yet; coming, coming!" He bent and kissed her,
"Bimbo's in a hurry; wants to see Little-Sam and Little-Womey."

Evie looked round everywhere, "Where, Taddy?"

"With Mother yet," Sam said tenderly.

He went to get up the boys. Ernie was out of bed like a shot
and pulling his pajama pants off his feet. He looked interested and
serious. He stopped with his day shirt half over his head, his two
big eyes out like Brer Rabbit's from the mudhole, questioning Big
Sam, at a noise from upstairs. But Big Sam did nothing, only put
himself everywhere at once, on all sides of the mattresses.
"Git-up, git-up," pulling and tugging at arms and legs, while the
twins, not yet aware, groaned and muttered, "You get out, Erno,
or I'll hit yer," and then at one moment shuttered up their eyes
finally and gladly stared at Sam, back from Malaya and Manila.

"Daddy!" they both cried.

"Git-up, git up!" he whispered joyously, mysteriously. They
shot up and began prancing on their mattresses. The sun shone,
but there was trouble above-stairs. Sam, however, instead of
pulling a long face and slewing towards them woebegone eyes,
was all merriment and gratulation, his eyes a playground for
scores of dancing little twitching elvish smiles, here and there,
come and gone; his tired, yellow, and flabby cheeks, flushed a

little; his ugly bloodshot eyes, which had gone creased, half shut and Indian, in the tropical sun, squinting at them, leering at them, with every token of a good time to come.

"New bimbo," half whispered Sam, "new bimbo; get ready, get ready."

To Louie who appeared, hastily dressed, he said, laughing, "Get 'em dressed, Looloo."

Little-Sam stood up straight, his eyes and ears straining towards the stairs, as Louie knelt to fasten his sandals. The sun blushed on them all, banana yellow on the blonds and ginger on the brunets. They were all amazed and sober, examining the faces of Louie and Sam attentively. Sam was unconcerned. He smiled and, bending to kiss Evie, crooned, "Ming! Sedgewing! Smudgewing! Wat oo so sober fower? Wat oo ready to bust in two tears fower? Mummy get a new urchin, Daddy get a new shrimp, Evie get a new cradle kid, Tommo get a new brudder, Louie get a new somebuddy to make *wawa!*"

Evie raised her pansy kitten-face and pored over his lineaments, trying to make sense out of it all, trying to suck information out of him. He looked at her adoringly, and suddenly swung her up into his arms.

"My Little-Womey! Should have come to Malay with Poor-Sam to see all the—little brown, little bronze, little copper, little sulphur, little corn-cake, little waffle babbies; should have come to nurse all the little brown babbies; shouldn't have stayed so far away from her poor little Sam."

She threw back her head like Henny, and laughed provokingly. "But you wouldn't take me, you wouldn't take me!"

Three ringing cries came from the room upstairs, above the ceiling of the sunroom. Evie looked frightened. Sam's face changed. He plumped her on to the floor.

"Quick, quick, all hands on deck!"

He ran amongst them, behind them, marshaling them, like a sheep dog, to the bottom of the stairs, where they stood with charmed expectant faces raised towards the landing.

Sam began to chant rather low, bending over them, with his hands on shoulders, bunching them together,

Mother's got a lot, but she bought a new cot!
Daddy's got Sedgewing, but he's got a new Thing!
Louie's got another little Creaker to her string!

All the children laughed, a babble of little chuckles and crows, like a summer wave rearing on the shingle; but stopped, with their mouths open to listen, as Henrietta screamed wildly, hoarsely, such a cry as they never thought she could make: Louie turned startled eyes to Samuel, believing that she had gone mad. Evie started to cry. Sam grew solemn and held up his hand,

"Kids, I want you to listen: she's been crying all night; this is the end; soon you'll hear a new kind of cry. That will be the new baby. Listen, listen!"

The children strained their faces upwards listening. Sam said softly, "This is the first sunrise and the first day on earth for one of our family. See what time it is, Looloo."

It was six-thirty. When the baby's cry came, they could not pick it out, and Sam, eagerly thrusting his face amongst their ears, said, "Listen, there, there, that's the new baby." He was red with delight and success. They heard voices, and their mother groaning still, and then, quite free and separate, the long thin wailing, and the voices again.

"Six-forty-five," called Louie.

"Did you hear, Ming," he asked, "did you hear?"

"Yes, Taddy, I heard."

"What is it?" asked Tommy.

"The new baby, listen, the new baby."

"We heard," Saul announced, for the twins.

They were still there puzzled, but believing in him, so that they were convinced that a baby had in some miraculous way arrived by the roof; when, in the soft stir upstairs, they heard their mother's speaking voice and a man answering her.

"Who is there, Taddy?" Tommy asked.

"Go tell Bonnie," Sam commanded with a little satiric grin; for Bonnie, in tears and full of objections, had refused to be with them in their waiting and had gone off to the back porch to cool her feelings.

The next moment the door opened upstairs, and a strange, severe man came to the top of the stairs, surveyed them all with distaste and choler, and unkindly said to Sam, "Mrs. Pollit wishes to see you."

Sam instantly swarmed through his children, putting them aside with his hands, disengaged his long legs from the mass of little legs, and bounded up the stairs. The doctor disappeared. At the top of the flight, Sam stopped and, turning round to them, gave them a wide grin, a chuckle, and said softly,

"Wait and see, kids: wait and see!"

The door closed. They heard their parents' voices.

"Is it a baby?" inquired Little-Sam again, much surprised.

"Of course, silly; Daddy said," Evie corrected him. They had understood nothing at all, except that Mother had been angry and miserable and now she was still; this was a blessed relief. They began to scatter through the hall after Louie had forbidden them to follow Sam upstairs. Suddenly Sam was at the bottom of the stairs again, flustered with a new love. He grabbed the twins by the shoulders and said excitedly, "Tribe, you have a new brother."

The children looked at each other. "What's his name?" inquired the twin Sam.

"He has no name," said big Sam comically, knowing how odd that seemed to them. "We got to give him a name. What'll we call him, kids?"

"Sam," said twin Saul promptly.

The rest of them, all but the twin Sam, laughed. They began to suggest names, calling the baby after friends at school and street friends; and then a strange, unpleasant woman who had flown in, in the night, came halfway down the stairs and said agreeably, "Mrs. Pollit wants to see Tommy."

The frightened Tommy made a step and hung back.

"Can I go? Can I go?" they all babbled.

"She said me," Tommy objected and made a slow progress to the stairs. But he refused the nurse's hand and looked sullen when she remarked with professional unction that he was a big boy now and had a little brother to look after.

"Charles Franklin," said big Sam, "that's what we'll call him probably, after Grandpa and after the President, the greatest man of our time, the Daniel of our days. May little Charles-Franklin grow up to be like him." '

"And like Grandpa," Ernie remarked.

"Grandpa is all right, but Grandpa is Grandpa; Grandpa had a hard row to hoe when he was a young man; but you kids have advantages. Grandpa came to this country with nothing but a tin box with his clothes in, but Charles-Franklin is going to have a better chance, and this is a better age. Things have changed since your grandpa's day. Grandpa specially asked for the baby to be called after him; it's just a little sentimental matter, you see, kids: Grandpa's old; we can't refuse him." He nodded his head over them and sent them outside to play till Bonnie and Hazel got breakfast ready.

"What's your name?" asked Evie, playing "mothers" with the twins.

"Ippa-pa-tixit!" declared Saul. "Mr. Ippa-pa-tixit!"

"Mrs. Ippa-pa-tixit," corrected Evie. "You're Sam's mother. What's your name, Ernie?"

"Oh, shut up," said Ernie, measuring himself against pencil marks on the veranda post.

"You're a lady, too, no," said Evie, ignoring the obstreperous Ernie, her usual antagonist and claiming Little-Sam. "You're his new baby. Mother has a new baby, and the lady in there has a new baby. Her name's Mrs. Arkus.

"Who's Mrs. Arkus?"

"Mrs. Ahss," said Ernie. The boys laughed, Evie frowned.

Up the Sandbox!

Anne Richardson Roiphe

In between the chapters devoted to her gloriously mad Walter Mitty-ish fantasies, the heroine of *Up the Sandbox!* gives us a fine-grained look inside her world as the upper West Side mother married to a young assistant professor of history. The literary device used by the author juxtaposes the dull domesticity of homemaking and motherhood against the exaggerated exploits that are carried out, all in the mother's imagination, in the outside world. Roiphe is pointing out that the woman you meet at the supermarket may have a rich, vivid inner life that is shielded from your scrutiny.

However, in this scene, she conveys far more than the dullness of many a housewife's role. We see that even the smallest happenings between mother and child are fraught with great drama, tension, a sense of contingency and imminent failure, and an aching, yearning love. We understand why parents come to invest so much emotion in their children's lives, how they can so closely identify with their children, even while recognizing that the future will bring conflict, disillusionment, and alienation; and even *now*, as she puts it, she is not happy. Yet they are so much a part of her that the least wound they suffer, the smallest frustration they experience, bruises and wounds her.

Other feelings are expertly captured; for example, the mother is aware that even the people on the street are judging her performance and dedication to the child's interest, her awareness of the best child-rearing techniques. We experience vicariously the sweet little girl's aggressive, sadistic impulse to pinch her brother. As Roiphe notes, ". . . she will never forgive me for having borne him."

From the very intensity with which she feels these successive emotions, we also perceive the extent to which the husband-father recedes somewhat in the background. He does enter her mind from time to time, as she thinks of

From Anne Richardson Roiphe, *Up the Sandbox!*, Simon & Schuster, Inc., New York, 1970.

his cold, of their sexual pleasures, or of the possibility of death, but the immediacy of the child's demands continues to dominate her responses.

Elizabeth is playing with the blue-and-white ball I have just bought her at the five-and-ten on Broadway. It rolls away and I see her chase it and suddenly trip on a toy truck and fall on the cement ground. I am attentive, taut, ready to charge forward. I put down the notebook and in another second I hear her scream as if her universe were empty and her sound would never find a human listener. I run to her and as I get close, I feel her scream in my chest, ready at the edge of an explosion. I see blood pouring from her mouth, covering her chin and staining the pink-and-white flowered dress she's wearing. Quickly I take her in my arms. "Nothing to be frightened of, just a little blood, nothing to worry about—Mommy will fix it." The screaming subsides to a sobbing and my own heart is pounding—so much blood is coming—my arms and the front of my dress are also red. I'm certain it's just a superficial mouth cut, but still my legs are trembling as I carry her to the water fountain. A friend lends me a diaper to use as a towel.—"It's nothing, it's nothing," I say over and over. My life is not my own any more, it belongs in part to her. I have committed myself to taking care of her and I must not fail. She must be the better part of me. She must be the more beautiful, the more graceful, the more loving part of me. I am in and of myself no longer complete, I need her. I wipe with the diaper. I use cold water and press against her pale face and stained mouth, and in a matter of moments she is quiet, leaning on my shoulder. The blood has stopped. Her teeth are all there and I can't even see in her mouth where such a terrible cut could have been. That pink soft tissue opens, profusely bleeds and then closes, leaving no trace of a slash. Elizabeth wants to sit on her seat in the stroller, and now the baby who has watched the drama with open eyes wants to be held and smiled at. I give them both cookies and sit back on the bench, the baby on my lap. The heat again feels like a weight, like someone stuffing cotton down one's chest. Sometimes as I sit watching the children I suddenly think of Paul, of the smell and feel of him. I don't know if the images I have are lascivious or tender, I think perhaps they are both. In and out of my mind all during the day move thoughts of him.

Paul's sleeping now on our bed, breathing heavily, his hair wet across his forehead. Not tonight, tonight I'll be too tired, he won't be well enough, but certainly tomorrow or perhaps in the early morning he'll reach over and touch my breasts and I'll roll toward him and for a while nothing else will matter, not his cold, not our children, not the book on revolutions—it will all wait for us to finish, to separate again.

The baby is struggling to move around. I put him down off my lap and take from his hand a cigarette about to go into his mouth. I watch as he crawls to the next bench, and quickly I jump up and grab him before his fingers get caught beneath a carriage wheel. I put him back in the stroller and he cries in fury. His face turns red, his period of freedom was too short, too delicious, to be given up so quickly. But I'm tired, I cannot watch him, protect him with total vigilance, and one accident a day is enough. The other mothers are looking at me. Why is that child screaming, why doesn't she do something? She's probably one of those cold, indifferent types, the kind that breed damaged children; hasn't she read Bettelheim, Spock, Gesell? I give him a smile, I push the stroller back and forth. Elizabeth leans forward and tickles his cheek—which usually makes him laugh. Nothing works. Elizabeth pinches him too hard, the pinch of anger, at his tears, at his very existence. He cries louder. I am an interfering, spoiling mother and from the sound of his crying I am never to be forgiven. From the strength of her pinch I can tell she will never forgive me for having borne him. It's early but I'm going to leave this hot playground and go to the air-conditioned pizza place on 115th Street. The children will cover themselves with tomato sauce. I will sit in the dark booth, my elbows on the shiny Formica tabletop, and play the jukebox. And then at last it will be time to go home.

I was thinking about Paul's cold earlier today. I noticed how pale and mottled his face was and the sticky damp dark spots on the sheets, and the frail sound of his nasal voice humming Mozart melodies as he watched the afternoon's soap opera on television—What when he is really ill, what when he or I lie in bed dying? It is absolutely certain that one of us will die before the other, and the stronger one will tend the sick one, grow to loathe the illness and the patient, and then suddenly be left alone, like a statue without arms, legs or nose, be permanently undone. That thought can't be tolerated long and yet it can't be pushed entirely aside, because the moment will arrive and I want my perceptions and attitudes to be ready, I want to be prepared.

Once last March Elizabeth ran a fever of 104 and her breath came heavy, slow and painful. The doctor came, not very disturbed, and used penicillin. A sharp disposable needle, a cry from Elizabeth, a pat on my back, a prescription on the table, and he was gone. I stayed up all that night, bringing her cold washcloths, rubbing her chest with alcohol, watching the vaporizer and the strange shapes that appeared in the steam. I wasn't really frightened, but as I stared at her flushed face and the dilated pupils, I realized that I couldn't be without her—that I had fiercely and passionately involved myself in the limbs and brain, the body and soul of my child. Why? Why was I proud when she learned numbers early, pleased when she fitted together pieces of a puzzle, proving an intelligence expected and necessary for survival? Why was I embarrassed when she wet her pants in the playground and the urine streamed down her legs, settling in puddles in her socks—why was I so angry and hurt the day the little boy called her "Cross-eyes" and wouldn't play daddy in her game of house? Why did I nearly cry as I held her in my arms and explained that he was just a bad boy? Is it something perhaps in the secret sticky protoplasm out of which I molded her—myself now devoted to a replica of myself, now slave, now master, caught in a bind; not pleasant, certainly *nowhere* happy, predictably bound for clashing of wills, disappointments, expectations unmet, pride hurt—all that I know will happen between a mother and a daughter, between me and Elizabeth. What do I want from her when she grows up? Whatever it is, I am sure I won't get it. Whatever she will do will be less than what I have planned, because I can't help planning so much, asking so much of her. I always used to share the joke and point the finger at the ambitious stage mother, or the possessive Jewish mother whose son could not go to the bathroom without her following behind to wipe and admire his parts. And now I think those are visible caricatures of the even more sinister reality, the more ordinary poisonous ooze that flows between parent and child—Elizabeth is marred because she is mine and each waking hour I transmit in a thousand unconscious ways the necessary code for her to absorb my personality, to identify with my sex, and to catch, like a communicable plague, all my inadequacies and mimic them or convert them to massive ugly splotches on her own still young soul. For example, I have never told her in any kind of words that I am afraid of the dark, and yet she will not let me put out her bedside lamp and I don't insist, because I remember giants and witches, evil blobs of unknown menace, lying directly at the cover's edge when it's dark. I still sometimes feel an unseen presence behind my back, readying itself to leap and force me into some unspeakable violence. Sometimes I think perhaps it's wrong, morally wrong to have children, when I am so uncertain whether or not I am a good person, enough of a person to create another. I so badly want my children to grow strong and be meaningfully rebellious, to take some corner of the earth and claim it for their own. I look around me in the playgound at all the other mothers and their children. We are united in our strong feelings of ambition for our children.

Elizabeth is sometimes afraid of dogs, large ones that pull on their leashes or little ones that bark too much. Sometimes she's afraid of the moon. She says it's like a ghost hand in the sky. Sometimes she curls up in my lap and says she wishes she were the tiny baby in the house, that growing up is a nasty thing. I point out all the wonders of maturity, but I still can't convince her. Sometimes she seems to want to contract until she's no more than a few cells, visible only through a microscope, nestling against the wall of my sealed-off uterus. I too sometimes would like to progress in reverse so my mother could brush my hair each morning and complain about my roller skates left out to rust in the backyard, so I could take my dolls to bed and draw pictures in my schoolbooks of a prince waiting to make me, Margaret Ferguson of Paramus, New Jersey, his bride.

How was I before Elizabeth was born? Even though it's only

a few short years, I seem to have always listened for the sound of a child's crying or calling. When I think of losing her, and of illness, long nights in the hushed corridors of bleak hospitals, the sound of children crying for their mothers or their teddy bears, and nurses rustling by in the dark whispering bad news to each other, I think about how I would drink dark coffee out of paper cups, and wait. Sometimes I am frightened of a possible car crash, a fall, a pot of boiling water overturned, a bobbypin experimentally poked into an electric socket. And then, after the death, I would be a woman with a limb amputated—worse, perhaps, I would be a woman with a hole in the center, in the bowels, a great gaping hole from breast to genitals, for the wind to blow through, for trash to collect in, for everyone to know I am emptied of myself.

I must pick up Elizabeth from the dirt by the water fountain where she is sitting with another little girl, drawing in the mud. There is a leak at the base of the fountain and it has created a miniature river whose geography is being carefully studied by the children. She is dirty, and I like to see her that way. The dirt is from the feeling and the touching of all possible surfaces, and a certain lack of concern, a certain pleasure in doing things uninhibited by prissy thoughts and stuffy manners. The baby is sleeping on his back, his hands flung out on either side of the stroller. Too late for pizza, instead I will take them both home and stop at the drugstore and pick up some cough medicine for Paul. Maybe if I can find enough change hidden in the corners of my bag, I can bring him the *New American Review* to take his mind off his nasal congestion.

Chapter 6

Siblings

Sociologists of the family have neglected the study of relations among siblings. They have focused most of their research attention on the relations between husband and wife and between parents and children, in part because the society as a whole uses these two sets of relationships as the core of the modern conjugal family unit.

Has literature helped depict the relationships among brothers and sisters? Surprisingly, no, or at least not a great deal. In the myths, legends, sagas, chronicles, and epic poetry of the distant past, sets of brothers often formed warring factions, mounted great raids and expeditions, vowed lifelong fealty to one another, or in dramatic circumstances became enemies. That emphasis reflected a different kind of society, one in which the husband-wife bond was less intense and relations with one's kin were paramount. In a matrilineal society, both brothers and sisters remained part of the same lineage throughout their lifetimes, whatever their marriages to "outsiders." In a patrilineal society, sisters were often lost to the lineage while brothers were linked closely, but even in such societies there remained, in both legend and fact, some tenderness and secret intimacy between brother and married sister.

But though great kindred are hardly to be met in contemporary life, and lineages are fast disappearing, the authors believe that in real life siblings mean more to one another than they do in literature or in sociology. A greater understanding of this topic would illumine our grasp of family relations, and perhaps of the larger society as well. In some ways, relations among brothers and sisters are a kind of "ascribed friendship," i.e., we are born into the relationship but by social definition we are supposed to remain friends throughout our lifetime.

Modern psychodynamics has made us perhaps overly sensitive to the phenomenon of "sibling rivalry." However, at its happiest the relations among brothers and sisters become that rarity in our experience, warmth without authority. Unlike their parents, they are not engaged in building or attaining a set of goals, but are rather focused simply on being together, on accepting one another for what they are rather than how much they contribute. Even an elder brother cannot assert much authority.

They are more likely to accept one another, because they have grown up together without questioning their togetherness, without indeed ever having to make a decision about it (as husbands and wives have done, and often continue to do). Moreover, because each recognizes the other's individuality, and the social destiny that will ultimately require him or her to establish an independent family, they have the choice of a wide range of intimacy, indeed a rare kind of intimacy, one in which each side can count on the other while living apart or even not seeing one another for long periods of time. Finally, insulated by the incest taboo from the deeper turmoil of passionate love, brothers and sisters are permitted an emotional intimacy that does not threaten either of them.

Although we do not wish to claim that such an ideal is often encountered in reality—every reader who has had a brother or sister will remember numerous childhood conflicts—we believe that many elements in this ideal version have been a frequent experience for most of us. Many women have been able to tolerate their marriages better because they could use their brother occasionally as a sympathetic listener. Many men have been saved by their brothers from financial ruin, or have established great enterprises with them. We are troubled when we hear of siblings betraying one another, or becoming steadfast enemies. On the other hand, we recognize that when such a betrayal occurs, or is believed to have occurred, the enmity that results may be extremely powerful, for it is fed by a set of strong affectional forces.

Of course, in asserting that writers have neglected sibling relations, we are aware that brothers and sisters *do* frequently appear in novels and short stories, because most of fiction focuses on family behavior, and brothers and sisters are part of families. However, their relations are not often presented as the central focus of any story. The reader may wonder what kinds of stories could be written with such an emphasis within contemporary society, and what kind of sociological research might illuminate these relationships.

The Story of Cain and Abel
The Old Testament

One of the oldest tales in Western literature is that of Cain and Abel, the first sons of Adam and Eve after they were expelled from the Garden of Eden. It expresses several themes of enduring interest. One of these, of course, is sibling rivalry. Siblings, but especially siblings of the same sex, compete for the same "goods," i.e., their parents' love, the right to inherit property, the command over any magic in the family line, and so on.

A second theme has been dropped from modern literature as it has come to focus increasingly on life in cities—the conflict between the nomadic shepherd and the sedentary farmer. Although our own images of herdsmen suggest peace, quiet, communing with the stars, and solitude, the literature of the past often emphasized violence instead. Herdspeople watched over their horses, camels, cattle, or sheep, guarding them against animal predators, bandits or rustlers, and the clever machinations of wily and decadent city dwellers. They could not count on help from policemen or the emperor's army; they had to stand fast or perish.

Thus, the sedentary agricultural Chinese felt it was necessary to build the Great Wall against the nomadic Mongols. Western cattlemen cut the barbed wire fences of farmers and drove their cattle through the tilled fields. Arab cities were under recurrent threat from the desert nomads. The literature about war often recounted the clash of the stolid, unimaginative city dwellers, whose fields lay just outside their settlements, and the daring barbarians who lived with their flocks in the wastelands.

The Old Testament story has a special perspective that perhaps occurs less often in world literature. It is the shepherd Abel who is the victim of violence, and it is his offering of which the Lord takes notice. Cain's agricultural produce is ignored. Thus, the Lord feeds whatever sibling rivalry may have existed (surely exhibiting poor managerial principles), and moreover he chides Cain for being downcast, pointing out that Cain (being the elder) enjoys authority over his brother.

The result was a murder, and the Lord's judgment was that Cain would forever bear a mark on his forehead to warn all that they should not kill him; he would be always cursed and banished. The first murder, then, was not punished by death, but the social context suggests that Cain would suffer for his crime until he died.

The literary version underscores certain universal truths, on which the power of such myths rests: That we are more likely to kill members of our own family, both because they are available to kill and because what they do arouses stronger emotions in us than what other people do; that though we are sometimes driven to contemplate murdering our sister or brother, such an act would be a most unnatural crime and we should always regret it. When such a conflict arises between siblings, its causes seem to the outsider much too weak and fortuitous for so momentous an event. Any reader who has grown up with a brother or sister will be able to relive the emotions underlying this spare account of a historic family tragedy.

The man had intercourse with his wife Eve; so she conceived and bore Cain. Then she said,

"I have won back my husband; the Lord is with me!"

Later she bore his brother, Abel. Abel was a shepherd, while Cain was a tiller of the soil.

In the course of time Cain brought some produce of the soil as an offering to the Lord, while Abel on his part brought some firstlings from his flock, that is, some fat pieces from them. The Lord took notice of Abel and his offering; but of Cain and his offering he took no notice. So Cain became very angry and downcast. Then the Lord said to Cain,

"Why are you angry, and why are you downcast? If you have been doing right, should you not be happy? But if you have not, sin will be lurking at the door. And yet he is devoted to you, while you rule over him."

Then Cain said to his brother Abel,

"Let us go off into the country."

When they were out in the country, Cain attacked his brother Abel, and murdered him.

Then the Lord said to Cain,
"Where is your brother Abel?"
"I do not know," he said. "Am I my brother's keeper?"
Whereupon he said,
"What have you done? Hark, your brother's blood is crying
to me from the ground! And now, cursed shall you be in
banishment from the soil which has opened its mouth to receive
your brother's blood from your hand. Though you were to till the
soil, never again would it yield you its full produce; a vagrant and
vagabond shall you be on the earth."
Cain said to the Lord,
"My punishment is too great to bear. Seeing that thou hast
today driven me off the soil, I must remain hidden from thee; I
must be a vagrant and a vagabond in the earth, and then anyone
who comes across me will kill me."
So the Lord said to him,
"In that case, sevenfold vengeance shall be taken on anyone
who kills Cain."
Then the Lord prescribed a mark for Cain, to prevent anyone
who chanced upon him from hurting him. So Cain left the
presence of the Lord, and settled in the land of Nod, east of
Eden.

God's Little Acre

Erskine Caldwell

Unlike the sociologist, the literary artist does not make a
contract to describe social reality accurately. The characters in a novel, as well as its setting in the larger society in
which the action takes place, cannot be viewed as a set of
hypotheses to be tested by scientific research. Moreover, as
anyone can ascertain by looking at popular novels, public
response is not determined by its sociological correctness.

But if the writer does not have to be truthful, he must

Erskine Caldwell, *God's Little Acre*, Copyright 1933 by Erskine Caldwell. Copyright renewed 1961. Reprinted by permission of Little, Brown and Company, Boston.

somehow achieve verisimilitude. Things must "seem correct," even if they are very atypical. The artist may even use correct sociological data in order to convince us of the reality of his characters; for example, Hemingway often gives considerable detail about the techniques of bullfighting, hunting, or fishing, in order to create a believable setting for his stories. In *God's Little Acre*, Erskine Caldwell has created a most unlikely set of characters, but millions of readers have accepted this world as real enough. It is far removed from the much more profound vision of the world that William Faulkner created.

However, it is possible that readers do not "believe in" this world. Rather, we enjoy the moral regression we perceive in Caldwell's characters, a letting down of moral barriers, an opening up of opportunities that are forbidden to us because of the restraints that jobs and repression put upon us in real life. Caldwell has created a set of caricatures who correspond to our stereotypes of "backward, rural Southerners," who live by immediate impulse, who break off the porch banisters in order to feed the fire in wintertime, who express openly their incestuous desires, who reach for every sexual opportunity, and who would rather enjoy an immediate pleasure than work hard at a tedious job.

In this setting, men and women fight and love one another without much calculation. In the following scene we see a violent encounter between two brothers. Jim Leslie is the only one of Ty Ty's sons who has become "successful." He has gone to the urban center and has become well-to-do, but in conformity with the stereotype he is strong, aggressive, hard and cold, contemptuous of his kin, and unloving with his wife and other women. Like many another man before him, he lusts after his brother's beautiful wife. Here he has suddenly appeared at the family farm, determined to use brute force in taking Griselda away with him. In his reserved way, he does not announce what he proposes to do, but his brother Buck and their father Ty Ty both know.

"This here now squabbling over women has got to stop on my land," Ty Ty said with sudden determination. He had at last realized how hopeless his efforts to make peace had been. "I've tried to settle this argument peacefully, but I ain't going to stand for you boys scrapping each other over women no longer. It's going to stop right now. You get in your car, son, Jim Leslie, and go on back to Augusta. Buck, you and Shaw go on back to the hole and dig. I've let this scrapping go as far as I'm going to stand for. Go on now, all of you. This here now squabbling over women has got to stop on my land."

"I'll kill the son-of-a-bitch, now," Buck said. "I'll kill him if he goes in that house, now. He can't come out here and take Griselda off, now."

"Boys, this here now squabbling over women on my land has got to stop. You all boys go on and do like I told you to do just now."

Jim Leslie saw his opportunity, and he sprang for the door and was in the house before they could stop him. Buck was only three steps behind him, however, and Ty Ty and Shaw ran after them. Jim Leslie ran through the first door he reached, and on into another room. He did not know where Griselda was, and he continued through the house in search of her.

"Stop him, Buck!" Shaw shouted. "Make him come back through the hall—don't let him get away through the back door!"

In the dining-room when Ty Ty reached it a moment later, Jim Leslie was in the middle of the room, with the table between Buck and himself, and they were cursing each other. Over in the corner the three girls were huddled behind a chair they had pulled in front of them. Griselda was crying, and so was Rosamond. Darling Jill looked as if she did not know whether to cry or to laugh. Ty Ty could not stop to look at them any longer, and he did not try to protect them so long as they were in no immediate danger, but began shouting at the boys again. He soon saw it was useless. They did not hear a word he said; they appeared to be unaware of his presence in the room.

"Come out of that corner, Griselda," Jim Leslie told her. "You're going with me. Come out of that corner and get into the car before I have to come and pull you out."

"You stay where you are and don't move," Buck told her out of the corner of his mouth, his eyes still on his brother.

Ty Ty turned to Shaw in desperation.

"You'd better go get Black Sam and Uncle Felix to help us. It looks like we can't handle him alone."

"You stay here, Shaw," Buck said. "I don't need any help. I can handle him by myself."

"Come out of that corner before I drag you out, Griselda," Jim Leslie said again.

"You came to get her, huh? Why didn't you say that in the yard? I knew damn well what it was, but I've just been waiting to hear you say it. You came to get her, huh?"

"This here now squabbling over women on my land has got to quit," Ty Ty said determinedly. "I just ain't going to stand for it no longer."

"Come out of that corner, Griselda," Jim Leslie said for the third time.

"I'll kill the son-of-a-bitch, now," Buck said.

He stepped back, relaxing his muscles.

"This here now squabbling over women on my land has got to stop," Ty Ty said, banging his fists on the table between his two sons.

Buck stepped back to the wall behind him and reached for the shotgun on the rack. He unbreeched it, looking down a moment to see if both barrels were loaded.

When Jim Leslie saw Buck with the gun, he ran out the door into the hall and on through the house to the front yard. Buck was behind him, holding out the gun in front of him as though it were a snake on a stick.

Out in the yard, Ty Ty realized it was useless for him to try to stop Buck. He could not wrestle the gun away from him; Buck was too strong. He would throw him aside without much effort. So, instead of running out into the yard, Ty Ty sank to his knees on the porch and began praying.

Behind him in the hall stood Griselda and Rosamond and Darling Jill, afraid to come any further, but scared to stay alone in the house. They huddled behind the front door, peeping through the crack to see what was happening in the yard.

Ty Ty looked up from his prayer, one eye open in fright, one eye closed in supplication, when he heard Buck shout to Jim

Leslie to stop running. Jim Leslie was in front of his automobile, and he could easily have jumped behind it for protection, but instead he stopped where he was and shook his fist at Buck.

"I reckon you'll leave her alone now," Buck said.

The gun was already leveled at Jim Leslie. Ty Ty could almost see through the sights from where he was on the porch, and he was certain he could feel Buck's finger tighten on the trigger. He closed his eyes prayerfully a second before the explosion in the barrel. He opened his eyes to see Jim Leslie reach forward for something to grip for support, and heard almost immediately the explosion of the second shell. Jim Leslie stood upright for a few short seconds, and then his body twisted to one side and he fell heavily on the hard white sand under the water-oak tree.

Memoirs of a Dutiful Daughter

Simone de Beauvoir

In their reports to parents about their own activities, siblings screen and censor their intimate activities. Few parents really know "what is going on" in their children's relations with one another. It is likely to be a rich, secret life. Typically all the siblings have a moral stake in keeping their world inviolate, from both their parents and other children.

De Beauvoir in *Memoirs of a Dutiful Daughter*, lets us view a relationship that is not often described, the interaction between sisters. Since she is the narrator, we do not know what her sister felt, but we do experience her great and continuing pleasure in the clever, beautiful younger sister whom she calls "my liege-man, my alter ego, my double." As elder sister, she could command her baby sibling, but because she needed her sister's willing presence each strove to please the other. Living in the world of

Simone de Beauvoir, *Memoirs of a Dutiful Daughter*, translated by James Kirkup, The World Publishing Company, Cleveland, 1959, pp.45–50.

her imagination, which later was to bring her international fame, de Beauvoir enjoyed having a devoted accomplice who could act out with her a wide variety of social roles, trying on numerous identities in successive entertainments that were kept private from the elders. She felt a nearly unquestioned superiority, because of her accomplishments and age, a security that was threatened only now and then when she glimpsed the affection her parents had for Poupette. Following this description of her relationship, we append a later scene, when they are both somewhat older, and de Beauvoir has finally acquired a genuine close friend. Then, as is common in sibling relations, the two sisters become less close. The two older girls now form a peership, and with the characteristic cruelty of children they express their contempt for the "baby." Poupette then becomes resentful and alienated. On the other hand, at a much deeper level, it is not only that the younger sister cannot simply discard her elder sibling. The elder cannot do without the friendship of the younger, either. It is as though both sense, beyond the immediate particularity of their lives, that in a world of transient passions and loves, occupational and group ties, many periods will occur in the future when siblings will need one another greatly after all.

For the time being, I felt I was being protected and guided both in matters of this life and of the life beyond. I was glad, too, that I was not entirely at the mercy of grown-ups; I was not alone in my children's world; I had an equal: my sister, who began to play a considerable role in my life about my sixth birthday.

We called her Poupette; she was two and a half years younger than I. People said she took after Papa. She was fair-haired, and in the photographs taken during our childhood her blue eyes always appear to be filled with tears. Her birth had been a disappointment, because the whole family had been hoping for a boy; certainly no one ever held it against her for being a girl, but it is perhaps not altogether without significance that her cradle was the center of regretful comment. Great pains were taken to treat us both with scrupulous fairness; we wore identical clothes, we nearly always went out together; we shared a single existence, though as the elder sister I did in fact enjoy certain advantages. I had my own room, which I shared with Louise, and I slept in a big carved wooden bed, a copy of an antique, over which hung a reproduction of Murillo's *Assumption of the Blessed Virgin*. A cot was set up for my sister in a narrow corridor. While Papa was undergoing his army training, it was I who accompanied Mama when she went to see him. Relegated to a secondary position, the "little one" felt almost superfluous. I was a new experience for my parents: my sister found it much more difficult to surprise and astonish them; I had never been compared with anyone: she was always being compared with me. At the Cours Désir the ladies in charge made a habit of holding up the older children as examples to the younger ones; whatever Poupette might do, and however well she might do it, the passing of time and the sublimations of the legend all contributed to the idea that I had done everything much better. No amount of effort or achievement was sufficient to break through that impenetrable barrier. The victim of some obscure curse, she was hurt and perplexed, and often in the evening she would sit crying on her little chair. She was accused of having a sulky disposition; one more inferiority she had to put up with. She might have taken a thorough dislike to me, but paradoxically she only felt sure of herself when she was with me. Comfortably settled in my role of elder sister, I preened myself only on the superiority accorded to my greater age; I thought Poupette was remarkably bright for her years; I accepted her for what she was—someone like myself, only a little younger; she was grateful for my approval, and responded to it with an absolute devotion. She was my liege-man, my alter ego, my double; we could not do without each other.

I was sorry for children who had no brother or sister; solitary amusements seemed insipid to me: no better than a means of killing time. But when there were two, hopscotch or a game of ball were adventurous undertakings, and rolling hoops an exciting competition. Even when I was just doing decalcomanias or daubing the pictures in a book with water colors I felt the need of an associate. Collaborating and vying with one another, we each found a purpose in our work that saved it from being pointless. The games I was fondest of were those in which I assumed another character; and in these I had to have an accomplice. We hadn't many toys; our parents used to lock away the nicest ones—the leaping tiger and the elephant that could stand on his hind legs; they would occasionally bring them out to show to admiring guests, I didn't mind. I was flattered to possess objects which could amuse grown-ups; and I loved them because they were precious: familiarity would have bred contempt. In any case the rest of our playthings—grocer's shop, kitchen utensils, nurse's outfit—gave very little encouragement to the imagination. A partner was absolutely essential to me if I was to bring my imaginary stories to life.

A great number of the anecdotes and situations which we dramatized were, we realized, rather banal; the presence of the grown-ups did not disturb us when we were selling hats or defying the Boches' artillery fire. But other scenarios, the ones we liked best, required secret performances. They were, on the surface, perfectly innocent; but in sublimating the adventure of our childhood or anticipating the future, they drew upon something secret and intimate within us which would not bear the searching light of adult gazes. I shall speak later of those games which, from my point of view, were the most significant. In fact, I was always the one who expressed myself through them; I imposed them upon my sister, assigning her the minor roles which she accepted with complete docility. At that evening hour when the stillness, the dark weight, and the tedium of our middle-class domesticity began to invade the hall, I would unleash my phantasms; we would make them materialize with great gestures and copious speeches, and sometimes, spellbound by our play, we succeeded in taking off from the earth and leaving it far behind until an imperious voice suddenly brought us back to reality. Next day we would start all over again. "We'll play *you know what*," we would whisper to each other as we prepared for bed. The day would come when a certain theme, worked over too long, would no longer have the power to inspire us; then we would choose another, to which we would remain faithful for a few hours or even for weeks.

I owe a great debt to my sister for helping me to externalize many of my dreams in play: she also helped me to rescue my

daily life from silence; through her I got into the habit of wanting
to communicate with people. When she was not there I hovered
between two extremes: words were either insignificant noises
which I made with my mouth, or, whenever I addressed my
parents, they became deeds of the utmost gravity; but when
Poupette and I talked together, words had a meaning yet did not
weigh too heavily upon us. I never knew with her the pleasure of
sharing or exchanging things, because we always held everything
in common; but as we recounted to one another the day's
incidents and emotions, they took on added interest and importance. There was nothing wrong in what we told each other;
nevertheless, because of the importance we both attached to our
conversations, they created a bond between us which isolated us
from the grown-ups; when we were together, we had our own
secret garden.

We found this arrangement very useful. The traditions of our
family compelled us to take part in a large number of duty visits,
especially around the new year; we had to attend interminable
family dinners with aunts and first cousins removed to the
hundredth degree, and pay visits to decrepit old ladies. We often
found release from boredom by running into the hall and playing
at "*you know what.*" In summer, Papa was very keen on
organizing expeditions to the woods at Chaville or Meudon; the
only means we had of enlivening the boredom of these long walks
was our private chatter; we would make plans and recall all the
things that had happened to us in the past; Poupette would ask me
questions; I would relate episodes from French or Roman history
or stories which I made up myself.

What I appreciated most in our relationship was that I had a
real hold over her. The grown-ups had me at their mercy. If I
demanded praise from them, it was still up to them to decide
whether to praise me or not. Certain aspects of my behavior
seemed to have an immediate effect upon my mother, an effect
which had not the slightest connection with what I had intended.
But between my sister and myself things happened naturally. We
would disagree, she would cry, I would become cross, and we
would hurl the supreme insult at one another: "You're stupid!"
and then we'd make up. Her tears were real, and if she laughed at

one of my jokes, I knew she wasn't trying to humor me. She alone endowed me with authority; adults sometimes gave in to me: she obeyed me.

One of the most durable bonds that bound us together was that which exists between master and pupil. I loved studying so much that I found teaching enthralling. Playing school with my dolls did not satisfy me at all: I didn't just want to go through the motions of teaching: I really wanted to pass on the knowledge I had acquired.

Teaching my sister to read, write, and count gave me, from the age of six onward, a sense of pride in my own efficiency. I liked scribbling phrases or pictures on sheets of paper: but then I knew only how to create imitation objects. When I started to change ignorance into knowledge, when I started to impress truths upon a virgin mind, I felt I was at last creating something real. I was not just imitating grown-ups: I was on their level, and my success had nothing to do with their indulgence. It satisfied in me an aspiration that was more than mere vanity. Until then, I had contented myself with responding dutifully to the care that was lavished upon me: but now, for the first time, I, too, was being of service to someone. I was breaking away from the passivity of childhood and entering the great human circle in which everyone is useful to everyone else. Since I had started working seriously time no longer flew by, but left its mark on me: by sharing my knowledge with another, I was fixing time on another's memory, making it doubly secure.

Thanks to my sister I was asserting my right to personal freedom; she was my accomplice, my subject, my creature. It is plain that I only thought of her as being "the same, but different," which is one way of claiming one's pre-eminence. Without ever formulating it in so many words, I assumed that my parents accepted this hierarchy, and that I was their favorite. My room gave on to the corridor where my sister slept and at the end of which was my father's study; from my bed I could hear my father talking to my mother in the evenings, and this peaceful murmur often lulled me to sleep. But one evening my heart almost stopped beating; in a calm voice which held barely a trace of curiosity, Mama asked: "Which of the two do you like best?" I waited for

Papa to say my name, but he hesitated for a moment that seemed like an eternity: "Simone is more serious-minded, but Poupette is so affectionate . . ." They went on weighing the pros and the cons of our case, speaking their inmost thoughts quite freely; finally they agreed that they loved us both equally well: it was just like what you read in books about wise parents whose love is the same for all their children. Nevertheless I felt a certain resentment. I could not have borne it if one of them had preferred my sister to me; if I was resigned to enjoying an equal share of their affection, it was because I felt that it was to my advantage to do so. But I was older, wiser, and more experienced than my sister: if my parents felt an equal affection for us, then at least I was entitled to more consideration from them; they ought to feel how much closer I was to their maturity than my sister was.

I thought it was a remarkable coincidence that heaven should have given me just these parents, this sister, this life. Without any doubt, I had every reason to be pleased with what fate had brought me. Besides, I was endowed with what is known as a happy disposition; I have always found reality more rewarding than illusion; therefore the things whose existence was most real to me were the things I possessed myself: the value I attached to them protected me from all disappointments, yearnings, and regrets; my affection for them overcame all baser longings. Blondine, my doll, was old-fashioned, dilapidated, and badly dressed; but I wouldn't have traded her for the most gorgeous doll queening it in a fancy shopwindow: the love I had for her made her unique and irreplaceable. I wouldn't have changed the park at Meyrignac for any earthly paradise, or our apartment for any palace. The idea that Louise, my sister, and my parents might be any different from what they were never entered my head. And as for myself, I couldn't imagine myself with any other face or with any other body: I felt quite satisfied with the way I was.

My father gradually lost his good temper. They never really quarreled, but they used to shout very loudly at one another over the merest trifles, and often vented their irritation upon my sister and me.

We stood staunchly by one another whenever we were confronted by grown-ups; if one of us upset a bottle of ink, we both took the blame and claimed a common responsibility for what had happened. All the same, since I had come to know Zaza, our relationship had changed a little: my new friend's every word was law. Zaza made fun of everybody; she didn't spare Poupette, and looked upon her as a "baby"; I followed her example. My sister became so unhappy that she tried to break away from my domination. One afternoon we were alone together in the study; we had just had a row, and she suddenly said to me in a dramatic tone of voice: "I have something to confess to you!" I had opened an English textbook on the desk pad and had started to read; I barely moved my head to listen to her outburst: "Well," my sister began, "I don't think I love you as much as I used to! There!" In a quiet, steady voice she went on to explain the growing indifference in her heart; I listened in silence and the tears rolled down my cheeks. She flung her arms round my neck: "It's not true!" she cried. "It's not true!" We kissed and hugged one another and I dried my tears. "I didn't really believe you, you know!" I told her. And yet there had been some truth in what she had said; she was beginning to revolt against her position as the younger sister, and as I seemed to be drifting away from her she included me in her rebellion. She was in the same class as our cousin Jeanne, whom she liked well enough, but whose tastes she did not share; yet she was obliged to associate with Jeanne's friends; they were all silly, pretentious little girls, she hated them and was furious that they should be considered worthy of her friendship; to no avail. At the Cours Désir Poupette continued to be regarded as a mere reflection, necessarily imperfect, of her elder sister: she often felt humiliated, so she was said to be haughty, and the teachers, in the name of education, humiliated her still further. I was more advanced, and so my father took more interest in my progress: though my sister did not share the devotion I felt for him, she was hurt by this partiality; one summer, at Meyrignac, to prove that she had just as good a memory as I had, she memorized a list of all Napoleon's marshals, with their names and titles; she rattled it off perfectly, and my parents only smiled. In her exasperation, she began to look upon me with a different eye: she picked out all my faults. It vexed me that she should seek, even half-heartedly, to rival, criticize, and do without me. We had always had rows, because I was brutal and she cried very easily; now she did not cry so much, but our quarrels became more and more serious: it became a question of pride; each of us wanted to have the final word. Yet in the end we always made up: we needed one another. We both held the same opinion of our friends, our teachers, and the members of our family; we didn't hide anything from each other; and we still took as much pleasure in playing together. When our parents went out in the evening, we would have a spread: we would concoct an omelette soufflé, which we would eat in the kitchen, then turn the flat upside down, shouting at the tops of our voices. Now that we had to sleep in the same room, our games and conversations used to go on long after we had gone to bed.

An Accidental Man

Iris Murdoch

Iris Murdoch creates a difficulty for some literary critics: such a prolific and entertaining novelist need not be taken seriously, yet her writing often approaches the masterly. Although her "social center" is the upper middle class, the range of her observation is much wider than that, and she has created a host of memorable characters.

In *An Accidental Man*, as in all her novels, a most complex set of plots and subplots is developed. One central theme focuses on the relations between Austin, the "accidental" man, and his brother Matthew. Austin is spoiled, exploitative, cunning, self-indulgent—a seedy failure amidst people who recurrently try to help him up, to take care of him, to apologize for his bad behavior. They do not drop him; they are only embarrassed by him.

Matthew left England as a young man and has spent

Iris Murdoch, *An Accidental Man*, The Viking Press, Inc., New York, 1971.

years in the Far East, where he has amassed a fortune while studying the refinements of Chinese and Japanese culture. He has seriously thought of becoming a Zen monk, and has brought back with him a great collection of Oriental bowls and vases (which Austin destroys in a fit of rage).

In the following scenes, we see them at several stages of the story. In the first, Austin recounts to a blowsy Mitzi (who was once a fine athlete, but after a crippling accident has been unable to cope) *his* version of why he harbors so great a hatred for his brother. We see his asthmatic attack occur because he learns Matthew has come to see him, and we watch his wild behavior as he tries to escape the love that Matthew offers.

In a later scene, we are inside Austin's mind as, full of self-loathing, he engages in feckless wishes about solving his problems. He reviews in his mind the same scene he recounted to Mitzi, and we see that the events are now different. He also dreams about his first wife Betty, who in the dream is kidnapped and drugged—but she must not awaken. Only later in the story do we learn why: He has killed her.

Murdoch's irony is evident in each of the subplots. Austin runs over a child while indulging himself in driving Matthew's new car too fast, and later kills the stepfather who has come to blackmail him, but he evades punishment in both cases. He is never punished for drowning Betty. He ends by living with Mavis, the stepsister of his second wife, although Mavis is in love with Matthew and they had planned to marry.

However, the greater irony, evident in the following scenes, is that Matthew had come back to England to remove the corroding hatred from Austin's heart, to establish a loving relationship with his brother; alas, not only has everything gone wrong, but while Austin has managed to rid himself of the hatred with no effort, no soul struggle, Matthew himself has come to see the entire hegira as empty and meaningless.

Although the complexities of Murdoch's world seem greater than our own, very likely it is because the novelist knows what has happened to her characters, while we do not know the inner worlds of those about us. Perhaps many

of the people we know live the lives of families in soap
operas, but there is in real life a deeper tragedy and a
greater sense of emptiness about the events once they have
happened. Surely, the theme of brothers hating, wandering
apart, and coming together again (but without any ultimate
joining in brotherly love) is a not uncommon experience in
modern life.

"Austin, you're drunk, you'd better go to bed."

"But not with you, my pettikins. Even big girls can't have
everything they want. Keep your dressing gown buttoned, duck-
ie, I don't want to see your nightie. Shall I sit on your knee?"

"Austin—"

"I'm not as drunk as you think. I'm just telling dull care to
begone. Shall I tell you a story?"

"The bottle's empty."

"Shall I tell you a *story?*"

"All right, but—"

"Once upon a time there were two brothers. Now this story
isn't about me and Matthew. I know you think it is but it isn't.
There were these two brothers and they lived on the top of a high
mountain, and down at the bottom of the mountain there was a
deep blue lake and at the bottom of the lake there lived a lady—"

"How did she breathe?"

"Shut up. And this lady was the most beautiful and desirable
thing in the whole world and one day the younger brother said to
the elder brother, Brother, let us go down and get this lady, let us
appropriate this lady, and the elder brother said, One lady
between two is no good, I resign my part in the lady, go you and
get the lady for yourself. So the younger brother climbed down
the mountain, which was very steep, did I mention that, it was
very steep, and he got the lady—"

"How?"

"Never mind. Then when he was climbing up the mountain
with the lady the elder brother looked down and saw and he
couldn't bear it and he took a great boulder and rolled it down the
hill and killed the younger brother—"

"Killed him?"

"Yes. Squashed him out as flat as a kipper."

"And what happened to the lady? Was she killed too or did she marry the elder brother?"

"That was the funny part. It turned out there wasn't really a lady at all. It was all made of plastic, like plastic flowers. And the younger brother was bringing it back to show it to the elder brother just for a laugh."

"So the elder brother killed him for nothing."

"It's not so simple. You keep saying things but it's never as simple as you think. Mitzi, what's that?"

"What?"

"That noise. Mitzi, there's somebody out on the landing— Quickly, go and look, quickly—"

Matthew, who had been listening at the door for some minutes, turned and scuttled away down the stairs. If he could immediately have undone the street door he would have darted out and run away into the night, but as he was still fumbling with the catch Mitzi appeared on the landing and switched the light on.

Matthew looked up. He saw a tall portly woman, with short pale bobbed hair and a large pink face, dressed in an old dressing gown. In the dim light and the shapeless robe she looked rotund and heavy, armless and legless and big-breasted like an archaic stone goddess. Mitzi looked down. She saw a stout bald elderly man with bulging bloodshot eyes and a frightened expression, holding a brief case. He looked like a tax inspector. They had never met each other before.

"What is it?" said Mitzi.

"I am extremely sorry," said Matthew. "I just came in through the door and was about to call up the stairs. The bell appears to be out of order. I fear in any case that I may have entered the wrong house. I am looking for a Mr. Gibson Grey, a Mr. Austin Gibson Grey."

"The bell hasn't worked since the blitz," said Mitzi. "Could you wait? I'll see if Mr. Gibson Grey is in." She had decided that this individual was about to serve a writ on Austin for nonpayment of a debt.

There was no sign of Austin. He had gone through into the adjoining kitchen. She found him there leaning over the sink and panting. He had been dashing water onto his face and his hair was wet and dripping.

"There's a—"

"I know. It's my brother."

"Your brother?"

"I'll go down and see him in a minute."

"What are you doing?"

"Just breathing."

"Do you think he heard?"

"Yes."

"Does it matter?"

"Yes. Could you give me some of that brandy? The whisky's all gone."

Mitzi took it from the cupboard and poured him some. He drank it in single draught and started coughing.

"Where is he?"

"In the hall."

"Go and look, would you? He may be just outside."

Mitzi came back. "He's sitting on the stairs at the bottom. Shall I—"

Austin strode past her and out of the room. As he came to the landing he took his glasses off and put them in his pocket. Matthew rose and they met at the bottom of the stairs. Austin extended his left hand.

"Matthew! How delightful!"

"Austin— Austin—" Matthew took the hand in both of his.

"Forgive me," said Austin, "I have to go out this very minute to make an urgent telephone call. You must excuse me. I would have loved a talk but it must wait. Please excuse this rush."

"May I come with you?"

"It's just at the corner. Perhaps I can get in touch with you. Where are you staying?"

"Brown's Hotel."

"Good. Well, here we are and I must make my call. I'm afraid it'll be rather a long one. So nice to see you. We must get in touch. Please don't wait."

Austin got inside the telephone box. It was very brightly lighted inside. Outside it was dark. Matthew had vanished. The bright lights were hurting Austin's eyes. He lifted the receiver and started dialling nines. Then a violent airy impulse took him about the waist and swung him far away. He pursued himself through space. He was lying on a tilting board which turned out to be the door of the telephone box. Just before it was going to tilt him into a pit he lurched forward until his face was pressed upon a black pane of glass. Through the glass he saw two shimmering orbs, like the face of an owl. Matthew was peering in at him from outside. He tried to turn his back but he seemed to have six rubbery legs which were gradually being folded up. He was a space craft landing on the moon. No, he was on that swing again, flying back the other way. His vision was darkening into a night sky of pullulating dots. One knee struck a concrete wall and there was pain somewhere. One foot seemed to be trying to run away down a rat hole. Something funny was spinning round and round in front of his face. It looked like a telephone receiver swinging round and round and round upon its flex. He must be on the floor. But then where were his legs?

"Are you all right?" said Matthew.

The telephone receiver was saying something too.

A woman's voice said, "Do you want the police?"

"Yes," said Austin, "I want to report a murder."

Nerves, thought Matthew, pure nerves. Typical. I couldn't leave it till tomorrow, could I. After that talk with Garth I imagined Austin thinking, he came straight to Garth, he talked me over with Garth, that he hadn't time to come and see me, oh no, I'm second best, he spends the evening with Garth and decides to see me later, everyone takes precedence over me, he wouldn't come hot-foot from the airport just to see me, would he. That's what I thought of him thinking. I can do Austin better than Austin does himself. So I come rushing round here in a nervous frenzy and commit that crime on the stairs. Did he know I was listening? And now this telephone box crime. Why couldn't I go quietly back to my hotel? Am I afraid of him, or what?

. . . .

My dear Austin,

I am sorry that I visited you so precipitately and so late on the evening of my arrival. My heart was full of you and I had to come to you directly, it could not have waited till the morning. Please forgive my rather abrupt appearance and departure. I have called twice since but got no reply, though I think Miss Ricardo was in on the second occasion. Your telephone appears to be out of order. May I suggest that we have lunch soon, somewhere quiet, perhaps my club? I think I should tell you this much of my plans. I am looking for a house and propose to settle here for good. I do not intend to hunt for old acquaintances and I shall not be calling at Valmorana. I have diplomatic cronies in London if I crave for company, which I do not expect to do. But I very much want to see you. I found (this condenses a long story which I will tell you at more leisure) that it was impossible to settle elsewhere with any peace of mind while our old difficulties remained as an unresolved cloud upon the horizon. I do not presume to imagine that I can help you. But you can certainly help me. And if I speak in this context of fraternal affection these are not, as far as I am concerned, empty words.

As ever,
your devoted brother,
MATTHEW

. . . .

He cared what Dorina thought, he cared what Matthew thought, he cared what Garth thought, he even cared what the bloody Tisbournes thought. Why should he be always the slave of his audience? Well, he was. What was so relaxing about Mitzi was that he did not care a fuck what Mitzi thought. Or Ludwig. There was peace there. But the others were his torment. How the Tisbournes would dance and sing if he became a nurse. "Darling, Austin's got a job, guess what!" And Dorina. How could he bear to be such a failure in her eyes? He had felt so proud on his wedding day. How had his marriage then become so vulnerable and exposed? He must be able once again to mystify and impress Dorina. She would lend herself to the mystification as she had always done.

He must get a job. He must get the flat back. He hadn't even let it yet. He must make Dorina stop being whatever she was being. Afraid of him? How he feared that fear, how he feared her horrible ghost-haunted thoughts, she was for him a fatal and destructive girl. Yet how precious she was and how much he loved her. He would kill anyone who came near her. How much longer could he keep her immobilized and spellbound at Valmorana? Of course she understood, she knew his jealousy, perhaps she feared it. She would keep still, as still as a frightened mouse, as still as prey. But supposing somebody were to kidnap her? The vile Tisbournes had asked her to stay with them. Supposing Mavis were to interfere or Garth or—

He could hear Mitzi stirring, hear the sound of her door opening. He switched off the light. There was a soft knock and Mitzi said, "Austin, are you awake?" He lay back silently. The door opened an inch or two. "Austin." He closed his eyes. He had read in a book that the eyeball reflects light. She must not see his terrible open eyes. The door creaked as it opened wider. He lay tense and stiff, feeling that he would scream if he were touched. The door closed again quietly and the feet shuffled away. He was on Calypso's isle. But was Ithaca still real? He turned sideways pulling a blanket up. Suppose Ludwig were to write him a testimonial? What happened if the money simply ran out? Was it conceivable that he could ask Matthew to lend him money? No. Would Ludwig lend him some of Gracie's hundreds of thousands?

He was beginning to see those clear coloured images, the gentle precursors of sleep. Now he saw again the blue lake in the quarry to which he had climbed down on that hot summer's day. Matthew would not come. Matthew was a timid boy. Scrambling down was easy, but to climb up was impossible, the loose stones came away, running past him in long rattling sluices. Matthew was laughing. Weakness, impotence, rage made him limp, the sun blazed in starry tears in his dazzled eyes, he could not get up. Now Matthew was throwing stones down at him and laughing. Weeping with rage he climbed and climbed. Something struck him and he fell and an avalanche of rattling stones cascaded him down to the very edge of the blue water. He had hurt his hand.

Sleep took him and he began to dream a dream which he had had many times before. Betty was not dead after all. She had been kidnapped and taken away and kept in a big house by somebody who gave her drugs. She was alive still but drugged.

He saw with horror her dazed vacant face. Yet he did not want her to awaken. That must never be.

. . . .

The park was in meadowy summer glory, with long plumes of uncut grass making a luscious light yellowy green between the splashed shadows. The air was thick with soft polleny smells which made breathing a luxury. Trees hazed the Albert Memorial and smudged the rosy front of Kensington Palace and long golden vistas showed multicoloured strollers with their dogs. Nearer to the water pink-footed geese and white-faced coots paraded in the groves of rhus and bamboo. A jay called in the bushes and signalled with its blue wing.

Matthew wondered in what modest hotel room, made hot and hideous by the sunshine, Charlotte was sitting tensely beside her suitcase, so determined to hurt and to be hurt. He wondered about Austin. He wondered about himself.

Talking to Taigu in Kyoto it had all seemed to become clear. Taigu was sad, but he had helped Matthew to his decision all the same. In matters of the spirit the difference between false and true can be as narrow as a needle, but only for the very great does it disappear altogether. Matthew had so long dreamed of the *place* which awaited him at that tiny monastery, a seat kept there for him, not quite so glorious as the empty thrones which Giotto imagined in paradise, but just as certainly reserved. Almost like an economist he had reckoned it out, how his future would pay for his present. He had advanced the day of his retirement with the impatience of a man awaiting his beloved. The anticipated savour of that time was as honey to him. Then he would be at peace and his life would begin.

But, as in almost every human life, something had gone wrong somewhere and the *malin génie* had got in and twisted something, ever so slightly, with huge huge results. Shifting his bulk about restlessly, Matthew had sat upon the floor of Taigu's little paper-screened room, while Taigu sat motionless cross-legged, and they talked the thing to a conclusion. Outside the snow fell, then sun yellowed the shoulders of the mountains against a pale blue sky. A single branch of evergreen curled agonizingly against the wall behind Taigu's shaven head. Matthew's feet were laden with cold, his legs aching with hours of sitting on the floor. Wind rattled the screens. A bell rang. Taigu sighed. It was not good. A human being has only one life. And Matthew had had his.

Yet what had that life amounted to, he wondered. How could a successful career vanish and seem to leave so little behind? There were his youthful hopes and vanities, his happy sense of himself as exceptional, and here was this—heap. While others had employed these twenty, thirty years in art, in marriage, in raising a family, he seemed to have done nothing that had achieved any permanent form at all. There were no jewelled external things: works of art, acts. There were not even any people who had really stood the test: loves, but no love. Of course he had made a great deal of money. Could something as vulgar as that matter? "He had great possessions," he quoted gloomily once to Taigu, who picked up the reference and laughed. Taigu often laughed at inappropriate moments. Matthew could not see the joke.

Not that he had been bored ever. But it appeared that a life could be interesting, amusing, full of the urgencies of state, and ultimately trivial. He had seen important things, he had seen terrible things. He had seen poverty and war, violence, oppression, cruelty, injustice and hunger. He had seen decisive moments in men's lives. He had witnessed a scene in the Red Square when demonstrators were arrested, and when an ordinary citizen, an accidental passerby, had suddenly gone across to join them and had been arrested too. Matthew knew some of the men involved. They were still in labour camps. Some were in "hospitals." Their lives were ruined. Oh he had seen these things, but always as an outsider, as a tourist with diplomatic immunity from the misery of the world, returning to evening drinks in a carpeted embassy hung with minor masterpieces by Gainsborough and Lawrence. He had never truly lived in places where duties were terrible and their consequences life-destroying and long.

Thus he had been cheated by the *malin génie*. A life which had seemed an interval, and which now was seen to have been

filled with trash, had made him what he was, a person profitlessly
spoiled. To have settled down now in Kyoto, to have lived in that
strange world with the idea of which he had so long ago fallen in
love, would be a falsity. He could only have played at the
contemplative life, only enacted it, producing something which
might be very like the real thing but could not be the real thing.
Could not be, because a human being has only one lifetime and
cannot but be fashioned by it. There are no intervals and one is
what one has thought and done. For Matthew, it was too late. He
had made his beloved wait too long. This was the bitter truth
which Taigu made him at last clearly see as he twisted and turned
his fat bulk restlessly upon the tatami.

Of course there were various second bests, but Matthew was
in no mood for second bests. He could rent a little flat in Kyoto,
and live there quietly, hanging around the monasteries, talking
Buddhism with the masters, writing a book about it all. He could
take up an art or craft, painting perhaps, or pottery. Wisdom was
to be had so. Or something humbler. "You might work in the
garden here," Taigu said to him, immobile with calm eyes. But if
one were never to have the pearl of great price? No.

Then there was Austin. Matthew sometimes felt that Austin
would be amazed if he knew how much, on the other side of the
world, he had been thought about. In a way it was a consolation to
Matthew to know that his preoccupation with Austin was not,
though it might have been, the only barrier to his vocation. Could
one have taken such an unresolved personal anguish into that
great silence? To have had his life, at this stage, wrecked simply
by Austin would have been—ridiculous. But now, since what he
had so greatly desired was not to be, there were older and in some
ways more natural duties which asked to be heard. Matthew
knew that if he had always carried Austin within him as a
poisonous and unassimilable alien body, the Matthew which
Austin carried must be that much greater and more venomous.

In a way, Matthew thought, it all rests on nothing, it's all in
Austin's imagination. In reality he had done nothing to Austin. Or
had he? Even at the quarry, Austin said that Matthew had thrown
stones, but this was not true. Or had he perhaps shuffled his feet a
little to make the stones run down the gulley? He remembered

seeing those stones cascading down and feeling pleased, before he heard Austin cry out. He had certainly, at the beginning, laughed. Could a man receive a life sentence for laughing? Yes. The rest had seemed like that, based on nothing, or practically nothing, or perhaps everything. Would he ever be able to talk about it with his brother, gently and with good will?

Running straight to Austin on that first night, with that almost uncannily grotesque outcome, had been a silly nervous thing to do. The sense of inevitable blunder, inevitable resentment, was unnervingly familiar. Someone who was always contriving things like that deserved to be hated. Since then, politely, Austin had evaded him, never at home, never free, courteously, on picture postcards, refusing, for excellently plausible reasons, all Matthew's invitations. I shall have to change my tactics, Matthew thought. The thing had already begun to seem like a quest. It was ironic that the great task of his retirement seemed to be simply to cure his younger brother of a crippling hatred. Yet if it could be done was this not a great thing? For him, yes, thought Matthew. But for me, emptiness. Thus duty often is, he told himself, for the doer, emptiness.

. . . .

"Well, I'm going," said Charlotte, picking up her handbag. "I won't bother you any more. I came to warn you about Austin. I really think he's capable of killing you. I didn't intend the declaration of love. But as you don't believe it it won't worry you. Good-bye."

"Charlotte, wait a minute—"

With a swing of blue and white skirt she was gone and the front door banged as Matthew reached the hall.

He returned to the drawing-room. The chipped white gung-bowl with the peony pattern was sitting in the middle of the mantelpiece. He picked it up and looked down into the creamy white ocean of its depth. He saw again the scene in the Square, the black gawky group of protesters and the man walking across to join them and the miraculous shaking of hands and the trodden snow and the empty scene after the police had taken them all away.

. . . .

"It must have been accidental," said Mavis.

She and Austin were sitting over tea in the drawing-room.

"Oh God, it haunts my dreams so," said Austin.

"Yes. Have some more cake."

"I blame myself—"

"I don't see that you should."

"Oh I do. I think—some people—think I blame everyone except myself, but it's not so."

"For this, no one was to blame."

"Oh well, who know how networks of causes can make one blameworthy. I expect that every time we do anything even slightly bad it sets up a sort of wave which ends with someone committing suicide or murder or something."

"That could be," said Mavis. "That was the sort of thing which when I believed in God I handed over to Him."

"But now—"

"There's nothing to be done. Except to try as usual. One can't see the network."

"Still, one is haunted."

"But I can't see how it can really be your fault."

"Well, I was showing off. He was so fat, you see."

"Fat?"

"Yes, even then. He wasn't as agile as I was and he was afraid to do the climb down. The pool looked so attractive at the bottom of the quarry, all turquoise blue, you know, among golden rocks, and the day was so hot. I got down there and paddled and splashed around and sort of taunted him and he sat up at the top in the heat. He must have hated it. I meant him to."

"And then—"

"Then I took off all my clothes and swam. I can remember it now. One of those hot days when one's body remains warm inside the cool water and the water is like a sort of silver skin. Strange. That must have been about the last happy moment of my life."

"Surely not. And then—"

"I thought he'd come down then, he must have been so envious. I could see him casting around, trying to find an easy way down, but he funked it. Then I got my clothes on and started to climb up, and he threw stones down at me as I was climbing and I fell."

"Wait a moment, Austin. Are you sure he threw the stones? Perhaps you loosened the stones yourself."

"I'm sure he threw one stone at least—it doesn't matter—I can't remember."

"But, Austin, it does matter. You say you've always blamed him for this— But if he didn't really do anything at all—"

"He laughed—"

"But only before you fell."

"He saw that I was in difficulties and he laughed."

"But that's not bad. You'd been mocking him just before—"

"I'm sure he threw a stone—anyway—it doesn't matter—it was terribly much harder to get up than to get down—I got into a panic—then lots of stones started rolling down on top of me—a sort of avalanche—and I couldn't hold on—and I fell all the way down to the bottom and—there it was."

Austin, who had been sitting stiffly staring at the wall as he spoke, put his cup down with a clack, gasped, and was suddenly breathless. He panted, lowering his head and supporting his brow, then half sidled half slipped out of his chair onto the carpet beside the window. He pushed the sash up a little and sat there, leaning his head against the bottom of the window, panting and gasping.

Mavis thought, he is going to have hysterics, in a moment he will be screaming. She ran to the door, ran back again, stared down at him. His face was contorted and he drew long slow shuddering breaths. Then she saw that he was trying to smile.

"Sorry," said Austin, "it's just the pollen."

"The what?"

"The pollen. Asthma, you know. I'll take a tablet in a minute or two. Funny thing, I know the garden's full of beastly pollen, but it does help to breathe fresh air. When one gets a fit any room seems too airless. Of course it's worse for other people, it must look as if I'm dying or something."

"Can I get you anything?"

"A little milk—perhaps I could have the milk jug—thanks—milk helps—don't know why—probably psychological—"

Mavis watched Austin sitting on the floor beside the window drinking milk in gulps out of the Crown Derby milk jug. She felt very odd herself, suddenly breathless and weird. Austin smiled up at her, almost perkily. His golden hair was brushed up, his handsome face scarcely wrinkled, bronzed and glowing. He had left off his spectacles. He looked like a successful actor. She sat down on the floor opposite to him on the other side of the window, tucking her dress in under her knees.

"Better now?"

"Better now. Sorry if I startled you."

"Not at all."

"Where was I? Oh yes. Well, there it was. I broke my right wrist—I fell like that, you see, stretching out my arm—and I broke a lot of little bones in the hand, rather unusual—and it all went stiff—then I couldn't write for ages and ages—and that was, well that was really the end of me."

"Oh nonsense, Austin, you're a fighter, there's a huge will inside you."

"I've got to survive—that's what my will's been for—it's been all used upon that—it's always been touch and go."

"Anyway it wasn't his fault. Even if he threw a stone it wasn't. He didn't mean to hurt you. And you aren't even sure he did throw a stone."

"Oh well—if it wasn't this it was something else—he would have—it's done now—"

"You're so vague. You mustn't be."

"One can be vague about the details. The main thing is overwhelming."

"But if all the details are wrong the main thing may be just in your imagination."

"Well, the imagination is real too."

"But Austin, think, it may be real to you, but that doesn't mean anything is somebody else's fault. I mean, there is a rather important difference between an awful thing and an imaginary awful thing!"

"There's always fault in such cases. Imagination sniffs out what's real. It's a good diagnostician."

"This sounds to me like madness," said Mavis.

"No, no. There's too much proof. Look at my poor old hand. That's real enough. Stiff as a branch of a tree. I can bend it this way and that, but I can't close my fingers. See. No wonder people shun me. It's like a claw, a beastly witch mark."

"There's nothing repulsive about it," said Mavis.

"But you notice it?"

"Well—yes—but only because I know you."

"Oddly enough I don't think it's ever made me unattractive to women. Rather the opposite in fact."

"You've had treatment for it?"

"Then. Not now. Not for years. It's hopeless."

"You might try again," said Mavis. "They find out things. Let me look at it."

Austin stretched out his right hand, revealing a grubby frayed shirt cuff. Mavis took his hand in both of hers. Austin's fingers were red and plump at the end from continual nail-biting. Mavis moved the stiff fingers a little to and fro. "Does that hurt?"

"No."

"It doesn't seem too stiff. I'm sure you should see a specialist. I'll inquire about people."

She went on gently fingering the stiff hand and moving it about.

"Funny thing," said Austin.

"What?"

"It never occurred—to any other woman—to do that—to my hand."

. . . .

Matthew was doing his meditating in the upstairs passenger lounge. It was not yet time for him to meet Ludwig in the bar. They had talked so much at Oxford, there was a slight shyness and by tacit agreement they let each other alone during parts of the day. Then there were the regular rendezvous to be looked forward to. Matthew wished that the voyage might never end.

While Matthew had been helping Ludwig to clarify his
motives for leaving, he had hoped somehow at the same time to
clarify his own; for he had realized, a day or two before he went
to Oxford, that he would probably have to go. He had not of
course discussed his own situation with Ludwig, and Ludwig with
the sweet egoism of youth had not inquired or, Matthew believed,
even wondered. When Matthew announced that, if Ludwig had
no objection, he would accompany him, Ludwig had cried, "Gee,
that's great of you!" and seemed to imagine that the pleasure of
his company would be quite a good enough reason for Matthew to
take the trip. And in a way, thought Matthew, he was right, even
righter than he dreamed. But of course there were other things.
And he had not told Ludwig that he was going away forever.

His departure had come to seem to him inevitable. But what
did that mean? Had Austin, with unerring instinct, made the one
move which would render his brother powerless? Had he not only
broken the spell but turned the tables? Matthew's quaint sadness
at having been unable to be the instrument of his brother's
salvation seemed something puny now when there was so much
more to regret. Had he lived all these years with himself to find
himself at the end still so unpredictable? Was he now just running
away out of chagrin?

Something or other had, in however ghastly a sense, done
Austin "good." Perhaps it was simply Dorina's death. And
perhaps the "good" was temporary, a prelude to some new and
different phase of obsession. If Austin now seemed "free"
without going through any of the procedures of spiritual reconciliation and liberation recognized by Matthew, could it still be
that he was, in this respect at least, really free? Was it genuinely
the case that Austin didn't care any more? It almost seemed to
Matthew at one point that Austin had simply forgotten, as if some
banal almost impersonal relationship had been slipped into the
place where the horror had been. The fear seemed to have gone
and the hatred was changed. To say that the hatred was gone
would be to say too much. But again, in some way quite outside
Matthew's calculations, it had changed.

At that stage, and when that was clear, that change of some
quite unauthorized kind was taking place, had taken place,

Matthew felt with a blessed simplicity that it was time for him to leave off. Any further close interest or concern from him would be not only fruitless but intrusive and improper. Nature could now take its course in some soothingly vulgar way. There could be drifting apart. He could even allow himself to come, and he laughed suddenly at this, to detest Austin heartily. That was where his high purposes had got him, and the best they could apparently do. Oddly enough, Taigu would have appreciated this. So it would drift on, London was quite large enough now to contain them both, and the quality of this failure would be the quality of his own final acceptance of an utter ordinariness of life.

But then, with the inner gasp of a man told by his doctor that he has a serious illness, Matthew realized how very much more awful the situation really was. Of course he had not minded Mavis looking after Austin, of course he had waited and understood. Of course Mavis was in some harmoniously inevitable way Matthew's future. This was the resting place and this the end. Time had circled to this point. And when Matthew had swallowed the knowledge that there was nothing more he could ever do for Austin except let him alone, and that this would be quite adequate, he associated Mavis instinctively with this sense of defeat and the inception of a humbler, more domestic sort of life quite devoid of the drama which he realized he had with a certain eagerness returned to England to find. The unexpected simplicity of his love for Mavis had even seemed to symbolize the modest enlightenment which he had achieved.

But at a certain moment, with the sudden alteration of quantity into quality which dialecticians speak of, he saw. One way of putting it was that Austin had simply stayed with Mavis too long and had contaminated her, Matthew felt stirrings of a sudden blind painful rage which made him feel, for the first time in his life, that he resembled his brother. With a strange precision Austin had taken his revenge for the pollution of Dorina. Of course Austin had not really done this "on purpose." It had all been, like so many other things in the story, accidental. But it was too beautiful not to have been also the product of instinct. Of course too they were not, he supposed, in love with each other. They did not need to be in love with each other, any more than he and Dorina had needed to be. Nor had Mavis's love for him swerved or faded. It did not need to fade, for everything to have become suddenly so dreadful. Naturally, Mavis had become fond of Austin, as women so often did become fond of Austin, sorry for him, maternal, and so on. As Matthew had sincerely said in a letter, such plain affection was just what Austin needed at this juncture of his life. But then what? Mavis's affection could not be treated like a sticking plaster and pulled off when the wound had healed.

Austin was cunning. And Mavis, it became increasingly clear, expected Matthew somehow to "deal." She could not manage without an initiative from Matthew which would inevitably seem like a re-enactment of the past. Of course Austin was not "cured," Matthew could now see, of course the deep things were exactly as they had always been, and exactly as they would always be, whatever pious hopes the self-styled good might have about the matter. Mavis must be claimed or lost. Austin must be allowed once more to play the role of victim. This he expected and perhaps even wanted. The stage had been set again by whatever deep mythological forces control the destinies of men.

Part Three

Kin, Near-Kin, and Generations

In no society does a nuclear family *system* exist; that is, in no society do most families maintain few or no relations with their more extended kin. In all, including our own, other kin play an important role. A few subgroups within the larger society, such as the Shakers or the Oneida in the United States, have tried to reduce the family structure and even the family itself to almost nothing; and some revolutionists (including Plato) have preached such a doctrine, but extended kinship relations resist these efforts.

In most societies without large governmental or economic structures, the need to organize many people for large enterprises, such as building roads or a temple, establishing a market relationship with a distant port or country, or administering a large estate, led to the creation of lineages, clans, or other collective kin units.

Matrilineages trace kinship through the maternal line, and patrilineages through the paternal line, but in both the husband-wife bond is less central than in our own. Extended kin have a larger voice in the affairs of any given nuclear or conjugal family unit. Elder kin are given more respect. In many patrilineal societies, it is difficult for a young man to marry without the social and economic support of his lineage.

In an industrial society young adults can be hired and promoted independently of their elder kin. Legally, they can be free of the extended kinship network. Although most of us have taken the family name of our fathers, the patriline is not a unit or collectivity, and we can ignore it in favor of our mother's line if we like them better. Western societies did not give a prominent place to lineages even in the distant past, and kindreds have not been important for hundreds of years. Even if great kin groupings have been of central significance in Western society, they would very likely have been undermined by industrialization.

Nevertheless, the popular and literary view of the modern family as isolated, rootless, free from both the burdens and pleasure of extended kin, and thus totally unlike rural families of the past, is not correct at all. Research over the past two decades has shown that almost all family units maintain social contact with a wide range of relatives. Almost every family lives in a network of extended kin and maintains sporadic or frequent contact with from 100 to 200 different people in this category.

It is easy to see why this is so. Many of the relatives *outside* the conjugal unit cannot be excluded or totally ignored without also hurting or angering some member within it. For example, a young wife cannot insult or exclude her mother's mother or mother's sister, her brother's wife or brother's wife's sister, without also annoying members of her immediate family. More-over, precisely to the extent that business and economic relations within modern society are emotionally unsatisfying, the kin network offers at least a slightly higher chance of small friend-ships without great cost.

Although "mother-in-law jokes" abound in this and in many other cultures, and in-laws are often viewed in literature as in conversation as a source of strain, it is safe to say that most people enjoy these interactions because they combine some security without forced intimacy. The fact that if we trace our kin relations in all directions and through all the in-law possibilities, we will encounter a relatively large number of people, means that we can pick and choose among this pool of human beings, and while remaining dutiful to our kin obligations locate a number of people whose company we do enjoy.

Moreover, a closer look at economic and business relations in our time suggests that far more business transactions, and certainly far more job possibilities, are opened up through kin relations than current discussions about "promotion and hiring through merit" might suggest. For example, for some decades most jobs in the building trades have gone to relatives. It is likely that few people begin small businesses without persuading one or more relatives to invest in their enterprise. Even where bureaucratic rules are supposed to be followed, an individual who would reject a relative's plea for help in processing an application, or getting a lower-level job, would be criticized by others, not alone by his or her kin. If we exhibit some favoritism in bureaucratic or business dealings with a relative, most people will accept our plea of kinship pressures as an adequate excuse.

Although modern essayists are correct in asserting that great family picnics have almost disappeared, we cannot infer that people have less interaction with their relatives than in the past when our society was rural. We no longer help our relatives pitch hay or raise a barn, but relatives help one another in various other ways. More fundamentally, the ease of modern transportation and communication may in fact mean that relatives see and interact with one another even more than they did 100 years ago in the United States.

Beyond that, the simple *generational* line of kinship remains strong. Of course, someone who claims to be founding a "family dynasty," or who is "building an estate" for his children, might today be viewed as unusual if not odd. Nevertheless, there seems to be no great diminution in the concern that fathers feel for their sons, or grandfathers for their grandchildren. Few people want to have no children, or even want to cut entirely their relations with their grandparents. It is common now for young people to leave home and to live independently for a while, but very few continue that rejection of the older generation. Rebellion against the political views, the hovering concern, or the stifling emotionality of family life constitute a common *phase* in the lives of young people today, but most of them (especially when they themselves become parents) work out later a new mode of life in which they accept, and are accepted by, their parents and grandparents. Most literary writing of our time has focused on the rebellious phase, but the return phase is equally important and deserves as much of our attention. Mark Twain captured some part of this reversal of attitude and opinion many years ago in noting that when he was a young boy, he thought his father was the stupidest man he ever met. Much later in life he met his father again, and was astounded at how much smarter his father had become.

Chapter 7

Extended Family and In-Laws

Although we are accustomed to think of the maintenance of relations with our more distant kin as a kind of "rural survival," a set of obligations that we sometimes carry out resentfully because we do not wish to annoy or hurt the feelings of our parents, not many social institutions survive for long unless there are *contemporary* supports for them. The extended family network is a kind of social invention, and it is maintained because of its own strengths and weaknesses, not merely because of some vague force called "tradition." In a world where a large number of services and aids come to us only if we fit a rigid bureaucratic rule, relatives constitute a much more flexible set of resources. Similarly, we may need help *now*, while the bank wants to take some time to ascertain our financial reliability. Or, because we all have idiosyncratic traits and needs, we can more easily count on our relatives being willing to recognize these particular foibles and to accept them, while bureaucratic regulations often will not.

The extended network also has a greater continuity than the individual family, precisely because in modern times it is a rather amorphous, sprawling set of possible relationships, rather than a neatly defined unit. If the father or the mother dies in a conjugal family, one half of the adults have disappeared, and can be counted on no longer. However, in an extended family network, though a greater *number* of people will die over a period of years, the impact of any one person's death is much less. The help that we can get from relatives is, of course, not as great as the help we could expect from our siblings or parents, but that amount may be crucial, and in times of crisis they may even rise to a genuine collective effort.

Sociologists of the family have not dealt adequately with the place of in-laws and extended family in modern society. Anthropologists have dealt with this theme extensively in tribal societies, but that is because these relationships constitute much of the social structure in those societies.

Consider, however, the difficulty of treating these relationships adequately in a literary work. Even in a large novel, the focus is likely to be on a love relationship between a man and a woman, or on an individual man or woman in his or her successive love relationships, while other people are chiefly drawn in as they interact with a central couple. In modern works, especially, with their strong attack on urban, bureaucratic, industrial society, that complex environment must be given substantial attention. Consequently, a novel that would give some role to the vast range of people in our kinship network would seem to pose an almost insuperable problem of exposition. We read words successively, and the plot (if any) is linear, while our network spreads out simultaneously in all directions: It is a network, a structure. Consequently, when modern literary artists discuss relatives in this network, they are likely to choose only a small number, with particular traits and qualities that make them fascinating as individuals, rather than as representative of an extended family structure.

In Praise of Aunts

Phyllis McGinley

Although the context and the tonalities in this poem suggest an upper-middle-class or upper-class world (where, indeed, extended kin relations are likely to be firmer and more extensive), perhaps most readers will be reminded of some of their experiences with their aunts—or uncles, for that matter.

The category itself, however, seems a little surprising; that is, though we can remember our *individual* relations with this or that aunt, and may remember aunts of friends of ours, we do not think of "aunts" as a class at all nowadays, because we do not use the rhetoric of kinship much. Note, too, the crucial line in the poem, which also applies to some other relatives: "Aunts care, but only mildly care." Their emotional feelings are warm, but their stake in our every decision and attitude is not so great that they are impelled to oppress us.

Of all that tribe the young must do
Familial obedience to,
Whom we salute on anniversaries,
Whose names we learn while new in nurseries
Or borrow at baptismal fonts,
The soothingest are aunts.

Aunts are discreet, a little shy
By instinct. They forbear to pry
Into recesses of the spirit
Where apprehensions lie.
Yet, given a tale to hear, they *hear* it.

Aunts spinster pamper us with praise,
And seats for worldly matinées
With coffee after. Married aunts,

From Phyllis McGinley, *Times Three*, The Viking Press, Inc., New York, 1960, pp. 43–44.

Attentive to material wants,
Run rather to the shared comestible,
Taboo or indigestible;
Are lenient but cool;
And let us, if we must, play fool.

Aunts carry no duty in their faces.
Their letters, mailed from far-off places,
Are merely letters meant to read
(Answerable at a moderate speed),
Not cries of need
Or vessels heavy with their hopes.
Aunts also send,
Tucked into casual envelopes,
Money entirely ours to spend.

At night they do not lie awake
Shuddering for our sorrows' sake.
Beneath our flesh we seldom wear
Their skeletons, nor need we stare
Into a looking glass and see
Their images begin to be.
Aunts care, but only mildly care,
About our winter moods,
Posture, or social attitudes,
And whether we've made a friend or dropped one.

All should have aunts, or else adopt one.

Black Spring
Henry Miller

Even in the modern period of easily available pornography, Henry Miller's exaltations of sex continue to attract readers. Here, however, in *Black Spring,* he introduces us to another set of his experiences, the turmoil, excitement, and delights of his extended family. As is typical of Miller, he reminds us not so much of the surface civilities of family life as of its deeper pleasures and the pathologies, giving us a long list of the psychological and physical ills of family members.

Here, too, is the common focus of extended family on a grand meal, a symbol of togetherness and a concrete manifestation of giving delight to one another.

He then turns, however, to an experience that many have had, even in families that have been relatively fortunate. For if we include in our circle of kin a very large number of relatives by blood or marriage, it is likely that at least a few will suffer great misfortune and tragedy, even insanity.

Thus we move from the general evocation of the closeness, warmth, and acceptance among family members to a collective focus on a decision to exclude one member by putting her in an asylum.

Although Miller himself is one of the least responsible members of his family, he is perhaps chosen to take Mele to the mental institution because, whatever his wildness, he feels a special warmth for Mele, which she reciprocates by trust. Most large families have one or more "kin-keepers," adults who seem to encourage others to maintain their kin relations intact, who help out the less fortunate, and who act generally as expressive leaders. Miller is not one of these. Miller is not a kin-keeper, and indeed his autobiographical writings show how, ruthlessly or in anger, he slips away from these bonds. However, in most cases it is not typically the kin-keeper who carries out such a disagreeable task. In any event, as we noted earlier, the problem of easing the

Henry Miller, *Black Spring*, Obelisk Press, 1954; Grove Press, Inc., New York, 1963, pp. 103–110.

transition from family life to the asylum is not given over to a
bureaucracy, but is assumed by a member of the family.

However, *always merry and bright*! If it was before the war and
the thermometer down to zero or below, if it happened to be
Thanksgiving Day, or New Year's or a birthday, or just any old
excuse to get together, then off we'd trot, the whole family, to
join the other freaks who made up the living family tree. It always
seemed astounding to me how jolly they were in our family
despite the calamities that were always threatening. Jolly in spite
of everything. There was cancer, dropsy, cirrhosis of the liver,
insanity, thievery, mendacity, buggery, incest, paralysis, tape-
worms, abortions, triplets, idiots, drunkards, ne'er-do-wells,
fanatics, sailors, tailors, watch-makers, scarlet fever, whooping
cough, meningitis, running ears, chorea, stutterers, jailbirds,
dreamers, story-tellers, bartenders—and finally there was Uncle
George and Tante Melia. The morgue and the insane asylum. A
merry crew and the table loaded with good things—with red
cabbage and green spinach, with roast pork and turkey and
sauerkraut, with kartoffel-klösze and sour black gravy, with
radishes and celery, with stuffed goose and peas and carrots, with
beautiful white cauliflower, with apple sauce and figs from
Smyrna, with bananas big as a blackjack, with cinnamon cake and
Streussel Kuchen, with chocolate layer cake and nuts, all kinds of
nuts, walnuts, butternuts, almonds, pecans, hickory nuts, with
lager beer and bottled beer, with white wines and red, with
champagne, kümmel, malaga, port, with schnapps, with fiery
cheeses, with dull, innocent store cheese, with flat Holland
cheeses, with limburger and schmierkäse, with home made wines,
elderberry wine, with cider, hard and sweet, with rice pudding
and tapioca, with roast chestnuts, mandarines, olives, pickles,
with red caviar and black, with smoked sturgeon, with lemon
meringue pie, with lady fingers and chocolate eclairs, with
macarons and cream puffs, with black cigars and long thin
stogies, with Bull Durham and Long Tom and meerschaums with
corn-cobs and tooth-picks, wooden tooth-picks which gave you
gum-boils the day after, and napkins a yard wide with your initials

stitched in the corner, and a blazing coal fire and the windows steaming, everything in the world before your eyes except a finger bowl.

Zero weather and crazy George, with one arm bitten off by a horse, dressed in dead men's remnants. Zero weather and Tante Melia looking for the birds she left in her hat. Zero, zero, and the tugs snorting below in the harbor, the ice floes bobbing up and down, and long thin streams of smoke curling fore and aft. The wind blowing down at seventy miles an hour; tons and tons of snow all chopped up into tiny flakes and each one carrying a dagger. The icicles hanging like cork-screws outside the window, the wind roaring, the panes rattling. Uncle Henry is singing "Hurrah for the German Fifth!" His vest is open, his suspenders are down, the veins stand out on his temples. *Hurrah for the German Fifth!*

Up in the loft the creaking table is spread; down below is the warm stable, the horses whinnying in the stalls, whinnying and champing and pawing and stomping, and the fine aromatic smell of manure and horse piss, of hay and oats, of steaming blankets and dry cruds, the smell of malt and old wood, of leather harness and tanbark floats up and rests like incense over our heads.

The table is standing on horses and the horses are standing in warm piss and every now and then they get frisky and whisk their tails and they fart and whinny. The stove is glowing like a ruby, the air is blue with smoke. The bottles are under the table, on the dresser, in the sink. Crazy George is trying to scratch his neck with an empty sleeve. Ned Martini, the ne'er-do-well, is fiddling with the phonograph; his wife Carrie is guzzling it from the tin growler. The brats are downstairs in the stable playing stinkfinger in the dark. In the street, where the shanties begin, the kids are making a sliding-pond. It's blue everywhere, with cold and smoke and snow. Tante Melia is sitting in a corner fingering a rosary. Uncle Ned is repairing a harness. The three grandfathers and the two great-grandfathers are huddled near the stove talking about the Franco-Prussian war. Crazy George is lapping up the dregs. The women are getting closer together, their voices low, their

tongues clacking. Everything fits together like a jig-saw puzzle—
faces, voices, gestures, bodies. Each one gravitates within his
own orbit. The phonograph is working again, the voices get
louder and shriller. The phonograph stops suddenly. I oughtn't to
have been there when they blurted it out, but I was there and I
heard it. I heard that big Maggie, the one who kept a saloon out in
Flushing, well that Maggie had slept with her own brother and
that's why George was crazy. She slept with everybody—except
her own husband. And then I heard that she used to beat George
with a leather belt, used to beat him until he foamed at the mouth.
That's what brought on the fits. And then Mele sitting there in the
corner—she was another case. She was queer even as a child. So
was the mother, for that matter. It was too bad that Paul had died.
Paul was Mele's husband. Yes, everything would have been all
right if that woman from Hamburg hadn't shown up and cor-
rupted Paul. What could Mele do against a clever woman like
that—against a shrewd strumpet! Something would have to be
done about Mele. It was getting dangerous to have her around.
Just the other day they caught her sitting on the stove. Fortunately the fire was low. But supposing she took it into her head
to set fire to the house—when they were all asleep? It was a pity
that she couldn't hold a job any more. The last place they had
found for her was such a nice berth, such a kind woman. Mele
was getting lazy. She had had it too easy with Paul.

The air was clear and frosty when we stepped outdoors. The
stars were crisp and sparkly and everywhere, lying over the
bannisters and steps and window-ledges and gratings, was the
pure white snow, the driven snow, the white mantle that covers
the dirty, sinful earth. Clear and frosty the air, pure, like deep
draughts of ammonia, and the skin smooth as chamois. Blue stars,
beds and beds of them, drifting with the antelopes. Such a
beautiful deep silent night, as if under the snow there lay hearts of
gold, as if this warm German blood was running away in the
gutter to stop the mouth of hungry babes, to wash the crime and
ugliness of the world away. Deep night and the river choked with
ice, the stars dancing, swirling, spinning like tops. Along the
broken street we straggled, the whole family. Walking along the
pure white crust of the earth, leaving tracks, foot-stains. The old

German family sweeping the snow with a Christmas tree. The whole family there, uncles, cousins, brothers, sisters, fathers, grandfathers. The whole family is warm and winey and no one thinks of the other, of the sun that will come in the morning, of the errands to run, of the doctor's verdict, of all the cruel, ghastly duties that foul the day and make this night holy, this holy night of blue stars and deep drifts, of arnica blossoms and ammonia, of asphodels and carborundum.

No one knew that Tante Melia was going completely off her nut, that when we reached the corner she would leap forward like a reindeer and bite a piece out of the moon. At the corner she leapt forward like a reindeer and she shrieked. "The moon, the moon!" she cried, and with that her soul broke loose, jumped clean out of her body. Eighty-six million miles a minute it travelled. Out, out, to the moon, and nobody could think quick enough to stop it. Just like that it happened. In the twinkle of a star.

And now I'm going to tell you what those bastards said to me . . .

They said—*Henry, you take her to the asylum tomorrow. And don't tell them that we can afford to pay for her.*

Fine! *Always merry and bright!* The next morning we boarded the trolley together and we rode out into the country. If Mele asked where we were going I was to say—"To visit Aunt Monica." But Mele didn't ask any questions. She sat quietly beside me and pointed to the cows now and then. She saw blue cows and green ones. She knew their names. She asked what happened to the moon in the day-time. And did I have a piece of liverwurst by any chance?

During the journey I wept—I couldn't help it. When people are too good in this world they have to be put under lock and key. There's something wrong with people who are too good. It's true Mele was lazy. She was born lazy. It's true that Mele was a poor housekeeper. It's true Mele didn't know how to hold on to a husband when they found her one. When Paul ran off with the woman from Hamburg Mele sat in a corner and wept. The others wanted her to do something—put a bullet in him, raise a rumpus, sue for alimony. Mele sat quiet. Mele wept. Mele hung her head.

What little intelligence she had deserted her. She was like a pair of torn socks that are kicked around here, there, everywhere. Always turning up at the wrong moment.

Then one day Paul took a rope and hanged himself. Mele must have understood what had happened because now she went completely crazy. The day before they found her eating her own dung. The day before that they found her sitting on the stove.

And now she's very tranquil and she calls the cows by their first name. The moon fascinates her. She has no fear because I'm with her and she always trusted me. I was her favorite. Even though she was a halfwit she was good to me. The others were more intelligent, but their hearts were bad.

When brother Adolphe used to take her for a carriage ride the others used to say—"Mele's got her eye on him!" But I think that Mele must have talked just as innocently then as she's talking to me now. I think that Mele, when she was performing her marriage duties, must have been dreaming innocently of the beautiful gifts she would give to everybody. I don't think that Mele had any knowledge of sin or of guilt or remorse. I think that Mele was born a half-witted angel. I think Mele was a saint.

Sometimes when she was fired from a job they used to send me to fetch her. Mele never knew her way home. And I remember how happy she was whenever she saw me coming. She would say innocently that she wanted to stay with us. Why couldn't she stay with us? I used to ask myself that over and over. Why couldn't they make a place for her by the fire, let her sit there and dream, if that's what she wanted to do? Why must everybody *work*—even the saints and the angels? Why must half-wits set a good example?

I'm thinking now that after all it may be good for Mele where I'm taking her. No more work. Just the same, I'd rather they had made a corner for her somewhere.

Walking down the gravel path towards the big gates Mele becomes uneasy. Even a puppy knows when it is being carried to a pond to be drowned. Mele is trembling now. At the gate they are waiting for us. The gate yawns. Mele is on the inside, I am on the outside. They are trying to coax her along. They are gentle with her now. They speak to her so gently. But Mele is terror-stricken. She turns and runs towards the gate. I am still standing there. She puts her arms through the bars and clutches my neck. I kiss her tenderly on the forehead. Gently I unlock her arms. The others are going to take her again. I can't bear seeing that. I must go. I must run. For a full minute, however, I stand and look at her. Her eyes seem to have grown enormous. Two great round eyes, full and black as the night, staring at me uncomprehendingly. No maniac can look that way. No idiot can look that way. Only an angel or a saint.

When I ran away from the gate I stopped beside a high wall and burying my head in my arms, my arms against the wall, I sobbed as I had never sobbed since I was a child. Meanwhile they were giving Mele a bath and putting her into regulation dress; they parted her hair in the middle, brushed it down flat and tied it into a knot at the nape of the neck. Thus no one looks exceptional. All have the same crazy look, whether they are half crazy or three-quarters crazy, or just slightly cracked. When you say "may I have pen and ink to write a letter" they say "yes" and they hand you a broom to sweep the floor. If you pee on the floor absent-mindedly you have to wipe it up. You can sob all you like but you mustn't violate the rules of the house. A bug-house has to be run in orderly fashion just as any other house.

Once a week Mele would be allowed to receive. For thirty years the sisters had been visiting the bug-house. They were fed up with it. When they were tiny tots they used to visit their mother on Blackwell's Island. The mother always said to be careful of Mele, to watch over her. When Mele stood at the gate with eyes so round and bright her mind must have travelled back like an express train. Everything must have leaped to her mind at once. Her eyes were so big and bright, as if they saw more than they could comprehend. Bright with terror, and beneath the terror a limitless confusion. That's what made them so beautifully bright. You have to be crazy to see things so lucidly, so all at once. If you're great you can stay that way and people will believe in you, swear by you, turn the world upside down for you. But if you're only partly great, or just a nobody, then what happens to you is lost.

Loving Hands at Home

Diane Johnson

Diane Johnson affords us a glimpse at the extremely familistic life of a subgroup in the United States that most of us have not experienced, that of the Mormons. However, several additional aspects of this account should be noted. First, although she is a "participant observer" living intimately with her in-laws, in *Loving Hands at Home,* she is defined by the Mormons and by her in-laws as an outsider. She does not have a full understanding of their religious or social patterns. On the other hand, because of that, she is more sensitive to some of their differences and their assumptions about life that they themselves do not question at all.

In addition, they feel a class superiority over her, for though she is obviously well educated, they consider her basically "underprivileged" and are a bit fearful that she will commit some social or cultural blunder.

In most great societies, the "in-marrying wife" must do most of the adjusting. She no longer has her relatives about her, to support either her individual foibles or the values and attitudes she has acquired since childhood. Here the narrator is aided somewhat, for she is devoted to her husband and genuinely respects her relatives. At the same time, we are quickly made aware of the extent to which she rejects their style of life, their complacency, and even the ways they oppress one another.

Central, of course, is her feeling of awkwardness and general incompetence at the traditional maternal skills, from keeping a house tidy to cooking, and her awareness that she can never hope to emulate the matriarchal mother-in-law—whom she cannot reject openly, of course, because thereby she would undermine her relationship with her husband.

Consider too, how typically familistic is the extent to which one's relatives "never give up" in their efforts to

From Diane Johnson, *Loving Hands at Home,* Harcourt, Brace Jovanovich, New York, 1968.

reform one's attitudes and behavior. The matriarch is constantly reminding her, either directly or subtly, of her failures. It is easiest to fight back by rejecting all of those
traditional home skills as irrelevant or silly, but the wife does
not. She neither aspires to become like her mother-in-law
nor wishes to engage in open rebellion. Ideally, she would
like to be accepted for what she is, but she sees that there is
little chance of that deeper acceptance. At best, she can
suffer through the lengthy Sunday dinner, with its accom-
panying byplay of surveillance, report, approval or disapproval, and plans for the immediate future. The reader may
find it worthwhile, if a little painful, to recall similar family
dinners in his or her own experience.

I had fallen off the motorcycle on Friday. On Sunday we went as
usual to family dinner at Garth's parents', along with Mahonri and
Joan, Sebastian and Patty, and the eleven children. The Mahonris
have seven. On the way there I felt wary, alerted by my bruised
bottom to the suspicion that, if all was not right in my nice life,
things might also be wrong in theirs, but as soon as we got there I
lapsed into the mouse disguise I always seemed to wear with
them. I could never be the person the family expected—a model
Mormon wife for Garth—or myself, which had at least the virtue
of coming easy to me, so that I never blamed them for disapproving of me. I just accepted Family Dinner. So did they.

Like most Mormon families, the Fry family is very close. We
spent all our Sundays together, and at least one evening during
the week, and saw one another during the day to swap baby-
sitting and the like. And we were always full of love and
co-operation and peace and concord. I had supposed we were
happy as well. At least I thought that they were. I was the only
non-Mormon, and tended to define myself in their context, like a
second-class citizen—denied the vote but happy by association
and content with my lot.

Besides my lack of religion, I think my underprivileged
background had contributed from the first to their reservations
about me. "Underprivileged" was linked in their minds with
phrases like "juvenile delinquent," "unwed mother," and, per-

haps, "mentally retarded." For a long time they were tense about me at concerts and fancy gatherings. Father Fry would launch into careful explanations of things the rest of them were bound to have known for years.

"Ah, the rondo is an amusing little form," he would say. "But just when you think it's over and are about to begin clapping, there comes the coda. I myself usually wait for everybody else to begin clapping first." Followed by jovial chuckles.

Another thing that has worried them is that my hair is dyed. Mother Fry associates "peroxide blonde" with "chippies," which is what she always calls them. I have never been sure she doesn't think I used to be one, and that Garth was involved, by marrying me, in a heroic rehabilitation effort, like someone in a Russian novel.

Of course she didn't really think that. I tend to make her sound Victorian and prim, when actually she was president of the Relief Society, and felt that after home and church the community is a proper object for woman's concern, and had many other modern attitudes. But about hair dye there remains a lot of superstition in the world.

The Fry family, again as is frequently true of Mormons, is a curious mixture of contemporary sophistication and farmy anachronism. Their house is an example of this. It is of the best all-electric, built-in-kitchen California kind, in which Mother Fry's Duncan Phyfe looks uncomfortable, and she keeps trying to grow tulips and lilacs outside it, like an Englishwoman who refuses to give in to India. The house was built at a time when dining rooms were out of fashion, so the mahogany table, eight chairs, and immense sideboard are squeezed into an L-shaped nook off the living room. It was here that Mother Fry did her best each Sunday to effect a stately, formal meal—damask, silver candlesticks, hand-hemstitched napkins, gracious talk. But it was always marred, because she and Joan and Patty and I were up and down, running to change courses and to supervise the eleven children, whom we put at a picnic table on the patio, or in the kitchen in bad weather.

Every Sunday each daughter-in-law was assigned her share of potluck, and this time I had brought a cake. Although it had fallen on one side, I had evened it up by putting extra frosting between the layers, and although, on the outside, the frosting knife had pulled away the surface of the cake in several places, giving it a littered, mouse-eaten look, I meant well. Cakes, I have heard someplace, are symbolic of love. I put it on the table, and Garth averted his eyes.

"Ah, my favorite, chocolate. With, ah, is it mint frosting?" Father Fry said. He was always tactful, not out of kindness so much as because tact best preserved inviolate his sanctum of private thoughts.

"Just a small piece for me. The waistline," said the oldest brother, Mahonri. He has the heavy, spreading body of the former athlete, and, from his guilty manner, seems always to hear the ghostly voices of old coaches behind him at the table. His wife, Joan, smiled, knowing he had never refused a large piece of *her* cake. She hypocritically praised my lime frosting. From the rest came only a moment of suspicious and embarrassed silence, and finally a stifled sigh from Mother Fry. The sad cake huddled in the center of the festive board, and we all received it silently, the way polite people receive an improper remark. Father Fry, temporizing, brandished the cake knife in reluctant preparation, and I vaguely knew, as always, that their disapproval of me had something to do with cakes. But that seemed silly, like a club which one is not invited to join. Father Fry impassively cut and handed around pieces of cake. The cut pieces revealed great internal holes, as in Swiss cheese. The silence was still strained, but strove for cheerfulness. Suddenly we heard a loud crunch and an exclamation from the middle brother, Sebastian. With an apologetic glance at me, as if to say he hated making this fuss, he took a small brown bottle cap from his mouth, and, in full view of everyone, strove unsuccessfully to secrete it under the edge of his plate. It was the cap off the vanilla bottle. I honestly have never figured out why these things happened to me.

"It would be a great relief, Mother," Garth said, "if Karen and I could just chip in and pay for our share on Sundays, rather than having her make these embarrassing messes every week." His voice aspired to a jocular, affectionate tone, but fell back with a defeated quiver of irritation.

Now the embarrassment, which had been hovering like a fog, capable of dispersion by the bright touch of a tactful remark, descended gloomy and damp. If someone had laughed and said "Poor old Karen," we might have been able to think of my domestic incompetence as a regrettable but endearing fault. Instead it was stonily avoided, the way the truly unforgivable always is. Domestic accomplishments had for the Frys a mystical significance related to femininity and the life force. The hearth, cakes, the cradle are still viable symbols, and lurk like native gods in the breasts of women outwardly converted to the League of Women Voters, and in the breasts of their husbands, the disenfranchised priests of an older worship. Actually the Fry men are not disenfranchised. Mormonism, like all successful creeds, protects and incorporates the old symbols. Although I was no Mormon, I was no apostate about femininity. It was simply that my cakes never turned out.

"Of course, if you'd rather not bring anything," Mother Fry said, looking annoyed, as if she'd been caught exploiting an imbecile child, "there's no need to 'chip in,' as you put it. Joan and Patty and I can take care of things perfectly well. I always supposed that Karen *preferred* to do her share."

I knew I ought to assure them that I did prefer, but truthfully I did not. I had grown discouraged. I could never in the world approach the accomplishments of Mother Fry and my sisters-in-law. They made their own clothing, pies, preserves, rugs, curtains, gifts, hats, greeting cards, dishes (Mother Fry and Patty dabbled in ceramics), soap (just Mother Fry), leather sandals, purses, simple furniture (Patty), and bread.

"There's nothing wrong with this cake," Father Fry said. "Has a fine, chocolatey flavor." A tense lump of resentment and tears in my throat dissolved gratefully. Father Fry was almost the only person in the family I loved, or would have had he not been too remote to inspire love. It seemed to me that he had been badly misled by Mother Fry, and because of her believed that good women not only ought to be but were interested mainly in housekeeping. Homemaking, he termed it, having gathered from somewhere that this was more tactful. There were other anachronistic things about Father Fry, too; he used adjectives like "corny." "Trim" is the word that describes *him* best—trim clothes, shape, manners, words. He is well-dressed, -shaven, -spoken, -thought-of. He is long and long-faced, with pleasant reddish golf-course coloring and white hair, gone at the top of his head but fluffy at the sides. The bare part of his forehead is creased with intellectual wrinkles, and he has square eyebrows. If he has not shaved since morning, his cheeks look as if they were sprinkled with silver dust. All this silver-and-rose color gives him a valuable look.

And he has a valuable air, as subtly befits an economist. His clothes cost money, his stereo costs, his car costs. Father Fry, though not in any way ostentatious, is used to being well-appointed; everything about him is so well-appointed and so effortless, one feels that at his birth his parents must have somehow endowed him with perpetual care, like a California burial plot. In spite of everything, I thought him basically kind and simple, very admiring of Mother Fry's hooked rugs, very enthusiastic about her home-pickled pickles.

"Those holes result from underbeating," Mother Fry said, her essential pedantry conquering her hostility.

"It's such a mystery to me. I think it's clever of you to be able to tell," I heard myself say in an affected, superior voice. I knew I sounded hateful, but I was determined not to sound cowed. Secretly I wondered how you do tell what ails a cake. I longed to know, both because I liked cake and because I believed a person has no right to despise what he cannot do.

Mother Fry, voice sweetened with maternal self-consciousness, began to discourse upon baking. Her husband and sons, regarding her with the rigid smiles of people who are not listening, looked nonetheless pleased at her expertise. Mother Fry has an M.A. in home economics, and it has always been a source of pleasure to her men that her special province is so motherly and suitable. She is a splendid cook, though she runs to molded gelatin salads and the use of marshmallows, and takes perverse pleasure in the concoction of archaic dishes (like head cheese) which require repulsive preparation. Now, about cakes, her deep voice grew richer, with overtones of experience.

Mother Fry is a handsome woman, but aggressively grizzled,

as if she cherishes her wrinkles and stiff gray hairs like merit badges of a useful life. She wears no powder or lipstick, does nothing to blur the lineaments of pioneer womanhood one sees in her face. Mother Fry has a genuine pioneer temperament as well, and once enjoyed modest fame as the author of an article in a church magazine to the effect that babies should be born at home because this provides a more natural and thrilling experience for everyone, including the older children, who, I suppose, would derive from the groans and shrieks of their mothers a sense of the miracle of birth. The three Fry boys were, in fact, born in hospitals.

Mother Fry was now describing the principle behind clarifying the butter, and her eyes had brightened fanatically. Her air of indifference to her person and of dedication to some higher endeavor had always made her look to me like an old feminist. She has the sturdy marching body of the Bloomerette, and proudly observes that she can do in a day enough work to kill the average man. It was surprising, in view of this, to hear her voice ring so true on the difference between single- and double-acting baking powder. Mother Fry is of course too young to have been a Bloomerette. I knew from an old photograph that she had in fact been a flapper, very slim and pink-kneed, with smudgy eyes beneath the deep rim of her hat. This photograph, which always made me feel sad, made no prediction of domestic fanaticism. In it one pale hand lay open, limp and dainty, on her lap. Now she is fond of saying, "Look at these hands," and thrusting out, for her sons and daughters-in-law to admire, her knobby, strong, man's hands, proof that she has been equal to the demands of life. And beside the solemnity with which Joan and Patty regarded Mother Fry's hands, and also the demands of life (bake! bear!) I had always felt myself effete and unpleasant, tainted with cynicism and ambition, the incarnation of one of those awful American women Frenchmen are always deploring.

Everyone had by now struggled through the cake, and we had arrived at the ceremonious pause, sitting among the litter of forks and crumpled napkins exchanging well-fed observations on the dinner. I emerged from a fantasy about making them an incredible cake, a pink croquembouche nine feet high, to hear Mother Fry saying, "I think cranberry jelly is really the best thing to baste ham with and I always keep coming back to it." But she got no response at all to this, which meant she had exhausted the men's ability to respond with any more compliments. "Well, let's polish off these dishes," she said, and that was the sign that dinner was officially over. Father Fry and Mahonri and Garth bolted to the music room, and we cleared the table to the muffled strains of Bartók. All the Fry men are devoted lovers and patrons of music.

The kitchen after family dinner always had the congratulatory atmosphere of a locker room after a track meet, and I, of course, was always pretty much in the position of a relay man who has dropped a baton. Even Joan and Patty, with whom I was on perfectly good terms the rest of the week, were apt to be unconsciously distant. And I always, always, broke one of Mother Fry's dishes. I was psychologically very suspect, because I never broke dishes at home, but Mother Fry and Joan and Patty could not have helped but think I must shatter whatever I touched, and this certainly lent support to Mother Fry's conviction that I was shattering Garth's life.

I dropped and broke a dish. In spite of my protests, Joan helped me sweep up the pieces. Then I cut my finger on a sharp fragment and was retired to a kitchen stool, which made me feel more uncomfortable and useless than ever. But I reassured myself by thinking of Joan, and of how I would not like to be thirty-two and hippy, with seven children and frizzy hair and no light at all in a bleak world of duty and scrub brushes. Mahonri, the junior partner in a busy law firm, makes thirty thousand a year. He has a Buick station wagon and a Corvette. He has a stereo only a few hundred dollars inferior to his father's. He belongs to an expensive golf club and plays two afternoons a week. And Joan, Joan four times a week packed up the accumulated bushels of dirty clothes, including Mahonri's shirts, and carted them off to the laundromat because she hadn't saved enough from her housekeeping money to repair the washer. Joan was to me what the starving people of war-torn Europe were to me as a child; I thought upon her and became thrifty, tidy, and grateful.

It began to grow dark. The dishes were finished, dried, put away. The counters were wiped, the stove was cleaned, the floor was swept, invisible fingerprints were polished off cabinets and refrigerator. Now it was almost time for Sacrament Meeting. Joan and Mahonri went on ahead in the station wagon with their three oldest children. Father Fry took Garth to the study to look at a new camera. Katy was happy watching television, which she was not permitted at home, but Toby was fussy and tired, toddling in complaining circles, shaking his head and wailing. I tried to quiet him with cookies, though this is not approved. Patty, nursing her baby, sat stiffly on a kitchen chair, like those mothers one sees in bus stations, with a blanket tucked lightly over baby and breast. Neither she nor Joan suffers embarrassment over natural functions, and Patty is an active member of La Leche Society, a group dedicated to disseminating information about lactation.

Mother Fry was puttering in the cupboard, saying things like "Ah, what a lovely day," and "I don't see how Joan does it, manages so beautifully, and the children all so well-behaved and neat." Joan's children were well-behaved, but had an over-whelmed air, as if each child could see that there were too many of them, feared it was perhaps he who was superfluous. But they always had buttons, and both shoes, and she sewed them all dear little dresses and shirts, and this was a triumph in itself.

The family had ceased to talk to me about the quilting and women's study group and Sunday school, and all the other things you do when you are a Mormon. Perhaps they had realized that having one nonchurchgoer is convenient. Father Fry and Garth came in, talking of Pentaflexes. Mother Fry took off her apron, and Patty handed me the baby.

"He hasn't burped yet," she said. I put him over my shoulder.

"I'm a very lucky woman, having all my family so near," Mother Fry said."

"Yes, we all have a lot to be thankful for," Father Fry agreed as he held the kitchen door open. And for the first time I was not convinced; I was aware of too many little clouds—Patty's whine, Garth's outburst, Sebastian speeding off to the mysterious millionairess, Joan's stolid silences. And, above all, all that thankfulness.

"Aunt Karen, will you play with us?" Joan's Sara asked.

"Of course," I said. "Have a nice time," I told the others as they left. It was always a longish three hours for me on Sunday evening. I never seemed to know enough games to last eight children three hours.

The Turn of the Screw
Phyllis McGinley

The poet's complaint here is itself a sociological commentary, especially on the *ascriptiveness* of relatives. Even adults can only ignore or escape their relatives; they cannot turn them in for new ones. Children, dragged along by parents, must accept the cousins that the cosmos has given them. If one is a girl, one can lose in the competition that parents create, for one's own parents point out how superior one's girl cousins are.

But boy cousins are no solace either; by age or condition, they are unlikely to fit one's needs.

Girl cousins condescend. They wear
Earrings, and dress like fashion's sample,
Have speaking eyes and curly hair.
And parents point to their example.
But the boy cousins one's allotted
Are years too young for one. Or spotted.

From Phyllis McGinley, *Times Three*, The Viking Press, Inc., New York, 1960, p. 43.

Chapter 8

Generational Relations

Precisely because of the love they feel toward one another, their identification with each other, and the inner tensions between affection and authority that both experience, each generation is engaged to some extent in conflict with the next. But though all literatures exploit this theme, often as a tragedy in the fighting between father and son, our contemporary world probably exhibits more parent-youth conflict than most societies of the past.

Traditional parent-youth conflict grows from the great demands that parents make on their children, and vice versa, at each point in the life cycle of the child. Even when he or she is an adult, both want unremitting loyalty and devotion, as well as a constant stream of services and even material gifts. Parents want to live a life of their own, as do their children, but each wants the other to be available at any moment, totally committed. The parent wants the child to be fully responsible and adult in all the obligations that are imposed upon him or her, but also to subordinate his or her own needs to those of the parent. Children feel the same way, even when they are adults.

However, in traditional societies this conflict is muted somewhat by the fact that the parents at least have had experiences similar to those of their children. They know what it is to be awkwardly adolescent, to feel the angry frustrations of being unable to accomplish a difficult task, to suffer the embarrassment of encounters with outsiders of the opposite sex, and so on.

However, in a time of rapid social change, the experiences that the younger generation has are very different from those of the older, so that parental claims that they "do understand" are likely to be viewed as hollow or false. Contemporary parents did not typically grow up in a world that has known, for example, the continued threat of the atomic bomb, the everyday utilization of prescription and psychedelic drugs of all kinds by both sober citizens and rebels, the widespread use of the contraceptive pill, the pervasive militarization of national political life. Consequently, the gap between the generations may be greater now than in the past.

This gap is great during any period of vast social change, and of course it is accentuated during a revolution where the political authorities attempt to set the generations against each other.

In both a traditional society and one undergoing rapid social change, a further gap should be noted. The adult, approaching the older years, moves into a realm that was experienced by his or her own father or mother but is nevertheless new to that individual—a realm as yet beyond the experience of the younger generation. Grandparents sometimes engage in "anticipatory socialization," by trying to pass on to either their own adult children or their grandchildren something of the family traditions, the cultural heritage of the region or ethnic group, or their own accumulated wisdom. In a traditional society that wisdom is likely to yield them some respect and attention: It may be technically useful, or it may represent a distillation of thought that younger people cannot achieve with their shorter and more limited life span. In many societies, too, and often in our own, the relations between grandparents and grandchildren yield satisfactions that the parent-child relationship does not afford. For though both feel a deep commitment to one another, grandparents do not (except in a strongly patriarchal tradition) feel a great need to control their grandchildren strictly. They do not need to temper their love because of their wish to exert authority.

A Bill to my Father

Edward Field

A common literary cliché of the past generation has supposed that family relations among the lower classes and
peasants were warm, loyal, spontaneous, impulsive, and
"sexually natural." The same cliché has been applied to
primitive societies for well over two centuries. The first of
these clichés is largely incorrect, and the second is too
often incorrect to be considered reliable.

In Western society, modern relations between parents
and children permit and encourage more overt expressions
of love and tenderness than at any time in the known past,
when authority relations were considered much more important, the power of the parents much less questioned, and
reserve between parents and children much more desirable.
We cannot now know how young people or adults felt about
the amount of love they received from their parents. It is
clear that one of the commonest complaints of people who
now seek psychiatric help is that their parents did not show
them enough love. Whether the lower expectations of
children in the past made them repress this need for more
tenderness and cuddling we cannot now ascertain. Perhaps
the modern rhetoric of "loving" merely means that people
are more sensitive to any lack of love from others in their
family.

We are assured by most modern psychologists that
reward is more effective than punishment, and cuddling is
better for the child's emotional health than is beating. If that
is so, then perhaps the next generation will be healthier
than any in the past. On the other hand, the reader may well
pause to reflect how far this trend has gone, and to consider
what may be the restrictions (social and psychological) on
the parents' freedom of action that might permit them to
give less love than they believed to be appropriate.

The author of this poem utilizes a figure of speech—the
bills that creditors send—to note both the alternate identity

From Edward Field, *Stand Up, Friend, with Me*, Grove Press, Inc., New York, 1963,
p. 28.

his father possesses that is alien to the child's experience
and the extent to which he feels himself that his father will
never pay him the "love-debt" that is owed.

I am typing up bills for a firm to be sent to their
    clients.
It occurs to me that firms are sending bills to my father
Who has that way an identity I do not often realize.
He is a person who buys, owes, and pays,
Not papa like he is to me.
His creditors reproach him for not paying on time
With a bill marked "Please Remit."
I reproach him for never having shown his love for me
But only his disapproval.
He has a debt to me too
Although I have long since ceased asking him to come
    across;
He does not know how and so I do without it.
But in this impersonal world of business
He can be communicated with:
With absolute assurance of being paid
The boss writes "Send me my money"
And my father sends it.

An Ideal Family

Katherine Mansfield

In this story the generational gap is not marked by conflict—after all, it is "an ideal family." Everyone in it is
charming, well-mannered, accomplished, and admired by
everyone. They avoid dark and ugly topics in discussion as
they avoid inappropriate actions. Their position in society is

From *The Garden Party and Other Stories* by Katherine Mansfield, Alfred A. Knopf,
Inc., New York, 1927, pp. 237–247.

secure, as is the wealth that the elderly father has created by his lifetime of hard work.

Katherine Mansfield has not presented this picture in order to show us that underneath all is evil and threatening. Rather, she wishes us to enter the thin, fragile, and ultimately sad realm which Mr. Neave inhabits as he approaches death. The challenges he now faces are too much for him: he cannot force his spoiled son to take care of the business that he has built up, he needs help that is not forthcoming when he goes down to dinner, and even the exhilarating press of springtime is too much.

His children have come to accept him as they would part of the background, the furniture, the house. They fuss over him briefly, but the focus of their attention is elsewhere. They have little perception of his inner world, and do not wish to know about it. Far removed from the class assumptions, the political conflicts, the sexual revolution of our era, they nevertheless represent a "now generation" that dismisses the old as essentially irrelevant.

That evening for the first time in his life, as he pressed through the swing door and descended the three broad steps to the pavement, old Mr. Neave felt he was too old for the spring. Spring—warm, eager, restless—was there, waiting for him in the golden light, ready in front of everybody to run up, to blow in his white beard, to drag sweetly on his arm. And he couldn't meet her, no; he couldn't square up once more and stride off, jaunty as a young man. He was tired and, although the late sun was still shining, curiously cold, with a numbed feeling all over. Quite suddenly he hadn't the energy, he hadn't the heart to stand this gaiety and bright movement any longer; it confused him. He wanted to stand still, to wave it away with his stick, to say, "Be off with you!" Suddenly it was a terrible effort to greet as usual—tipping his wide-awake with his stick—all the people whom he knew, the friends, acquaintances, shopkeepers, postmen, drivers. But the gay glance that went with the gesture, the kindly twinkle that seemed to say, "I'm a match and more for any of you"—that old Mr. Neave could not manage at all. He stumped along, lifting his knees high as if he were walking through air that had somehow grown heavy and solid like water. And the home-ward-going crowd hurried by, the trams clanked, the light carts clattered, the big swinging cabs bowled along with that reckless, defiant indifference that one knows only in dreams. . . .

It had been a day like other days at the office. Nothing special had happened. Harold hadn't come back from lunch until close on four. Where had he been? What had he been up to? He wasn't going to let his father know. Old Mr. Neave had happened to be in the vestibule, saying good-bye to a caller, when Harold sauntered in, perfectly turned out as usual, cool, suave, smiling the peculiar little half-smile that women found so fascinating.

Ah, Harold was too handsome, too handsome by far; that had been the trouble all along. No man had a right to such eyes, such lashes, and such lips; it was uncanny. As for his mother, his sisters, and the servants, it was not too much to say they made a young god of him; they worshipped Harold, they forgave him everything; and he had needed some forgiving ever since the time when he was thirteen and he had stolen his mother's purse, taken the money, and hidden the purse in the cook's bedroom. Old Mr. Neave struck sharply with his stick upon the pavement edge. But it wasn't only his family who spoiled Harold, he reflected, it was everybody; he had only to look and to smile, and down they went before him. So perhaps it wasn't to be wondered at that he expected the office to carry on the tradition. H'm, h'm! But it couldn't be done. No business—not even a successful, estab-lished, big paying concern—could be played with. A man had either to put his whole heart and soul into it, or it went all to pieces before his eyes. . . .

And then Charlotte and the girls were always at him to make the whole thing over to Harold, to retire, and to spend his time enjoying himself. Enjoying himself! Old Mr. Neave stopped dead under a group of ancient cabbage palms outside the Government buildings! Enjoying himself! The wind of evening shook the dark leaves to a thin airy cackle. Sitting at home, twiddling his thumbs, conscious all the while that his life's work was slipping away, dissolving, disappearing through Harold's fine fingers, while Harold smiled. . . .

"Why will you be so unreasonable, father? There's absolutely no need for you to go to the office. It only makes it very awkward for us when people persist in saying how tired you're looking. Here's this huge house and garden. Surely you could be happy in—in—appreciating it for a change. Or you could take up some hobby."

And Lola the baby had chimed in loftily, "All men ought to have hobbies. It makes life impossible if they haven't."

Well, well! He couldn't help a grim smile as painfully he began to climb the hill that led into Harcourt Avenue. Where would Lola and her sisters and Charlotte be if he'd gone in for hobbies, he'd like to know? Hobbies couldn't pay for the town house and the seaside bungalow, and their horses, and their golf, and their sixty-guinea gramophone in the music-room for them to dance to. Not that he grudged them these things. No, they were smart, good-looking girls, and Charlotte was a remarkable woman; it was natural for them to be in the swim. As a matter of fact, no other house in the town was as popular as theirs; no other family entertained so much. And how many times old Mr. Neave, pushing the cigar box across the smoking-room table, had listened to praises of his wife, his girls, of himself even.

"You're an ideal family, sir, an ideal family. It's like something one reads about or sees on the stage."

"That's all right, my boy," old Mr. Neave would reply. "Try one of those; I think you'll like them. And if you care to smoke in the garden, you'll find the girls on the lawn, I dare say."

That was why the girls had never married, so people said. They could have married anybody. But they had too good a time at home. They were too happy together, the girls and Charlotte. H'm, h'm! Well, well! Perhaps so. . . .

By this time he had walked the length of fashionable Harcourt Avenue; he had reached the corner house, their house. The carriage gates were pushed back; there were fresh marks of wheels on the drive. And then he faced the big white-painted house, with its wide-open windows, its tulle curtains floating outwards, its blue jars of hyacinths on the broad sills. On either side of the carriage porch their hydrangeas—famous in the town—were coming into flower; the pinkish, bluish masses of flower lay like light among the spreading leaves. And somehow, it seemed to old Mr. Neave that the house and the flowers, and even the fresh marks on the drive, were saying, "There is young life here. There are girls—"

The hall, as always, was dusky with wraps, parasols, gloves, piled on the oak chests. From the music-room sounded the piano, quick, loud and impatient. Through the drawing-room door that was ajar voices floated.

"And were there ices?" came from Charlotte. Then the creak, creak of her rocker.

"Ices!" cried Ethel. "My dear mother, you never saw such ices. Only two kinds. And one a common little strawberry shop ice, in a sopping wet frill."

"The food altogether was too appalling," came from Marion.

"Still, it's rather early for ices," said Charlotte easily.

"But why, if one has them at all . . ." began Ethel.

"Oh, quite so, darling," crooned Charlotte.

Suddenly the music-room door opened and Lola dashed out. She started, she nearly screamed, at the sight of old Mr. Neave.

"Gracious, father! What a fright you gave me! Have you just come home? Why isn't Charles here to help you off with your coat?"

Her cheeks were crimson from playing, her eyes glittered, the hair fell over her forehead. And she breathed as though she had come running through the dark and was frightened. Old Mr. Neave stared at his youngest daughter; he felt he had never seen her before. So that was Lola, was it? But she seemed to have forgotten her father; it was not for him that she was waiting there. Now she put the tip of her crumpled handkerchief between her teeth and tugged at it angrily. The telephone rang. A-ah! Lola gave a cry like a sob and dashed past him. The door of the telephone-room slammed, and at the same moment Charlotte called, "Is that you, father?"

"You're tired again," said Charlotte reproachfully, and she stopped the rocker and offered him her warm plum-like cheek. Bright-haired Ethel pecked his beard; Marion's lips brushed his ear.

"Did you walk back, father?" asked Charlotte.

"Yes, I walked home," said old Mr. Neave, and he sank into one of the immense drawing-room chairs.

"But why didn't you take a cab?" said Ethel. "There are hundreds of cabs about at that time."

"My dear Ethel," cried Marion, "if father prefers to tire himself out, I really don't see what business of ours it is to interfere."

"Children, children?" coaxed Charlotte.

But Marion wouldn't be stopped. "No, mother, you spoil father, and it's not right. You ought to be stricter with him. He's very naughty." She laughed her hard, bright laugh and patted her hair in a mirror. Strange! When she was a little girl she had such a soft, hesitating voice; she had even stuttered, and now, whatever she said—even if it was only "Jam, please, father"—it rang out as though she were on the stage.

"Did Harold leave the office before you, dear?" asked Charlotte, beginning to rock again.

"I'm not sure," said old Mr. Neave. "I'm not sure. I didn't see him after four o'clock."

"He said—" began Charlotte.

But at that moment Ethel, who was twitching over the leaves of some paper or other, ran to her mother and sank down beside her chair.

"There, you see," she cried. "That's what I mean, mummy. Yellow, with touches of silver. Don't you agree?"

"Give it to me, love," said Charlotte. She fumbled for her tortoise-shell spectacles and put them on, gave the page a little dab with her plump small fingers, and pursed up her lips. "Very sweet!" she crooned vaguely; she looked at Ethel over her spectacles. "But I shouldn't have the train."

"Not the train!" wailed Ethel tragically. "But the train's the whole point."

"Here, mother, let me decide." Marion snatched the paper playfully from Charlotte. "I agree with mother," she cried triumphantly. "The train overweights it."

Old Mr. Neave, forgotten, sank into the broad lap of his chair, and, dozing, heard them as though he dreamed. There was no doubt about it, he was tired out; he had lost his hold. Even Charlotte and the girls were too much for him to-night. They were too . . . too. . . . But all his drowsing brain could think of was—too *rich* for him. And somewhere at the back of everything he was watching a little withered ancient man climbing up endless flights of stairs. Who was he?

"I shan't dress to-night," he muttered.

"What do you say, father?"

"Eh, what, what?" Old Mr. Neave woke with a start and stared across at them. "I shan't dress to-night," he repeated.

"But, father, we've got Lucile coming, and Henry Davenport, and Mrs. Teddie Walker."

"It will look so *very* out of the picture."

"Don't you feel well, dear?"

"You needn't make any effort. What is Charles *for*?"

"But if you're really not up to it," Charlotte wavered.

"Very well! Very well!" Old Mr. Neave got up and went to join that little old climbing fellow just as far as his dressing-room. . . .

There young Charles was waiting for him. Carefully, as though everything depended on it, he was tucking a towel round the hot-water can. Young Charles had been a favourite of his ever since as a little red-faced boy he had come into the house to look after the fires. Old Mr. Neave lowered himself into the cane lounge by the window, stretched out his legs, and made his little evening joke, "Dress him up, Charles!" And Charles, breathing intensely and frowning, bent forward to take the pin out of his tie.

H'm, h'm! Well, well! It was pleasant by the open window, very pleasant—a fine mild evening. They were cutting the grass on the tennis court below; he heard the soft churr of the mower. Soon the girls would begin their tennis parties again. And at the thought he seemed to hear Marion's voice ring out, "Good for you partner. . . . Oh, *played*, partner. . . . Oh, *very* nice indeed." Then Charlotte calling from the veranda, "Where is Harold?" And Ethel, "He's certainly not here, mother." And Charlotte's vague, "He said—"

Old Mr. Neave sighed, got up, and putting one hand under his beard, he took the comb from young Charles, and carefully combed the white beard over. Charles gave him a folded handkerchief, his watch and seals, and spectacle case.

"That will do, my lad." The door shut, he sank back, he was alone. . . .

And now that little ancient fellow was climbing down endless flights that led to a glittering, gay dining-room. What legs he had! They were like a spider's—thin, withered.

"You're an ideal family, sir, an ideal family."

But if that were true, why didn't Charlotte or the girls stop him? Why was he all alone, climbing up and down? Where was Harold? Ah, it was no good expecting anything from Harold. Down, down went the little old spider, and then, to his horror, old Mr. Neave saw him slip past the dining-room and make for the porch, the dark drive, the carriage gates, the office. Stop him, stop him, somebody!

Old Mr. Neave started up. It was dark in his dressing-room; the window shone pale. How long had he been asleep? He listened, and through the big, airy, darkened house there floated far-away voices, far-away sounds. Perhaps, he thought vaguely, he had been asleep for a long time. He'd been forgotten. What had all this to do with him—this house and Charlotte, the girls and Harold—what did he know about them? They were strangers to him. Life had passed him by. Charlotte was not his wife. His wife!

. . . A dark porch, half hidden by a passion-vine, that dropped sorrowful, mournful, as though it understood. Small, warm arms were round his neck. A face, little and pale, lifted to his, and a voice breathed, "Good-bye, my treasure."

"My treasure! "Good-bye my treasure!" Which of them had spoken? Why had they said good-bye? There had been some terrible mistake. *She* was his wife, that little pale girl, and all the rest of his life had been a dream.

Then the door opened, and young Charles, standing in the light, put his hands by his side and shouted like a young soldier, "Dinner is on the table, sir."

"I'm coming, I'm coming," said old Mr. Neave.

The Feasts of Memories

Elias Kulukundis

Only a few sociologists (Alice Rossi and Nicholas Tavuchis are exceptions) have tried to ascertain the importance of *naming* in modern society. In some subgroups, children are not permitted to be named after a living parent, while in others the custom of giving the father's name to the son expresses a sense of generational continuity. We come to consider our own names and those of others as expressive of personality traits and ethnic backgrounds.

Here, Kulukundis attempts (with only modest success, for it is difficult to enter his assumptions and understand all his rules) to explain to us how Greek familial position and fate determine the name one bears. He tells us, for example, that the first son must be named for the father's father. Knowing this, and the other rules he gives us, we can understand a wide variety of family relations past and present from the names of contemporaries in Greek society. Furthermore, as he notes, the naming customs are determined in part by the rules of inheritance—a son thus receives his father's father's name, because he inherits the *ancestral* property, which has been passed down from generation to generation.

We are also reminded of the common pattern of looking at a child and making assertions about which of his or her traits come from this or that ancestor, or are like those of an aunt, uncle, or cousin.

The deeper meaning of the author's comments is, however, the extent to which our present lives are part of an unbroken chain of generations extending into the past, although we often do not know who those ancestors were, or by what delicate process their social or emotional characteristics came down to us. In a traditional society, they are part of common family conversation. In our own, those comments may occur less often, but the process of inheritance takes place just the same.

Elias Kulukundis, *The Feasts of Memories*, Holt, Rinehart and Winston, Inc., New York, 1967.

A name is a paradox. A name is what a person is, but it is the one thing he cannot decide. Our names are the titles that other people give to our existence, and we are all what we are—George, Michael, Elias—not by our choice but by the workings of some whimsy that is not our own.

In Kasos, even parents are not free to choose their children's names. Instead, by Kasiot custom, the name itself chooses the infant. I am Elias because I am the first son of my father, and because my father is the son of a first son, and my father's father was also the first son of a first son, and that original first son, the one who precedes all the rest and antedates my own arrival by almost a hundred and fifty years, was also Elias Kulukundis.

The custom is honored all over Greece, not only Kasos, that the first son be named for the father's father. Old Elias made no exception: he named his first son George, for his father. And when this second George became a father, his own first-born was Elias again, for *his* father. That second Elias was Captain Elias who shared the house of the blue shutters with his wife Eleni. When Eleni bore him a son, that latest first-born was named George again: Uncle George of the bananas and plaster cats. And when Uncle George became a father in London, his own first-born was Elias again, nicknamed Eddie.

In Kasos, the second son is named for the mother's father. Thereafter, the sons are named for the brothers of the parents, the third son for the father's eldest brother, the fourth for the mother's, the fifth for the father's next eldest brother, sixth for the mother's.

The daughters follow the same pattern, in reverse. The first daughter is named for the mother's mother, the second for the father's, the third for the mother's eldest sister, and so on. My family tree provides numerous examples of the male naming patterns, but few of the female. That is because the old Kulukundis fathers were very good at getting their way in the lottery of the genders, and sons were always preferred.

"How many children do you have?" someone might ask a Kasiot father.

"Four," the father might reply, "four children, and two daughters."

. . . .

The naming customs relate directly to inheritance codes. A parent was free to pass on all property acquired in his lifetime according to his will, and he would usually distribute it equally among all his children. But whatever property the parent had in turn inherited himself—his *ancestral* property—had to follow a code which was parallel to the naming customs. By this code, a first son inherited all his father's ancestral property, in other words, the property ultimately of his father's father, whose name he bore. Similarly, a first daughter would inherit all her mother's ancestral property, including her mother's house. (Houses in Kasos were owned maternally.)

. . . .

How the customs came about is a matter of speculation. Some scholars contend they are remnants of feudal law introduced into the islands by the Venetians. Others observe that the customs do not exist in Peloponnesos and mainland Greece, areas which were also settled by Venetians, only on Kasos and certain other islands. Instead, according to these other scholars, the customs must be older than the Venetians and probably originated in the religion of the ancients. In ancient Greece, a first son was also named for his father's father. After the father's death, this first son would tend his grave and perform services in ministration for his soul. For this reason, by religious precept, the son would acquire the land adjacent to his father's grave, which would then become his ancestral property to be handed on to his own first son.

But a set of customs may originate for certain reasons and be preserved for totally different ones. Like any custom, this naming and inheritance code had the practical effect of removing the necessity of human choice. Unconsciously, parents might actually come to favor those children named for their side of the family, and in this way, affection could be divided equitably. Naturally, one would have to look far beneath the surface of any family to observe such preferences, but sometimes they became apparent.

Eleni's second son, Basil, died at thirteen. When he died, his grandmother, Old Yia-Yia, seized his brother Nicholas by the throat and said, "Why didn't you die instead of Basil?" Little Nicholas was bewildered. "Why should I die instead of Basil?" he said. And what poor Nicholas was far from guessing was that in her frenzy, Old Yia-Yia was admitting that she considered Basil *her* grandson in a way Nicholas could never be: Basil was named for her late husband, Vasilios Mavroleon, whereas Nicholas was named, not for anyone in her family, but for his father's eldest brother.

Human choice would be even more divisive in the question of inheritance. Without a house, a Kasiot girl could not marry. Only a wealthy man could afford to build houses for several daughters, but in any family, there was already at least one house, the mother's. Without the custom, the family would find it very difficult to decide which daughter should have it. What mortal could confer the joys of wedlock on one girl and deny them to another? Instead, the question was left to custom to decide: the first daughter would have the house, and afterward, all her unmarriageable sisters could live with her, like my aunts in Syros, as a retinue of attendant maidens. Bearing no grudge, either against their elder sister or their parents, they would embrace their fate of fealty. The elder sister did not seek the privilege, and her parents did not confer it on her. It simply fell to her in the way the universe was ordered, by an inexorable tradition, according to the lottery of birth.

But the names are more than a custom; they are a manifestation of eternity. The child is not simply named for his grandfather. He *is* the grandfather incarnate. In the person of the child, the elder relatives see the grandfather before them.

"The eyes," says one.

"The mouth," another.

"The forehead," a third, in chorus.

Manchild in the Promised Land

Claude Brown

We are accustomed to think that only the younger generation opens up new experiences, that they discover new
things before their parents do, and that old people represent only a gradual closing of many doors. However, Claude
Brown reminds us that to explore the world of one's
grandparents may equally open up a new realm, though it
may be a world the younger generation does not wish to
enter.

As a Harlem boy, alive to the excitement of the very
latest in everything, Claude Brown moves back in generational time and even in cultural time. He comes to know his
grandparents, but they live in the South, in a social environment that is historically more distant from New York City
than the two generations between Claude and his grandparents would suggest. He thinks of them as "dumb country
people" because they do not know any boogie songs or
jump songs; they know only the songs they themselves have
been singing for years and years.

Nevertheless, distance does not mean discontinuity. He
comes to have an unexpressed admiration for his grandfather, who still enjoys a reputation as a "real bad and evil
nigger" because of his behavior as a young man. By living
with his rural grandfather for a time, the boy has an
experience that used to be common in rural society, but
perhaps is less so in modern urban society: the heavy,
awe-inspiring *physical* authority of the elderly grandfather.

Deeper than this wisdom, however, is his awareness
that the people he meets want to *place* him in the generational chain. They wish to ascertain whether he has inherited
some of his grandfather's traits. Indeed, his grandmother is somewhat afraid that he may be like his grandfather. It is in fact through her apprehension that he comes
to perceive that the old woman does in fact love him, and

that in spite of his awe for her he loves her as well. Thus, the familial and affectional links once more bridge the gap between different cultures, geographical locations, and generations.

Sometimes Grandpa used to hum some of the church songs when he was sitting in his rocking chair out on the porch patting his foot and watching the sun go down behind Mr. Hayward's tobacco barn. He would close his eyes and just start humming away. Maybe he was thinking about a funeral where he sang a song real good for somebody. Or maybe he was thinking about a funeral that didn't happen yet, a funeral where he wouldn't hear the songs, wouldn't know who was singing them, and wouldn't hear the preacher talking . . . talking about him . . . real loud. Maybe he was thinking about who would sing his favorite song for him and hoping that Mr. Charlie Jackson would live long enough to do the singing for him.

I couldn't understand why they sang nothing but those sad old church songs. They sure seemed to be some dumb country people to me. They didn't know any boogie songs or jump songs—they didn't even know any good blues songs. Nobody had a record player, and nobody had records. All the songs they sang, they'd been singing for years and years.

Somebody would sing real good at Grandpa's funeral, and a lot of people would be there. It would have to be a big funeral, because Grandpa was a real bad and evil nigger when he was a young man. He had the devil in him, and everybody knew it, even people who didn't know him. When Grandma took me to town or to church, people would come up to me and stare at me for a while, then ask, "Boy, is Mr. Son Brown yo' grandaddy?" And after a while, I knew why they were looking at me so hard; they were trying to see if I had the devil in me too.

For a long time, I used to be scared of Grandpa. He used to go walking in the woods in the evening, and when I asked Grandma where Grandpa was always going, she said he was hunting the devil. I only asked one time. I started to follow him once, but I got scared and changed my mind.

People used to say I was going to be just like Grandpa, since
I had the devil in me too. I never paid attention to what people
said about being like Grandpa until one day. That day, my cousin
McKinley Wilson and me were out in the yard seeing who could
pick up the biggest and heaviest sack of corn. While I was
straining to pick up a sack, I heard Grandma scream and felt a
stinging feeling on my neck that made me drop the sack, jump up
and down, and grab my neck. When I turned around to see what
had happened to me, I saw Grandma standing there with a switch
in her hand. She was screaming and hollering a whole lot of things
at me, but all I could make out was that she was going to kill me if
I ever did that again. I didn't know what to think except that
maybe she was going crazy. She had never said anything when I
messed with the wasps' nests and got stung and cried and kept on
messing with them. I couldn't understand why she had hit me, and
Grandma didn't talk much. I knew she had mistreated me, and I
had to do something about it, so I started walking, walking back
to New York.

When Grandma caught up with me on the highway, she had a
bigger switch, and she was real mad. After she finished beating
me for running away, she said she had hit me because she didn't
want me to be walking like Grandpa. I asked her if Grandpa had
gotten his stroke from lifting corn.

She said, "It wasn' no stroke that makes Grandpa walk the
way he do. The stroke just stiffened up his right side. But you see
the way he gotta swing his left leg way out every time he take a
step?"

I said, "Yeah, I seen him do that."

Grandma said that Grandpa walked that way because he was
toting corn one day. I didn't understand, but I kept on listening.
Then Grandma started telling me about the things I saw Grandpa
cut out of the pig to keep the bacon from getting rank when they
killed the pig. And she told me that right above the things that
make the bacon rank are the chitterlings and that chitterlings
press against a thin window in pigs and boys and men. I never
knew I had chitterlings in me until that day. Grandma said if
somebody lifted something too heavy for him, the chitterlings
would press right through that window and the man would have a

hard time walking and doing a lot of other things for the rest of his life. She said one time Grandpa was in the woods making liquor, and his dog started barking. Grandpa picked up his still and started running with it. The still was too heavy—the window broke, and now Grandpa had to walk real slow. She was saying that she didn't mean to hit me. She just didn't want me to break my window.

We walked back home up the highway. Grandma had her arm around my shoulder, and I had my arm around her waist. That was the only time I ever touched Grandma—and the only time I recall wanting her to touch me and liking her touch. When I saw the house coming at us up the road, I was kind of sad. I looked at Grandma's wrinkled face and liked it. I knew I had fallen in love with that mean old wrinkled lady who, I used to think, had a mouth like a monkey. I had fallen in love with a mean old lady because she hit me across the neck for trying to lift a sack of corn.

Part Four

Rifts and Resolutions

Family life seems especially to illustrate the maxim that there are only a few ways for a system to work well, and thousands of ways for it to dissolve or break apart. On the other hand, to the extent that it does form a system, it may resist those threatening forces, or parts of it may link together again after the break. Some families do not come apart although their members engage in almost daily fights. Others stay together and observe the outward forms of convention (the empty-shell family) while all of them feel alone and unloved. Others are riven by a conflict that seems to the outsider to be trivial, or their members may suddenly recognize that they no longer need one another, and thus they drift apart without having faced any crisis at all.

The sociologist of the family typically tries to view the rifts within a family as the outcome of many kinds of centripetal forces—differences in social background and thus tastes and values; personality needs; precipitating events such as drunkenness or a new love relationship; the reduced social pressures on the modern family to avoid divorce, and so on. Divorce is a kind of escape valve for such tensions; it is not to be viewed as a moral violation that an erring spouse has caused. The wisest of literary artists have also tried to let us understand the inner motivations of family members deeply enough so that we can perceive family conflict as the sometimes tragic working out of forces over which lovers or spouses had only little control and therefore for which they should not be made to bear the sole blame. Even the moralist Tolstoy, holding up for our scorn the emptiness and decadence of mid-nineteenth-century St. Petersburg society, makes us understand that Anna Karenina was not an evil person, and that we ourselves might also have acted as she did.

Our stance is, of course, very different when we are participants in our own family conflicts. We feel the urgency of our own needs, wants, and injustices. We do not easily perceive the rightness of other people's demands. Unlike the novelist, we do not know the inner motivations of others and cannot enter their perceptions, so that they seem most unreasonable. More important, we not only want others to *conform*, to bow to our wishes outwardly; we also want them to *want* to do the right thing, to *feel* the appropriate emotions. Unfortunately, no one has so great a control over his or her own actions, much less feelings.

Both sociologists and writers have neglected to a considerable extent the family strains among the lower classes. Indeed, it was only about two decades ago that sociologists came to understand clearly that the divorce rate is much higher among the lower classes than in other social strata. Both have also neglected family conflict among blacks, and in literature this has rarely been presented as the tragic or deeply felt conflict that it is. More commonly, fights between black husband and wife have been pictured as slightly comic. Much of sociology, like much of literature, has rather focused on the family life and thus family disorganization within the middle classes.

Sociologists and writers have also neglected the direct experiences of children in most types of family rifts—fighting, divorce, death, mental disease. Sociologists and psychologists have charted to a considerable extent the unfortunate effects of family breakups on the subsequent life experiences of children, but they have not ascertained from the children themselves how those experiences were lived. Novelists have filled that gap to only a minor extent, for they have primarily focused on the husband-wife relationship. On the other hand, because so many novels are thinly disguised autobiographies, and because many writers have grown up in a family ripped apart by strains or by divorce, literature does offer us richer materials than sociology has produced so far.

However, neither art nor sociology can capture the whole of living. Bound by the convention that the story must end, and that as readers we must feel it is complete, the artist must aim for a neatness and even orderliness that life will not often produce if left to itself. The sociologist attempts, by contrast, to analyze a relatively thin slice of conflict and resolution, often at a single point in time or at best over a short period, so that what he or she describes is also likely to be pressed into a conventional mold of completeness.

On the other hand, in real life people continue to move on to new conflicts and new resolutions, even when they occur with different people. They carry with them not merely the childhood backgrounds that figure so largely in novels or in the cross tabulations of sociologists. They also carry with them all of the lessons they wisely or unwisely learned from the conflict, the new attitudes and roles they have taken on, the new persons they have become, so that the chronicle of an individual's conflicts and resolutions within his or her lifetime cannot be fully captured by either of these endeavors, the artistic or the social-scientific.

Chapter 9

Family Strain
and Disorganization

Family strain and disorganization does not always result in separation or divorce; the range of family difficulties is much wider.[1] They include at least:

1 Illegitimacy. Although here a family is not "dissolved," the situation does in fact represent a failure on the part of one or both parties to assume the traditional role obligations of family members. Often a major factor in illegitimacy is a role failure on the part of the parents of the two people who produced the illegitimate child.

2 Annulment, separation, divorce, and desertion. In these cases, one spouse (or both) decides to leave, and thus refuses to

[1]William J. Goode, *The Family*, Prentice-Hall, Inc., Englewood Cliffs, N.J., 1964, Chap. 9.

assume his or her family obligations to the other or sometimes to their children.

3 "Empty-shell family." As we have noted elsewhere, in this type the members carry out the conventional forms of civility and role obligation, but typically do not give emotional support to one another.

4 "Unwilled" absence of one spouse. Sometimes the family breaks apart because the husband or wife has died, has gone to jail, or has been removed by some catastrophe such as war, depression, or persecution.

5 "Unwilled" major role failures. Severe physical, emotional, or mental pathologies may cause role failures on the part of either those suffering from these difficulties or those who must adjust to them.

From such a typology, we see at once that everyone will experience some family disorganization within his own life. As sociologists, we could also predict that every society attempts to work out various solutions for them. Clearly, too, the "solutions" that are offered or imposed may change in time. Thus, for example, a severely mentally retarded child would once have probably become the "village idiot" laughed at by many and neglected by most, while most familes today would be advised by a social worker to place such a child in a home for the retarded.

Literature has neglected most of the situations listed above in favor of the high drama of divorce. It is much neater than annulment, separation, or desertion, and its dramatic impact seems greater. On the other hand, literature has paid little attention to the problem of adjustment after divorce.

Although illegitimacy remains a potential for tragedy in our own time as it was in the past, and in most countries is still viewed as a scandal, its potential for literary drama has diminished to almost zero. When illegitimacy was a stigma that could never be erased, and sex relations contained the threat of this stigma, tragic plots could hinge on the occurrence of a conception outside wedlock, as in Dreiser's *An American Tragedy*. However, and in part because literary artists are likely to hold attitudes much in advance of their own society, such a pregnancy no longer seems to be worthy of serious drama. The girl who becomes pregnant when her male partner has no interest in marriage is more likely to be viewed as frivolous or careless, rather than the victim of fate. Or, she is lower-class or black, and in both those cases the artist is less likely to feel it is the stuff of tragedy.

Another circumstance that has largely disappeared from literature is the hopeless love between two people who cannot marry because at least one of them is married to someone else—divorce being unthinkable. As with illegitimacy, this situation does occur in our time, but the writer no longer feels that he can convince readers of its reality. In both instances he would have to create a traditional or old-fashioned family in which such values and attitudes were affirmed, in contrast to the looser attitudes of our age. In the past, similarly, the threat of "scandal" could destroy a marriage, or lead to murder (as it still does in real life).

These changes in esthetic attitudes do reflect changes in the larger society, but they also suggest a small puzzle. The literary artist typically focuses on the individual and personal meaning of such events, and in modern life they are likely to cause grave emotional consequences. The changes in *social* consequences seem, by contrast, to be much greater. That is, divorce is very painful for the spouses, and often for the children, but few people are ostracized, as they once were, for seeking that solution to their problems. If a girl is discovered in a boy's college dormitory room at night, people will simply say "hello" to her. She will not be expelled from college. The social answer to an illegitimate pregnancy is simply abortion; few writers would dare to risk ridicule by having the girl's parents cast her out into the winter snow. In short, much of the stuff of literature of the past remains *personally* moving, hurtful, or exciting, but some part of that has been reduced in *social* importance, and can be used only in literature about the past.

The death of the father often occasioned a total reorganization of the lives of family members. Once, literature could exploit this sudden tragedy visited on the widow and her children (Dickens did this with great success) by following up the now separate fates of the family members and by describing their adjustment to selfish relatives and unfeeling society. Although the modern essayist reminds us constantly of our harsh, materialistic modern society, in real life he or she would expect social workers, welfare agencies, or other governmental assistance to help mitigate such a tragedy. Writers can no longer take for granted that their readers will believe the death of the husband would create so stark and tragic a set of consequences.

Similarly, even death itself has been removed to some extent from literary treatment, though the reasons seem in part obscure. The truth is that in real life more marriages end in death than in divorce. Surely, death is no less a personal tragedy than it once was, even if (like illegitimacy, sex scandals, divorce, and so on) its consequences have been rendered somewhat less crippling. Perhaps the central reason is simply the writer's awareness that mortality rates have fallen—in other words, within any given time period a smaller percentage of a population will die than, say, 100 years ago. Consequently, the writer would strain the reader's credulity if he or she were to solve many of the problems in the plot by death. Indeed, just as the writer is bound to some extent by an elementary knowledge of sociological facts, so is he to some extent by medical facts. For example, he can no longer kill off his characters by means of "brain fever" or "a broken heart." The reader requires that he produce a specific, believable disease.

At a deeper level the writer may simply reflect a determined unawareness of death on the part of our society. Funerals are not socially as important as they once were. Children are permitted to stay away from funerals, and sometimes even forbidden to go to them. Everyone is in fact aware of death, and everyone fears the possible death of his or her beloved, but that kind of discussion is frowned upon within the family or in larger social gatherings. People who grieve deeply are encouraged to take tranquilizers. Perhaps, then, the modern literary artist is reflecting not so much a change in the mortality statistics as an alteration in the social position of death in our society.

All in the Family

Edwin O'Connor

Edwin O'Connor thrusts shatteringly before us the tragedy experienced by a young boy when his mother and younger brother are drowned. Up to this point he has portrayed an idyllic world, loving parents, a beautiful mother who was an actress, a privileged life of glamorous people, fun, camping trips, and even a chauffeur-helper who knows judo and is fiercely loyal to the family.

Since we experience the tragedy through the boy's eyes, we are forced to attend to the succession of *events* rather than to their deeper meaning. However, because the events themselves so focus his attention, and they are retold through the mind of the author, we are also made aware of some curious inner facts as well. The mother is happy and carefree when she leaves, but she makes what seems to be a light-hearted threat never to come back. She usually continued to clean the cabin until she finished, but this time she breaks off the cleaning in order to put on a bathing suit. When Jackie and his father finally arrive at the canoe from which his brother and mother have seemingly fallen into the lake, the scarf she wore about her head is still in the canoe, and so is the turtle that young Tom had taken along. The boy does not think about this, but we at once recognize that canoes tip over easily, and people fall out of them, but that turn of events usually disarranges the canoe and its contents. In short, we are already led to suspect that there are some mysteries in the family, even if we never learn precisely what they are. We begin to suspect that the mother has drowned herself and simultaneously drowned her young son.

Note that Jackie cries three times, once in innocent sympathy at the thought of his mother and Tom underneath the ice, and a second time in sheer terror when his father jumps over the side of the rowboat in order to locate the bodies below. He does not experience the full impact of

Edwin O'Connor, *All in the Family*, Bantam Books, New York, 1967, pp. 15–26.

losing his mother and brother until he is in bed late that evening, and finally learns that bodies have been found. In between, he experiences a void, an ache, even a feeling of suspense and excitement. In psychological terms we would say that he is finally engaged in the "work of grief," the catharsis of giving way totally to sorrow.

Jackie and his father had enjoyed a warm, close relationship, and now it is transformed because they must reconstitute the family. The father will not leave his son with relatives who will rear him. Their resolution of the trauma is to cling more closely together.

It came to an end on a morning in March, when I was eleven years old. It came to an end most sadly and most unexpectedly; it came to an end in an instant.

We had gone up to the cabin for the weekend. March was always unreliable, and the winter had been bad, but for more than a week there had been a warm spell, and when we reached the cabin, late on a Friday afternoon, the ice which had edged the lakes on our last visit was gone, the sharp wet smell of winter had left the air, the ground was soft, birds we had not heard in months were chirping away somewhere in the trees, and out on the water a fish jumped. Spring had not really and firmly begun, but winter was over, and when we woke the next morning the air was very warm and slow and slightly hazy, as though we had skipped a season overnight and were now in mid-July.

After breakfast, wearing only our shorts on this extraordinary March morning, my father and I went outside and began to work around the cabin, doing the little things that always needed to be done at the end of every winter—there were screens to be replaced, shingles had blown off, paint had flaked away in spots, and a squirrel had started a hole in the back wall near the fireplace. My mother, who always cleaned the cabin each time we came up as if no one had been here for years, stayed inside and, with Tom as an unreliable and occasionally disappearing helper, opened windows, aired bedding, and swept dirt that I could not even see off the floor. When she began her cleaning she usually stayed with it until she finished, but this morning she surprised us by suddenly joining us in the yard. More surprising still, she was wearing her bathing suit.

"Ha!" my father said. "Who's rushing the season? Don't let that sun fool you—the last thing in those lakes was an iceberg."

"I'm having spring fever," my mother said, "for the first time in years. It's all so beautiful I'm taking time off. No swimming, just the canoe. The first ride of the year. Want to come?"

"All right," my father said. He began to get up—he had been plugging the squirrel hole—but then he stopped and said, "On second thought, no. I'd better wait for this stuff to dry. Otherwise I'll have to start all over again. Take Jackie with you: he's a good man in a canoe."

But I was my father's helper; loyally I said, "I want to see this stuff dry, too."

"I can go," Tom said. He was now six years old, a round-headed little boy who came up to my shoulder, with blond hair so light it was almost white, and gray-green eyes just like my mother's. For a long time now I had been making bets—sometimes with Arthur, but mostly with myself—that whenever people came to our house and met Tom and me for the first time, they would always say that Tom was the image of my mother, just as they would always say that I was the image of my father. Tom had been wandering in the woods on the other side of the cabin, and when he came walking toward us now he held in his hand a very small box turtle. "Look what I found," he said. "I could take it in the canoe."

He went over to my mother, who put her hand lightly on his head and mussed his hair a bit. "Good for you, Tommy," she said. "That gives me one customer. That's all, is it? Just the one?"

"And a turtle," my father said. "Don't forget that. And look—don't be too long, will you? I'd like to drive in to the village sometime before noon."

My mother had already started for the lake, with Tom at her side. As they went around the corner of the cabin Tom turned and held up his turtle to show me once more, and my mother, with a little wave of her hand, called back, "We may surprise you: we may never come back!"

And as she called this out to us, her voice was light and very gay. It was almost as if she were singing.

We were working away about ten minutes later when my father paused and said, "Wait: listen. Did you hear anything?"

We both listened; we both heard a shout. My father jumped

up and ran down to the point; I followed as fast as I could. We looked out on the east lake, which was the one my mother liked best, and there, some distance out and closer to the far shore than to us, we saw the dark green canoe. We could see it very clearly. It was floating upright, and it was empty. Of my mother and Tom there was no sight at all. My father called my mother's name three times, very loudly; there was no answer. There was no sound of any kind: I don't think that at that moment we even heard a bird. We simply stood there in the complete stillness of the beautiful morning: I, not yet realizing just what had happened, and my father, who must have realized it from the very first shout.

Suddenly my father went "*Aaaggghh!*" It wasn't a call, it wasn't a shout to my mother, it wasn't anything: just a loud and terrible sound. Then without even looking at me or asking me to follow him—but I did anyway—he spun around and ran for the little boathouse, about fifty yards away on the shore of the lake. Here there were a small rowboat and a blue canoe, neither of which had been used since last year; my father began to tug at the rowboat and pulled it into the water. Still without looking at me, with his eyes out on the lake, he said, "Hurry up, get in. Take this can: you'll have to bail. This thing can't be tight. Hurry up, hurry up, *come on!*"

So I jumped in, and by now I was frightened. I had never heard my father like this before, I had never seen him look like this before, and now at last I knew what must have happened. My father began to row very fast, and water began to seep into the boat through the seams—not much, but I had to bail. We moved out over the water, the spray from the oars sometimes hitting me in the face, and as I felt the icy drops I knew how cold the water really was. I thought of my mother and Tom in that water, and suddenly I began to cry. At first my father paid no attention to this, merely keeping on with his rowing and looking constantly over his shoulder at our target: the dark green canoe which continued to float and swing gently about, not moving much in the still morning air. I continued to bail and also to cry, and my father continued to pay no attention, but at one point he looked up from his rowing and stared at me with such a strange expression that for a moment I was sure he was terribly angry with me. But he was not, it must have been something else, for he closed his eyes tight, then opened them and said in a quiet voice, "Don't cry, Jackie. Don't cry. It'll be all right. You'll see. We'll both see. It'll be all right." After this he seemed to row faster than before, breathing quite hard now, and still looking back over his shoulder at the canoe as if he were afraid it would go away before we reached it.

I don't know how long it took us to get there: probably no more than a few minutes, but it seemed a very long time. We came alongside, and my father reached over and grabbed the canoe, pulling it right up against us, and there, on its floor, we saw the pale blue kerchief that my mother had worn around her head, and we saw also, carefully crawling its way across the varnished ribs, Tom's turtle. So the canoe had not turned over: we knew that much. My father stood up in the boat; I started to do the same, but he said, quickly and harshly, "Sit down! And stay down! Don't move until I tell you to!" I sat at once and began to look over the side of the boat, more frightened than ever by the thought of what we were looking for and what I might have to see. The water was dark but quite clear, and although we must have been several feet over my head, I could see to the bottom, but I could see nothing except sand and dark patches of leaves and weeds and a couple of large smooth shapes which I knew were rocks.

My father now knelt in the bow, his head bent forward as if he were trying to reach down through the water with his eyes. Straining to see, he was so close to the water that he seemed to be mostly out of the boat, and suddenly I had the terrible feeling that at any moment he might topple overboard and get lost, like my mother and Tom, and in that case what would become of me? It was a thought that filled me with panic, but I didn't dare to say a word, and after no more than a few seconds my father straightened up and, without taking his eyes from the water, reached around behind him and grabbed one of the oars. Using it as a paddle he began to send us forward quickly but not too quickly, dipping the oar each time very carefully so that it made no ripples to interfere with our seeing. We went in straight toward the shore, then came back out; we zigzagged; we swung around in a big circle, then came back to the center in smaller circles. We covered all the nearby water, with my father kneeling in the bow and with me seated on a thwart in the stern; we saw nothing. Once I asked my father a question, but he gave no sign of having heard me. He continued to paddle, never missing a stroke, and as I sat there behind him, seeing only the blank and silent surface of his slim, strong, freshly sunburned back, my own hope died away, I knew at last that my mother and Tom were gone for good, and I began to cry again, but this time to myself.

My father was paddling faster now, taking less care not to disturb the water, but this did not matter much any more, for while we had been looking a wind had come up out of the north. It was a cold wind, the kind of wind that brings clouds, and these were now scattered all over the sky, huge and gray, all rushing together to block out the sun. The still lake was now fairly rough, the boat began to bump along, and while we continued to search, I realized all at once that with the choppy water and the loss of sunlight I could no longer see the bottom—I could barely see to any depth at all. My father could have been no better off, for suddenly he jumped to his feet, threw the oar down on the floor of the boat, and stood looking all around him, out over all the lake, and then back into the boat and right at me, but looking at me in such a different way that I wasn't even sure he saw me. Then, without a word, he dived over the side and disappeared in the cold dark tossing water!

I screamed at him, but I don't think he heard me. I stood up, still screaming and at the same time crying, for I was terrified now: too much had happened that I did not understand, and I had no idea what was going to happen next. Then, just as suddenly as he had gone, my father was back, pulling himself over the side, standing, breathing deeply, and diving over the side again. I looked over after him, saw him swim down and out of sight, and knew now that he was not leaving me or swimming away: he was going down to the bottom himself to try to find my mother and Tom.

This knowledge was of no help, however, because for the first time it had occurred to me that I was going to drown. The wind had become stronger and the water rougher; the boat was rocking badly, and except for my father's frantic reappearances, I was alone: I was certain that within the next few minutes the boat would capsize and I would be dumped into the freezing water and would never come up again. Meanwhile, my father kept on diving from the boat and a minute or so later scrambling back in— clearly not in answer to my screams, for each time he came back he said nothing to me and didn't even seem to know I was there. The pattern was always the same: my father throwing himself over the side, the splash as he entered the water, my screams, my father bobbing up on the other side and then pulling himself in, waving me away, almost *pushing* me away if I tried to help. Each time he climbed in, the boat tipped more dangerously than before, and twice I slipped and fell to the floor, sprawling out on my back in water which had leaked in through the seams or come in over the sides, while my father stood over me, ignoring me, and breathing in and out noisily, filling his lungs before he hurled himself into the water again. It got worse and worse, and I remember screaming and crying and yelling "Dad! Dad!" whenever he came back in the boat, and thinking that at any moment now we would both go over and that would be the end of me. I was so frightened by my own danger that I could think of absolutely nothing else, and from the beginning to the end of this awful interval I completely forgot the reason, the terrible reason, for our being out in the lake in the first place. I did not once think of my mother or of Tom.

Then, at last, my father climbed into the boat once more, but slowly this time, and very carefully, as if it had only now occurred to him that he might tip the boat over. I had slipped and fallen again and was lying on the floor; my arm hurt where I had cracked it against one of the oars, and I was cold. My father stood over me, dripping water on me, just as before, but now he seemed more like himself, and instead of looking all around him in a wild way and breathing in and out in great harsh gasps, he just stood still, breathing deeply but quietly, his shorts soaking wet and torn by something—a nail in an underwater board, maybe, or a branch. All at once he said loudly, but mainly to himself, "Nothing. Nothing nothing nothing."

At this I sniffled, and he looked down at me with a funny expression on his face; he said, "Jackie."

"I'm cold," I sobbed. "I'm freezing."

"You're freezing?" he said. And he said it almost with surprise, as if he didn't even know that it was cold. Yet the wind was very strong now, there was no sun at all, the temperature must have been dropping all the time; like me he had on only his shorts, and he had been in the icy water. When I looked up at him for comfort I saw that he was shaking and that his skin was pinched and blue. I was shaking too, trembling all over: my teeth had started to chatter and I couldn't stop them. My father looked down at me, and all at once he bent over and lifted me up and held me very close to him, hugging me against his cold wet chest. He held me there for a few seconds, and I could feel him shivering. Then, very gently, he put me down in the stern, propping me up against a wet cushion.

"All right, Jackie," he said. "We're going in now."

And so we went in, with my father rowing as hard as he could, and being helped by the wind which was blowing strong behind us. It must have been a fast trip; it seemed very slow. There were little whitecaps on the water now, the sky was completely covered with low thick dull gray clouds, and it had begun to feel like snow. The beautiful March morning had gone in an hour, and I was so cold I ached. I was still shaking, I kept rubbing my arms and legs, and every second the cold seemed to get worse: great layers of it that passed right through me, freezing the inside of my bones. I could think of nothing but this cold, the warm cabin seemed a very long distance away, and I wondered miserably if I would be frozen to death in the boat before we reached the shore.

My father spoke only once, and that was when he stopped rowing for a moment and looked across at me as if he had just hurt me. "Jackie," he said. "Jackie, I . . . good God forgive me, I don't know what to say to you!"

I said, lying bravely, "It's all right. I'm not so cold any more."

But he just looked at me with the same hurt look and said nothing to this; he went on with his rowing. It didn't dawn on me that he hadn't been talking about the cold at all.

When we got to the shore my father leaped from the boat, picked me up, and carried me to the cabin, running all the way.

He ripped my shorts off and, with a heavy, rough bath towel, began to rub me dry. He rubbed so hard it hurt, and then he dried off too, and we both put on heavy winter clothes. All this time he was silent; finally he looked at me and said, "You ought to be in bed, but I can't—come on," and we ran out and got into the car and drove to the village.

Here, while I sat in the car, warm and safe now, my father hurried about, gathering people together, pulling them along with him: the priest, the doctor, the man with no jaw who ran the gas station. I watched all this, and as I watched, the odd and awful thing was that I couldn't feel what I should have felt at all. By now I understood everything that had happened, I knew just what my father was doing and what he was going to do, but it was as if a part of me—an important part of me—had not been able to catch up with what the rest of me knew. What I felt was mainly suspense, a kind of excitement: I was like a spectator at some game which was interesting but with which I had no great personal connection. As yet I had not begun to feel anything more than the faintest trembling beginnings of what I was to feel so devastatingly, and for the first time in my life, later in the day.

My father jumped into the car, bringing some of the men with him, and we drove back to the cabin, more men following us in two trucks loaded with some kind of equipment. When we reached the cabin my father took me inside; he built up the fire and told me to stay in front of it until he came back. Then he went off to the lake with the other men.

I stayed in the cabin all afternoon. Most of the time I was alone, and most of the time, as my father had directed, I stayed in the main room near the fireplace. Obedience was easy; there was really no place else to go. Once I went outside, into the clearing in front of the cabin, but the weather was worse now, a cold drizzle had begun to fall, and when I peered through the mist across the lake all I could see was men in boats over near the far shore where my father and I had been. And inside, beyond the main room, there were only the two bedrooms. I went into mine briefly. It was just as it had been when we had got up that morning: Tom's pajamas were still on the bed, and his lopsided fort, which he had made out of pillows and blankets, was still standing. I left the room quickly and did not go back. Later, reluctantly but somehow feeling that I ought to, maybe even that I *had* to, I went into the other bedroom. The first thing I saw, directly opposite the door and hanging over the back of a chair in front of my mother's dressing table, was a bathing suit—one she must have taken out, then decided not to wear: in that moment it looked to me exactly like the one she had worn. On the table was a scattering of her things—combs, brushes, little white jars of face creams, a slim gold bottle of the perfume which she liked best and which my father, for some reason, always called One Night in the Alps—and on the edge of the mirror, stuck in under the frame, was the birthday card from me. It was the first card I had ever sent her, long ago, before Tom was born, and I remember that my father had guided my hand while underneath the printed greeting I wrote a message of my own: *Dear Mom I love you and hope you have a very good birthday. Your son Jackie.*

And so I left this room quickly too. I sat by the fireplace and wished my father would come back. I started to read a book, I pushed around the pieces of a huge family jigsaw puzzle called Big Game of North America, I picked up a pack of cards and began to scale them, one by one, across the room. I did all these things halfheartedly, in fact without any interest at all, because by now I had begun to feel quite different: uneasy, very strange. Here by myself in the silent cabin where I had never been alone before, where nothing I touched or even looked at was all mine but was a part of my father and mother and Tom as well, where into my head now came not vague and passing thoughts but a sudden succession of hard and marvelously clear pictures of things we had all done together and could never do again—here now, I felt as if something had begun a slow incessant twisting inside me, like a key which was winding me up, turning and turning and turning, tightening me more every second, and this was all so real that all at once the tension shot me out of my chair and I sprang to my feet, stiff and trembling a little and waiting apprehensively for the one final twist that would surely be unbearable. But suddenly it stopped, the tautness let go completely, and when it did it seemed that everything that was in me, even my breath, left me in a single great gushing rush, and I stood there boneless and helpless and absolutely empty. And it was in this desperate, desolate, *total* way that the death of my mother and my brother came home to me at last, and in this awful, cataclysmic misery I thought my heart would really break.

Strangely, I did not cry. I sat back in the chair once more, very lonely and full of a great dull swelling ache. After a while—it might have been minutes, it might have been an hour—my father came back. He came into the cabin alone, he came over to me and hugged me hard again, and then, quietly but very quickly, he told me that a few minutes ago they had found my mother and Tom. And when I heard this it was just as if I had been expecting to hear it, and it made no difference: it just landed in the empty ache, and I didn't feel any worse because, I suppose, I couldn't feel at all. Then the priest came in and took my hand and patted it a few times.

"A brave li'l boys like you," he said, "he don' wan' to cry, eh? You know what for? Because dat brave li'l boys, he know his mamma and his li'l brudder, dey're wit' de angels now!"

His name was Father LaPlante; he was a French-Canadian priest who sometimes in the pulpit on Sunday talked English, but most often did not. Everybody else came in then, and some of them said things to me and some of them just looked, but in a little while everyone went away, and they took my mother and Tom with them. I asked my father if I could see them before they went, but he said it would be better a little later.

And so my father and I were alone in the cabin again, but not for long. He went into his bedroom and I heard him moving about; when I looked in I saw him putting some of my mother's things into a suitcase. After this he came out and took me by the hand, just as if I were a baby, and led me out to the car. It was dark, and the cold drizzle had changed to a light and lazy snow. We drove off, and as we took the first turn on the dirt road I looked back through the slow flakes at the cabin, and I saw that my father had not even closed the door.

I never saw the cabin again.

We drove toward the city: a long, silent, immensely sad drive. To my surprise we did not go home; instead, about twenty

miles from the city, we left the main road and turned into a small
seaside town and stopped in front of an old hotel. My father said
simply, "We're going to stay here. Just for tonight."

I had never been in a hotel before, but I knew that this was
not a very good one. At the desk downstairs a thin, tired-looking
man with watery eyes watched my father sign a big book; over his
head was a card which said: PEOPLE *may come and* PEOPLE *may
go, but the* BULL *in this place goes on forever.* Upstairs, our room
was big and dark and smelled of the sea. There was a wide brass
bed, everything was old but looked clean, and on the floor,
underneath one of the windows and attached to the foot of the
radiator, was a coil of thick rope with big knots in it. Above the
rope was a sign in big red letters reading: IN CASE OF FIRE.

It was late, I hadn't eaten since morning, but I wasn't hungry
at all; my father said it was time to go to bed. I undressed and
knelt by the bed and said my prayers, and I think that this was the
worst part of all. For the prayers for the dead were familiar to me,
I had said them every night since I had begun to pray, but they
had never been in any sense *personal* prayers: no one I knew had
ever died. Suddenly I was saying them for my own mother and
for Tom, and even now I found this impossible to believe, even
though I knew it was agonizingly, shatteringly true.

Finally I got into bed, and after a minute my father got in too.
We lay there in the dark and the silence. There were no night
noises from the streets of the town; the only outside sound was
from the sea: a dull and regular thudding as the surf broke on the
hard shore. There was a thud, then silence, then another thud,
then more silence, and in between I could hear only the beating of
my heart, which seemed to me very loud and very fast. My father
said nothing. He was lying on his back, looking straight up at the
ceiling. Suddenly I felt his hand touch mine, then take it and hold
it, very lightly and tenderly, and when this happened something
seemed to turn completely over inside me, and I twisted around in
bed and flung myself up against my father, clinging to him
desperately, and as he quickly put his arms around me and held
me, I cried for the first time since my father had told me that my
mother and Tom had been found.

I cried and kept crying: very hard, and for a very long time.
My father just held me, not saying anything, not trying to comfort

me with words, and when at last I stopped—or at least gave signs of stopping—he still held me, but he began to talk, and to talk only about my mother. He went back to the beginning: he told me about how he had met her, how she had looked on the stage, where they had been married, and who had married them—the bishop had been at the reception, my mother had been thrilled by the telegram of congratulations from the President, my mother had been terrified when my Uncle Jimmy (at the time, my father explained, a drinking man) had first threatened to punch the governor of the state in the nose, and then in fact had done so. My father told me about their life together before I was born and afterward, of their trips and travels, of the wonders they had seen and the love they had shared. He talked and talked about my mother, and he seemed not to be able to stop talking, and I listened, hanging on every word, just as I had always listened to his stories at night in the cabin, and then, imperceptibly, I began to grow drowsy, and finally—again, just as I had done so often in the cabin—I simply collapsed into sleep with his words still sounding in my ears.

At one point during the night I woke and realized with sudden fright that my father was no longer in bed with me. But then I saw him: he was on the far side of the room, but I could see him clearly. The weather must have broken, for there was a moon, and in its pale light I could see that my father had thrown open the window wide and was in front of it, not standing but kneeling, motionless, his hands joined, and looking out into the still, dark, windless night. I watched him for a moment, and then I must have fallen asleep again, for the next time I saw him he was back in bed and it was morning.

We left the hotel and went home. Ellen and Arthur were waiting for us: Ellen was weeping, Arthur was pale and very quiet. Later in the day my mother and Tom were brought home, and I saw them at last. During the next two days, until the morning of the funeral, I saw them often. Sometimes I was by myself with them, sometimes I was with a crowd of people who came to the wake. On the third morning we all went to the church and from there to the cemetery, and at last it was over, and I knew that from now on I would see them only in my memory.

The Desert

Allen Wheelis

The author, a psychiatrist, tells here the story of a psychiatrist who becomes fatally involved in a genuinely pathological marriage. Like many another mature man, he has gradually fallen in love with a married woman who appears to fulfill his deepest needs, and who seems to be already emotionally independent of her husband. Thus, there is no real obstacle to their marriage. After the husband has returned from a long trip, the wife and the psychiatrist continue their relationship openly.

However, the lover soon perceives what she had successfully hidden from him when her husband was gone, namely that in fact the husband-wife bond is extremely strong. Moreover, it is apparent that the husband is a dangerous psychotic and that she is bound to him through her need to protect him from his own excesses. As the husband's psychosis advances, her protectiveness increases, and the protagonist begins to be excluded from their life. She is willing to sacrifice her love, and herself, by remaining in bondage to her sadistic husband. We begin to suspect that eventually his actions will lead to her death.

The specific details of the plot may seem excessive, and the author's philosophical contemplations of natural beauty in the desert in contrast to the ugliness of the lives he describes may seem at times inflated, but the phenomenon of one spouse's bondage to another who suffers from some deep pathology (alcoholism, psychosis, drugs, gambling, or murderous hostility) is not uncommon. Often we may come to know a couple for a long period of time before we penetrate the disguises and facades they have created to prevent others from understanding this deeper dynamic. A husband and his alcoholic wife may act as though theirs is a normal, happy marriage. Alternately, one spouse may make others feel that he or she is carrying out the appropriate marital duties out of a sense of traditional obligation while

Allen Wheelis, *The Desert*, Basic Books, Inc., New York, 1970.

still remaining emotionally free to leave at any time—when in fact both are bound together in the service of that pathology.

The author also teaches us to beware of the extent to which the "outsider," even after many intimate hours with his or her beloved, may find it difficult to believe in the power of this pathological relationship. We have no way of understanding how husband and wife may be bound to one another, for we do not see them when they are alone. If we interact with one of them separately, that person behaves differently, and we therefore perceive—and perceive correctly—a different and healthier person. In this instance, the wife's love for the psychiatrist transforms her when she is with him; but similarly her bondage to her husband transforms her once again when he needs her.

A day passes, another. She doesn't call. On the third day I determine not to call her, go that night to North Beach to find a girl, thinking I'll take her to Ariana's apartment and bed. What I find in a din of jazz is a nineteen-year-old Haitian with short curly hair, red lips, round expressionless face. I change my mind about where to take her, give the driver my own address. In the cab I don't touch her, neither of us speaks. I think of the brown couch in my apartment, the gray chair in the bedroom where Ariana leaves her clothes, see her white slip with lace, the stockings, the bra sliding to the floor, her presence on everything. I glance at the girl. "What's your name?" "Jeanine." She wears a red jersey dress, very tight, reaches only to midthigh; I see it thrown across the gray chair—lean forward suddenly, "Driver, take us to the West Wind Motel."

I lock the door, sit on the bed, think of the tricks she may know, but can't respond, watch sadly as she peels the tight dress up over her head. Black satin skin with scarlet traverses: red bikini with black lace, tiny red bra which just covers nipples and areolae. The lithe body lazily bumps and grinds. She raises her arms, turns around, hunches shoulders forward, the bra falls, she pushes down the bikini; but it's not for me, I pull her to the bed, try to make conversation. She's restive, wants to work on me. I shake my head, tell her to get dressed. Her feelings are hurt, and paying doesn't help; she leaves without a word and I find myself sitting on the bed in pants and undershirt, staring senselessly at a glass in a wax paper bag, feeling things are going awry, something important is slipping, don't know how to stop it, and whatever I try becomes a flailing about that makes it worse.

The next afternoon I cancel my patients, drive to San Anselmo. The day is warm, sunny, windless. The yard before the Craig house is a sea of daffodils, flame tulips along the walk. Ariana has heard the car, comes from around the house to meet me, wears a sleeveless dress with broad diagonal stripes of black and white, takes my arm, for a moment puts her head on my shoulder. Strain has lined her face, she has not slept, I think. Minute drops of perspiration stand in the down of her lip. We do not speak, she holds my arm tightly. I feel sorry for her as we walk around the house to the patio.

A small table is set with yellow brocade cloth, a vase of daffodils, tea service—a scene from Chekhov. "Country life has its charms," I say. "Very cozy."

Ariana flushes, brings another chair. Scott stands awkwardly, holds out his hand. Wants to be forgiven, wants everything the same. "Have the police come yet?" I ask, dismissing the hand with a shake of my head.

"Yes."

"And what did you tell them?"

"Nothing."

"Did they ask about those marks on Zoë's belly?"

"I knew nothing."

"So you lied."

"You think I owe honesty to policemen?"

Ariana has brought another cup and plate, another napkin of yellow brocade. I sit on a yellow vinyl cushion which sighs under my weight, a chair of white wrought-iron tracery like lace. Tea is poured, a plate of *petits fours* is passed. I can't reconcile this scene with Zoë's body, the crushed head, the matted hair. One or the other is unreal, is a lie—and it's this one. I drink the tea, eat the pastry, become furious, as if tricked into taking the sacrament of a religion I despise. Ariana makes efforts at conversation which Scott picks up hysterically; I am silent. After a while Ariana gives up, sits across from me with lowered head. Scott is intensely nervous, puts his hand on hers, his soft white fingers making quick entreaties. Her brown hand does not respond but is not withdrawn, and this weight of him on her, and her acceptance of it, goads me.

"I have things to tell you, Scott. Alone." I have to get away from this absurd, insulting table. "Come for a walk with me."

"I . . . well. . . ." Again he puts his soft wet hand on hers. "Will you come?" he whispers.

She looks at him calmly. "He wants to talk to you alone."

Scott stands with a sudden jerk, still holding her hand. I stand. "No! No!" he says shrilly. "I won't go." He sits again, just as suddenly. "You can say it here. Whatever it is. I have no secrets from my wife."

"No, just from the police, you bastard! And have the insufferable nerve to say 'my wife,' to brag of a frankness you've never used except to torment her—except now when you use it in fear." In lieu of hitting him I jerk my chair from the table, overturning it.

A bee buzzes around the daffodils. Ariana pays no attention, Scott flails at it.

"All right," I say, "we'll talk here. You are sick, you have to go to a hospital."

"Ariana and I have discussed that," he says—I recognize a prepared speech. "I've given it a lot of thought . . . have decided not to go."

"He did consider it," Ariana says, "kept it open till today."

"When did the police come?" I ask.

"Yesterday," Ariana says.

"But of course! If they'd had something on him he'd go—as a dodge. If he's in the clear, he won't."

"I won't go," Scott says in an effort at dignity, "because I'm not sick."

"You are not competent to judge," I snap.

"Are you," he says, "as my wife's lover, competent?"

He has scored, better watch my temper. "You are sick in a way that makes you dangerous, that was fatal for Zoë."

"That's a charge, not a diagnosis."

"I'm not going to argue with you, Scott. It's not necessary. You *know* you're sick. The only question is what to do about it. You want to play around. I'm *telling* you: you have to go to a hospital."

"No."

I look at Ariana: head lowered, miserable, abstaining. "If you won't go willingly, you have to be committed."

"You can't do that. Only a court . . ."

"Yes, only a court. But a court *will*."

"I don't think so." His voice is rising. "I'll have the best lawyer, I'll . . ."

"You will be in more trouble," I say, "if you are judged sane. Then there will be criminal charges."

"They've got nothing on me," he shrills. "She was not forced. Everything was for pleasure."

I feel sick. "You push the limits of pleasure rather far, don't you?"

His chin is trembling. Ariana looks at her folded hands as in a trance. The bee buzzes before us in the daffodils. After a while I walk around the house to the car, sit behind the wheel. Ariana comes, stands beside me.

Inside the house Scott looks out at us, moves from window to window. I take Ariana's hand, draw her into the car. "Come with me," I plead. "I can't leave you here."

Scott comes flying out. "Go back," she says to him, as to a child; "I'm not leaving." He hesitates. "Go in the house," she says firmly; "I'll be there soon."

Reluctantly, with backward glances, he obeys. Again moves from room to room, watching.

"You can't help him," I say.

"I have to try."

"You've tried for ten years and he's become more and more the sadist. You can't give him anything new. He wants only to hide behind your skirts till he's over this scare."

"Will a hospital help him?"

"I don't know, I . . ."

"What do you think?" she insists. "Really? . . ."

I hesitate. "I think nothing will help him."

I try to draw her to me, but she sits straight. Inside the house Scott moves from window to window. I look at her face, the clear profile, the curve of lashes, the line of nose; run my hand through the soft black hair, see it below me on white sheet. "I can't let you stay. It's not safe." She looks straight ahead. A jet passes over us, northbound for Seattle. "I'd have some hope if he felt guilt, but he doesn't, just fear." Still no reply.

"I have to go now," she says after a while.

I take her arm. "If you won't commit him, I'll have to do it without you."

"Please don't!"

"I have to. I can't just forget what happened . . . what could happen to you."

She searches my face, kisses me, walks slowly back to the house.

I do nothing about Scott that day, or the next, and the longer I wait the more difficult it becomes. With the signature of one other psychiatrist I can have him picked up. Whom shall I ask? Lars? Julian? Can I, without disclosing my involvement, ask anyone? Perhaps I must disqualify myself altogether, ask the two of them to do it. But would they not turn me down, discounting the danger to Ariana as the apprehensiveness of a lover, or, if I insist, refer me to the police? I could sign a complaint as friend of the family . . . but with the wife opposed, that would come to nothing.

But suppose, somehow, I *do* get him picked up. He could be held for three days against his will in the County Hospital. What then? The judge would have to rule. And might not commit. I imagine Scott explaining himself to the judge—the cultivated speech, the achievements in film, his great distress at Zoë's suicide, the disclosure of my affair with his wife—"Case dismissed!" At that point, indeed, the judge might ask the State Medical Board to look into my professional deportment. The more carefully I consider what to do the more empty my threats seem to have been; I'm dismayed to find that my involvement has robbed me of authority. Yet I know for sure he is dangerous.

I consider going to the police. But with what evidence? I can't prove it was he who used the whip. And if I could it wouldn't hold him long. The orgy is hearsay. I could destroy the alibi Ariana has provided, but could not establish that he was in Zoë's room, nor ever know what happened there before she climbed out on the ledge. I could have him questioned again, perhaps locked up for a few hours, and that's all. His menace is as much too subtle for the law as for psychiatry.

When I have finished with my patients on the third day I begin packing a suitcase before I realize fully the decision I have come to: If Ariana won't leave, if I can't tear Scott away, then I must join them. It amuses me that Ariana will see nothing odd in this, will find it natural that I should move in to help her. I will be the doctor, she the nurse—a mental hospital for one. Rather exclusive care Scott will have arranged for himself, but in his style; he never travels second-class. As I cross the bridge I think how incredulous my colleagues would be, how disapproving the State Medical Board: to treat the husband of my mistress in his own home. Yet the more I think of it the more possible it seems, perhaps because I can imagine no other course. I even feel hopeful—not for fundamental change, but to get him on his feet. And who knows? Maybe a little more. At least to the point of not clinging to Ariana. I whistle as I drive, realize I am doing exactly what she has planned from the beginning. But feel no bitterness, am content that she has won.

It is twilight when I reach the house in San Anselmo. No answer to my knock, the bell sounds hollow, no car in the garage. I peer through the windows, beat on the door. At the back of the house I find an unlocked window, force my way in. They are gone. I walk through every room looking for a note, though I know there will be none.

I drive then to Ariana's apartment on Telegraph Hill. My things are still there, her clothes are gone. No note. I feel a depression beginning, something being tied in a knot, pulled tight. I close the door of her apartment, close my heart, go back to my own place, turn the key.

Howards End

E. M. Forster

Howards End may well be, as Lionel Trilling alleged, a novel about England's decline and the power of one class over another; certainly it contains many symbols of underlying clashes—industrialism and commercialism versus beauty, freedom of the spirit versus selfish caution, and so on. However, the impact of Forster's novel is felt more keenly because he does not stress the symbols but lets us see the inner life of real individuals: we are caught up in their lives and want to know what is going to happen next. We are made aware of the larger social structure not because Forster analyzes it separately, but because we see how it shapes the specific fates of the people who are part of it.

The following scene, toward the end of the novel, brings together several of these larger themes. Margaret's sister Helen loves the house known as Howards End and wants to spend a night there before returning to Germany, where she will bear her illegitimate child. It is a child of love, and Helen "represents" the warm acceptance of life's impulses no matter what punishment society may threaten. Margaret is more practical, bending more to society's demands, but her inner feelings are in harmony with her sister's. Margaret is Mr. Wilcox's second wife, and this second marriage perhaps represents one of the few evidences of his ability to reach out and (in Forster's word) "connect" with others; otherwise, he is self-righteous, little engaged in self-examination, a staunch defender, on the surface, of the social system as it is.

In this scene, Mr. Wilcox both recognizes and rejects Margaret's influence, her willingness to protect her sister. Ultimately, he lives within the fortress of property: Howards End is *his*, not his wife's, and it will belong to his son Charles. It is *his* authority that can and should decide. Helen represents a danger to his little world, and if he is capable of stating his sympathy without feeling any, he is equally

E. M. Forster, *Howards End*, Alfred A. Knopf, Inc., New York, 1921.

capable of stating and (by not examining his own emotions) even feeling a false protectiveness toward the memory of his first wife, who once lived at Howards End.

What he cannot comprehend is that his sins and cruelties are greater than Helen's, that as a human being he has no right to do what, as a husband, he has the legal authority to do. Margaret's sharp and finally complete rejection of him is not so much on the ground that he has hurt others, but that at the deepest levels of his soul he is incapable of feeling any sympathy with the needs or hurts of others: they are no part of him.

"Leave it that you don't see," cried Margaret. "Call it fancy. But realize that fancy is a scientific fact. Helen is fanciful, and wants to."

Then he surprised her—a rare occurrence. He shot an unexpected bolt. "If she wants to sleep one night, she may want to sleep two. We shall never get her out of the house, perhaps."

"Well?" said Margaret, with the precipice in sight. "And suppose we don't get her out of the house? Would it matter? She would do no one any harm."

Again the irritated gesture.

"No, Henry," she panted, receding. "I didn't mean that. We will only trouble Howards End for this one night. I take her to London tomorrow—"

"Do you intend to sleep in a damp house, too?"

"She cannot be left alone."

"That's quite impossible! Madness. You must be here to meet Charles."

"I have already told you that your message to Charles was unnecessary, and I have no desire to meet him."

"Margaret—my Margaret—"

"What has this business to do with Charles? If it concerns me little, it concerns you less, and Charles not at all."

"As the future owner of Howards End," said Mr. Wilcox, arching his fingers, "I should say that it did concern Charles."

"In what way? Will Helen's condition depreciate the property?"

"My dear, you are forgetting yourself."

"I think you yourself recommended plain speaking."

They looked at each other in amazement. The precipice was at their feet now.

"Helen commands my sympathy," said Henry. "As your husband, I shall do all for her that I can, and I have no doubt that she will prove more sinned against than sinning. But I cannot treat her as if nothing has happened. I should be false to my position in society if I did."

She controlled herself for the last time. "No, let us go back to Helen's request," she said. "It is unreasonable, but the request of an unhappy girl. Tomorrow she will go to Germany, and trouble society no longer. Tonight she asks to sleep in your empty house—a house which you do not care about, and which you have not occupied for over a year. May she? Will you give my sister leave? Will you forgive her—as you hope to be forgiven, and as you have actually been forgiven? Forgive her for one night only. That will be enough."

"As I have actually been forgiven—?"

"Never mind for the moment what I mean by that," said Margaret. "Answer my question."

Perhaps some hint of her meaning did dawn on him. If so, he blotted it out. Straight from his fortress he answered: "I seem rather unaccommodating, but I have some experience of life, and know how one thing leads to another. I am afraid that your sister had better sleep at the hotel. I have my children and the memory of my dear wife to consider. I am sorry, but see that she leaves my house at once."

"You mentioned Mrs. Wilcox."

"I beg your pardon?"

"A rare occurrence. In reply, may I mention Mrs. Bast?"

"You have not been yourself all day," said Henry, and rose from his seat with face unmoved. Margaret rushed at him and seized both his hands. She was transfigured.

"Not any more of this!" she cried. "You shall see the connection if it kills you, Henry! You have had a mistress—I forgave you. My sister has a lover—you drive her from the house. Do you see the connection? Stupid, hypocritical, cruel—oh,

contemptible!—a man who insults his wife when she's alive and
cants with her memory when she's dead. A man who ruins a
woman for his pleasure, and casts her off to ruin other men. And
gives bad financial advice, and then says he is not responsible.
These, man, are you. You can't recognize them, because you
cannot connect. I've had enough of your unweeded kindness. I've
spoilt you long enough. All your life you have been spoiled. Mrs.
Wilcox spoiled you. No one has ever told you what you are—
muddled, criminally muddled. Men like you use repentance as a
blind, so don't repent. Only say to yourself: 'What Helen has
done, I've done.' "

"The two cases are different," Henry stammered. His real
retort was not quite ready. His brain was still in a whirl, and he
wanted a little longer.

"In what way different? You have betrayed Mrs. Wilcox,
Helen only herself. You remain in society, Helen can't. You have
had only pleasure, she may die. You have the insolence to talk to
me of differences, Henry?"

Oh, the uselessness of it! Henry's retort came.

"I perceive you are attempting blackmail. It is scarcely a
pretty weapon for a wife to use against her husband. My rule
through life has been never to pay the least attention to threats,
and I can only repeat what I said before: I do not give you and
your sister leave to sleep at Howards End."

Margaret loosed his hands. He went into the house, wiping
first one and then the other on his handkerchief. For a little she
stood looking at the Six Hills, tombs of warriors, breasts of the
spring. Then she passed out into what was now the evening.

Seize the Day
Saul Bellow

Few readers will want to identify with Wilhelm Adler, the
central figure in this section. His own father is cold and
severe, and has no intention of helping him out of his
troubles. This son is a slob, a *nebbish*, a spineless weakling.
He fails everyone, himself most of all. In *Seize the Day*, Saul
Bellow unsparingly forces us to watch Adler, already middle-aged and long accustomed to defeat, as he encounters
his past and present without dignity, without competence.

The writer is clinical with his merciless details. He
almost never steps aside to tell the reader, "Here's what that
means"; instead, we simply *watch*, appalled at Wilhelm's
ups and downs as he experiences the day. We know it is not
our life; we are not like Wilhelm. He lets others determine
who and what he is, while we keep our self intact through
the buffeting of circumstance.

What makes Wilhelm painful and not laughable is that
now and then we *do* see a glimpse of ourselves in him, and
we *can* imagine ourselves at times behaving and feeling as
he does. He is not *radically* different from us. Indeed, he
resembles too well the kind of person mid-century America
seemed to produce in quantity. He is always chasing the
quick, easy buck, and so he becomes a sucker for people
brighter and more ruthless than he. He expects (as each of
us does, at times) that his appearance, his facility for glib
talk will be just what is needed to earn him a good living—at
the next step, the next opportunity. If someone will bail him
out just *this* time, he will make it on the next try. He is only a
slight distance from making it, or so he thinks, and thus he
feels tantalized while slowly sinking into seedy failure.

A Dr. Tamkin has defrauded him of what little money he
had. He has just been coldly denied by his own well-to-do
father, Dr. Adler. He is now called urgently by his wife, and
again he appears not only to be an incompetent: he is a

Saul Bellow, *Seize the Day*, The Viking Press, Inc., New York, 1956, pp. 120–125.

moral failure, seen as a fool and a weakling by others. Worse, he is not even lovable. No one will console him.

The telephone conversation tells us, with no analysis, what the marriage has been. His wife feels morally invulnerable, and his feeble attempts to slash back at her have no effect. We can see that she, too, is not admirable; we would not want her for spouse or mother. Both are caught, however, in a common enough situation at the end of a marriage: neither can possibly satisfy the other's needs any longer. For Wilhelm, as for most people at this stage of marital disorganization, there *is* no solution.

He inquired at the desk for Dr. Tamkin.

The clerk said, "No, I haven't seen him. But I think there's something in the box for you."

"Me? Give it here," said Wilhelm and opened a telephone message from his wife. It read, "Please phone Mrs. Wilhelm on return. Urgent."

Whenever he received an urgent message from his wife he was always thrown into a great fear for the children. He ran to the phone booth, spilled out the change from his pockets onto the little curved steel shelf under the telephone, and dialed the Digby number.

"Yes?" said his wife. Scissors barked in the parlor.

"Margaret?"

"Yes, hello." They never exchanged any other greeting. She instantly knew his voice.

"The boys all right?"

"They're out on their bicycles. Why shouldn't they be all right? Scissors, quiet!"

"Your message scared me," he said. "I wish you wouldn't make 'urgent' so common."

"I had something to tell you."

Her familiar unbending voice awakened in him a kind of hungry longing, not for Margaret but for the peace he had once known.

"You sent me a postdated check," she said. "I can't allow

that. It's already five days past the first. You dated your check for the twelfth."

"Well, I have no money. I haven't got it. You can't send me to prison for that. I'll be lucky if I can raise it by the twelfth."

She answered, "You better get it, Tommy."

"Yes? What for?" he said. "Tell me. For the sake of what? To tell lies about me to everyone? You—"

She cut him off. "You know what for. I've got the boys to bring up."

Wilhelm in the narrow booth broke into a heavy sweat. He dropped his head and shrugged while with his fingers he arranged nickels, dimes, and quarters in rows. "I'm doing my best," he said. "I've had some bad luck. As a matter of fact, it's been so bad that I don't know where I am. I couldn't tell you what day of the week this is. I can't think straight. I'd better not even try. This has been one of those days, Margaret. May I never live to go through another like it. I mean that with all my heart. So I'm not going to try to do any thinking today. Tomorrow I'm going to see some guys. One is a sales manager. The other is in television. But not to act," he hastily added. "On the business end."

"That's just some more of your talk, Tommy," she said. "You ought to patch things up with Rojax Corporation. They'd take you back. You've got to stop thinking like a youngster."

"What do you mean?"

"Well," she said, measured and unbending, remorselessly unbending, "you still think like a youngster. But you can't do that any more. Every other day you want to make a new start. But in eighteen years you'll be eligible for retirement. Nobody wants to hire a new man of your age."

"I know. But listen, you don't have to sound so hard. I can't get on my knees to them. And really you don't have to sound so hard. I haven't done you so much harm."

"Tommy, I have to chase you and ask you for money that you owe us, and I hate it."

She hated also to be told that her voice was hard.

"I'm making an effort to control myself," she told him.

He could picture her, her graying bangs cut with strict fixity above her pretty, decisive face. She prided herself on being fair-minded. We could not bear, he thought, to know what we do. Even though blood is spilled. Even though the breath of life is taken from someone's nostrils. This is the way of the weak; quiet and fair. And then smash! They smash!

"Rojax take me back? I'd have to crawl back. They don't need me. After so many years I should have got stock in the firm. How can I support the three of you, and live myself, on half the territory? And why should I even try when you won't lift a finger to help? I sent you back to school, didn't I? At that time you said—"

His voice was rising. She did not like that and intercepted him. "You misunderstood me," she said.

"You must realize you're killing me. You can't be as blind as all that. Thou shalt not kill! Don't you remember that?"

She said, "You're just raving now. When you calm down it'll be different. I have great confidence in your earning ability."

"Margaret, you don't grasp the situation. You'll have to get a job."

"Absolutely not. I'm not going to have two young children running loose."

"They're not babies," Wilhelm said. "Tommy is fourteen. Paulie is going to be ten."

"Look," Margaret said in her deliberate manner. "We can't continue this conversation if you're going to yell so, Tommy. They're at a dangerous age. There are teen-aged gangs—the parents working, or the families broken up."

Once again she was reminding him that it was he who had left her. She had the bringing up of the children as her burden, while he must expect to pay the price of his freedom.

Freedom! he thought with consuming bitterness. Ashes in his mouth, not freedom. Give me my children. For they are mine too.

Can you be the woman I lived with? he started to say. Have you forgotten that we slept so long together? Must you now deal with me like this, and have no mercy?

He would be better off with Margaret again than he was today. This was what she wanted to make him feel, and she drove it home. "Are you in misery?" she was saying. "But you have deserved it." And he could not return to her any more than he could beg Rojax to take him back. If it cost him his life, he could not. Margaret had ruined him with Olive. She hit him and hit him, beat him, battered him, wanted to beat the very life out of him.

"Margaret, I want you please to reconsider about work. You have that degree now. Why did I pay your tuition?"

"Because it seemed practical. But it isn't. Growing boys need parental authority and a home."

He begged her, "Margaret, go easy on me. You ought to. I'm at the end of my rope and feel that I'm suffocating. You don't want to be responsible for a person's destruction. You've got to let up. I feel I'm about to burst." His face had expanded. He struck a blow upon the tin and wood and nails of the wall of the booth. "You've got to let me breathe. If I should keel over, what then? And it's something I can never understand about you. How you can treat someone like this whom you lived with so long. Who gave you the best of himself. Who tried. Who loved you." Merely to pronounce the word "love" made him tremble.

"Ah," she said with a sharp breath. "Now we're coming to it. How did you imagine it was going to be—big shot? Everything made smooth for you? I thought you were leading up to this."

She had not, perhaps, intended to reply as harshly as she did, but she brooded a great deal and now she could not forbear to punish him and make him feel pains like those she had to undergo.

He struck the wall again, this time with his knuckles, and he had scarcely enough air in his lungs to speak in a whisper, because his heart pushed upward with a frightful pressure. He got up and stamped his feet in the narrow enclosure.

"Haven't I always done my best?" he yelled, though his voice sounded weak and thin to his own ears. "Everything comes from me and nothing back again to me. There's no law that'll punish this, but you are committing a crime against me. Before God—and that's no joke. I mean that. Before God! Sooner or later the boys will know it."

In a firm tone, levelly, Margaret said to him, "I won't stand to be howled at. When you can speak normally and have something sensible to say I'll listen. But not to this." She hung up.

Wilhelm tried to tear the apparatus from the wall. He ground his teeth and seized the black box with insane digging fingers and made a stifled cry and pulled. Then he saw an elderly lady staring through the glass door, utterly appalled by him, and he ran from the booth, leaving a large amount of change on the shelf. He hurried down the stairs and into the street.

On Broadway it was still bright afternoon and the gassy air was almost motionless under the leaden spokes of sunlight, and sawdust footprints lay about the doorways of butcher shops and fruit stores. And the great, great crowd, the inexhaustible current of millions of every race and kind pouring out, pressing round, of every age, of every genius, possessors of every human secret, antique and future, in every face the refinement of one particular motive or essence—*I labor, I spend, I strive, I design, I love, I cling, I uphold, I give way, I envy, I long, I scorn, I die, I hide, I want.* Faster, much faster than any man could make the tally. The sidewalks were wider than any causeway; the street itself was immense, and it quaked and gleamed and it seemed to Wilhelm to throb at the last limit of endurance. And although the sunlight appeared like a broad tissue, its actual weight made him feel like a drunkard.

"I'll get a divorce if its' the last thing I do," he swore. "As for Dad— As for Dad— I'll have to sell the car for junk and pay the hotel. I'll have to go on my knees to Olive and say, 'Stand by me a while. Don't let her win. Olive!'" And he thought, I'll try to start again with Olive. In fact, I must. Olive loves me. Olive—

Chapter 10

Adjustment to the End of Marriage

Parallels have often been noted in the problems people must face when they adjust to the end of a marriage by either death or divorce: the loss of friendship, love, or security; the lack of sexual satisfaction; the lack of an adult role model for the children to follow; the greater work load for the remaining spouse; economic difficulties, especially if a husband has either died or abandoned the home. These two endings to marriage are, however, fundamentally different in one important respect: in few societies is the adjustment to divorce eased by a set of institutional arrangements and social definitions, but perhaps all societies develop rituals that focus on death, support the bereaved in his or her sorrow, instill a feeling of family obligation to rally around the broken family, and in general offer a set of proscriptions, prescriptions, and prohibitions about what is appropriate when a death in the family has taken place.

However, most tribal societies in which divorce was permitted gave more guidance than our own does. In most, custody was not problematic, because the child belonged to one definite lineage or another, and a collective responsibility was felt for that child. In a matrilineage, a woman remained part of her lineage after divorce as she did before her marriage, and her lineage would feel an obligation to arrange for a next marriage, too. Where there was a bride price, rules specified (even though there was argument in individual cases) the conditions under which the bride price should be returned.

The lack of social guidance in modern society, and especially the failure to impose on certain people the obligation to help the divorced person adjust, is primarily caused by the *recency* of divorce as a general solution for marital difficulty. In addition, however, ours is an age that has increasingly widened the options that people may choose, in many different kinds of situations. Our era specifies much less closely what is the appropriate behavior for old people. Western countries have generally dropped any detailed rules about appropriate mourning periods, how long a spouse should wait before remarrying after his or her spouse dies, etc. Thus it is not surprising that new "traditions" have not grown up about how to behave when there is a divorce.

Millions of people must go through it each year, but "adjustment" is a pale and uninspiring term. It looms as a deep personal problem, and may be experienced as tragedy, but it is difficult to create exciting literature (or sociology for that matter) out of that period. The creation of a life or love, or their destruction, gives us a climax or ending, but few writers have been able to create an appropriate esthetic form for the slow reconstruction of a new person, life, or marriage from the ashes of the old.

The Other Two

Edith Wharton

Although the women's liberation movement has inspired many wives to rebel, women must still adjust more than men do when they marry. They are persuaded to accept the situation partly because they have been reared from childhood to do so, partly because their material interests lie in that direction as well. They are economically more dependent on their husbands' goodwill than their husbands are on theirs, and the role obligations imposed on them by the society specify that they should sacrifice many of their wishes to the needs and desires of husband and children.

Nevertheless, many disgruntled husbands have wondered, upon reading such a statement, how they could have failed to find the docile, sweet, self-effacing, nurturant woman all this social energy was supposed to produce. Edith Wharton presents just such a wife in *The Other Two*. In these pages, we encounter Mrs. Waythorn after she has married a third time. The third husband must interact with the father of her child, because that husband has visitation rights. The third has had some social and business relations with the second husband. He is not at all dissatisfied with his wife, and he is not jealous of the other two, for she is devoted to him.

Indeed, she has so fully adjusted to his needs and wants that he finds it difficult to accomplish what he would prefer, that is, have no contact with the other two husbands at all. However, she makes those contacts easy and natural, while he has ruefully come to recognize that at least some part of her graciousness and pliancy toward him has grown from her experiences in her previous marriages. *Her* adjustment to divorce seems complete, and now he must also "adjust to divorce"—but to her divorces.

Although we may smile at Mrs. Waythorn's victory through yielding, both our observations and sociological research inform us that we are not the same person after a

Edith Wharton, *Roman Fever and Other Stories*, Charles Scribner's Sons, New York, 1964.

marriage as we were before. Perhaps we are not even better. On the other hand, it does seem likely that we are better able to adjust to the problems of living with another person than we were before. Indeed, it is possible that many of us follow Mrs. Waythorn's example to some extent: since we have learned some things at the expense of our first spouses, our later spouses are grateful for it.

She paused a moment. "I'll do just as you wish," she returned pliantly. "I thought it would be less awkward to speak to him when we meet."

Her pliancy was beginning to sicken him. Had she really no will of her own—no theory about her relation to these men? She had accepted Haskett—did she mean to accept Varick? It was "less awkward," as she had said, and her instinct was to evade difficulties or to circumvent them. With sudden vividness Waythorn saw how the instinct had developed. She was "as easy as an old shoe"—a shoe that too many feet had worn. Her elasticity was the result of tension in too many different directions. Alice Haskett—Alice Varick—Alice Waythorn—she had been each in turn, and had left hanging to each name a little of her privacy, a little of her personality, a little of the inmost self where the unknown god abides.

"Yes—it's better to speak to Varick," said Waythorn wearily.

The winter wore on, and society took advantage of the Waythorns' acceptance of Varick. Harassed hostesses were grateful to them for bridging over a social difficulty, and Mrs. Waythorn was held up as a miracle of good taste. Some experimental spirits could not resist the diversion of throwing Varick and his former wife together, and there were those who thought he found a zest in the propinquity. But Mrs. Waythorn's conduct remained irreproachable. She neither avoided Varick nor sought him out. Even Waythorn could not but admit that she had discovered the solution of the newest social problem.

He had married her without giving much thought to that problem. He had fancied that a woman can shed her past like a man. But now he saw that Alice was bound to hers both by the circumstances which forced her into continued relation with it, and by the traces it had left on her nature. With grim irony Waythorn compared himself to a member of a syndicate. He held so many shares in his wife's personality and his predecessors were his partners in the business. If there had been any element of passion in the transaction he would have felt less deteriorated by it. The fact that Alice took her change of husbands like a change of weather reduced the situation to mediocrity. He could have forgiven her for blunders, for excesses; for resisting Haskett, for yielding to Varick; for anything but her acquiescence and her tact. She reminded him of a juggler tossing knives; but the knives were blunt and she knew they would never cut her.

And then, gradually, habit formed a protecting surface for his sensibilities. If he paid for each day's comfort with the small change of his illusions, he grew daily to value the comfort more and set less store upon the coin. He had drifted into a dulling propinquity with Haskett and Varick and he took refuge in the cheap revenge of satirising the situation. He even began to reckon up the advantages which accrued from it, to ask himself if it were not better to own a third of a wife who knew how to make a man happy than a whole one who had lacked opportunity to acquire the art. For it *was* an art, and made up, like all others, of concessions, eliminations and embellishments; of lights judiciously thrown and shadows skilfully softened. His wife knew exactly how to manage the lights, and he knew exactly to what training she owed her skill. He even tried to trace the source of his obligations, to discriminate between the influences which had combined to produce his domestic happiness: he perceived that Haskett's commonness had made Alice worship good breeding, while Varick's liberal construction of the marriage bond had taught her to value the conjugal virtues; so that he was directly indebted to his predecessors for the devotion which made his life easy if not inspiring.

From this phase he passed into that of complete acceptance. He ceased to satirise himself because time dulled the irony of the situation and the joke lost its humour with its sting. Even the sight of Haskett's hat on the hall table had ceased to touch the springs of epigram. The hat was often seen there now, for it had been decided that it was better for Lily's father to visit her than for the little girl to go to his boarding-house. Waythorn, having acquiesced in this arrangement, had been surprised to find how little difference it made. Haskett was never obtrusive, and the few visitors who met him on the stairs were unaware of his identity. Waythorn did not know how often he saw Alice, but with himself Haskett was seldom in contact.

One afternoon, however, he learned on entering that Lily's father was waiting to see him. In the library he found Haskett occupying a chair in his usual provisional way. Waythorn always felt grateful to him for not leaning back.

"I hope you'll excuse me, Mr. Waythorn," he said rising. "I wanted to see Mrs. Waythorn about Lily, and your man asked me to wait here till she came in."

"Of course," said Waythorn, remembering that a sudden leak had that morning given over the drawing-room to the plumbers.

He opened his cigar-case and held it out to his visitor, and Haskett's acceptance seemed to mark a fresh stage in their intercourse. The spring evening was chilly, and Waythorn invited his guest to draw up his chair to the fire. He meant to find an excuse to leave Haskett in a moment; but he was tired and cold, and after all the little man no longer jarred on him.

The two were enclosed in the intimacy of their blended cigar-smoke when the door opened and Varick walked into the room. Waythorn rose abruptly. It was the first time that Varick had come to the house, and the surprise of seeing him, combined with the singular inopportuneness of his arrival, gave a new edge to Waythorn's blunted sensibilities. He stared at his visitor without speaking.

Varick seemed too preoccupied to notice his host's embarrassment.

"My dear fellow," he exclaimed in his most expansive tone, "I must apologise for tumbling in on you in this way, but I was too late to catch you down town, and so I thought—"

He stopped short, catching sight of Haskett, and his sanguine colour deepened to a flush which spread vividly under his scant blond hair. But in a moment he recovered himself and nodded slightly. Haskett returned the bow in silence, and Waythorn was still groping for speech when the footman came in carrying a tea-table.

The intrusion offered a welcome vent to Waythorn's nerves. "What the deuce are you bringing this here for?" he said sharply.

"I beg your pardon, sir, but the plumbers are still in the drawing-room, and Mrs. Waythorn said she would have tea in the library." The footman's perfectly respectful tone implied a reflection on Waythorn's reasonableness.

"Oh, very well," said the latter resignedly, and the footman proceeded to open the folding tea-table and set out its complicated appointments. While this interminable process continued the three men stood motionless, watching it with a fascinated stare, till Waythorn, to break the silence, said to Varick: "Won't you have a cigar?"

He held out the case he had just tendered to Haskett, and Varick helped himself with a smile. Waythorn looked about for a match, and finding none, proffered a light from his own cigar. Haskett, in the background, held his ground mildly, examining his cigar-tip now and then, and stepping forward at the right moment to knock its ashes into the fire.

The footman at last withdrew, and Varick immediately began: "If I could just say half a word to you about this business—"

"Certainly," stammered Waythorn; "in the dining-room—"

But as he placed his hand on the door it opened from without, and his wife appeared on the threshold.

She came in fresh and smiling, in her street dress and hat, shedding a fragrance from the boa which she loosened in advancing.

"Shall we have tea in her, dear?" she began; and then she caught sight of Varick. Her smile deepened, veiling a slight tremor of surprise.

"Why, how do you do?" she said with a distinct note of pleasure.

As she shook hands with Varick she saw Haskett standing behind him. Her smile faded for a moment, but she recalled it quickly, with a scarcely perceptible side-glance at Waythorn.

"How do you do, Mr. Haskett?" she said, and shook hands with him a shade less cordially.

The three men stood awkwardly before her, till Varick, always the most self-possessed, dashed into an explanatory phrase.

"We—I had to see Waythorn a moment on business," he stammered, brick-red from chin to nape.

Haskett stepped forward with his air of mild obstinacy. "I am sorry to intrude; but you appointed five o'clock—he directed his resigned glance to the time-piece on the mantel.

She swept aside their embarrassment with a charming gesture of hospitality.

"I'm so sorry—I'm always late; but the afternoon was so lovely." She stood drawing off her gloves, propitiatory and graceful, diffusing about her a sense of ease and familiarity in which the situation lost its grotesqueness. "But before talking business," she added brightly, "I'm sure every one wants a cup of tea."

She dropped into her low chair by the tea-table, and the two visitors, as if drawn by her smile, advanced to receive the cups she held out.

She glanced about for Waythorn, and he took the third cup with a laugh.

The Soft Touch of Grass
Luigi Pirandello

Contrary to the opinions of many essayists of our day, Americans do not worship youth—witness the age distribution of the people in important positions within our society. What the elderly have lost, by contrast with a traditional society in the past such as India, China, or Japan, is a perception of life as a kind of cycle or well-accepted series of *phases*, in which each age-position from birth to death is granted some privileges and must accept some obligations. In a modern society, it is not clear whether the elderly are supposed to retire into a dim room to contemplate their past, or to continue to pursue actively a new set of goals or build a new life upon retirement.

This lack of role definition is especially visible when death removes a husband or wife, for that spouse while living helped to affirm the existence and selfhood of the other. The trauma of grief and the yearning for a lifelong companion undermines the widow or widower's security about what is the appropriate thing to do, but this is intensified by the loss of the other spouse, who is no longer there to bolster the survivor's sense of identity. In the succeeding story, Luigi Pirandello asks us to perceive the world through the eyes of an elderly man who has just lost his lifelong companion, a wife whom he misses greatly. Of course, his son has also lost a mother, but he knows that his grown, married son is not so alone as he himself is. His own world is now empty.

The old man expects to be pushed aside, to be treated like a little child of no consequence, and he does not suppose that he himself can impose his will on others, or work out a new plan for living.

However, the young people are more sensitive and loving than he had anticipated, and indeed (though they completely change the house itself, signaling the end of an era) they decorate his new room with the best pieces of furniture in the house, selecting a room that will give him privacy. They encourage him, in short, to think of a new and independent life.

However, the very independence that he now enjoys leaves him with no sense of who he is, of what would be appropriate behavior for him. He is too old for young people, yet does not feel that he shares anything with oldsters.

When we lack a sure sense of our own identity, we do not necessarily cease to act at all, but the responses of others to our acts may determine how we perceive what we actually do. Here, Pirandello shows us the quick transitions of self-feelings the old man experiences, when he succumbs to the temptation to remove his socks and walk on the grass in his bare feet, just as the children do. His inner feelings are innocent, but his actions are misinterpreted by a young girl. His hurt, anger, and confusion remind us how insecure an individual's identity can be if the people in his or her social network no longer offer clear messages about his or her role definition.

They went into the next room, where he was sleeping in a big chair, to ask if he wanted to look at her for the last time before the lid was put on the coffin.

"It's dark. What time is it?" he asked.

It was nine-thirty in the morning, but the day was overcast and the light dim. The funeral had been set for ten o'clock.

Signor Pardi stared up at them with dull eyes. It hardly seemed possible that he could have slept so long and well all night. He was still numb with sleep and the sorrow of these last days. He would have liked to cover his face with his hands to shut out the faces of his neighbors grouped about his chair in the thin light; but sleep had weighted his body like lead, and although there was a tingling in his toes urging him to rise, it quickly went away. Should he still give way to his grief? He happened to say aloud, "Always . . ." but he said it like someone settling himself under the covers to go back to sleep. They all looked at him questioningly. Always what?

Always dark, even in the daytime, he had wanted to say, but

it made no sense. The day after her death, the day of her funeral, he would always remember this wan light and his deep sleep, too, with her lying dead in the next room. Perhaps the windows. . . .

"The windows?"

Yes, they were still closed. They had not been opened during the night, and the warm glow of those big dripping candles lingered. The bed had been taken away, and she was there in her padded casket, rigid and ashen against the creamy satin.

No. Enough. He had seen her.

He closed his eyes, for they burned from all the crying he had done these past few days. Enough. He had slept, and everything had been washed away with that sleep. Now he was relaxed, with a sense of sorrowful emptiness. Let the casket be closed and carried away with all it held of his past life.

But since she was still there. . . .

He jumped to his feet and tottered. They caught him, and with eyes still closed he allowed himself to be led to the open casket. When he opened his eyes and saw her, he called her by name, her name that lived for him alone, the name in which he saw her and knew her in all the fullness of the life they had shared together. He glared resentfully at the others daring to stare at her lying still in death. What did they know about her? They could not even imagine what it meant to him to be deprived of her. He felt like screaming, and it must have been apparent, for his son hurried over to take him away. He was quick to see the meaning of this and felt a chill as though he were stripped bare. For shame—those foolish ideas up to the very last, even after his night-long sleep. Now they must hurry so as not to keep the friends waiting who had come to follow the coffin to the church.

"Come on, Papa. Be reasonable."

With angry, piteous eyes, the bereaved man turned back to his big chair.

Reasonable, yes; it was useless to cry out the anguish that welled within him and that could never be expressed by words or deeds. For a husband who is left a widower at a certain age, a man still yearning for his wife, can the loss be the same as that of a son for whom—at a certain point—it is almost timely to be left an orphan? Timely, since he was on the point of getting married and would, as soon as the three months' mourning were passed, now that he had the added excuse that it was better for both of them to have a woman to look after the house.

"Pardi! Pardi!" they shouted from the entrance hall.

His chill became more intense when he understood clearly for the first time that they were not calling him but his son. From now on their surname would belong more to his son than to him. And he, like a fool, had gone in there to cry out the living name of his mate, like a profanation. For shame! Yes, useless, foolish ideas, he now realized, after that long sleep which had washed him clean of everything.

Now the one vital thing to keep him going was his curiosity as to how their new home would be arranged. Where, for example, were they going to have him sleep? The big double bed had been removed. Would he have a small bed? he wondered. Yes, probably his son's single bed. Now he would have the small bed. And his son would soon be lying in a big bed, his wife beside him within arm's reach. He, alone, in his little bed, would stretch out his arms into thin air.

He felt torpid, perplexed, with a sensation of emptiness inside and all around him. His body was numb from sitting so long. If he tried now to get up, he felt sure that he would rise light as a feather in all that emptiness, now that his life was reduced to nothing. There was hardly any difference between himself and the big chair. Yet that chair appeared secure on its four legs, whereas he no longer knew where his feet and legs belonged nor what to do with his hands. What did he care about his life? He did not care particularly about the lives of others, either. Yet, as he was still alive, he must go on. Begin again—some sort of life which he could not yet conceive and which he certainly would never have contemplated if things had not changed in his own world. Now, deposed like this all of a sudden, not old and yet no longer young. . . .

He smiled and shrugged his shoulders. For his son, all at once, he had become a child. But after all, as everyone knows, fathers are children to their grown sons who are full of worldly ambition and have successfully outdistanced them in positions of importance. They keep their fathers in idleness to repay all they have received when they themselves were small, and their fathers in turn become young again.

The single bed. . . .

But they did not even give him the little room where his son had slept. Instead, they said, he would feel more independent in another, almost hidden on the courtyard; he would feel free there to do as he liked. They refurnished it with all the best pieces, so it would not occur to anyone that it had once been a servant's room. After the marriage, all the front rooms were pretentiously decorated and newly furnished, even to the luxury of carpets. Not a trace remained of the way the old house had looked. Even with his own furniture relegated to that little dark room, out of the mainstream of the young people's existence, he did not feel at home. Yet, oddly enough, he did not resent the disregard he seemed to have reaped along with the old furniture, because he admired the new rooms and was satisfied with his son's success.

But there was another deeper reason, not too clear as yet, a promise of another life, all shining and colorful, which was erasing the memory of the old one. He even drew a secret hope from it that a new life might begin for him, too. Unconsciously, he sensed the luminous opening of a door at his back whence he might escape at the right moment, easy enough now that no one bothered about him, leaving him as if on holiday in the sanctuary of his little room "to do as he pleased." He felt lighter than air. His eyes had a gleam in them that colored everything, leading him from marvel to marvel, as though he really were a child again. He had the eyes of a child—lively and open wide on a world which was still new.

He took the habit of going out early in the morning to begin his holiday which was to last as long as his life lasted. Relieved of all responsibilities, he agreed to pay his son so much every month out of his pension for his maintenance. It was very little. Though he needed nothing, his son thought he should keep some money for himself to satisfy any need he might have. But need for what? He was satisfied now just to look on at life.

Having shaken off the weight of experience, he no longer knew how to get along with oldsters. He avoided them. And the younger people considered him too old, so he went to the park where the children played.

That was how he started his new life—in the meadow among the children in the grass. What an exhilarating scent the grass had, and so fresh where it grew thick and high. The children played hide-and-seek there. The constant trickle of some hidden stream outpurled the rustle of the leaves. Forgetting their game, the children pulled off their shoes and stockings. What a delicious feeling to sink into all that freshness of soft new grass with bare feet!

He took off one shoe and was stealthily removing the other when a young girl appeared before him, her face flaming. "You pig!" she cried, her eyes flashing.

Her dress was caught up in front on a bush, and she quickly pulled it down over her legs, because he was looking up at her from where he sat on the ground.

He was stunned. What had she imagined? Already she had disappeared. He had wanted to enjoy the children's innocent fun. Bending down, he put his two hands over his hard, bare feet. What had she seen wrong? Was he too old to share a child's delight in going barefoot in the grass? Must one immediately think evil because he was old? Ah, he knew that he could change in a flash from being a child to becoming a man again, if he must. He was still a man, after all, but he didn't want to think about it. He refused to think about it. It was really as a child that he had taken off his shoes. How wrong it was of that wretched girl to insult him like that! He threw himself face down on the grass. All his grief, his loss, his daily loneliness had brought about this gesture, interpreted now in the light of vulgar malice. His gorge rose in disgust and bitterness. Stupid girl! If he had wanted that—even his son admitted he might have "some desires"—he had plenty of money in his pocket for such needs.

Indignant, he pulled himself upright. Shamefacedly, with trembling hands, he put on his shoes again. All the blood had gone to his head, and the pulse now beat hot behind his eyes. Yes, he knew where to go for that. He knew.

Calmer now, he got up and went back to the house. In the

welter of furniture which seemed to have been placed there on purpose to drive him mad, he threw himself on the bed and turned his face to the wall.

A Clean, Well-lighted Place

Ernest Hemingway

In addition to describing the quiet, stoic despair of the aged man who is left without a wife and whose only "entertainment" is coming to a "clean, well-lighted place" to drink all evening, Hemingway seeks to enlarge our understanding of the nothingness that almost everyone must face. The young waiter exudes confidence; he has a wife waiting at home for him. The eighty-year-old is fortunate in still having money and in having a niece who will still care for him, but he no longer has a reason for existence, and his money cannot give meaning to his life.

After the customer has been pushed out, the older and the younger waiters talk. The older one, who also lives alone, expresses his sympathy for the old man who has just left. He too suffers from sleeplessness, meaninglessness, a lack of confidence—and he also has no wife.

Beyond that, he understands the social difference between drinking at home and drinking in pleasant surroundings where at least the presence of others affirms one's existence and temporarily makes one forget that when the café is closed people must once again go home to nothingness. However, like the older customer, the waiter makes no complaint; after all, many of us share this fate.

It was late and every one had left the café except an old man who sat in the shadow the leaves of the tree made against the electric

Ernest Hemingway, *The Fifth Column and the First Forty-Nine Stories*, Charles Scribner's Sons, New York, 1938, pp. 477–481.

light. In the day time the street was dusty, but at night the dew settled the dust and the old man liked to sit late because he was deaf and now at night it was quiet and he felt the difference. The two waiters inside the café knew that the old man was a little drunk, and while he was a good client they knew that if he became too drunk he would leave without paying, so they kept watch on him.

"Last week he tried to commit suicide," one waiter said.

"Why?"

"He was in despair."

"What about?"

"Nothing."

"How do you know it was nothing?"

"He has plenty of money."

They sat together at a table that was close against the wall near the door of the café and looked at the terrace where the tables were all empty except where the old man sat in the shadow of the leaves of the tree that moved slightly in the wind. A girl and a soldier went by in the street. The street light shone on the brass number on his collar. The girl wore no head covering and hurried beside him.

"The guard will pick him up," one waiter said.

"What does it matter if he gets what he's after?"

"He had better get off the street now. The guard will get him. They went by five minutes ago."

The old man sitting in the shadow rapped on his saucer with his glass. The younger waiter went over to him.

"What do you want?"

The old man looked at him. "Another brandy," he said.

"You'll be drunk," the waiter said. The old man looked at him. The waiter went away.

"He'll stay all night," he said to his colleague. "I'm sleepy now. I never get into bed before three o'clock. He should have killed himself last week."

The waiter took the brandy bottle and another saucer from the counter inside the café and marched out to the old man's table. He put down the saucer and poured the glass full of brandy.

"You should have killed yourself last week," he said to the deaf man. The old man motioned with his finger. "A little more," he said. The waiter poured on into the glass so that the brandy slopped over and ran down the stem into the top saucer of the pile. "Thank you," the old man said. The waiter took the bottle back inside the café. He sat down at the table with his colleague again.

"He's drunk now," he said.

"He's drunk every night."

"What did he want to kill himself for?"

"How should I know."

"How did he do it?"

"He hung himself with a rope."

"Who cut him down?"

"His niece."

"Why did they do it?"

"Fear for his soul."

"How much money has he got?"

"He's got plenty."

"He must be eighty years old."

"Anyway I should say he was eighty."

"I wish he would go home. I never get to bed before three o'clock. What kind of hour is that to go to bed?"

"He stays up because he likes it."

"He's lonely. I'm not lonely. I have a wife waiting in bed for me."

"He had a wife once too."

"A wife would be no good to him now."

"You can't tell. He might be better with a wife."

"His niece looks after him."

"I know. You said she cut him down."

"I wouldn't want to be that old. An old man is a nasty thing."

"Not always. This old man is clean. He drinks without spilling. Even now, drunk. Look at him."

"I don't want to look at him. I wish he would go home. He has no regard for those who must work."

The old man looked from his glass across the square, then over at the waiters.

"Another brandy," he said, pointing to his glass. The waiter who was in a hurry came over.

"Finished," he said, speaking with that omission of syntax

stupid people employ when talking to drunken people or foreigners. "No more tonight. Close now."

"Another," said the old man.

"No. Finished." The waiter wiped the edge of the table with a towel and shook his head.

The old man stood up, slowly counted the saucers, took a leather coin purse from his pocket and paid for the drinks, leaving half a peseta tip.

The waiter watched him go down the street, a very old man walking unsteadily but with dignity.

"Why didn't you let him stay and drink?" the unhurried waiter asked. They were putting up the shutters. "It is not half-past two."

"I want to go home to bed."

"What is an hour?"

"More to me than to him."

"An hour is the same."

"You talk like an old man yourself. He can buy a bottle and drink at home."

"It's not the same."

"No, it is not," agreed with waiter with a wife. He did not wish to be unjust. He was only in a hurry.

"And you? You have no fear of going home before your usual hour?"

"Are you trying to insult me?"

"No, hombre, only to make a joke."

"No," the waiter who was in a hurry said, rising from pulling down the metal shutters. "I have confidence. I am all confidence."

"You have youth, confidence, and a job," the older waiter said. "You have everything."

"And what do you lack?"

"Everything but work."

"You have everything I have."

"No. I have never had confidence and I am not young."

"Come on. Stop talking nonsense and lock up."

"I am of those who like to stay late at the café," the older waiter said. "With all those who do not want to go to bed. With all those who need a light for the night."

"I want to go home and into bed."

"We are of two different kinds," the older waiter said. He was now dressed to go home. "It is not only a question of youth and confidence although those things are very beautiful. Each night I am reluctant to close up because there may be some one who needs the café."

"Hombre, there are bodegas open all night long."

"You do not understand. This is a clean and pleasant café. It is well lighted. The light is very good and also, now, there are shadows of the leaves."

"Good night," said the younger waiter.

"Good night," the other said. Turning off the electric light he continued the conversation with himself. It is the light of course but it is necessary that the place be clean and pleasant. You do not want music. Certainly you do not want music. Nor can you stand before a bar with dignity although that is all that is provided for these hours. What did he fear? It was not fear or dread. It was a nothing that he knew too well. It was all a nothing and a man was nothing too. It was only that and light was all it needed and a certain cleanness and order. Some lived in it and never felt it but he knew it all was nada y pues nada y nada y pues nada. Our nada who art in nada, nada be thy name thy kingdom nada thy will be nada in nada as it is in nada. Give us this nada our daily nada and nada us our nada as we nada our nadas and nada us not into nada but deliver us from nada; pues nada. Hail nothing full of nothing, nothing is with thee. He smiled and stood before a bar with a shining steam pressure coffee machine.

"What's yours?" asked the barman.

"Nada."

"Otro loco mas," said the barman and turned away.

"A little cup," said the waiter.

The barman poured it for him.

"The light is very bright and pleasant but the bar is unpolished," the waiter said.

The barman looked at him but did not answer. It was too late at night for conversation.

"You want another copita?" the barman asked?

"No, thank you," said the waiter and went out. He disliked bars and bodegas. A clean, well-lighted café was a very different thing. Now, without thinking further, he would go home to his room. He would lie in bed and finally, with daylight, he would go to sleep. After all, he said to himself, it is probably only insomnia. Many must have it.

Chapter 11

Economy and Family Relations

Many family sociologists have argued that family processes cannot simply be determined by economic relations, but that they represent an independent set of forces; that a knowledge of only economic factors would lead one astray in understanding the family.

In general, writers have agreed with them, if one judges only from the emphasis in their stories. Their main focus is likely to be the inner feelings of people, and only secondarily the occupational or economic factors that define the larger framework of our lives.

Economic patterns are more likely to be presented as background or setting rather than the prime mover. Even a Balzac is likely to translate economic motivation into a different, baser element, *greed*. It is the rare novelist—George Eliot is an example—who manages to integrate both of these great sets of independent factors, showing on the one hand how economic forces may determine which kinds of choices and problems we face, but on the other how the personal or family motivations transmute those larger elements into a more specific human meaning: some people are indeed the pawns of economic forces, while others transcend them.

In any event, few novelists have been able to create literature from the intricacies of economic transactions, however fascinating they are to each of us personally. Zola arouses our horrified fascination with the details of peasants engaged in land acquisition, and Faulkner has often built comic episodes on the elaborate financial schemes of Southern lower-class blacks and whites; *poverty* as a general condition has played an important part in many stories. However, economic behavior has not in general been a fruitful source of literature. Almost certainly the reason lies in the simple fact that even if most people would prefer to have more rather than less, an economic analysis of human behavior is but a thin slice of the total, while the writer strives to portray human beings in all their richness and complexity.

Dark Eye

Harry Mark Petrakis

Although they are privileged in many ways, most men in an industrial society have never had the experience of deciding whether they ought to go to work or stay home and take care of the children. They are taught from childhood that work is a burden not to be questioned. With it goes a still heavier burden, the foundation of the former: if they fail at their task, or fail to have a job at all, they lose some of their sense of self. Much of a man's identity rests on his engaging in an occupation of some sort.

Although we can suppose this set of feelings has its origin in middle-class protestantism and runs contrary to the ideals of the nobility, which extolled the cultivation of leisure, we cannot be certain of that conclusion without better knowledge. For though the lord of the manor did spend much of his time in falconry, hunting, and court games, and sneered at business, the nobleman who neglected his estates and tenantry, who did not master the skills of war, or who avoided the responsible posts the monarch offered also lost respect. Some of the tasks the Japanese nobility assumed during the Tokugawa now seem empty formalisms to us, but they were socially defined as genuine responsibilities, while the nobleman who devoted all his time to sensual delights did not earn the esteem of others.

In a depression, when millions of men are jobless through no fault of their own, men feel (and often the members of their family share this attitude) not only humiliated by fate but also impoverished by their own fecklessness or incompetence. Although in recent times numerous social commentators have preached a new hedonism, asserting that occupational compulsiveness is irrational and that people should be supported even if they have no job, most men still feel they are less than whole if they cannot get work.

In this story by Harry Mark Petrakis, we observe the

Harry Mark Petrakis, *The Waves of Night and Other Short Stories*, David McKay Company, Inc., New York, 1969.

destructive effect upon a man who, by family heritage, has acquired a difficult art that commands no audience in the United States, not even among his fellow immigrant Greeks. Once honored in his own country for his profession, he is reduced to unskilled labor. He demands and gets overt deference from his own family, but we see him through the eyes of his son, who only much later comes to understand the father's helpless rage at his occupational fate.

My father was a tall, burly man who might once have been regarded by some as handsome, until indulgence and self-pity had scarred his face with weak, ugly circles. Whether drunk or sober, he moved in a shuffling and uncertain walk, defeat and failure rising like a fetid mist from his pores.

Although he worked at many different jobs, never able to hold even the menial ones for very long, he regarded himself as a Karaghiozis, the profession he had practiced in the old country, a puppetmaster of the shadow puppets once so popular throughout Greece. The art of the Karaghiozis was handed down from father to son and my father had learned his craft from his father. As a young man in Greece, he performed frequently at festivals and fairs, but the popularity of the plays declined. Just a few years after he married my mother, the plays were being requested only on a few special holidays. A new generation of children turned to other pursuits and only the old and infirm lamented the passing of the Karaghiozis.

My father must have come to America thinking that in a new country of myriad opportunities, he would be able to practice his craft. But the children who had never seen a Karaghiozis had other allegiances to Laurel and Hardy, Buster Keaton and baseball. And their parents were too involved with the artifacts of home and the rigors of business to bother with an old-country art.

Once, when I was eight or nine, and this was the only time, I remember my father performing the Karaghiozis. It was in the week before Christmas and I sat in the assembly hall of the church with perhaps a hundred other children on long low benches around me. A scattering of adults sat in chairs along the walls. On a small platform in front of us was a rectangular screen of thin, translucent muslin.

When the lights in the hall were turned off, the room was totally darkened except for the radiant screen casting eerie flickering lights across the faces of the children. From behind the screen came a rattling sound, as if pieces of wood were being shaken in a sack. A few men clapped, and then on the glowing screen a palace appeared, a courtyard and gardens, and in the foreground, a fountain. The brightly attired figure of a soldier appeared. He pranced a few steps and then cried, "Karaghiozis! Wake up, Karaghiozis! The sultan is coming!"

From behind the fountain snapped a great bald head, the face in profile containing a single huge dark eye. The head drew back down for a moment and then the silhouette of Karaghiozis leaped swiftly into view. A powerful body with one arm shrunk to no more than a hand emerging from his chest, the other arm long and apelike.

The sight of the weird figure caused the children to cry out, and with a wrenching of my flesh in fear, I joined my shriek to their cries.

A frantic sequence of scenes followed, characters appearing who shouted, danced, sang, quarreled, laughed and beat one another. There were dancers and beggars, soldiers and wrestlers, fishermen and sultans, gods and devils, a rabid throng inhabiting the screen with a violent and teeming world that my father created and controlled. His nimble hands directed their leaps and jumps and somersaults; his voice delivered their cries, harsh, shrill, tearful, deceiving, demonic. Above all the players loomed the figure of Karaghiozis, his dark eye piercing the screen. It seemed to look directly at me and I screamed in terror even while the children around me shouted and shrieked in glee.

When the lights went on at the end of the performance, I sat mute and exhausted. A vigorous clapping brought my father from behind the screen, his face flushed with power and triumph as he bowed, acknowledging the cheers and the applause. He stood afterward in the center of a group of admiring men, who slapped his shoulders and shook his hands. My mother hung smiling to his arm. I went to her to be consoled for my distress, but even while she held me against her body, I felt her love directed only toward my exultant father.

He never performed the Karaghiozis in public again. In the years that followed, he kept the cardboard figures of the players, perhaps twenty-five or thirty of them, in a footlocker at the rear of his closet. Sometimes, when he was drunk, he would pull out the footlocker, open it and sit down on the floor beside it. He would bring out the mad Karaghiozis and all his companions. He'd spread them around on the floor, pick them up, move their heads and arms. They often spoke only in his head, but when he could not contain himself, he cried voices between them. In the end, exhausted and unfulfilled, he would store them carefully away and go lamenting to his bed.

My father lost his job in the grocery, worked for a while in a laundry and then lost that job as well. During this period, my mother took work as a waitress to pay our rent and food. When he could not find money on which to drink, my father spent his time brooding.

I remember a night when my mother was still at work. My father had been locked alone in his bedroom for hours until he called me in. I found him on the floor beside the open footlocker with the Karaghiozis players spread around him. He wasn't drunk then, but his face was flushed and a frenzy glittered in his eyes. He motioned for me to sit beside him and, frightened, I obeyed.

"In the old country," he said, "a father teaches the Karaghiozis to his son. In this way, it is passed from generation to generation. My father taught me and I will teach you."

I trembled and nodded slowly.

"They don't want the Karaghiozis now," my father said with bitterness, "but someday it will be revived. The crowds will gather again and cheer and laugh and cry out for Karaghiozis." He looked at me with burning eyes. "You must be ready for that time."

He motioned to one of the cardboard players. "This one is Hachivat, Karaghiozis' friend; and this is Celebit, the dandy; and Tusuz Deli Bekir, the bellowing bully; Tiryaki, the opium smoker; Zenne, the dancer . . . and this one, this one is Karaghiozis."

He picked up the cardboard Karaghiozis and held him tenderly in his hands. I had never seen him look at any living creature with the warmth and love his face held as he looked at Karaghiozis. He moved slowly to hand the figure to me. "Hold him now and I'll show you how to control his head and arms."

The huge dark eye in the profiled face terrified me and I shrank away.

"What's the matter?" my father cried. "What are you afraid of? He won't hurt you! This is Karaghiozis!"

His anger fled and he tried to speak softly to reassure me.

"It will take time to teach you all the plays," he said. "You must learn them slowly and learn them well. Then you will be able to improvise plays of your own." He stared at me with naked and earnest eyes. "Do you know that once I could continue a dialog between Karaghiozis and his friend, Hachivat, for more than fifteen hours? Do you know that once the mayor of our village, watching me perform, hearing Karaghiozis talk of politics, the mayor offered me a position in his office? Do you know . . . ?"

His voice trailed off as he looked sadly at my locked and frightened face.

"Get out, little bastard," he said wearily. "Get out of my sight. Go to bed."

I hurried from the room to undress and climb shaking under the covers. I called to my mother when she came home and she came and sat beside me, consoling me by her presence until I had fallen asleep.

That night marked a change in my father. His last hope had fled and he seemed more furiously bent on his own destruction. His credit was dried up at the taverns on our street and he made futile pilgrimages to other neighborhoods. When he could not bully or steal money from my mother or my cousin Frosos, he begged and borrowed from friends and strangers along the street. Abandoning all efforts to find any kind of work, he whirled in a wind of drunken despair.

Any redeeming memory I had of him, any bond of blood remaining between us was demolished in the blustering, whining, raging moments when he cursed fate, the misfortune of his marriage, the madness that made him leave the old country. And in his frenzy his voice altered, becoming shrill and hoarse, taunting and pleading, demanding and denouncing, as if all the myriad tongues of the Karaghiozis players were crying through his lips.

My mother suffered as he suffered, prayed for him constantly and accepted all his curses and imprecations in silence. On those evenings when his helpless rage seemed to be tearing him apart, my mother said my prayers with me and put me to bed. She closed the doors between my room, the hall and their bedroom. I still heard faintly my father shouting and cursing for a while. Then a silence fell over the rooms, an ominous and terrible silence, although I did not understand until years later the way in which my mother took my father's rage and frenzy into her own frail body.

Once, only once, did I condemn my father to my mother. I was about twelve and it was after one of the worst of his rampages, when he had broken several dishes he knew my mother treasured, and finally, like a great beast, had collapsed in a heap on the floor. He lay sprawled on his back, his mouth open, harsh drunken snores erupting from his loose, limp face. I whispered a wish to my mother that he might die.

She had never struck me before, but she beat me then. She beat me savagely with a belt while I screamed in shock and pain.

"Listen to me," she said, her face white and her eyes like knives. "Say such a thing again and I'll have the flesh hot from your back. In the old country your father was an artist, a great Karaghiozis. They came from villages a hundred miles away to see him perform. Now nobody cares for his skill and he rages and drinks to forget his grief and loss. Do you think a man whose soul is being torn apart can help himself? We can only love him and have faith in him. He has nothing else."

But I could not understand, and for turning my mother against me, for the beating she gave me, I hated him more.

Cheated

August Strindberg

In eighteenth-century France, the aspiring rich bourgeoisie who had acquired enough social skills to "live nobly" did mix socially to some extent with members of the nobility, but to enter into the still more intimate relationship of marriage they had to offer large sums of money as a dowry. The higher the nobleman's rank, the larger the amount of the dowry a marriageable daughter had to convey. These arrangements were explicit and widely understood. They formed a market system in which social prestige was exchanged for money. As in many markets for elite goods, not everyone could enter. An especially uncultured young woman or a family tainted by scandal might find it difficult to locate *any* nobleman willing to engage in such a trade. On the other hand, the rich family with great political power, or an especially beautiful young woman, would find this commerce easier to arrange.

Since moralists make it their business to keep us from enjoying some of the simpler pleasures of life, they have frequently attacked such exchanges, pointing to the hollowness of the quest for social rank, the vulgarity of money, and the fragility of the marital relation itself. Here, August Strindberg uses the style of the fable as a literary device for conveying the timelessness of this family pattern. Although he gives us a few details here and there which might enable us to place the setting (e.g., the dresses and uniforms which are worn), he has deliberately removed specific historical or national descriptions from his story so that the reader is compelled to imagine these relationships between money and family as occurring in any place, at any time. The characters do not have names, and they are intended to be *types*: the businessman's sensible daughter who is nevertheless deluded by the glitter of society, and the noble lieutenant who wants to devote his life to idle pleasure.

August Strindberg, *Getting Married*, Parts I and II, translated by Mary Sandbarch, Victor Gollancz Ltd., London, 1972, pp. 321–324.

In our own generation, less willing to recognize the extent to which our emotions are ruled by money, marrying for money or exchanging money openly for prestige is viewed as a violation of authentic love, besides being in bad taste. Nevertheless, the reader should not merely ask whether such exchanges continue to be widespread (if not openly admitted), but also whether he or she might in fact be tempted by the possibility of such an exchange.

When the fish were playing, and the cock-birds beginning to sing, the children of man went out to their playgrounds to find mates. Mothers decked out their young females to entice the males; dressmakers sewed wadding into bodices, and tailors put pads into jackets and frock-coats. And then out they went into 'nature' to choose surroundings suitable for the natural act for which they were preparing. One was the sea-side. There it was that the businessman's wife came with her daughter, and the lieutenant with his uniform and his debts.

And one evening, while the midges danced, and the cats caterwauled, the girls danced too in the ball-room of the Assembly rooms. They had cut the tops of their dresses low, and ordered the blinds to be drawn, so that the lights could shine down on them. And the lieutenant bent over the businessman's daughter in a window recess, and his eyes asked:

"Will you pay my debts?" But his lips said: "Will you love me for better or for worse?"

And the businessman's daughter answered with her eyes: "Yes, if you will make me a countess, and introduce me to your grand friends, and if you will let Papa play cards with your generals, and Mama call your countesses by their Christian names, and if you will keep me until death us do part, and let me enjoy myself."

Yes, he would, and so the bargain was struck.

Two years had passed. They were sitting in their dressing-gowns, listless, bored, exchanging a few home truths.

"Wadding," he said, pointing to the puffed-out dress that hung over the back of the chair.

"Wadding," she answered, and pointed her slipper at his riding coat, that dangled from the towel-rail.

He pulled his dressing-gown closer round him, and did not answer.

Two years later the businessman went bankrupt. That put an end to the card-playing with generals that he had been promised, and the countesses broke off relations with his wife. Their daughter was made less welcome, and the lieutenant developed a taste for private life in the home, especially as the subsidies from his father-in-law were no longer forthcoming. One day, when he had been particularly truthful to his countess, the latter found herself obliged to deal with the matter in detail.

"Now that I'm poor, you're not as polite as you used to be," she said.

"I wasn't polite before either," he replied, "so it's not only a case of your being poor."

"Yes, but you were more polite to Papa before."

"Certainly, because he had one merit, he was rich. Now that he's lost that estimable quality, I see no reason to show him any exaggerated marks of respect."

"So, you admit, quite crudely, that you married me for money?"

"Of course! Isn't it nice of me to own up to—hm—being myself?"

"And you're not ashamed to talk to me like that?"

"Oh yes, I am, but surely you're not trying to make me believe that you married me for—what do they call it—love? I'm much more inclined to think that you paid my miserable debt of ten thousand crowns in exchange for the title of countess. It was a good bargain. Dickson had to give a couple of hundred thousand for the privilege of becoming a mere member of the nobility, and L. O. Smith had to pay sixty thousand for the Order of Vasa. I haven't cheated you over the deal, for you are a countess. But you've cheated me, for you hung out a rich father-in-law, and here I am with a poor one. Wadding, wadding, from beginning to end!"

"Yes, but I didn't marry just for money."

"No, for a title, and—but it comes to the same thing."

"Go on please. A man with the courage to make away with a poor woman's money . . . he'll stop at nothing."

"Listen to me, my little chick."

"I'm not a chick."

"You contributed ten thousand crowns. But do you know what I've spent during the past four years? Forty thousand! Your father coughed up another five. That should tell you just how much of the poor lieutenant's money you've made away with shouldn't it?"

"Aren't you ashamed of yourself? Perhaps a wife's expected to keep her husband these days?"

"No, but she mustn't accuse her husband of making away with her money when they've used it up together, and anyhow, what do you mean by *her* money? Where did that money come from? Had she earned it? None of *you* have any business to talk about money, when it's what you all marry for."

"Are you trying to tell me that you keep me, as you might any other 'kept' woman?"

"There's no need for me to say it as you've admitted it yourself. However, it's just as well that you have, for if you want to hear the truth of the matter, we shall have to change our way of life after what's happened. Wouldn't you like to seize the opportunity to liberate yourself, to emancipate yourself from the humiliation of eating the bread of charity?"

"Indeed I should."

"Do it then. Work."

"I've never learnt to do anything."

"Do what you can. Look after your house."

"That's not work."

"How right you are. In that case you'll just have to go on doing nothing. That's the role allotted to you by society."

"What a splendid role!"

"So you admit it now, do you?"

"Yes, I admit it. I'm doomed until I die to eat a man's bread. When my father couldn't keep me any longer my mother took me to market, to find someone who could."

"Yes, and she found me. I boosted your father's credit, and

probably procured him many times as much as he spent on me. That's how matters stand now. What do you want me to do about it?"

"Nothing."

"No, I can't really see that there's anything that can be done. It's the same story all along the line: a hollow sham. Wadding! Wadding! Every bit of it."

The lieutenant became peevish, and his wife miserable. After two years of it they got a divorce, and the lieutenant was ordered to pay his wife alimony for life.

"Yes, it's an expensive business, that is," said the captain one day, as he was dining at the restaurant.

"What is legitimate is always expensive," said the lieutenant. "But as it's so dear, one ought at least to be able to have it on approval."

Of Time and the River
Thomas Wolfe

Wolfe himself is the main character in his books. Yet we do not feel ourselves confined within a narrow world when we read them, for he absorbed and conveyed so completely the time and the places he inhabited.

This work is a grand, generational chronicle about a large family representing the cultures of both North and South. In it he introduces the importance of wealth in family relations and at the same time shows how his father had transcended it. The people of the town have gathered at his father's funeral to express their sorrow, affection, and respect. As is typical, the mourners unthinkingly segregate themselves by wealth; even family members do so.

The daughter, Helen, observes the separation and feels a spontaneous impulse to join the "better citizens." She

Thomas Wolfe, *Of Time and the River*, Charles Scribner's Sons, New York, 1935.

stops herself when she suddenly recognizes that the "working people"—not, be it noted, *lower-class*, for some are businessmen and property owners—had been her father's best friends.

She then engages in a far-ranging soliloquy about the class position of her father, who was a stonecutter, a businessman, and a property owner. Her first conclusion is that he belongs among the working men, his real friends.

However, she perceives a further truth, that only two of these men, and none of Mr. Gant's children, had ever addressed him by his first name. Clearly, his *personal* authority commanded a respect far beyond the esteem that a modest prosperity would bring in a North Carolina town. In fact, throughout Mr. Gant's adult lifetime among these people he had remained a lonely stranger, mature beyond his years, and somehow both embodying and conveying to others his kinship with all other men as well as his fated aloneness.

No matter how unique this father or the personal qualities that made others respect him, however, most of us have known people who resemble Mr. Gant—men and women whose position in life is partly determined by their wealth and occupational competence, but whose special characteristics allow them to transcend these marks of status and occupy perhaps an unexpected place in their family or social network.

In a curious and indefinable way the two groups of men in the hallway had become divided: the wealthier group of prominent citizens, which was composed of the brothers William, James, and Crockett Pentland, Mr. Sluder and Eliza, stood in a group near the front hall door, engaged in earnest conversation. The second group, which was composed of working men, who had known Gant well, and worked for or with him—a group composed of Jannadeau the jeweller, old Alec Ramsay and Saul Gudger, who were stonecutters, Gant's nephew, Ollie Gant, who was a plasterer, Ernest Pegram, the city plumber, and Mike Fogarty, who was perhaps Gant's closest friend, a building contractor—this group, composed of men who had all their lives done stern labor with their hands, and who were really the men who had known the stone-cutter best, stood apart from the group of prominent and wealthy men who were talking so earnestly to Eliza.

And in this circumstance, in this unconscious division, in the air of constraint, vague uneasiness and awkward silence that was evident among these working men, as they stood there in the hallway dressed in their "good clothes," nervously fingering their hats in their big hands, there was something immensely moving. The men had the look that working people the world over have always had when they found themselves suddenly gathered together on terms of social intimacy with their employers or with members of the governing class.

And Helen, coming out at this instant from her father's room into the hall, suddenly saw and felt the awkward division between these two groups of men, as she had never before felt or noticed it, as sharply as if they had been divided with a knife.

And, it must be admitted, her first feeling was an unworthy one—an instinctive wish to approach the more "important" group, to join her life to the lives of these "influential" people who represented to her a "higher" social level. She found herself walking towards the group of wealthy and prominent men at the front of the hall, and away from the group of working men who had really been Gant's best friends.

But seeing the brick-red face of Alec Ramsay, the mountainous figure of Mike Fogarty, suddenly with a sense of disbelief, and almost terrified revelation of the truth, she thought: "Why-why-why—these men are really the closest friends he's got—not rich men like Uncle Will or Uncle Jim or even Mr. Sluder—but men like Mike Fogarty—and Jannadeau—and Mr. Duncan—and Alec Ramsay—and Ernest Pegram—and Ollie Gant—but—but—good heavens, no!" she thought, almost desperately—"surely these are not his closest friends—why-why—of course, they're decent people—they're honest men—but they're only common people—I've always considered them as just *working* men—and-and-and—my God!" she thought, with that terrible feeling of discovery we have when we suddenly see ourselves as others see us—"do you suppose that's the way people in this town think of

Papa? Do you suppose they have always thought of him as just a common working man—oh, no! but of course not!" she went on impatiently, trying to put the troubling thought out of her mind. "Papa's not a working man—Papa is a *business* man—a well thought of business man in this community. Papa has always owned property since he came here—he has always had his own shop"—she did not like the sound of the word shop, and in her mind she hastily amended it to "place"—"he's always had his own place, up on the public square—he's—he's rented places to other people—he's—he's—oh, of course not!—Papa is different from men like Ernest Pegram, and Ollie, and Jannadeau and Alec Ramsay—why, they're just working men—they work with their hands—Ollie's just an ordinary plasterer—and-and—Mr. Ramsay is nothing but a stone-cutter."

And a small insistent voice inside her said most quietly: "And your father?"

And suddenly Helen remembered Gant's great hands of power and strength, and how they now lay quietly beside him on the bed, and lived and would not die, even when the rest of him had died, and she remembered the thousands of times she had gone to his shop in the afternoon and found the stonecutter in his long striped apron bending with delicate concentration over a stone inscription on a trestle, holding in his great hands the chisel and the heavy wooden mallet the stonecutters use, and remembering, the whole rich and living compact of the past came back to her, in a rush of tenderness and joy and terror, and on that flood a proud and bitter honesty returned. She thought: "Yes, he was a stonecutter, no different from these other men, and these men were his real friends."

And going directly to old Alec Ramsay she grasped his blunt thick fingers, the nails of which were always whitened a little with stone dust, and greeted him in her large and spacious way:

"Mr. Ramsay," she said, "I want you to know how glad we are that you could come. And that goes for all of you—Mr. Jannadeau, and Mr. Duncan, and Mr. Fogarty, and you, Ernest, and you, too, Ollie—you are the best friends Papa has, there's no one he thinks more of, and no one he would rather see."

Mr. Ramsay's brick-red face and brick-red neck became

even redder before he spoke, and beneath his grizzled brows his blue eyes suddenly were smoke blue. He put his blunt hand to his mustache for a moment, and tugged at it, then he said in his gruff, quiet, and matter-of-fact voice:

"I guess we know Will about as well as any one, Miss Helen. I've worked for him off and on for thirty years."

At the same moment, she heard Ollie Gant's easy, deep, and powerful laugh, and saw him slowly lift his cigarette in his coarse paw; she saw Jannadeau's great yellow face and massive domy brow, and heard him laugh with guttural pleasure, saying, "Ah-h! I tell you vat! Dat girl has alvays looked out for her datty—she's de only vun dat coult hantle him; efer since she vas ten years olt it has been de same." And she was overwhelmingly conscious of that immeasurable mountain of a man, Mike Fogarty, beside her, the sweet clarity of his blue eyes, and the almost purring music of his voice as he gently laid his mutton of a hand upon her shoulder for a moment, saying,

"Ah, Miss Helen, I don't know how Will could have got along all these years without ye—for he has said the same himself a thousand times—aye! that he has!"

And instantly, having heard these words, and feeling the strong calm presences of these powerful men around her, it seemed to Helen she had somehow re-entered a magic world that she thought was gone forever. And she was immensely content.

At the same moment, with a sense of wonder, she discovered an astonishing thing, that she had never noticed before, but that she must have heard a thousand times;—this was that of all these people, who knew Gant best, and had a deep and true affection for him, there were only two—Mr. Fogarty and Mr. Ramsay—who had ever addressed him by his first name. And so far as she could now remember, these two men, together with Gant's mother, his brothers, his sister Augusta, and a few of the others who had known him in his boyhood in Pennsylvania, were the only people who ever had. And this revelation cast a strange, a lonely and a troubling light upon the great gaunt figure of the stonecutter, which moved her powerfully and which she had never felt before. And most strange of all was the variety of names by which these various people called her father.

As for Eliza, had any of her children ever heard her address her husband as anything but "Mr. Gant"—had she ever called him by one of his first names—their anguish of shame and impropriety would have been so great that they could hardly have endured it. But such a lapse would have been incredible: Eliza could no more have addressed Gant by his first name, than she could have quoted Homer's Greek; had she tried to address him so, the muscles of her tongue would have found it physically impossible to pronounce the word. And in this fact there was somehow, now that Gant was dying, an enormous pathos. It gave to Eliza's life with him a pitiable and moving dignity, the compensation of a proud and wounded spirit for all the insults and injuries that had been heaped upon it. She had been a young country woman of twenty-four when she had met him, she had been ignorant of life, and innocent of the cruelty, the violence, the drunkenness and abuse of which men are capable, she had borne this man fifteen children, of whom eight had come to life, and had for forty years eaten the bread of blood and tears and joy and grief and terror, she had wanted affection and had been given taunts, abuse, and curses, and somehow her proud and wounded spirit had endured with an anguished but unshaken fortitude all the wrongs and cruelties and injustices of which he had been guilty toward her. And now at the very end her pride still had this pitiable distinction, her spirit still preserved this last integrity: she had not betrayed her wounded soul to a shameful familiarity, he had remained to her—in mind and heart and living word—what he had been from the first day that she met him; the author of her grief and misery, the agent of her suffering, the gaunt and lonely stranger who had come into her hills from a strange land and a distant people—that furious, gaunt, and lonely stranger with whom by fatal accident her destiny—past hate or love or birth or death or human error and confusion—had been insolubly enmeshed, with whom for forty years she had lived, a wife, a mother, and a stranger—and who would to the end remain to her a stranger—"Mr. Gant."

What was it? What was the secret of this strange and bitter mystery of life that had made of Gant a stranger to all men, and most of all a stranger to his wife? Perhaps some of the answer might have been found in Eliza's own unconscious words when she described her meeting with him forty years before:

"It was not that he was old," she said,—"he was only thirty-three—but he *looked* old—his *ways* were old—he had lived so much among old people.—Pshaw!" she continued, with a little puckered smile, "if any one had told me that night I saw him sitting there with Lydia and old Mrs. Mason—that was the very day they moved into the house, the night he gave the big dinner—and Lydia was still alive and, of course, she was ten years older than he was, and that may have had something to do with it—but I got to studying him as he sat there, of course, he was tired and run down and depressed and worried over all that trouble that he'd had in Sidney before he came up here, when he lost everything, and he knew that Lydia was dying, and that was preyin' on his mind—but he *looked* old, thin as a rake you know, and sallow and run down, and with those *old* ways he had acquired, I reckon, from associatin' with Lydia and old Mrs. Mason and people like that—but I just sat there studying him as he sat there with them and I said—'Well, you're an old man, aren't you, sure enough?'—pshaw! if any one had told me that night that some day I'd be married to him I'd have laughed at them—I'd have considered that I was marrying an old man—and that's just exactly what a lot of people thought, sir, when the news got out that I was goin' to marry him—I know Martha Patton came running to me, all excited and out of breath—said, 'Eliza! You're not going to marry that old man—you know you're not!'—you see, his *ways* were old, he *looked* old, *dressed* old, *acted* old—everything he did was old; there was always, it seemed, something strange and old-like about him, almost like he had been born that way."

And it was at this time that Eliza met him, saw him first—"Mr. Gant"—an immensely tall, gaunt, cadaverous-looking man, with a face stern and sad with care, lank, drooping mustaches, sandy hair, and cold-gray staring eyes—"not so old, you know—he was only thirty-three—but he *looked* old, he *acted* old, his *ways* were old—he had lived so much among older people he seemed older than he was—I thought of him as an old man."

This, then, was "Mr. Gant" at thirty-three, and since then,

although his fortunes and position had improved, his character had changed little. And now Helen, faced by all these working men, who had known, liked, and respected him, and had now come to see him again before he died—suddenly knew the reason for his loneliness, the reason so few people—least of all, his wife—had ever dared address him by his first name. And with a swift and piercing revelation, his muttered words, which she had heard him use a thousand times when speaking of his childhood—"We had a tough time of it—I tell you what, we did!"— now came back to her with the unutterable poignancy of discovery. For the first time she understood what they meant. And suddenly, with the same swift and nameless pity, she remembered all the pictures which she had seen of her father as a boy and a young man. There were a half dozen of them in the big family album, together with pictures of his own and Eliza's family: they were the small daguerreotypes of fifty years before, in small frames of faded plush, with glass covers, touched with the faint pale pinks with which the photographers of an earlier time tried to paint with life the sallow hues of their photography. The first of these pictures showed Gant as a little boy; later, a boy of twelve, he was standing in a chair beside his brother Wesley, who was seated, with a wooden smile upon his face. Later, a picture of Gant in the years in Baltimore, standing, his feet crossed, leaning elegantly upon a marble slab beside a vase; later still, the young stonecutter before his little shop in the years at Sidney; finally, Gant, after his marriage with Eliza, standing with gaunt face and lank drooping mustaches before his shop upon the square, in the company of Will Pentland, who was at the time his business partner.

And all these pictures, from first to last, from the little boy to the man with the lank drooping mustaches, had been marked by the same expression: the sharp thin face was always stern and sad with care, the shallow cold-gray eyes always stared out of the bony cage-formation of the skull with a cold mournfulness—the whole impression was always one of gaunt sad loneliness. And it was not the loneliness of the dreamer, the poet, or the misjudged prophet, it was just the cold and terrible loneliness of man, of every man, and of the lost American who has been brought forth naked under immense and lonely skies, to "shift for himself," to grope his way blindly through the confusion and brutal chaos of a life as naked and unsure as he, to wander blindly down across the continent, to hunt forever for a goal, a wall, a dwelling place of warmth and certitude, a light, a door.

And for this reason, she now understood something about her father, this great gaunt figure of a stonecutter that she had never understood or thought about before: she suddenly understood his order, sense of decency and dispatch; his love of cleanness, roaring fires, and rich abundance, his foul drunkenness, violence, and howling fury, his naked shame and trembling penitence, his good clothes of heavy monumental black that he always kept well pressed, his clean boiled shirts, wing collars, and his love of hotels, ships, and trains, his love of gardens, new lands, cities, voyages. She knew suddenly that he was unlike any other man that ever lived, and that every man that ever lived was like her father. And remembering the cold and mournful look in his shallow staring eyes of cold hard gray, she suddenly knew the reason for that look, as she had never known it before, and understood now why so few men had ever called him by his first name—why he was known to all the world as "Mr. Gant."

How to Buy a House
Lawrence Durrell

Perhaps most family law and certainly the most bitterly fought court cases under it focus on the issue of property, and especially inheritance. Because family members often wish to control others and to exert their will even after their death, systems of inheritance are developed. The family is the keystone of the stratification system, in part because it is through family relations that the inheritance of property is decided.

Lawrence Durrell, *Bitter Lemons*, E. P. Dutton & Co., Inc., New York, 1957.

In many systems, family property descends to one son (usually the eldest), who is responsible for his brothers until they are adult and his sisters until they are married. However, because there is property other than "ancestral," and because the older generation often wishes to express its affection or gratitude to the younger, property continues to be divided. In fact, all inheritance systems represent a compromise between the aim of keeping the family strong by keeping the family property together, and the goal of providing for *all* the members of the younger generation.

In the small Cyprus community described here by Lawrence Durrell, so many families have intermarried with each other over hundreds of years that any given piece of property may be divided among dozens of different "rights": to the water, the garden, a fruit-bearing tree, and so on. Thus, what would be the simple purchase of a house in the United States becomes a large-scale family transaction. Everyone is interested in financial gain, but at a deeper level each also resists selling a piece of his or her family heritage.

Although such legal complexities are not common in this country, they can and do occur when property has descended through several generations. The reader should consider other economic situations where family members have a heavy emotional stake in the property (homestead, family picnic grounds, paintings, antiques) and where they have an interest in *who* is the purchaser, in short, where the interrelations among family members do affect economic transactions.

Then at last the summons came; I was to present myself at Sabri's office the next morning at eight. Panos brought me the message, smiling at my obvious anxiety, and telling me that Sabri was rather despondent because it now appeared that the house was owned not by the cobbler but by his wife. It had been her dowry, and she herself was going to conduct the sale. 'With women,' said my friend, 'it is always a Calvary to argue. A Golgotha.' Nevertheless Sabri had decided to go forward with the business. The intervening space of time had been valuable, however, because he had come into possession of a piece of vital information about the water supply. Water is so scarce in Cyprus that it is sold in parcels. You buy an hour here and an hour there from the owner of a spring—needless to say no quantity measure exists. The trouble lies here: that water-rights form part of property-titles of citizens and are divided up on the death of the owner among his dependents. This is true also of land and indeed of trees. Families being what they are, it is common for a single thing to be owned by upwards of thirty people, or a single tree to be shared out among a dozen members of a family. The whole problem, then, is one of obtaining common consent—usually one has to pay for the signatures of thirty people in order to achieve any agreement which is binding. Otherwise one dissident nephew and niece can veto the whole transaction. In the case of some trees, for example, one man may own the produce of the tree, another the ground on which it stands, a third the actual timber. As may be imagined the most elementary litigation assumes gigantic proportions—which explains why there are so many lawyers in Cyprus.

Now Sabri had got wind of the fact that the Government was planning to install the piped water supply to the village which had been promised for so long; moreover that the plans were already being drawn up. The architect of the Public Works happened to be a friend of his so he casually dropped into his office and asked to see where the various water-points were to be placed. It was a stroke of genius, for he saw with delight that there was to be a public water-point outside the very front door of the old house. This more than offset the gloomy intelligence that the only water the cobbler owned was about an hour a month from the main spring—perhaps sixty gallons: whereas the average water consumption of an ordinary family is about forty gallons a *day*. This was a trump card, for the cobbler's water belonged in equal part to the rest of his wife's family—all eighteen of them, including the idiot boy Pipi whose signature was always difficult to obtain on a legal document. . . .

I found my friend, freshly shaven and spruce, seated in the gloom of his office, surrounded by prams, and absolutely motionless. Before him on the blotter lay the great key of the house, which he poked from time to time in a reproachful way. He put his finger to his lips with a conspiratorial air and motioned me to a chair. 'They are all here, my dear,' he hissed, 'getting ready.' He pointed to the café across the road where the cobbler had gathered his family. They looked more like seconds. They sat on a semicircle of chairs, sipping coffee and arguing in low voices; a number of beards waggled, a number of heads nodded. They looked like a rugger scrum in an American film receiving last-minute instructions from their captain. Soon they would fall upon us like a ton of bricks and gouge us. I began to feel rather alarmed. 'Now, whatever happens,' said Sabri in a low voice, tremulous with emotion, 'do not surprise. You must never surprise. And you don't want the house at all, see?'

I repeated the words like a catechism. 'I don't want the house. I absolutely don't want the house.' Yet in my mind's eye I could see those great doors ('God,' Sabri had said, 'this is fine wood. From Anatolia. In the old days they floated the great timbers over the water behind boats. This is Anatolian timber, it will last for ever'). Yes, I could see those doors under a glossy coat of blue paint. . . . 'I don't want the house,' I repeated under my breath, feverishly trying to put myself into the appropriate frame of mind.

'Tell them we are ready,' said Sabri to the shadows and a barefooted youth flitted across the road to where our adversaries had gathered. They hummed like bees, and the cobbler's wife detached herself from the circle—or tried to, for many a hand clutched at her frock, detaining her for a last-minute consideration which was hissed at her secretively by the family elders. At last she wrenched herself free and walked boldly across the road, entering Sabri's shrine with a loud 'Good morning' spoken very confidently.

She was a formidable old faggot, with a handsome self-indulgent face, and a big erratic body. She wore the white headdress and dark skirt of the village woman, and her breasts were gathered into the traditional baggy bodice with a drawstring at the waist, which made it look like a loosely furled sail. She stood before us looking very composed as she gave us good morning. Sabri cleared his throat, and picking up the great key very delicately between finger and thumb—as if it were of the utmost fragility—put it down again on the edge of the desk nearest her with the air of a conjurer making his opening dispositions. 'We are speaking about your house,' he said softly, in a voice ever so faintly curdled with menace. 'Do you know that all the wood is . . .' he suddenly shouted the last word with such force that I nearly fell off my chair, 'rotten!' And picking up the key he banged it down to emphasize the point.

The woman threw up her head with contempt and taking up the key also banged it down in her turn exclaiming: 'It is not.'

'It *is*.' Sabri banged the key.

'It is *not*.' She banged it back.

'It *is*.' A bang.

'It is *not*.' A counter-bang.

All this was not on a very high intellectual level, and made me rather ill at ease. I also feared that the key itself would be banged out of shape so that finally none of us would be able to get into the house. But these were the opening chords, so to speak, the preliminary statement of theme.

The woman now took the key and held it up as if she were swearing by it. 'The house is a good house,' she cried. Then she put it back on the desk. Sabri took it up thoughtfully, blew into the end of it as if it were a six-shooter, aimed it and peered along it as if along a barrel. Then he put it down and fell into an abstraction. 'And suppose we wanted the house,' he said, 'which we don't, what would you ask for it?'

'Eight hundred pounds.'

Sabri gave a long and stagy laugh, wiping away imaginary tears and repeating 'Eight hundred pounds' as if it were the best joke in the world. He laughed at me and I laughed at him, a dreadful false laugh. He slapped his knee. I rolled about in my chair as if on the verge of acute gastritis. We laughed until we were exhausted. Then we grew serious again. Sabri was still fresh as a daisy, I could see that. He had put himself into the patient contemplative state of mind of a chess player.

'Take the key and go,' he snapped suddenly, and handing it to her, swirled round in his swivel chair to present her with his back; then as suddenly he completed the circuit and swivelled round again. 'What!' he said with surprise. 'You haven't gone.' In truth there had hardly been time for the woman to go. But she was somewhat slow-witted, though obstinate as a mule: that was clear. 'Right,' she now said in a ringing tone, and picking up the key put it into her bosom and turned about. She walked off stage in a somewhat lingering fashion. 'Take no notice,' whispered Sabri and busied himself with his papers.

The woman stopped irresolutely outside the shop, and was here joined by her husband who began to talk to her in a low cringing voice, pleading with her. He took her by the sleeve and led her unwillingly back into the shop where we sat pointedly reading letters. 'Ah! It's you,' said Sabri with well-simulated surprise. 'She wishes to discuss some more,' explained the cobbler in a weak conciliatory voice. Sabri sighed.

'What is there to speak of? She takes me for a fool.' Then he suddenly turned to her and bellowed, 'Two hundred pounds and not a piastre more.'

It was her turn to have a paroxysm of false laughter, but this was rather spoiled by her husband who started plucking at her sleeve as if he were persuading her to be sensible. Sabri was not slow to notice this. 'You tell her,' he said to the man. 'You are a man and these things are clear to you. She is only a woman and does not see the truth. Tell her what it is worth.'

The cobbler, who quite clearly lacked spirit, turned once more to his wife and was about to say something to her, but in a sudden swoop she produced the key and raised it above her head as if she intended to bring it down on his hairless dome. He backed away rapidly. 'Fool,' she growled. 'Can't you see they are making a fool of you? Let me handle this.' She made another pass at him with the key and he tiptoed off to join the rest of her relations in the coffee-shop opposite, completely crushed. She now turned to me and extended a wheedling hand, saying in Greek, 'Ah come along there, you an Englishman, striking a hard bargain with a woman. . . .' But I had given no indication of speaking Greek so that it was easy to pretend not to understand her. She turned back to Sabri, staring balefully, and banging the key down once more shouted 'Six hundred,' while Sabri in the same breath bellowed 'Two hundred.' The noise was deafening.

They panted and glared at each other for a long moment of

silence like boxers in a clinch waiting for the referee to part them. It was the perfect moment for Sabri to get in a quick one below the belt. 'Anyway, your house is mortgaged,' he hissed, and she reeled under the punch. 'Sixty pounds and three piastres,' he added, screwing the glove a little to try to draw blood. She held her groin as if in very truth he had landed her a blow in it. Sabri followed up swiftly: 'I offer you two hundred pounds plus the mortgage.'

She let out a yell. 'No. Never,' and banged the key. 'Yes, I say,' bellowed Sabri giving a counter-bang. She grabbed the key (by now it had become, as it were, the very symbol of our contention. The house was forgotten. We were trying to buy this old rusty key which looked like something fitter for Saint Peter's keyring than my own). She grabbed the key, I say, and put it to her breast like a child as she said: 'Never in this life.' She rocked it back and forth, suckled it, and put it down again.

Sabri now became masterful and put it in his pocket. At this she let out a yell and advanced on him shouting: 'You give me back my key and I shall leave you with the curses of all the saints upon you.' Sabri stood up like a showman and held the key high above his head, out of her reach, repeating inexorably: 'Two hundred. Two hundred. Two hundred.' She snapped and strained like a hooked fish, exclaiming all the time: 'Saint Catherine defend me. No. No.' Then quite suddenly they both stopped, he replaced the key on the desk and sat down, while she subsided like a pan of boiling milk when it is lifted off the fire. 'I shall consult,' she said briefly in another voice and leaving the key where it was she took herself off across the road to where her seconds waited with towels and sponges. The first round was a draw, though Sabri had made one or two good points.

'What happens now?' I said, and he chuckled. 'Just time for a coffee. I think, you know, my dear,' he added, 'that we will have to pay another hundred. I feel it.' He was like a countryman who can tell what the weather will be like from small signs invisible to the ordinary townsman. It was an enthralling spectacle, this long-drawn-out pantomime, and I was now prepared for the negotiations to go on for a week. 'They don't know about the water,' said Sabri. 'They will let us have the house cheap and then try to sting us for the water-rights. We must pretend to forget about the water and buy the house cheaper. Do you see?' I saw the full splendour of his plan as it unfolded before us. 'But,' he said, 'everything must be done today, now, for if she goes back to the village and makes the gossips nothing will be consummated.' It seemed to me that she was already making the gossips in the café opposite, for a furious altercation had broken out. She was accusing her husband of something and he was replying waspishly and waving his arms.

After a while Sabri whispered: 'Here she comes again,' and here she came, rolling along with sails spread and full of the cargo of her misfortunes. She had changed her course. She now gave us a long list of her family troubles, hoping to soften us up; but by now I felt as if my teeth had been sharpened into points. It was clear that she was weakening. It was a matter of time before we could start winding her in. It was, in fact, the psychological moment to let out the line, and this Sabri Tahir now did by offering her another hundred ('a whole hundred,' he repeated juicily in a honeyed voice) if she would clinch the deal there and then. 'Your husband is a fool,' he added, 'and your family ignorant. You will never find a buyer if you do not take this gentleman. Look at him. Already he is weakening. He will go elsewhere. Just look at his face.' I tried to compose my face in a suitable manner to play my full part in the pantomime. She stared at me in the manner of a hungry peasant assessing a turnip and suddenly sat herself down for the first time, bursting as she did so into heartrending sobs. Sabri was delighted and gave me a wink.

She drew her wimple round her face and went into convulsions, repeating audibly: 'O Jesus, what are they doing to me? Destruction has overtaken my house and my line. My issue has been murdered, my good name dragged in the dust.' Sabri was in a high good humour by this time. He leaned forward and began to talk to her in the voice of Mephistopheles himself, filling the interstices between her sentences with his insinuations. I could hear him droning on 'Mortgage . . . two hundred . . . husband a fool . . . never get such an opportunity.' Meanwhile she rocked and moaned like an Arab, thoroughly enjoying herself. From time to time she cast a furtive glance at our faces to see how we were taking it; she could not have drawn much consolation from Sabri's for he was full of a triumphant concentration now; in the looming shadows he reminded me of some great killer shark—the flash of a white belly as it turned over on its back to take her. 'We have not spoken of the water as yet,' he said, and among her diminishing sobs she was still able to gasp out. 'That will be another hundred.'

'We are speaking only of the house,' insisted Sabri, and at this a look of cunning came over his face. 'Afterwards we will speak of the water.' The tone in which he said this indicated subtly that he had now moved over on to her side. The foreigner, who spoke no Greek, could not possibly understand that without water-rights the house itself was useless. She shot a glance at me and then looked back at him, the look of cunning being replaced by a look almost of triumph. Had Sabri, in fact, changed sides? Was he perhaps also planning to make a killing, and once the house was bought. . . . She smiled now and stopped sobbing.

'All this can only be done immediately,' said Sabri quietly. 'Look. We will go to the widow and get the mortgage paper. We will pay her mortgage before you at the Land Registry. Then we will pay you before witnesses for the house.' Then he added in a low voice: 'After that the gentleman will discuss the water. Have you the papers?"

We were moving rather too swiftly for her. Conflicting feelings beset her; ignorance and doubt flitted across her face. An occasional involuntary sob shook her—like pre-ignition in an overheated engine which has already been switched off. 'My grandfather has the title-deeds.'

'Get them,' said Sabri curtly.

She rose, still deeply preoccupied, and went back across the street where a furious argument broke out among her seconds. The white-bearded old man waved a stick and perorated. Her husband spread his hands and waggled them. Sabri watched all this with a critical eye. 'There is only one danger—she must not get back to the village.' How right he was; for if her relations could make all this noise about the deed of sale, what could the village coffee-shop not do? Such little concentration as she could muster would be totally scattered by conflicting counsels. The whole thing would probably end in a riot followed by an island-wide strike. . . .

I gazed admiringly at my friend. What a diplomat he would make! 'Here she comes again,' he said in a low voice, and here she came to place the roll of title-deeds on the table beside the key. Sabri did not look at them. 'Have you discussed?' he said sternly. She groaned. 'My grandfather will not let me do it. He says you are making a fool of me.' Sabri snorted wildly.

'Is the house yours?'

'Yes, sir.'

'Do you want the money?'

'Yes.'

'Do you want it today?'

'Yes.'

My friend leaned back in his chair and gazed up at the cobwebs in the roof. 'Think of it,' he said, his voice full of the poetry of commerce. 'This gentleman will cut you a chekky. You will go to the Bank. There they will look with respect at it, for it will bear his name. They will open the safe. . . .' His voice trembled and she gazed thirstily at him, entranced by the story-book voice he had put on. 'They will take from it notes, thick notes, as thick as a honeycomb, as thick as salami' (here they both involuntarily licked their lips and I myself began to feel hungry at the thought of so much edible money). 'One . . . two . . . three,' counted Sabri in his mesmeric voice full of animal magnetism. 'Twenty . . . sixty . . . a hundred' gradually getting louder and louder until he ended at 'three hundred.' Throughout this recital she behaved like a chicken with her beak upon a chalk line. As he ended she gave a sigh of rapture and shook herself, as if to throw off the spell. 'The mortgage will have been paid. The widow Anthi will be full of joy and respect for you. You and your husband will have *three hundred pounds*.' He blew out his breath and mopped his head with a red handkerchief. 'All you have to do is to agree. Or take your key.'

He handed her the key and once more swivelled round, to remain facing the wall for a full ten seconds before completing the circle.

'Well?' he said. She was hovering on the edge of tears again.

'And my grandfather?' she asked tremulously. Sabri spread his hands. 'What can I do about your grandfather? Bury him?' he asked indignantly. 'But act quickly, for the gentleman is going.' At a signal from him I rose and stretched and said, 'Well I think I . . .' like the curate in the Leacock story.

'Quick. Quick. Speak or he will be gone,' said Sabri. A look of intense agony came over her face. 'O Saint Matthew and Saint Luke,' she exclaimed aloud, tortured beyond endurance by her doubts. It seemed a queer moment to take refuge in her religion, but obviously the decision weighed heavily upon her. 'O Luke, O Mark,' she rasped, with one hand extended towards me to prevent me from leaving.

Sabri was now like a great psychologist who divines that a difficult transference is at hand. 'She will come,' he whispered to me, and putting his fingers to his mouth blew a shrill blast which alerted everybody. At once with a rumble Jamal, who had apparently been lurking down a side street in his car, grated to the door in a cloud of dust. 'Lay hold of her,' Sabri said and grabbed the woman by the left elbow. Following instructions I grabbed the other arm. She did not actually resist but she definitely rested on her oars and it was something of an effort to roll her across the floor to the taxi. Apparently speed was necessary in this *coup de main* for he shouted: 'Get her inside' and put his shoulder to her back as we propelled her into the back of the car and climbed in on top of her.

She now began to moan and scream as if she were being abducted—doubtless for the benefit of the grandfather—and to make dumb appeals for help through the windows. Her supporters poured out into the road, headed by a nonagenarian waving a plate and her husband who also seemed in tears. 'Stop.' 'You can't do that,' they cried, alerting the whole street. Two children screamed: 'They are taking Mummy away,' and burst into tears.

'Don't pay any attention,' said Sabri now, looking like Napoleon on the eve of Wagram. 'Drive, Jamal, drive.' We set off with a roar, scattering pedestrians who were making their way to the scene of the drama, convinced perhaps that a shot-gun wedding was in progress. 'Where are we going?' I said.

'Lapithos—the widow Anthi,' said Sabri curtly. 'Drive, Jamal, drive.'

As we turned the corner I noticed with horror that the cobbler and his family had stopped another taxi and were piling into it with every intention of following us. The whole thing was turning into a film sequence. 'Don't worry,' said Sabri, 'the second taxi is Jamal's brother and he will have a puncture. I have thought of everything.'

In the brilliant sunshine we rumbled down the Lapithos road. The woman looked about her with interest, pointing out familiar landmarks with great good-humour. She had completely recovered her composure now and smiled upon us both. It was obviously some time since she had had a car-ride and she enjoyed every moment of it.it.

We burst into the house of the widow Anthi like a bomb and demanded the mortgage papers; but the widow herself was out and they were locked in a cupboard. More drama. Finally Sabri and the cobbler's wife forced the door of the cupboard with a flat-iron and we straggled back into the sunshine and climbed aboard again. There was no sign of the second taxi as we set off among the fragrant lemon-groves towards Kyrenia, but we soon came upon them all clustered about a derelict taxi with a puncture. A huge shout went up as they saw us, and some attempt was made to block the road but Jamal, who had entered into the spirit of the thing, now increased speed and we bore down upon them. I was alarmed about the safety of the grandfather, for he stood in the middle of the road waving his stick until the very last moment, and I feared he would not jump out of the way in time. I closed my eyes and breathed deeply through my nose: so did Sabri, for Jamal had only one eye and was unused to speeds greater than twenty miles an hour. But all was well. The old man must have been fairly spry for when I turned round to look out of the back window of the car I saw him spread-eagled in the ditch, but quite all right if one could judge by the language he was using.

The clerks in the Registry Office were a bit shaken by our appearance for by this time the cobbler's wife had decided to start crying again. I cannot for the life of me imagine why—there was nobody left to impress; perhaps she wanted to extract every ounce of drama from the situation. Then we found she could not write—Grandfather was the only one who could write, and she must wait for him. 'My God, if he comes, all is lost again, my dear,' said Sabri. We had to forcibly secure her thumbprint to the article of sale, which sounds easy, but in fact ended by us all being liberally coated with fingerprint ink.

She only subsided into normality when the ratified papers were handed to Sabri; and when I made out her cheque she positively beamed and somewhat to my surprise insisted on shaking hands with me, saying as she did so, 'You are a good man, may you be blessed in the house.'

It was in the most amiable manner that the three of us now sauntered out into the sunlight under the pepper trees. On the main road a dusty taxi had drawn up and was steadily disgorging the disgruntled remains of the defeated army. Catching sight of her they shouted vociferously and advanced in open order, waving sticks and gesticulating. The cobbler's wife gave a shriek and fell into her grandfather's arms, sobbing as if overtaken by irremediable tragedy. The old man, somewhat tousled by his expedition, and with grass in his eyebrows, growled protectively at her and thundered: 'Have you done it?' She sobbed louder and nodded, as if overcome. The air was rent with execrations, but Sabri was quite unmoved. All this was purely gratuitous drama and could be taken lightly. With an expressive gesture he ordered Coca-Cola all round which a small boy brought from a barrow. This had the double effect of soothing them and at the same time standing as a symbolic drink upon the closing of a bargain— shrewdly calculated as were all his strokes. They cursed us weakly as they seized the bottles but they drank thirstily. Indeed the drive to Lapithos is a somewhat dusty one.

'Anyway,' said the cobbler at last when they had all simmered down a bit, 'we still have the water-rights. We have not yet discussed those with the gentleman.' But the gentleman was feeling somewhat exhausted by now, and replete with all the new sensations of ownership. I possessed a house! Sabri nodded quietly. 'Later on,' he said, waving an expressive hand to Jamal, who was also drinking a well-earned Coca-Cola under a pepper tree. 'Now we will rest.' The family now saw us off with the

greatest good humour, as if I were a bridegroom, leaning into the
taxi to shake my hand and mutter blessings. 'It was a canonical
price,' said the old greybeard, as a parting blessing. One could not
say fairer than that.

Death of a Salesman

Arthur Miller

Few writers have dared to cross the grain of our literary
prejudices by trying to arouse our sympathy or admiration
for the bureaucrat or petty bourgeois. We easily identify
with noble lovers, with military heroes, with peasants and
workers who revolt against tyrants, or with the young
poet-novelist-artist who rejects a dull middle-class world for
the high calling of esthetic creation. But the traveling
salesman has been a stock character that stood for jokes,
vulgarity, fraudulence, and shallowness.

Miller takes a still greater risk by letting Willy Loman fit
all of our stereotypes. Both his sons and his wife see
through his pretentions, his false joviality, and his self-
deceptions. He is not portrayed as an antistereotype, a
traveling salesman who is inwardly a poet, philosophically
deep, or a brave man. His sons are in fact contemptuous of
him, and we see why.

Nevertheless, his wife demands that we respect him just
the same, though (as she puts it) he has not become
wealthy, achieved honor, or even, under the harsh pressures of living, created a personal character that we must
admire. "Attention must be finally paid to such a person,"
she says.

He has become the victim of economic forces beyond
his control. He has been modestly successful for thirty-six
years, but his company has now taken away his salary, the
number of his customers has dwindled, and he cannot make
a living from the few commissions he receives. He forces us

Arthur Miller, *Death of a Salesman*, The Viking Press, Inc., New York, 1949, pp.
53–60.

to concede that his façade is a kind of bravery, an optimism in the face of adversity. His steadiness in taking care of his family and his devotion to his sons must be viewed not as smug domesticity, but as devotion to duty. He has now arrived at the age of sixty-three and is a financial failure. One of his sons is "a philandering bum," and the other hates him. If, now, such a man talks to himself at night, and attempts death by an automobile accident, we have no right to sneer at his pitiful pretentions before the outside world that all goes well, or at the desperate expedients he was forced to use as a salesman in order to keep his family afloat financially.

How different would Miller's literary treatment be if the main protagonist were not a traveling salesman, but, say, an assembly-line worker? Consider also the ways in which family relations are affected by different occupational positions.

Biff: What is he doing out there?
Linda: Sh!
Biff: God Almighty, Mom, how long has he been doing this?
Linda: Don't, he'll hear you.
Biff: What the hell is the matter with him?
Linda: It'll pass by morning.
Biff: Shouldn't we do anything?
Linda: Oh, my dear, you should do a lot of things, but there's nothing to do, so go to sleep.
Happy comes down the stairs and sits on the steps.
Happy: I never heard him so loud, Mom.
Linda: Well, come around more often; you'll hear him. *She sits down at the table and mends the lining of Willy's jacket.*
Biff: Why didn't you ever write me about this, Mom?
Linda: How could I write to you? For over three months you had no address.
Biff: I was on the move. But you know I thought of you all the time. You know that, don't you, pal?
Linda: I know, dear, I know. But he likes to have a letter. Just to know that there's still a possibility for better things.

Biff: He's not like this all the time, is he?

Linda: It's when you come home he's always the worst.

Biff: When I come home?

Linda: When you write you're coming, he's all smiles, and talks about the future, and—he's just wonderful. And then the closer you seem to come, the more shaky he gets, and then, by the time you get here, he's arguing, and he seems angry at you. I think it's just that maybe he can't bring himself to—to open up to you. Why are you so hateful to each other? Why is that?

Biff, *evasively:* I'm not hateful, Mom.

Linda: But you no sooner come in the door than you're fighting!

Biff: I don't know why. I mean to change. I'm tryin', Mom, you understand?

Linda: Are you home to stay now?

Biff: I don't know. I want to look around, see what's doin'.

Linda: Biff, you can't look around all your life, can you?

Biff: I just can't take hold, Mom. I can't take hold of some kind of life.

Linda: Biff, a man is not a bird, to come and go with the springtime.

Biff: Your hair . . . *He touches her hair.* Your hair got so gray.

Linda: Oh, it's been gray since you were in high school. I just stopped dyeing it, that's all.

Biff: Dye it again, will ya? I don't want my pal looking old. *He smiles.*

Linda: You're such a boy! You think you can go away for a year and . . . You've got to get it into your head now that one day you'll knock on this door and there'll be strange people here—

Biff: What are you talking about? You're not even sixty, Mom.

Linda: But what about your father?

Biff, *lamely:* Well, I meant him too.

Happy: He admires Pop.

Linda: Biff, dear, if you don't have any feeling for him, then you can't have any feeling for me.

Biff: Sure I can, Mom.

Linda: No. You can't just come to see me, because I love him. *With a threat, but only a threat, of tears:* He's the dearest man in the world to me, and I won't have anyone making him feel unwanted and low and blue. You've got to make up your mind now, darling, there's no leeway any more. Either he's your father and you pay him that respect, or else you're not to come here. I know he's not easy to get along with—nobody knows that better than me—but . . .

Willy, *from the left, with a laugh:* Hey, hey Biffo!

Biff, *starting to go out after Willy:* What the hell is the matter with him? *Happy stops him.*

Linda: Don't—don't go near him!

Biff: Stop making excuses for him! He always, always wiped the floor with you. Never had an ounce of respect for you.

Happy: He's always had respect for—

Biff: What the hell do you know about it?

Happy, *surlily:* Just don't call him crazy.

Biff: He's got no character—Charley wouldn't do this. Not in his own house—spewing out that vomit from his mind.

Happy: Charley never had to cope with what he's got to.

Biff: People are worse off than Willy Loman. Believe me, I've seen them!

Linda: Then make Charley your father, Biff. You can't do that, can you? I don't say he's a great man. Willy Loman never made a lot of money. His name was never in the paper. He's not the finest character that ever lived. But he's a human being, and a terrible thing is happening to him. So attention must be paid. He's not to be allowed to fall into his grave like an old dog. Attention, attention must be finally paid to such a person. You called him crazy—

Biff: I didn't mean—

Linda: No, a lot of people think he's lost his—balance. But you don't have to be very smart to know what his trouble is. The man is exhausted.

Happy: Sure!

Linda: A small man can be just as exhausted as a great man. He works for a company thirty-six years this March, opens up unheard-of territories to their trademark, and now in his old age they take his salary away.

Happy, *indignantly:* I didn't know that, Mom.

Linda: You never asked, my dear! Now that you get your

spending money someplace else you don't trouble your mind with him.

Happy: But I gave you money last—

Linda: Christmas time, fifty dollars! To fix the hot water it cost ninety-seven fifty! For five weeks he's been on straight commission, like a beginner, an unknown!

Biff: Those ungrateful bastards!

Linda: Are they any worse than his sons? When he brought them business, when he was young, they were glad to see him. But now his old friends, the old buyers that loved him so and always found some order to hand him in a pinch—they're all dead, retired. He used to be able to make six, seven calls a day in Boston. Now he takes his valises out of the car and puts them back and takes them out again and he's exhausted. Instead of walking he talks now. He drives seven hundred miles, and when he gets there no one knows him any more, no one welcomes him. And what goes through a man's mind, driving seven hundred miles home without having earned a cent? Why shouldn't he talk to himself? Why? When he has to go to Charley and borrow fifty dollars a week and pretend to me that it's his pay? How long can that go on? How long? You see what I'm sitting here and waiting for? And you tell me he has no character? The man who never worked a day but for your benefit? When does he get the medal for that? Is this his reward—to turn around at the age of sixty-three and find his sons, who he loved better than his life, one a philandering bum—

Happy: Mom!

Linda: That's all you are, my baby! *To Biff:* And you! what happened to the love you had for him? You were such pals! How you used to talk to him on the phone every night! How lonely he was till he could come home to you!

Biff: All right, Mom. I'll live here in my room, and I'll get a job. I'll keep away from him, that's all.

Linda: No, Biff. You can't stay here and fight all the time.

Biff: He threw me out of this house, remember that.

Linda: Why did he do that? I never knew why.

Biff: Because I know he's a fake and he doesn't like anybody around who knows!

Linda: Why a fake? In what way? What do you mean?

Biff: Just don't lay it all at my feet. It's between me and him—that's all I have to say. I'll chip in from now on. He'll settle for half my pay check. He'll be all right. I'm going to bed. *He starts for the stairs.*

Linda: He won't be all right.

Biff, *turning on the stairs, furiously:* I hate this city and I'll stay here. Now what do you want?

Linda: He's dying, Biff.

Happy turns quickly to her, shocked.

Biff, *after a pause:* Why is he dying?

Linda: He's been trying to kill himself.

Biff, *with great horror:* How?

Linda: I live from day to day.

Biff: What're you talking about?

Linda: Remember I wrote you that he smashed up the car again? In February?

Biff: Well?

Linda: The insurance inspector came. He said that they have evidence. That all these accidents in the last year—weren't—weren't—accidents.

Happy: How can they tell that? That's a lie.

Linda: It seems there's a woman . . . *She takes a breath as*

⌠**Biff,** *sharply but contained:* What woman?

⌡**Linda,** *simultaneously:* . . . and this woman . . .

Linda: What?

Biff: Nothing. Go ahead.

Linda: What did you say?

Biff: Nothing. I just said what woman?

Happy: What about her?

Linda: Well, it seems she was walking down the road and saw his car. She says that he wasn't driving fast at all, and that he didn't skid. She says he came to that little bridge, and then deliberately smashed into the railing, and it was only the shallowness of the water that saved him.

Biff: Oh, no, he probably just fell asleep again.

Linda: I don't think he fell asleep.

Biff: Why not?

Linda: Last month . . . *With great difficulty:* Oh, boys, it's so hard to say a thing like this! He's just a big stupid man to you, but I tell you there's more good in him than in many other people. *She chokes, wipes her eyes.* I was looking for a fuse. The lights blew out, and I went down in the cellar. And behind the fuse box—it happened to fall out—was a length of rubber pipe—just short.

Happy: No kidding?

Linda: There's a little attachment on the end of it. I knew right away. And sure enough, on the bottom of the water heater there's a new little nipple on the gas pipe.

Happy, *angrily:* That—jerk!

Biff: Did you have it taken off?

Linda: I'm—I'm ashamed to. How can I mention it to him? Every day I go down and take away that little rubber pipe. But, when he comes home, I put it back where it was. How can I insult him that way? I don't know what to do. I live from day to day, boys. I tell you, I know every thought in his mind. It sounds so old-fashioned and silly, but I tell you he put his whole life into you and you've turned your backs on him. *She bent over in the chair, weeping, her face in her hands..* Biff, I swear to God! Biff, his life is in your hands!

Happy, *to Biff:* How do you like that damned fool!

Biff, *kissing her:* All right, pal, all right. It's all settled now. I've been remiss. I know that, Mom. But now I'll stay, and I swear to you, I'll apply myself. *Kneeling in front of her, in a fever of self-reproach:* It's just—you see, Mom, I don't fit in business. Not that I won't try. I'll try, and I'll make good.

Chapter 12

Women's Places

The "true history" of women can never be written, even by women, because the original data cannot be recaptured. Men created the records, writing mainly about themselves, not women. Men dominated the societies of the past, and historians saw no need to pay much attention to women. Reading history helps us to catch flashes and glimpses of women's worlds; how they truly thought, felt, or acted in the past becomes better known to us, but we still have encountered only little of that experience.

Women have played a much larger role in literature than in history. Granted, that literature was almost entirely written by men until very recently, and those writers innocently shared the biases and stereotypes of the men of their times. They saw women as obviously different, by birth, biology, or rearing. Perhaps most indicative of this attitude is the fact that men often attempted to puzzle out what women were really like, but saw no problem at all understanding men. Men were people; women were not. It is difficult to recall a single essay devoted to explaining men, but scores of writers have tried to fathom the mysteries of womanhood.

Nevertheless, though the grander roles in literature were usually given to heroes, not heroines, women had to be included if novels, plays, and stories were to imitate life at all. Because characters have a way of living independently of the author once he or she has created them, and because writers as a class are more sensitive to the feelings of all human beings, women have often emerged from the pages of a book as full-bodied persons whose will or whim determined the course of the plot. Even when writers heaped scorn on a woman (e.g., Helen of Troy, Cleopatra, Lady Macbeth, Lucrezia Borgia), they were paying grudging tribute to her importance.

This importance was based in the first instance on the extent to which the world's literature has focused on passionate love, mostly love between a man and a woman. Since all plots require conflict, the desires and actions of women could not be trivial. A further large part of literature has centered on conflicts (and sometimes love) between husbands and wives. Again, if the men's roles were not to be trivial, the women who were to be their foils could not be, either; writing failed as literature if the women characters were shallow and unimportant.

Beyond these esthetic needs, however, one can dimly perceive a further dynamic at work, which surfaces only sporadically until the nineteenth century and then begins to occur with increasing frequency. First, now and then there appears throughout literary history a recognition, amidst man's complacency about his natural propensity for greater wisdom, nobility, bravery, competence, and even ability to sacrifice self-interest for a greater principle, that at least *some* women are wiser than their husbands or lovers, nobler in spirit, or more concerned for the common good. In another form, similar concessions sometimes appear in comic Greek and Roman plays, as complaints by men about how rebellious their women have become. Sometimes the women are created as spiritually great because they are supposed to be fit companions for the heroes of the stories. Nevertheless, from time to time women do appear in literature who are genuine *heroines*, not merely passive pawns, frail vessels of fragility, or evil temptresses.

Second, and of much more importance, is the still rarer concession that there is in fact another *world*, that of women; that though oppressed and even seeming to defer to their oppressors, they have not inwardly capitulated, and that their own world is legitimate in its own right, not as a minor complement to the world of men. These themes are evident in as early a writer as Homer, especially in the thoughts and feelings of the women "left behind." They are expressed with still greater power and poignancy in Aeschylus' *The Trojan Women*. Perhaps one of the finest expressions of these themes is to be found in Chaucer's great *Tale of the Wife of Bath*. The latter is strikingly important because she is neither noble nor a heroine, but an authentic human being who serenely accepts her own foibles, passions, and strength without any need to utilize the stock, set speeches of grander women in high drama.

Although the main thrust of Shakespeare's large themes remains masculine, he possessed an uncanny ability not merely to create great women characters but—and perhaps that is the source of their greatness—to justify the woman's actions within her own world. Whether it is Portia, the woman lawyer, defending a woman's right to speak, or the evil Lady Macbeth, he forces us to see the world through their eyes. When they speak, we are persuaded momentarily to set aside the traditional masculine prejudices when we say "A woman is speaking"; instead we must concede, "A particular human being is speaking," with all that person's uniqueness.

But though such perceptions do flash into prominence from time to time in literature in the past, they are rare, and even now they may hardly be said to occur frequently. This is not merely because men have done most of the writing, although of course that is a prime cause. Nor is it entirely that writers have tried to depict the world as it is, and men have typically dominated that world. More deeply, it is because both men and women have seen the world through a framework or set of lenses that were made by men. They have not perceived any great need to understand the world of women. If the literature of the future is to be more liberated, it will be in part because there will be more women writers. But that alone will not be sufficient. It is further necessary that both men and women exercise their imaginations and most penetrating intuitions both to narrow the gulf between the sexes and to bridge it by trying to share each other's experiences, whether grand or banal.

Advice to Women on How to Be Attractive

Ovid

Ovid takes for granted that women operate in a love market where they must do their own advertising. Although his tone seems mocking, he is not simply making fun of women. He would like both men and women to be as attractive as possible, since he is in favor of light-hearted flirtation, frivolous affairs, in fact all aspects of the art of love. He could also be interpreted as slightly mocking toward men, for they cannot be very wise if they are so easily fooled. In truth, that is not his aim either. He wants to show that both sexes are victims of the illusions they weave to ensnare each other.

For all our rhetoric about the ideals we would like our sweethearts or spouses to embody, almost all of us easily fall victim to appearances, just as to some degree all of our fates are determined in part by the fortuitous features of our physical self. We know that at times we have been entranced by a pretty or handsome face, but most of us do not realize how much we are influenced by others' attractiveness (or lack of it) in a wide variety of human interaction, from dealing with a bank clerk to getting a job.

Even if we concede that important point, we can nevertheless ask how *correct* Ovid is, and how we might in our day rewrite his instructions, for either men or women.

Faults of the face or physique call for attempts at
    disguise.
If you are short, sit down, lest, standing, you seem to
    be sitting,
Little as you may be, stretch out full length on your
    couch

Ovid, *The Art of Love* and *The Loves*, translated by Rolfe Humphries, Indiana University Press, Bloomington, 1957, Bk. 3, ll. 255–279.

Even here, if you fear some critic might notice your
    stature,
See that a cover is thrown, hide yourself under a
    spread.
If you're the lanky type, wear somewhat billowy
    garments,   260
Loosely let the robe fall from the shoulders down.
If you're inclined to be pale, wear stripes of scarlet or
    crimson,
If you're inclined to be dark, white is an absolute must.
Let an ugly foot hide in a snow-covered sandal.
If your ankles are thick, don't be unlacing your shoes.   265
Do your collarbones show? Then wear a clasp at each
    shoulder.
Have you a bust too flat? Bandages ought to fix that.
If your fingers are fat, or your fingernails brittle and
    ugly,
Watch what you do when you talk; don't wave your
    hands in the air.
Eat a lozenge or two if you think your breath is
    offensive,   270
If you have something to say, speak from some
    distance away.
If a tooth is too black or too large, or the least bit
    uneven,
Pay no attention to jokes; laughter might give you
    away.
Who would believe it? The girls must learn to govern
    their laughter.
Even in this respect tact is required, and control.   275
Do not open the mouth too wide, like a braying
    she-jackass,
Show your dimples and teeth, hardly much more than a
    smile.
Do not shake your sides or slap your thigh in
    amusement—
Feminine, that's the idea; giggle or titter, no more.

The Taming of the Shrew
William Shakespeare

The rights and obligations that properly fall to men and women separately are nowhere so fully argued in Shakespeare as in *The Taming of the Shrew*. Generations have delighted in the comic battles within the play, and generations of men have doubtless gone home pleased at the outcome: Katharine is tamed, and not merely by a rational calculation that she will do better if she acts submissive. Nor is she merely tamed by love, putting aside her imperious will because Petruchio has won her heart. Rather, she submits because in fair battle she has lost, persuaded by the eloquence that Shakespeare gives to the characters in the play—especially by Petruchio's cleverness in defining every aggressive or hostile act she commits as an act of affection and tenderness.

If the following speech of submission had been made by the traditional docile, soft, pale young lady, it would appear almost a caricature. Played on the stage it is moving, precisely because we have known Katharine in her other manifestation. Present-day readers find the speech slightly offensive, because its content appears incorrect. Women are not truly like that, and probably they never were, unless forced to behave so.

Many readers and playgoers in the past have felt a nagging sense of disbelief at the final turn of events in *The Taming of the Shrew*. First of all, they suspect that such a strong human being can violate her sense of worth only temporarily, at great cost to herself and ultimately to her credulous spouse. Secondly, Shakespeare has given Katharine some very powerful arguments during the course of the play. Even if he himself did not believe these expositions of women's rights and these denunciations against male oppression, he frees his characters to speak for

From *Shakespeare: The Complete Works*, edited by G. B. Harrison, Harcourt Brace Jovanovich, Inc., New York, 1968, pp. 363-364, ll. 129–188. This excerpt is from Act V, Scene 2.

themselves; Katharine argues from a full heart and a clear mind. Consequently, even when she submits, as she does in this final speech, the reverberations of her previous speeches continue to trouble even those who feel smug in their masculine superiority. It is the needs of the plot that have caused the submission, but Katharine's last statement cannot erase the truth of what has gone before.

Petruchio: Katharine, I charge thee, tell these headstrong women
What duty they do owe their lords and husbands.
Widow: Come, come you're mocking: we will have no telling.
Petruchio: Come on, I say; and first begin with her.
Widow: She shall not.
Petruchio: I say she shall: and first begin with her.
Katharina: Fie, fie! unknit that threatening unkind brow;
And dart not scornful glances from those eyes,
To wound thy lord, thy king, thy governor:
It blots thy beauty as frosts do bite the meads,
Confounds thy frame as whirlwinds shake fair buds,
And in no sense is meet or amiable.
A woman moved is like a fountain troubled,
Muddy, ill-seeming, thick, bereft of beauty;
And while it is so, none so dry or thirsty
Will deign to sip or touch one drop of it.
Thy husband is thy lord, thy life, thy keeper,
Thy head, thy sovereign; one that cares for thee,
And for thy maintenance commits his body
To painful labour both by sea and land,
To watch the night in storms, the day in cold,
Whilst thou liest warm at home, secure and safe;
And craves no other tribute at thy hands
But love, fair looks, and true obedience;
Too little payment for so great a debt.
Such duty as the subject owes the prince
Even such a woman oweth to her husband;
And when she is froward, peevish, sullen, sour,

And not obedient to his honest will,
What is she but a foul contending rebel,
And graceless traitor to her loving lord?
I am ashamed that women are so simple
To offer war where they should kneel for peace;
Or seek for rule, supremacy, and sway,
When they are bound to serve, love, and obey.
Why are our bodies soft and weak and smooth,
Unapt to toil and trouble in the world,
But that our soft conditions and our hearts
Should well agree with our external parts?
Come, come, you froward and unable worms!
My mind hath been as big as one of yours,
My heart as great, my reason haply more,
To bandy word for word and frown for frown;
But now I see our lances are but straws,
Our strength as weak, our weakness past compare,
That seeming to be most which we indeed least are.
Then vail your stomachs, for it is no boot,
And place your hands below your husband's foot:
In token of duty, if he please,
My hand is ready, may it do him ease.

Petruchio: Why, there's a wench! Come on, and kiss me, Kate.
Lucentio: Well, go thy ways, old lad; for thou shalt ha't.
Vincentio: 'Tis a good hearing, when children are toward.
Lucentio: But a harsh hearing, when women are froward.
Petruchio: Come, Kate, we'll to bed.
We three are married, but you two are sped.
'Twas I won the wager, though you hit the white;

(To Lucentio)

And, being a winner, God give you good night!

(Exeunt Petruchio and Katharina)

Hortensio: Now, go thy ways; thou hast tamed a curst shrew.
Lucentio: 'Tis a wonder, by your leave, she will be tamed so.

(Exeunt)

Children of Violence

Doris Lessing

This writer has come to play an important role in the women's liberation movement, almost certainly without having planned it so. From the beginning of her career she has aimed high, avoiding the easy road of "women's literature," and composing with the fierce artistic integrity that has more often been the aspiration of the dedicated male literary artist. She has made her readers share the often repellent social and physical world of South Africa and has woven a complex fabric of intertwined lives and generations that demand our attention even if we do not wish to identify with any of these people. In later works her locale shifts to England, but in both places the characters we encounter have an unsettling effect upon us: we recognize that some of them resemble us partly (but only partly, we hope). Thus, at one level, her importance is as a literary artist, a model that women could emulate.

It is only gradually that people have come to see a somewhat radical orientation or viewpoint in Lessing's writings, for her specific message has not been feminist; that is, she has not used her work as a vehicle for stating radical arguments in favor of women's liberation. Instead, she has been able to create a special stance from which to view the unfolding of events in her novels.

It is a woman's view, and she pitilessly exposes the obtuseness, cowardice, weakness, and cruelty of men. But this is not a political exaggeration, matching the traditional male biases against women. Nor is it the traditional sentimentality or even wailing of a woman who delights in her own frivolity and complains affectionately about the men who dominate her.

She is not even writing for such women or men. For she exposes with equal lack of sentimentality or gush the self-destructive, headstrong, bad judgments of women. Her women are not soft creatures, grown-up babies; they sub-

Doris Lessing, *Children of Violence*, Simon & Schuster, Inc., New York, 1966, pp. 94–105.

mit only when they must. They are not antistereotypes, i.e., wonderful spirits to be set against the silly, pretentious men. She portrays them as they are, warts and boils and all, courageous and weak at times, and often foolish: in short, as human beings.

Thus she "defends" women not by trying to persuade us that they need a woman champion, but by making us see that their fate *matters*. Of course they are dominated by men's arrangements of force and wealth, but that immediate fact is neither to be disregarded nor to be made the sole object of our attention. For, however oppressed, their lives can be as fascinating to us as those of men, since they are of equal worth.

In the following reading, we enter the world of Martha Quest and her husband. It is almost embarrassing to watch their quick emotional swings, because we see that we too might at some time behave in this way. Martha moves from melancholy and pity for her mother, who had not wanted to bear the child that became Martha, to the insistence that she will "cut the cycle" of doom and have an abortion; then she decides to have the child after all. Her husband placidly accepts the notion of an abortion, and even encourages her, then he becomes elated at realizing that he is to become a father. We also observe one of society's little mechanisms for keeping women in their place: the traditional physician's response to a woman's appeal for an abortion.

Mrs. Quest was talking of matters on the farm, about the house in town they were shortly to buy, about her husband's health.

Martha scarcely listened. She was engaged in examining and repairing those intellectual's bastions of defence behind which she sheltered, that building whose shape had first been sketched so far back in her childhood she could no longer remember how it then looked. With every year it had become more complicated, more ramified; it was as if she, Martha, were a variety of soft, shell-less creature whose survival lay in the strength of those walls. Reaching out in all directions from behind it, she clutched at the bricks of arguments, the stones of words, discarding any that might not fit into the building.

She was looking at Mrs. Quest in a deep abstract speculation, as if neither she nor her mother had any validity as persons, but were mere pawns in the hands of an old fatality. She could see a sequence of events, unalterable, behind her, and stretching unalterably into the future. She saw her mother, a prim-faced Edwardian schoolgirl, confronting, in this case, the Victorian father, the patriarchal father, with rebellion. She saw herself sitting where her mother now sat, a woman horribly metamorphosed, entirely dependent on her children for any interest in life, resented by them, and resenting them; opposite her, a young woman of whom she could distinguish nothing clearly but a set, obstinate face; and beside these women, a series of shadowy dependent men, broken-willed and sick with compelled diseases. This the nightmare, this the nightmare of a class and generation: repetition. And although Martha had read nothing of the great interpreters of the nightmare, she had been soaked in the minor literature of the last thirty years, which had dealt with very little else: a series of doomed individuals, carrying their doom *inside* them, like the seeds of fatal disease. Nothing could alter the pattern.

But inside the stern web of fatality did flicker small hopeful flames. One thought was that after all it had not always been that these great life-and-death struggles were fought out inside the family; presumably things might change again. Another was that she had decided not to have a baby; and it was in her power to cut the cycle.

Which brought her back into the conversation with a question on her tongue.

Mrs. Quest was talking about the coming war. She had no doubt at all as to the shape it would assume. It was Britain's task to fight Hitler and Stalin combined. Martha suggested this might be rather a heavy task. Mrs. Quest said sharply that Martha had no patriotism, and never had had. Even without those lazy and useless Americans who never came into a war until they could make good pickings out of it, Britain would ultimately muddle through to victory, as she always did.

Martha was able to refrain from being *logical* only by her more personal preoccupations. She plunged straight in with an enquiry as to whether her mother had ever had an abortion. She hastened to add that she wanted to know because of a friend of hers.

Mrs. Quest, checked, took some moments to adjust to this level. She said vaguely, "It's illegal . . ." Having made this offering to the law, she considered the question on its merits and said, in a lowered voice, a look of distaste on her face, "Why— are you like that?"

Martha suppressed the hostility she felt at the evasion, and said, "No."

"Well, you look like it," said Mrs. Quest bluntly, with triumph.

"Well, I'm not." Martha added the appeal, "I do wish you'd tell me . . ." She had no idea what she really wanted to know!

Mrs. Quest looked at her, her vigorous face wearing the dubious, rather puzzled expression which meant she was trying to remember her own past.

Martha was telling herself that this appeal was doomed to produce all kinds of misunderstanding and discomfort. They always did. And what *did* she want her mother to say? She looked at her in silence, and wished that some miracle would occur and her mother would produce a few simple, straightforward remarks, a few *words*—not emotional, nothing deviating from the cool humorous understatement that would save them both from embarrassment. Martha needed the right words.

She reflected that Mrs. Quest had not wanted her. How, then, had she come to accept her? Was that what she wanted to know? But looking at her now, she could only think that Mrs. Quest had spent a free, energetic youth, had "lived her own life"—she had used the phrase herself long before it was proper for middle-class daughters to do so—and had, accordingly, quarrelled with her father. She had not married until very late.

For many years now, she had been this immensely efficient down-to-earth matron; but somewhere concealed in her was the mother who had borne Martha. From her white and feminine body she, Martha, had emerged—that was certainly a fact! She could remember seeing her mother naked; beautiful she had been, a beautiful, strong white body, with full hips, small high breasts—the Greek idea of beauty. And to that tender white body had belonged the strong soft white hands Martha remembered. Those hands had tended her, the baby. Well, then, why could her mother not resurrect that woman in her and speak the few simple, appropriate words?

But now she was turning Martha's flimsy nightgown between her thickened, clumsy hands, as if determined not to say she disapproved of it; and frowned. She looked uncomfortable. Martha quite desperately held on to that other image to set against this one. She could see that earlier woman distinctly. More, she could feel wafts of tenderness coming from her.

Then, suddenly, into this pure and simple emotion came something new: she felt pity like a clutching hand. She was remembering something else. She was lying in the dark in that house on the farm, listening to a piano being played several rooms away. She got up, and crept through the dark rooms to a doorway. She saw Mrs. Quest seated at the keyboard, a heavy knot of hair weighting her head and glistening gold where the light touched it from two candle flames which floated steadily above the long white transparent candles. Tears were running down her face while she set her lips and smiled. The romantic phrases of a Chopin nocturne rippled out into the African night, steadily accompanied by the crickets and the blood-thudding of the tomtoms from the compound. Martha smiled wryly: she could remember the gulfs of pity that sight had thrown her into.

Mrs. Quest looked up over the nightdress and enquired jealously, "What are you laughing at."

"Mother," she said desperately, "you didn't want to have me. Well, then . . ."

Mrs. Quest laughed, and said Martha had come as a surprise to her.

Martha waited, then prodded. "What did you *feel?*"

A slight look of caution came onto her mother's honest square face. "Oh, well . . ." But almost at once she launched into the gay and humorous account, which Martha had so often heard, of the difficulties of getting the proper clothes and so on; which almost at once merged with the difficulties of the birth itself—a painful business, this, as she had so often been told.

"But what did you *feel* about it all? I mean, it couldn't have been as easy as all that," said Martha.

"Oh, it wasn't easy—I was just telling you." Mrs. Quest began to repeat how awkward a baby Martha had been. "But it wasn't really your fault. First I didn't have enough milk, though I didn't know it; and then I gave you a mixture, and didn't know until the doctor told me that it was only half the right strength. So in one way and another I half starved you for the first nine months of your life." Mrs. Quest laughed ruefully, and said, "No wonder you never stopped crying day or night."

A familiar resentment filled Martha, and she at once pressed on. "But, Mother, when you first knew you were going to have a baby—"

Mrs. Quest interrupted. "And then I had your brother, he was such a good baby, not like you."

And now Martha abdicated, as she had so often done before; for it had always, for some reason, seemed right and inevitable that Mrs. Quest should prefer the delicate boy child to herself. Martha listened to the familiar story to the end, while she suppressed a violent and exasperated desire to take her mother by her shoulders and shake her until she produced, in a few sensible and consoling sentences, the truth which it was so essential Martha should have. But Mrs. Quest had forgotten how she had felt. She was no longer interested. And why should she be, this elderly woman with all the business of being a woman behind her?

In a short while she returned to the war, dismissed Chamberlain with a few just sentences, and recommended Mr. Churchill for his job. The Quests belonged to that section of the middle class who would be happy and contented to be conservatives if only the conservatives could be more efficient. As it was, they never ceased complaining about the inefficiency and corruption of the party they would unfailingly vote for if they lived in England.

Towards lunchtime she left, with the advice that Martha should go and see the doctor and get a good tonic. She looked dreadful—it wasn't fair to Douglas.

The result of that visit from her mother was that Martha

decided again she must not sink into being a mere housewife. She should at once learn a profession, or at least take some kind of job. But this decision was not as firm as it might seem from the energy she used in speaking about it to Douglas.

She was gripped by a lethargy so profound that in fact she spent most of her time limp on that divan, thinking about nothing. She felt heavy and uncomfortable and sick. And she was clinging to Douglas with the dependence of a child. She was miserable when he left in the morning; she was waiting anxiously for his return hours before he might be expected. Pride, however, forbade her to show it, or to ask him to come home for lunch. at night, the loud sad music from the fair was becoming an obsession. She found herself waking from sleep and crying, but what she was weeping for she had no idea at all. She drew the curtains so that she might not see the great wheel; and then lay watching the circling of light through their thin stuff. She accused herself of every kind of weak-mindedness and stupidity; nevertheless, the persistent monotony of that flickering cycle seemed a revelation of an appalling and intimate truth; it was like being hypnotized.

During the daytime she sat with a book, trying to read, and realized that she was not seeing one word of it. It was, she realized, as if she were listening for something; some kind of anxiety rang through every limb.

One morning she was very sick, and all at once the suspicion she had been ignoring for so long became a certainty—and from one moment to the next. When Douglas came home that night she said sullenly, as if it was his fault, that she must be pregnant; and insisted when he said that Dr. Stern could not be wrong. At last he suggested she should go and talk to Stella, whose virtuosity in these matters was obvious. She said she would; but when it came to the point, she shrank from the idea and instead went to Alice.

It was a hot, dusty morning. A warm wind swept flocks of yellowing leaves along the streets. The jacarandas were holding up jaded yellow arms. This drying, yellowing, fading month, this time when the year tensed and tightened towards the coming rains, always gave her a feeling of perverted autumn, and now filled her with an exquisite cold apprehension. The sky, above the haze of dust, was a glitter of hot blue light.

Alice was in her pink taffeta dressing gown in her large chair. She greeted Martha with cheerful indifference, and bade her sit down. On the table beside her was a pile of books, called variously *Mothercraft, Baby Handling,* and *Your Months of Preparation.*

Martha glanced towards them, and Alice said, "The nonsense they talk, dear, you wouldn't believe." She pushed them gently away. Then she got up, and stood before Martha, with her two hands held tenderly over her stomach. "I'm flat as a board still," she remarked with pride. She looked downwards with a preoccupied blue stare; she seemed to be listening. "According to the books, it doesn't quicken until—but now I've worked out my dates, and actually it quickens much earlier. At first I thought it must be wind," remarked Alice, faintly screwing up her face with the effort of listening.

"I think I'm pregnant, too," remarked Martha nervously.

"Are you, dear?" Alice sat down, keeping her hands in a protective curve, and said, "Oh, well, when you get used to it, it's quite interesting, really."

"Oh, I'm not going to *have* it," said Martha with energy.

Alice did not reply. Martha saw that she had gone completely into her private world of sensation, and that anything which happened outside was quite irrelevant. She recognized the feeling: what else had she been fighting against during the last few weeks?

After a pause Alice continued the conversation she was having with herself by remarking, "Oh, well, to hell with everything. Who cares, anyway?" She gave her dry, nervous laugh and reached for a cigarette.

"Well, you look very pleased with yourself," said Martha, half laughing.

Alice frowned as these words reached her, and said, "Help yourself to cigarettes, dear."

The morning drifted past. Alice, dim and safe in her private world, smoked constantly, stubbing out the cigarettes as she lit them, and from time to time dropped remarks such as "It ought to be November, I think." When Martha roused herself to go, Alice appeared to be reminding herself that she had not been as sympathetic as she could have been. She held the door half open, Martha already being outside it, and proceeded to offer various bits of advice in an apologetic voice, the most insistent being that she should at once go and see Stella.

Martha went home, reached for the telephone, but was unable to dial Stella's number. She shrank away from Stella with the most extraordinary dislike of her. She was thinking of Alice; and in spite of her own deep persistent misery, her knowledge that the web was tight around her, she knew, too, that she was most irrationally elated. Anyone would think that you were pleased, she said angrily to herself. With an efficiency which Stella must have applauded, she put on her dressing gown, locked the door, and took the telephone off the hook. She then drank, with calm determination, glass after glass of neat gin, until a full bottle was gone. Then she lay down and slept. When she woke it was four in the afternoon, and she felt nothing but a weakness in her knees. She filled the bath with water so hot that she could not put her hand into it, and, setting her teeth, got in. The pain was so intense that she nearly fainted. She was going through with this, however; and she sat in the bath until the water was tepid. When she reeled out, she was boiled scarlet, and could not touch her skin. Having rubbed cream all over herself, she lay on her bed, shrinking from the touch of the sheet, and cried a little from sheer pain. She slept again. Douglas was rattling at the locked door when she woke, and she staggered to let him in.

Faced with a touzled, bedraggled, red-faced female, reeking of gin, Douglas was naturally upset; but he was informed in a cold and efficient voice that this was necessary. He sat wincing while Martha climbed repeatedly onto the table and jumped off, crashing down on her heels with the full force of her weight. At the end of half an hour he could no longer stand it, and forcibly put her to bed. In a small triumphant voice Martha informed him that if *that* didn't shift it nothing would.

In the morning she woke, feeling as if her limbs had been

pulverized from within and as if her skin were a separate, agonized coating to her body, but otherwise whole. Douglas was astounded to hear her say, in a voice of unmistakable satisfaction, that she must be as strong and as healthy as a horse. He was unable to bear it: this female with set will, tight mouth, and cold and rejecting eyes was entirely horrifying to him.

"Well," demanded Martha practically, "do we or do we not want to have this baby?"

Douglas evaded this by saying that she should go forthwith to see Dr. Stern, and escaped to the office, trying to ignore the inescapable fact that Martha was contemptuous of him because of his male weakness.

Late that afternoon Martha entered Dr. Stern's consulting room, in a mood of such desperate panic that he recognized it at once and promptly offered her a drink, which he took from a cupboard. Martha watched him anxiously, and saw him look her up and down with that minute, expert inspection which she had seen before. On whose face? Mrs. Talbot's, of course!

Dr. Stern, kindness itself, then examined Martha. She told him, laughing, of the measures she had taken, to which he replied gravely, looking at her scarlet skin, that she shouldn't overdo these things. But never, not for one second, did he make the mistake of speaking in the anonymous voice of male authority, which she would have so passionately resented.

Finally he informed her that she was over four months pregnant; which shocked her into silence. Such was his bland assurance, such was the power of this man, the doctor in the white coat behind the big desk, that the words stammering on her tongue could not get themselves said. But he saw her reproachful look and said that doctors were not infallible; he added almost at once that a fine, healthy girl like herself should be delighted to have a baby. Martha was silent with misery. She said feebly after a pause that there was no point in having a baby when the war was coming. At which he smiled slightly and said that the birth rate, for reasons best known to itself, always rose in wartime. She felt caught up in an immense impersonal tide which paid no attention to her, Martha. She looked at this young man who was after all not so much older than herself; she looked at the grave responsible face, and hated him bitterly from the bottom of her heart.

She asked him bluntly if he would do an abortion.

He replied immediately that he could not.

There was a long and difficult silence. Dr. Stern regarded her steadily from expert eyes, and reached out for a small statuette which stood on his desk. It was in bronze, of a mermaidlike figure diving off a rock. He fingered it lightly and said, "Do you realize that your baby is as big as this already?" It was about five inches high.

The shock numbed her tongue. She had imagined this creature as "it," perhaps as a formless blob of jellylike substance, or, alternatively, as already born, a boneless infant in a shawl, but certainly not as a living being five inches long coiled in her flesh.

"Eyes, ears, arms, legs—all there." He fingered the statuette a little longer; then he dropped his hand and was silent.

Martha was so bitter that she could not yet move or speak a word. All she was for him, and probably for Douglas too, she thought, was a "healthy young woman."

Then he said with a tired humorous smile that if she knew the proportion of his women patients who came, as she did, when they found they were pregnant, not wanting a baby, only to be delighted when they had got used to it, she would be surprised.

Martha did not reply. She rose to leave. He got up, too, and said, with a real human kindness that she was able to appreciate only later, that she should think twice before rushing off to see one of the wise women: her baby was too big to play tricks with now. If she absolutely insisted on an abortion, she should go to Johannesburg, where, as everyone knew, there was a hospital which was a positive factory for this sort of thing. The word "factory" made her wince; and she saw at once, with a satirical appreciation of his skill in handling her, that it was deliberately chosen.

He shook hands with her, invited her to drop in and talk it all over if she felt like it at any time, and went back to his desk.

Martha returned to her flat in a trance of despair. Not the least of her bitterness was due to her knowledge that in some part of herself she was already weakening towards this baby. She could not forget that diving creature, bent in moulded bronze, about five inches long. In her bedroom, she found herself standing as she had seen Alice stand, hands curiously touching her stomach. It occurred to her that this child had quickened already; she understood that this long process had been one of determined self-deception—almost as if she had wanted this damned baby all the time, she thought quickly, and immediately pushing the idea from her mind. But how could she have mistaken those irregular but definite movements for anything else?

When Douglas came home she informed him that nothing would induce her to have this child, with which he at once agreed. She found herself slightly annoyed by this. It was agreed that she should go at once to Johannesburg. Douglas knew of an astounding number of women who had made the trip and returned none the worse for it.

Martha, left alone next day to make preparations for the trip, did nothing at all. Then her mother flew in. Against all her intentions, Martha blurted out that she was going to have a baby; and was immediately folded in Mrs. Quest's arms. Mrs. Quest was delighted; her face beamed pleasure; she said it was lovely, it was the best thing that could possibly happen, it would settle Martha down and give her no time for all her funny ideas. (Here she gave a small defiant, triumphant laugh.) Unfortunately, as she had to get back to the farm, she could not stay with her daughter, much as she wanted to. She embraced Martha again, and said in a warm, thrilled voice that it was the greatest experience in a woman's life. With this she left, wet-eyed and with a tremulous smile.

Martha was confounded; she sat thinking that her mother must be out of her mind; above all she was thinking angrily of the triumph she had shown. She roused herself again to pack and make telephone calls; but they again faded out in indecision. The child, five inches long, with eyes, nose, mouth, hands and feet, seemed very active. Martha sat feeling the imprisoned thing moving in her flesh, and was made more miserable by the knowledge that it had been moving for at least a week without her noticing it than by anything else. For what was the use of thinking, of planning, if emotions one did not recognize at all worked their own way against you? She was filled with a strong and seething rage against her mother, her husband, Dr. Stern, who had all joined the conspiracy against her. She addressed angry speeches of protest to them, fiery and eloquent speeches; but alas, there was no one there but herself.

Sometime later Stella came in, stepping blithely around the door, hips swaying lightly, eyes bright with interest. She had heard the news; the boys were already drinking Douglas's health in the clubs.

"Everyone's quite convinced that you *had* to get married," said Stella with a delighted chuckle.

An astonishing thought occurred to Martha for the first time. "Do you know," she cried out, half laughing, "if I'm as pregnant as Dr. Stern says I am, then I must have been when I got married!" At this she flung back and roared with laughter. Stella joined her briefly; then she regarded Martha impatiently, waiting for the rather helpless wail of laughter to end.

"Well," demanded Stella, "and what are we going to do about it?"

It was at this point that Martha, in the stubborn, calm voice of complete conviction, found herself explaining to Stella how foolish an abortion would be at this stage. Stella grew increasingly persuasive, and Martha obstinate. The arguments she now found for having this baby were as strong and unanswerable as those she had been using, only ten minutes ago, against it. She found herself intensely excited at the idea of having a baby.

"Well, I don't know," remarked Stella disgustedly at last. "You and Alice are mad. Both quite, quite mad."

She rose, and stood poised before Martha to deliver the final blow; but Martha intercepted it by suggesting teasingly that Stella herself ought to start a baby, as otherwise she'd be left out of it.

At this Stella allowed a brief gleam of a smile; but at once she substituted a disapproving frown. "I'm not going to have kids now, it wouldn't be fair to Andrew. But if *you* want to shut yourself into a nursery at your age, then it's your own affair." She gave the triumphant and amused Martha a long, withering look, dropped a goodbye, pulled on her gloves gracefully, and went out.

She sustained the sweep of her exit until she reached the street. She had meant to go shopping, but instead she went to Douglas's office. She told the typist to announce her, but was unable to wait, and followed the girl in, saying urgently, "Douggie—I must see you."

"Come in, Stell." He nodded to the typist, who went out again.

Stella sat down. "I've just seen Matty"

"Yes, it's a bit of a mess," he said at once. But he looked self-conscious, even proud.

Seeing it, Stella said impatiently, "She's much too young. She doesn't realize."

"Oh, I don't know—she's been putting the fear of God into me. She'll be ill. I wish you'd speak to her, Stell."

"But I have been speaking to her. She won't listen."

"After all, there's no danger in a proper operation in Johannesburg, but messing about with gin and all that nonsense . . ."

Stella shrugged this away, and said, "She's as stubborn as a mule. She's just a baby herself. She's pleased now, of course, but that's natural."

Douglas looked up sharply, and went red. His lips trembled. He stood up, then sat down again. Now he was white.

"What's the matter with you?" she asked, smiling but irritated.

"I'll talk to her again," he muttered. He understood. Now all he wanted was for her to go. For the first time he had imagined the baby being born. He was imagining himself a father. Pride was invading him. It had already swallowed up his small pang of hurt that Martha had made up her mind without him, his aggrieved annoyance at her inconsistency. He felt nothing but swelling exaltation.

Stella had risen. "You're both crazy," she said.

"There, Stella . . ." he said, hesitated, then kissed her.

"Well!" she exclaimed, laughing.

"Look, Stell, I'm awfully busy."

She nodded, and said, "Come and have a drink, both of you,

this evening. We'll celebrate. Though I think you're both mad."
With another unconsciously envious look at his flushed, proud
face, she went out.

The moment she had gone he rang Martha. Her voice came
gay over the air as she announced her conviction that having a
baby was the most sensible thing they could both do.

"Why, Matty!" he shouted. Then he let out a yell of pure
elation. He heard her laugh.

"Come home to lunch?" she asked. Then she added scrupu-
lously, "Not if you're busy."

"Well, actually, I've got an awful lot of work."

"Oh, very well, we'll celebrate this evening."

"Actually, Stella asked us over."

"Oh, but Stella . . ." She stopped.

"We can decide that later." They each held the receiver for a
while, waiting for the other to say something. Then he said, very
stern and efficient, "Matty, you're quite sure?"

She giggled at his tone, and said derisively, "I've been
perfectly sure for a whole hour."

"See you later, then." He put down the receiver—and nearly
lifted it to ring her again. Something more, surely, must be said or
done. He was seething with the need to release his elation, his
pride. It was impossible to sit quietly working in the office. He
walked across to the door of his chief's office, and stood outside
it. No—he would tell him later. He left a message that he would
be back in half an hour, and went into the street. He was walking
towards the flat, he realized. His steps slowed, then he stopped.
On a street corner he stood staring at nothing, breathing heavily,
smiling. There was a florist's shop opposite. He was drawn to the
window. He was looking at some deep-red carnations. He would
send Matty some flowers—yes, that was it. But as he was about to
go into the shop, he saw again her face as he had last seen it that
morning—set, angry, stiff-lipped. He did not enter the shop. A big
clock at the end of the street said it was after twelve. He
hesitated, turned, and set off towards the flat after all. He would
surprise her for lunch. Then again he stopped, standing irresolute
on the pavement. Nearly, he went back to the office. Almost, he
directed himself to Martha. He gave another long look at the mass

of deep-crimson carnations behind the glass. Then he thought, I could do with a drink. He walked off to the Club, where he usually had a drink before lunch.

The first person he saw was Perry at the bar, eating potato chips with a glass of beer. They nodded, and Perry pushed the plate of chips towards him.

Douglas shook his head. "My ulcer's been playing me up again."

"The more I ill-treat mine, the more it likes it." Perry directed very bright hard blue eyes at him, and asked, "What are you looking so pleased about?"

"We're having a kid," said Douglas proudly. He knew tears stood in his eyes: it was the climax of his exultation.

"You're joking," said Perry, polite but satiric.

Douglas laughed, then whooped, so that people turned around to stare and smile sympathetically. "It's a fact." He called to the barman, "Drinks on me. Drinks all round." In a moment the two were surrounded and Douglas was being thumped over the shoulders and back. "Stop it, silly sods," he said, grinning, "stop it."

Profession: Housewife

Sally Benson

Every status or rank contains some dilemmas and contradictions, but the modern woman's status contains more difficulties than most. Her relationship to work is surrounded by contradictory messages from others, both men and women.

As a child, she is encouraged to do well in school, and indeed girls do better than boys in school. However, her aspirations are constantly scaled down. If she does well in biology, she is encouraged to become a nurse, not a

Sally Benson, "Profession: Housewife," in Philip Van Doren Stern (ed.), *The Pocket Book of Modern American Short Stories*, Simon & Schuster, Inc., New York, 1943.

physician. If she does well in mathematics, she may be encouraged to be a computer technician, but not a physicist.

Almost all young women work, and indeed people are surprised if a young woman does not take a job for a while. She may even be encouraged to work after marriage, if she is "helping to build a home" or "helping out," but thoughts of independent, high aspirations are supposed to be gradually dropped.

If she does enter a challenging profession, she is likely to be given praise for doing ancillary activities rather than taking leadership. She will be welcomed as a junior collaborator on a book, or approved if she does the library work for a law brief. She should be responsible and hardworking, but as a subordinate. She is likely to receive less helpful criticism than a talented young man, for the improvement of his work is much more important.

However, the meaning of work has many facets. And both men and women work for other reasons than a high aspiration. Sally Benson in *Profession: Housewife* asks us to share the world of an unimportant woman, who is not even striving to become an office manager. Like so many of her peers, she has been caught by the dreams in women's magazines. That is, the man she loves has divorced his wife to marry her, and she has left her work in order to create a pretty setting for their life together.

Indeed, both were captured by that dream, and both imagined that when the divorce was over and the house redecorated, they would be the center of a gay social network. However, the physical objects do not create friendships. The friends of the former wife do not visit, and neither partner has developed a set of new friends. Indeed, we see that a work place (like a kinship network) furnishes easy, friendly interaction that could not otherwise be achieved without effort, and Dorothy has left the work place. She shares the experience of the upper-middle-class women Betty Friedan describes in *The Feminine Mystique* as having been betrayed by the propaganda of the 1950s; they did take the advice of women's magazines, made of homemaking a creative, full-time activity, and afterwards found that life was not fulfilling. (Note that the salesman who is a victim of her mood is peddling a book that symbolizes her imprisonment.)

Although the window by the breakfast nook was open, it was very warm. The yellow-and-white gingham curtains hung still and the blue oilcloth showed beads of moisture. Even the painted table top felt damp and sticky, and Joe Grannis was conscious of the discomfort of the hard bench on which he sat. He heard Dorothy tear open the letter and, leaning back as far as he could, he shook out his paper and held it before his face.

In a few minutes she slapped the letter down on the table so hard that the coffee in her cup spilled over into the saucer. "I might have known," she said. "They can't come. At least, she *says* they can't come."

Although it was what he had expected, Joe Grannis lowered his paper and managed to look surprised. "That's funny," he answered. "Maybe some other time."

"Some other time," his wife repeated. "Don't be dumb. The point is they don't want to come, now or any other time."

"I wouldn't say that," he said. "There's no reason why they shouldn't want to come."

Dorothy Grannis lifted her saucer and poured the coffee that had spilled back into the cup. Her face, normally a solid pink, had turned a bright cerise and her hair lay against her forehead with the metallic fixity of a doll's wig. "I'm sorry I asked them in the first place," she told him.

Joe Grannis made a mistake. "Well, you can't say I didn't warn you," he said. "You can't expect to make friends with people who were friends of Louise's. Those things never work out. People feel funny, sort of."

She pushed the sleeves of her chintz house coat further up on her arms with a hard, deliberate gesture and rested her elbows on the table. "Why?" she asked. "From the way you used to talk, I got the impression they were friends of yours. I got the impression that they didn't think so much of *Louise*, that you were the fair-haired boy with them. I got the impression that they couldn't wait until the divorce and everything was over so they could come here again."

She looked around the bright, shiny kitchen and laughed. "My God!" she went on. "If they saw this place now it might be too much for them. They might drop dead. Digging this place out was like excavating. It might be too much for them to see it clean for a change."

Joe Grannis took his watch from his pocket and looked at it. He edged from behind the table and stood up. "Time to go," he said.

"I suppose so," she told him. "You never know the answers to anything. Well, what are we going to do tonight? Sit here and listen to the radio?"

"Now, don't be sarcastic," he answered. "You've got friends of your own. Why don't you call Ruth and Van up and ask them out?"

"And have them wondering why nobody else ever drops in?" she asked indignantly. "That was all right at first. They didn't think anything of it the first few times. But the last time she acted plenty funny about it. Wanting to know if I didn't get lonesome here all day and everything. I'd rather rot."

He looked at her and his face grew set. "Suit yourself," he said. "And since you're speaking of impressions, I got some myself. I got the impression that all you needed to make you happy was a home of your own and to be able to quit work. God knows you sang that tune long enough. Three years, wasn't it? Well, you got what you wanted. You've spent money like a drunken sailor on this place and if you can't make friends for yourself, I can't help you."

"Well, really!" she exclaimed, her voice politely formal. "Really!"

She remained seated at the table until she heard the front door slam behind him, and then she got up and with brisk, efficient movements carried the breakfast dishes to the sink. The sink was of glaring yellow porcelain and the faucets were shiny and new. The hot water on her hands made her feel warmer and she pulled down the zipper of her house coat. Her grasp on the dishes was rough, but she arranged them almost gently in the wire rack to drain.

Pretty soon now the girls would come straggling into the office where she used to work, cool and neat in their new summer dresses. Because the day was warm, the atmosphere about the place would relax and Mannie, the office boy, would be sent to the drugstore for double cokes. There would be gossip and cigarettes in the washroom and speculation as to whether Mr. Ackerman would leave early for a round of golf.

She opened the drawer of the kitchen cabinet and took out a towel, yellow, with blue featherstitching, and dried the dishes hurriedly. Glancing at the clock and seeing that it was not yet nine, she tried to slow her movements. She wiped the breakfast table with a damp cloth and put away the oilcloth doilies.

The dining room was cool and bare. In the centre of the shiny mahogany table was placed an etched silver bowl around which huddled four thin silver candlesticks. Going to the sideboard, she opened the drawers one by one, looking with satisfaction at the rows of silver-plated knives, forks, and spoons lying on their squares of felt. In each drawer was a lump of camphor to prevent tarnishing.

The stairs led out of the dining room and she walked up them to the upstairs hall. Four doors opened out into the hall, but only two of them stood ajar—the door to the bathroom and the one to their bedroom. She liked to keep the extra bedrooms shut off until she felt she could do them over decently. There was little disorder in their own room. Joe's striped silk pajamas lay folded on his bed and her pale-green satin nightgown lay on a chair by the window. She hung these in the closet and then spread the beds, fitting their lavender taffeta covers smoothly.

As she finished, the front-door bell rang briefly, and looking out the window, she saw a man standing there, a leather briefcase under his arm. She loosened her hair slightly about her face and pulled the zipper up on her house coat.

The man who stood at the door was very young and very thin. His light-gray suit was shabby and the coat hung limply from his shoulders. He wore no hat and his fine, light hair was too long and fell untidily over his forehead. He had been looking down when she opened the door, his whole figure drooping, but hearing the sound of the latch, he straightened up to face her, jerking his head up alertly, smiling pleasantly.

"Good morning, Madam," he said.

She stood looking at him for so long without speaking that he shifted his feet in embarrassment, the smile growing fixed on his face.

"Yes?" she asked finally. "Yes?"

He took the briefcase from under his arm, and after struggling with the catch, opened it and drew forth a book, which he held toward her. Its bright, flowered cover looked worn and dirty, as though it had been often handled. She made no motion to take it from him, but he stood bravely facing her, the book in his hand.

"I'm not interested in buying any books," she told him. "Nor anything else."

"The young man laughed brightly. "This book, Madam," he said, "is not for sale. It is a gift to you from the company I represent."

"Yes, I know," she answered. "A gift if I subscribe to what?"

The young man lowered his arm, slightly abashed.

"Well?" she asked, raising her eyebrows and putting her head to one side. "Am I right?"

The young man gave another slight laugh. "I can see that you've learned, Madam, that we don't get anything in this world for nothing. A lot of people haven't learned that, and I guess you must be cleverer than average." For a minute he combed his mind to gather up the first rules of salesmanship, which lay scattered there. Then he went on with more assurance. "No, this book is not exactly free, and yet it is free in the sense that you will not actually be paying for this book. What you will be paying for is a three-year subscription to *Good Homes Magazine*. And you will be paying the exact price you would pay if you went to your local dealer. But by taking a subscription now from me, you also will receive this book of five hundred tested recipes, how to set your table for any occasion, and other helpful household hints. So, you see, in a manner of speaking, this book *is* absolutely free. And what is more, Madam, you are permitted to take it now, look it over, and return it to me if you decide you do not care to take a subscription to *Good Homes*."

He smiled triumphantly at her. "Could anything be fairer than that?"

Mrs. Grannis had heard his speech coldly, but now suddenly she opened the door wider and extended her hand for the book. "How long can I keep it before I decide?" she asked.

"For five days, Madam," he told her. Then he dropped his professional manner, and his voice changed. "To tell you the truth, we are supposed to leave them five days. And that's all right for guys that have a car and can come back for them. But I got to figure differently. It's like this—I go to one of these suburbs and spend a day there. I leave a book, if that's what the lady of the house wants, and then I stop by later in the day and pick it up. You see, we're responsible for the books we hand out, and if you don't take a subscription you can't keep the book. The company couldn't afford it. Why, these books cost three dollars to buy."

She stepped back and laid the book on the hall table. "I see," she said. "Well, I'll let you know."

There was something in her gesture that caused the young man to clear his throat anxiously before he spoke again. "May I ask what time will be most convenient for you?"

"Oh, any time," she answered. "I'll be in, all right."

His face cleared. "Well, let's see," he said. "It isn't ten yet and I'll come back about three. That'll give me plenty of time to cover this neighborhood, come back and write out your subscription, and grab a train back to New York. Now, don't think I am too confident, Madam, but I can safely say it will be worth your while to retain the book *plus* receiving *Good Homes* for three entire years."

He refastened the catch of his briefcase and tucked it under his arm. There was a dark spot where the moisture from his hand had stained the leather. He felt very thirsty and wondered if he dared ask for a drink of water. But the lady acted strange. To be sure, she had taken the book, but you never could tell how people were going to act if you asked for a favor. She might think he was trying to get fresh.

So with the sun beating on his head, he stepped back from the door, smiling. "Good day, Madam," he said. "I will be back later."

Halfway down the path, he turned and called to her. "You're the first lady that's taken a book today. It must be good luck or something."

Mrs. Grannis closed the door and walked into the living room. The glare of the sun hurt her eyes and she lowered the shades. Even then, because of the newness of the light, shiny maple furniture, the room had a sort of glint. She lay down on the couch and closed her eyes, trying to decide whether or not to put on her things and run in to see the girls at the office. She could tell them about the house, she thought, and might even ask them out to see it sometime, although she had almost decided to drop them gradually. Still, you had to see somebody, and with Joe's friends acting the way they did, there didn't seem to be much to look forward to in that direction. The dimness of the room soothed her and she fell asleep.

It was after twelve when she woke up, and her head felt stuffy. She made herself a glass of iced tea, heavily sugared, and toasted a cheese sandwich on the electric grill. Then she dressed leisurely and started for the centre of the village. It was almost three when she arrived back home, her hair freshly washed and waved, her face flushed from sitting under the drier. Remembering the young man, she glanced anxiously up and down the street, but he was not in sight. Upstairs, she took off her street things and slipped once more into her house coat. Then, carefully turning back the taffeta spread from her bed, she lay down and lit a cigarette. She heard the bell ring in the kitchen and, propping herself up on one elbow, she peered cautiously out the window. On the steps below stood the young man, who had come back for his book. His clothes were even limper than they had been in the morning and he leaned against the side of the door ready to spring into alert attention at the sound of footsteps. She let the curtain drop and lay back on the bed, smoking and staring at the ceiling. The bell rang again, and then, after a few minutes, more urgently.

For a long while she lay there listening to the bell and then she got up and walked silently down the stairs. She picked up the book from the hall table and carried it back to her room. In a few minutes she heard steps once more on the outside walk and the bell began, persistently now. She sat up on the edge of the bed and, taking the book, deliberately and slowly ripped the pages out. When they all lay scattered on the bed beside her, she began tearing them across. With some difficulty she bent the cover. Then, gathering the pieces together, she went to the window and opened it.

The young man looked up at her and the expression on his face changed. He began to smile. "Wake you up?" he asked pleasantly.

She fumbled with the screen and slowly let the torn pages of the book fall to the grass below.

For a minute the young man stared at them, dazed. Without a word he stooped to pick them up, but realizing the hopelessness of his task, he straightened and stood staring up at the window. For a dreadful moment they looked at one another. Then he turned and walked away.

She fastened the screen, lit a cigarette, and lay down again on the bed, smoking and staring at the ceiling.

Indian Summer

Dorothy Parker

Dorothy Parker's acerb wit spared none of her friends and turned as often against herself as against her foes. Here she gaily states a credo that contains a deeper truth: when a woman comes to accept her own worth (if she ever does), she is much less likely to violate her inner integrity with falsely ingratiating submission to the notions of a man; he

Dorothy Parker, *Enough Rope*, Boni and Liveright, New York, 1926, p. 78.

must respect and accept her for her own qualities, not as a mirror of his own.

In youth, it was a way I had
    To do my best to please,
And change, with every passing lad,
    To suit his theories.

But now I know the things I know,
    And do the things I do;
And if you do not like me so,
    To hell, my love, with you!

Point Counter Point

Aldous Huxley

In all civilizations the philandering of men is viewed more tolerantly than that of women. Men are encouraged to approach women sexually, and women are trained to resist, at least until they have managed to acquire some concessions or promises from men. Consequently it is not surprising that successful pornography (written almost entirely by men) exploits the fantasy of sexual delight without complications, the progression of sexuality without conflict, the smooth unfolding of a sexual experience without catastrophe.

In the modern epoch, real life has not yet come to imitate art in this respect, but men are psychologically unprepared for sexual equality. Accustomed to deciding whether they will take the initiative sexually, they find it embarrassing when they do not wish to engage in sex with a woman, but she proposes it just the same: the roles are reversed, and the man has no easy repertoire of evasive phrases.

Aldous Huxley, *Point Counter Point*, Harper & Row, Publishers, Incorporated, New York, 1923.

Similarly, because women are reared to "yield" only if there are material gifts, legal promises, or the justification of loving, men come to believe, at least partly, that when women engage in sex with them they are simultaneously saying, "I love you." That confession of love may be a slight burden, but it is one that men have been reared to accept.

Here Huxley portrays the unease of a man whose erotic fancy has first led him to philander, but thereupon has been transformed into a need to be loved, and especially a need to use the vocabulary of loving. His own wife cannot protest much because she recognizes her helplessness. He can live independently of her, but her resources are inadequate for an independent life. Thus, he is free to continue his relationship with Lucy.

But although his erotic relationship with Lucy is sensually delightful, he experiences the kinds of doubts and needs that women in the past have often expressed. That is, he wants the relationship to have a deeper meaning, and he continues to demand that she *love* him. In truth, if we read his comments and thoughts carefully, we see no evidence that he is in fact *in love with* her, though he uses the phrases of loving and expresses much adoring tenderness.

Basically, he objects to her viewing him in the way that men have often viewed women in a sexual affair: not as objects of contempt or cold condescension, but as partners in a relationship that can be enjoyed in its own right, standing for itself and requiring no submission to the other person as a condition for that continued sexual enjoyment.

•

Sensuality and sentiment, desire and tenderness are as often friends as they are enemies. There are some people who no sooner enjoy but they despise what they have enjoyed. But there are others in whom the enjoyment is associated with kindliness and affection. Walter's desire to justify his longings by love was only, on final analysis, the articulately moral expression of his natural tendency to associate the act of sexual enjoyment with a feeling of tenderness, at once chivalrously protective and childishly self-abased. In him sensuality produced tenderness; and conversely, where there was no sensuality, tenderness remained undeveloped. His relations with Marjorie were too sexless and platonic to be fully tender. Tenderness can only live in an atmosphere of tenderness. It was as a hard, angrily cynical sensualist that Walter had conquered Lucy. But put into action, his sensuality sentimentalized him. The Walter who had held Lucy naked in his arms was different from the Walter who had only desired to do so; and this new Walter required, in sheer self-preservation, to believe that Lucy felt no less tenderly under the influence of his caresses than he did himself. To have gone on believing, as the old Walter had believed, that she was hard, selfish, incapable of warm feeling would have killed the soft tenderness of the new Walter. It was essential for him to believe her tender. He did his best to deceive himself. Every movement of languor and abandonment was eagerly interpreted by him as a symptom of inner softening, of trustfulness and surrender. Every loving word—and Lucy was fashionably free with her "darlings" and "angels" and "beloveds," her rapturous or complimentary phrases—was treasured as a word come straight from the depths of the heart. To these marks of an imaginary softness and warmth of feeling he responded with a grateful redoubling of his own tenderness; and this redoubled tenderness was doubly anxious to find an answering tenderness in Lucy. Love produced a desire to be loved. Desire to be loved begot a strained precarious belief that he was loved. The belief that he was loved strengthened his love. And so, self-intensified, the circular process began again.

Lucy was touched by his adoring tenderness, touched and surprised. She had had him because she was bored, because his lips were soft and his hands knew how to caress and because, at the last moment, she had been amused and delighted by his sudden conversion from abjectness to conquering impertinence. What a queer evening it had been! Walter sitting opposite to her at dinner with that hard look on his face, as though he were terribly angry and wanted to grind his teeth; but being very amusing, telling the most malicious stories about everybody, producing the most fantastic and grotesque pieces of historical information, the most astonishing quotations from old books. When dinner was over, "We'll go back to your house," he said. But Lucy wanted to go and see Nellie Wallace's turn at the

Victoria Palace and then drop in at the Embassy for some food and a little dancing, and then perhaps drive round to Cuthbert Arkwright's on the chance that . . . Not that she had any real and active desire to go to the music hall, or dance, or listen to Cuthbert's conversation. She only wanted to assert her will against Walter's. She only wanted to dominate, to be the leader and make him do what she wanted, not what he wanted. But Walter was not to be shaken. He said nothing, merely smiled. And when the taxi came to the restaurant door, he gave the address in Bruton Street.

"But this is a rape," she protested.

Walter laughed. "Not yet," he answered. "But it's going to be."

And in the grey and rose-coloured sitting room it almost was. Lucy provoked and submitted to all the violences of sensuality. But what she had not expected to provoke was the adoring and passionate tenderness which succeeded those first violences. The hard look of anger faded from his face and it was as though a protection had been stripped from him and he were left bare, in the quivering, vulnerable nakedness of adoring love. His caresses were like the soothing of pain or terror, like the appeasements of anger, like delicate propitiations. His words were sometimes like whispered and fragmentary prayers to a god, sometimes words of whispered comfort to a sick child. Lucy was surprised, touched, almost put to shame by this passion of tenderness.

"No, I'm not like that, not like that," she protested in answer to his whispered adorations. She could not accept such love on false pretences. But his soft lips, brushing her skin, his lightly drawn finger tips were soothing and caressing her into tenderness, were magically transforming her into the gentle, loving, warm-hearted object of his adoration, were electrically charging her with all those qualities his whispers had attributed to her and the possession of which she had denied.

She drew his head onto her breast, she ran her fingers through his hair. "Darling Walter," she whispered, "darling Walter." There was a long silence, a warm still happiness. And then suddenly, just because this silent happiness was so deep and perfect and therefore, in her eyes, intrinsically rather absurd and even rather dangerous in its flawless impersonality, rather menacing to her conscious will, "Have you gone to sleep, Walter?" she asked, and tweaked his ear.

In the days that followed Walter desperately did his best to credit her with the emotions he himself experienced. But Lucy did not make it easy for him. She did not want to feel that deep tenderness which is a surrender of the will, a breaking down of personal separateness. She wanted to be herself, Lucy Tantamount, in full command of the situation, enjoying herself consciously to the last limit, ruthlessly having her fun; free, not only financially and legally, but emotionally too—emotionally free to have him or not to have him. To drop him as she had taken him, at any moment, whenever she liked. She had no wish to surrender herself. And that tenderness of his—why, it was touching, no doubt, and flattering and rather charming in itself, but a little absurd and, in its anxious demand for a response from her side, really rather tiresome. She would let herself go a little way toward surrender, would suffer herself to be charged by his caresses with some of his tenderness, only to suddenly draw herself back from him into a teasing, provocative detachment. And Walter would be wakened from his dream of love into a reality of what Lucy called "fun," into the cold daylight of sharply conscious, laughingly deliberate sensuality. She left him unjustified, his guiltiness unpalliated.

"Do you love me?" he asked her one night. He knew she didn't. But perversely he wanted to have his knowledge confirmed, made explicit.

"I think you're a darling," said Lucy. She smiled up at him. But Walter's eyes remained unansweringly sombre and despairing.

"But do you *love* me?" he insisted. Propped on his elbow, he hung over her almost menacingly. Lucy was lying on her back, her hands clasped under her head, her flat breasts lifted by the pull of the stretched muscles. He looked down at her; under his fingers was the curved elastic warmth of the body he had so completely and utterly possessed. But the owner of the body smiled up at him through half-closed eyelids, remote and unattained. "Do you *love* me?"

"You're enchanting." Something like mockery shone between the dark lashes.

"But that isn't an answer to my question. Do you love me?"

Lucy shrugged up her shoulders and made a little grimace. "Love?" she repeated. "It's rather a big word, isn't it?" Disengaging one of her hands from under her head, she raised it to give a little tug to the lock of brown hair that had fallen across Walter's forehead. "Your hair's too long," she said.

"Then why did you have me?" Walter insisted.

"If you knew how absurd you looked with your solemn face and your hair in your eyes!" She laughed. "Like a constipated sheep dog."

Walter brushed back the drooping lock. "I want to be answered," he went on obstinately. "Why did you have me?"

"Why? Because it amused me. Because I wanted to. Isn't that fairly obvious?"

"Without loving?"

"Why must you always bring in love?" she asked impatiently.

"Why?" he repeated. "But how can you leave it out?"

"But if I can have what I want without it, why should I put it in? And, besides, one doesn't put it in. It happens to one. How rarely! Or perhaps it never happens; I don't know. Anyhow, what's one to do in the intervals?" She took him again by the forelock and pulled his face down toward her own. "In the intervals, Walter darling, there's you."

His mouth was within an inch or two of hers. He stiffened his neck and would not let himself be pulled down any farther. "Not to mention all the others," he said.

Lucy tugged harder at his hair. "Idiot!" she said frowning. "Instead of being grateful for what you've got."

"But what *have* I got?" Her body curved away, silky and warm, under his hand; but he was looking into her mocking eyes. "What *have* I got?"

Lucy still frowned. "Why don't you kiss me?" she demanded, as though she were delivering an ultimatum. Walter did not answer, did not stir. "Oh, very well." She pushed him away. "Two can play at that game."

Repelled, Walter anxiously bent down to kiss her. Her voice had been hard with menace; he was terrified of losing her. "I'm not a fool," he said.

"You are." Lucy averted her face.

"I'm sorry."

But she would not make peace. "No, no," she said, and when, with a hand under her cheek, he tried to turn her face back toward his kisses, she made a quick fierce movement and bit him in the ball of the thumb. Full of hatred and desire, he took her by force.

"Still bothering about love?" she asked at last, breaking the silence of that languid convalescence which succeeds the fever of accomplished desires.

Reluctantly, almost with pain, Walter roused himself to answer. Her question in that deep silence was like the spurt of a match in the darkness of the night. The night is limitless, enormous, pricked with stars. The match is struck and all the stars are instantly abolished; there are no more distances and profundities. The universe is reduced to a little luminous cave scooped out of solid blackness, crowded with brightly lit faces, with hands and bodies and the near familiar objects of common life. In that deep night of silence Walter had been happy. Convalescent after the fever, he held her in his arms, hating no more, but filled with a drowsy tenderness. His spirit seemed to float in the warm serenity between being and annihilation. She stirred within his arms, she spoke, and that marvellous unearthly serenity wavered and broke like a smooth reflecting surface of water suddenly disturbed.

"I wasn't bothering about anything." He opened his eyes to find her looking at him, amused and curious. Walter frowned. "Why do you stare at me?" he asked.

"I didn't know it was prohibited."

"Have you been looking at me like that all this time?" The idea was strangely unpleasant to him.

"For hours," Lucy answered. "But admiringly, I assure you. I thought you looked really charming. Quite a sleeping beauty." She was smiling mockingly; but she spoke the truth. Aesthetically, with a connoisseur's appreciation, she had really been admiring him as he lay there, pale, with closed eyes, and as though dead, at her side.

Walter was not mollified by the flattery. "I don't like you to exult over me," he said, still frowning.

"Exult?"

"As though you'd killed me."

"What an incorrigible romantic!" She laughed. But it was true, all the same. He *had* looked dead; and death, in these circumstances, had something slightly ridiculous and humiliating about it. Herself alive, wakefully and consciously alive, she had studied his beautiful deadness. Admiringly, but with amused detachment, she had looked at this pale exquisite creature which she had used for her delight and which was now dead. "What a fool!" she had thought. And "Why do people make themselves miserable, instead of taking the fun that comes to them?" She had expressed her thoughts in the mocking question which recalled Walter from his eternity. Bothering about love—what a fool!

"All the same," insisted Walter, "you were exulting."

"Romantic, romantic!" she jeered. "You think in such an absurdly unmodern way about everything. Killing and exulting over corpses and love and all the rest of it. It's absurd. You might as well walk about in a stock and a swallow-tail coat. Try to be a little more up-to-date."

"I prefer to be human."

"Living modernly's living quickly," she went on. "You can't cart a wagon-load of ideals and romanticisms about with you these days. When you travel by airplane, you must leave your heavy baggage behind. The good old-fashioned soul was all right when people lived slowly. But it's too ponderous nowadays. There's no room for it in the airplane."

"Not even for a heart?" asked Walter. "I don't so much care about the soul." He had cared a great deal about the soul once. But now that his life no more consisted in reading the philosophers, he was somehow less interested in it. "But the heart," he added, "the heart . . . ."

Lucy shook her head. "Perhaps it's a pity," she admitted. "But you can't get something for nothing. If you like speed, if you want to cover the ground, you can't have luggage. The thing is to

know what you want and to be ready to pay for it. I know exactly
what I want; so I sacrifice the luggage. If you choose to travel in a
furniture van, you may. But don't expect me to come along with
you, my sweet Walter. And don't expect me to take your grand
piano in my two-seater monoplane."

There was a long silence. Walter shut his eyes. He wished he
were dead. The touch of Lucy's hand on his face made him start.
He felt her taking his lower lip between her thumb and forefinger.
She pinched it gently.

"You have the most delicious mouth," she said.

Letters from the Earth

Mark Twain

Mark Twain the iconoclast continually warred with Twain
the lovable old curmudgeon. He *felt* strongly pressured
toward propriety in his writings, but he also thoughtfully
provided himself with intimates who wanted his stories and
essays to be innocent. He gained a partial revenge by
circulating unpublished writings in which his pornographic
or more nihilistic impulses were expressed. Among these
was the manuscript *Letters from the Earth*, written (as Twain
assures us) by Satan on the basis of his observations about
the curious animal called Man.

Twain firmly held two diametrically opposed views of
women, an intellectual effort that few men find difficult at all
(perhaps women return the compliment). One view could be
called both Victorian and Southern but the other was closer
to reality. The first view dominated his daily life, perhaps,
but the second is embodied far more in his writings. In the
following report from Satan, Twain emphasizes the sexuality of women in a way that only a few of his most enlightened
contemporaries would have accepted. Yet even in his "respectable" writings his characterizations of women are rich

Mark Twain, *Letters from the Earth*, edited by Bernard de Voto, Harper & Row,
Incorporated, New York, 1938.

and strong. They are almost never flat portraits of mindless, virtuous paragons, but are full of life and complexity.

Like so many other men, Twain felt dominated by women throughout his lifetime. Like others he struck back with satires and ironies about feminine foibles, weaknesses, and irrationalities. Unlike most men, however, even those who were aware of the inequities caused by the class system, caste, or U.S. imperialism, Twain also recognized the injustices under which women lived. In dozens of sketches, he made fun of the standard male bombast and pretension, and especially the poses adopted when strutting before the female.

Satan's general thesis is that since Man supposes God is omniscient and omnipotent, surely God's law must be expressed in Man's temperament and natural needs: surely God will not punish human beings for eating, loving, and so on, for after all He made them that way. Satan notes with astonishment (and expects his readers in Heaven to be equally incredulous) that the human view of God's law is always the *reverse*: If it's "natural," then God has surely forbidden it, under dire threats of punishment in Hell.

In his commentary on what is natural to men and women, not only does Satan-Twain take note of the great physical differences between them; he also follows his own logic about the law by inferring that the two sexes ought to be governed by different rules. As might be expected, one's response to Twain's analysis may well depend upon one's sex: fewer men than women will find it palatable. It is worthwhile to ponder the extent to which marriage and family law, and thus the laws that affect sex roles greatly, have been created and enforced largely by men and not women.

It is as I have said: every statute in the Bible and in the lawbooks is an attempt to defeat a law of God—in other words an unalterable and indestructible law of nature. These people's God has shown them by a million acts that he respects none of the Bible's statutes. He breaks every one of them himself, adultery and all.

The law of God, as quite plainly expressed in woman's

construction, is this: There shall be no limit put upon your intercourse with the other sex sexually, at any time of life.

The law of God, as quite plainly expressed in man's construction, is this: During your entire life you shall be under inflexible limits and restrictions, sexually.

During twenty-three days in every month (in the absence of pregnancy) from the time a woman is seven years old till she dies of old age, she is ready for action, and *competent*. As competent as the candlestick is to receive the candle. Competent every day, competent every night. Also, she *wants* that candle—yearns for it, longs for it, hankers after it, as commanded by the law of God in her heart.

But man is only briefly competent; and only then in the moderate measure applicable to the word in *his* sex's case. He is competent from the age of sixteen or seventeen thenceforward for thirty-five years. After fifty his performance is of poor quality, the intervals between are wide, and its satisfactions of no great value to either party; whereas his great-grandmother is as good as new. There is nothing the matter with her plant. Her candlestick is as firm as ever, whereas his candle is increasingly softened and weakened by the weather of age, as the years go by, until at last it can no longer stand, and is mournfully laid to rest in the hope of a blessed resurrection which is never to come.

By the woman's make, her plant has to be out of service three days in the month and during a part of her pregnancy. These are times of discomfort, often of suffering. For fair and just compensation she has the high privilege of unlimited adultery all the other days of her life.

That is the law of God, as revealed in her make. What becomes of this high privilege? Does she live in the free enjoyment of it? No. Nowhere in the whole world. She is robbed of it everywhere. Who does this? Man. Man's statutes—if the Bible *is* the Word of God.

Now there you have a sample of man's "reasoning powers," as he calls them. He observes certain facts. For instance, that in all his life he never sees the day that she can't overwork, and defeat, and put out of commission any ten masculine plants that can be put to bed to her.[1] He puts those strikingly suggestive and luminous facts together, and from them draws this astonishing conclusion: The Creator intended the woman to be restricted to one man.

So he concretes that singular conclusion into a *law*, for good and all.

And he does it without consulting the woman, although she has a thousand times more at stake in the matter than he has. His procreative competency is limited to an average of a hundred exercises per year for fifty years, hers is good for three thousand a year for that whole time—and as many years longer as she may live. Thus his life interest in the matter is five thousand refreshments, while hers is a hundred and fifty thousand; yet instead of fairly and honorably leaving the making of the law to the person who has an overwhelming interest at stake in it, this immeasurable hog, who has nothing at stake in it worth considering, makes it himself!

You have heretofore found out, by my teachings, that man is a fool; you are now aware that woman is a damned fool.

Now if you or any other really intelligent person were arranging the fairnesses and justices between man and woman, you would give the man a one-fiftieth interest in one woman, and the woman a harem. Now wouldn't you? Necessarily. I give you my word, this creature with the decrepit candle has arranged it exactly the other way. Solomon, who was one of the Deity's favorites, had a copulation cabinet composed of seven hundred wives and three hundred concubines. To save his life he could not have kept two of those young creatures satisfactorily refreshed, even if he had had fifteen experts to help him. Necessarily almost the entire thousand had to go hungry years and years on a stretch. Conceive of a man hardhearted enough to look daily upon all that

---

[1]In the Sandwich Islands in 1866 a buxom royal princess died. Occupying a place of distinguished honor at her funeral were thirty-six splendidly built young native men. In a laudatory song which celebrated the various merits, achievements and accomplishments of the late princess those thirty-six stallions were called her *harem*, and the song said it had been her pride and boast that she kept the whole of them busy, and that several times it had happened that more than one of them had been able to charge overtime. [M. T.]

suffering and not be moved to mitigate it. He even wantonly added a sharp pang to that pathetic misery; for he kept within those women's sight, always, stalwart watchmen whose splendid masculine forms made the poor lassies' mouths water but who hadn't anything to solace a candlestick with, these gentry being eunuchs. A eunuch is a person whose candle has been put out. By art.

From time to time, as I go along, I will take up a Biblical statute and show you that it always violates a law of God, and then is imported into the lawbooks of the nations, where it continues its violations. But those things will keep; there is no hurry.